Economists and Societies

PRINCETON STUDIES IN CULTURAL SOCIOLOGY

Paul J. DiMaggio, Michèle Lamont, Robert J. Wuthnow, and Viviana A. Zelizer, Series Editors

A list of titles in this series appears at the back of the book

Economists and Societies

DISCIPLINE AND PROFESSION IN THE UNITED STATES, BRITAIN, AND FRANCE, 1890s TO 1990s

Marion Fourcade

PRINCETON UNIVERSITY PRESS

PRINCETON AND OXFORD

Copyright © 2009 by Princeton University Press

Published by Princeton University Press, 41 William Street, Princeton, New Jersey 08540

In the United Kingdom: Princeton University Press, 6 Oxford Street, Woodstock, Oxfordshire OX20 1TW

Library of Congress Cataloging-in-Publication Data

Fourcade, Marion, 1968–
    Economists and societies : discipline and profession in the United States,
Britain, and France, 1890s to 1990s / Marion Fourcade.
        p. cm. — (Princeton studies in cultural sociology)
    Includes bibliographical references and index.
    ISBN 978-0-691-11760-7 (hbk. : alk. paper)   1. Economists—United States.
2. Economists—Great Britain.   3. Economists—France.   4. Economics—United States—
History—20th century.   5. Economics—Great Britain—History—20th century.
6. Economics—France—History—20th century.   I. Title.
    HB119.A2F685 2009
    330.09' 04—dc22   2008026664

British Library Cataloging-in-Publication Data is available

This book has been composed in Sabon

Printed on acid-free paper. ∞

press.princeton.edu

Printed in the United States of America

3 5 7 9 10 8 6 4 2

Contents

List of Figures

List of Tables

Preface

The Department of Economics at the University of California, Berkeley occupies the fifth and sixth floors of a tall building colored a slightly unpleasant dark green. Evans Hall was built in 1971 to serve as a primary home to the statistics and mathematics departments. Today this physical arrangement may reflect a natural disciplinary affinity between these disciplines and economics (indeed, some Berkeley economists have joint appointments in mathematics or statistics). This was not always the case, however. Back in the 1960s, the economics department had a different location and a different set of neighbors. It was housed just a few hundred yards away, in Barrows Hall, alongside other social science departments. Politics and sociology are still there today, and this is where my own office is located.

Metaphorically, of course, the migration of the Berkeley economics department from one building to the other mirrored the entire profession's intellectual evolution over the course of the twentieth century as it grew more distant from the rest of the social sciences and humanities and became increasingly reliant on mathematical formalization. By the 1970s, the transformation of economics had proceeded so far that economics Nobel Prize winner Wassily Leontief wrote a letter to the magazine *Science* lamenting that "page after page of professional economic journals are filled with mathematical formulas leading the reader from sets of more or less plausible but entirely arbitrary assumptions to precisely stated but irrelevant theoretical conclusions" (1982, 104). Indeed, it is precisely this formal, abstract orientation that sociologists have repeatedly taken issue with.

To understand how this transformation happened, let us go back to Berkeley. The economics department's migration from Barrows to Evans Hall took place in two steps. Space in Evans Hall was limited at first, so the move involved only about seven or eight people (most of these individuals, in fact, already had separate offices off campus, which a grant had helped secure). The Evans Hall group consisted exclusively of the most mathematically inclined faculty, with a strong component of mathematical economists and econometricians. Staying behind in Barrows Hall were specialists in area studies, economic history (Albert Fishlow), public finance, labor (Lloyd Ulman), development, and industrial organization (Joe S. Bain). Fishlow, Bain, and Ulman were certainly not antitechnical, but their use of statistics was mainly descriptive, and they eschewed the most complex formal modeling. They were also heavily involved in practical work with governments, foundations, regulatory agencies, and unions. This was less true of the mathematical group, which, however, would later boast a different form of distinction: a greater concentration of the field's highest scientific honors. Three of its members later went on to win the Nobel Prize in Economic Sciences: Gérard Debreu (1983), Daniel McFadden (2000), and George Akerlof (2001). These same three (and others from the same group) were also fellows of the Econometric Society and later became presidents of the American Economic Association.

The two wings of the Berkeley economics department were reunited in 1989, when the Barrows Hall people quietly transferred to Evans. By then the broader American field had been thoroughly transformed: according to Leontief, by the early 1980s 54 percent of the papers in the *American Economic Review* contained "models without data." So it seems that American economics was getting ever more deeply entrenched in mathematical formalism, and that Berkeley was just another instance of a broader trend.

The story of economics at Berkeley is not simply one of drift toward formalization, however. Nor is it a purely American story. To be sure, both available space and the proximity of mathematics were important motives behind the relocation of some Berkeley economists to Evans Hall. Yet the protagonists in the process were a quite heterogeneous group and were not even distinctively American. One of the most enthusiastic supporters of the move was Gérard Debreu, who, while endorsing some diversity in the practice of economics, had a rather peculiar view of the nature and purpose of economic *theory*. Importantly, Debreu was not trained in the United States. He was primarily a mathematician who had graduated from the École Normale Supérieure in France. Like many of his European colleagues, he had entered U.S. academia shortly after the war thanks to a fellowship from the Rockefeller Foundation. In 1951 he was drafted into the Cowles Commission and worked there for eleven years before joining the Berkeley economics department. The person who helped recruit him (and other future leaders of mathematical economics) at Berkeley was another foreigner: Andreas Papandreou, the Harvard-educated economist who in later life became socialist prime minister of Greece.

Debreu was the product of a very particular social and intellectual environment. During his early years in France, he had been deeply influenced by the axiomatic method of the mathematical collective that called itself "Nicolas Bourbaki." He had also become acquainted with the general equilibrium synthesis of Maurice Allais, whose economic treatise (published as *Traité d'économie pure*) Debreu had stumbled across in 1946 and whose seminar he later attended in Paris, thereby deepening his connection to the engineering world. Debreu's way into economics thus reflected a unique set of intellectual and institutional affiliations, quite separate from the mainstream of economics dominant in French universities. He saw economics as a pure deductive science that should embrace Bourbakist principles of absolute mathematical rigor, simplicity, and generality. Not surprisingly, he would one day help found the *Journal of Mathematical Economics*.

The formalist turn, with which Debreu's name is closely associated, and which so many have decried as the hallmark of what is wrong with economics as it is practiced in the United States, is thus not a distinctively American story. To an important extent, it had roots elsewhere. There were unquestionably plenty of distinguished builders of formal models among American economists, like Paul Samuelson or Kenneth Arrow. But *pure* mathematical formalism never dominated the U.S. field. First, the homegrown institutionalist tradition, which was dominant before World War II and persisted after the war in certain applied fields, was antithetical to the formalist method. Second, some of the most powerful intellectual centers had nothing but scorn for formalism. For instance, the Chicago economics department largely ignored the Cowles Commission, the center of formalism, when the two entities were housed in the same building. Finally, the formalist moment seems well past its prime. As Robert Solow put it, "the past fifty years have indeed seen formalist economics grow and prosper. But it has not grown very much. Only a small minority within the profession practices economic theory in this style. To tell the truth, not many more pay any attention at all to formalist theory" (1998, 61). At Berkeley, too, the pure formalist orientation has largely faded away. By the 1990s, a solid majority of the articles published in the main American economic reviews had an empirical component, in contrast with the theoretical hegemony Leontief identified only two decades earlier. Indeed, if we are to judge the influence of the Berkeley department on the current state of American economics by its Nobel Prizes, then we probably have to turn to George Akerlof, whose work has inspired the incorporation of considerations of asymmetric information in economic modeling as well as a behavioral evolution of the field with increasingly sophisticated claims about the cognitive, psychological, and sociological underpinnings of human action; or to Daniel McFadden, whose econometric methods have sustained the rise of a generation of quantitative analysts working on all kinds of specialized empirical questions, from transportation to housing, health, the environment, or economic development. Indeed, seen from today's vantage point, American economics is, predominantly, a world of measurement techniques claiming to provide decision-making criteria in every possible domain of policy and social life.

This narrative about economics at Berkeley illustrates some of the themes upon which I expand throughout the rest of this book. While serving as a useful reminder that the history of disciplines is necessarily contingent upon complex social relations (e.g., across fields, across national boundaries), this story also illustrates the power of national institutions in giving individual pursuits a lastingly distinct flavor. For instance, several of the people I spoke to in the course of this research characterized Debreu's intellectual project as very "French"—in spite of the fact that he spent most of his career in the main centers of American economics. By making these casual comments, my interlocutors thus implied that Debreu, in his practice of economics, was acting out social and institutional forces beyond himself; in other words, they suggested that there were broader historical and sociological conditions of possibility to a Gérard Debreu that lay beyond the disciplinary situation of his day.

Economists and Societies is an exploration of the processes whereby national institutional dynamics structure disciplines by reliably structuring the individuals who carry them out. More specifically, this book tells the story of the political and economic forces that have shaped the professional identities, practical activities, and disciplinary projects of economists in the United States, Britain, and France in the twentieth century. It analyzes the logics at work within each national field by examining the scientific claims of economic knowledge, its relationship to administrative authority, and its inscription in the market. The assumption throughout is that something can be gained from taking a broad view: while a wide-ranging approach may sometimes obscure the subtleties of each case, it also enables us to develop a better understanding of the inscription of scientific struggles and individual trajectories into larger patterns of social organization.

This book started from the recognition of one simple fact: that economic knowledge, like any form of knowledge, is always deeply intertwined with politics. This claim does not refer only to the local politics of scientific fields but also to what we may call the politics of polity organization—the ways each society sets up, and reproduces, the rules (i.e., the institutions) through which conflict is organized and settled, and authority is asserted. Because political life in that sense varies so much from country to country (cf. the key role of central administrative agencies in France vs. that of the courts and the public policy industry in the United States, for instance), people's experience and understanding of the economy, their battles over it, and the authority of economic discourse itself have crystallized around different institutional logics and different social missions in each country, with important intellectual consequences for the shape of their economics discipline. In the United States, for instance, the porosity of administrative structures and the democratic need of governmental and private actors to justify their behavior have produced a professional culture that is unified in its commitment to the mastery of scientific language and technical instruments and has extended its influence imperialistically, in all areas of social practice. In France, by contrast, the categorical work of state institutions has long sustained a divided field with divided claims and intellectual traditions. The jurisdiction of economics in French society has consequently been more suspect, and the discipline's main route to legitimation has involved a close association with the administrative and industrial functions of the central state as the representative of the general interest and a logistic approach to economic problems, drawn mainly out of engineering. Finally, in Britain, economics was part of the generalist culture of educated elites and helped articulate these elites' moral mission vis-à-vis British society in a quite different way: as the wardens of the welfare of all. This feature of British political culture has sustained the discipline's characteristic macroeconomic orientation and its strong preoccupation with ethical (and, in particular, distributional) issues.

Over the years and the writing of this book I have had the privilege to rely extensively on the generosity of countless institutions, colleagues, friends, family, and benevolent strangers. My first debt is to all the individuals who took my subject seriously enough to lend themselves to an interview. I owe incalculable thanks to the economists who opened their offices, their private homes, sometimes their libraries to me; who shared their views, their stories, but also their coffees and lunches; who introduced me to their friends and colleagues; who walked me back to the bus or the subway station for fear I would get lost—and even, once, insisted on lending me a hat to keep me from getting wet in the rain (I duly returned it the next day). As daunting as the interviewing process seemed at its beginnings, I came to cherish every moment of it and regard it as one of this project's most rewarding achievements, both intellectually and personally. Finally, beyond the formal interviews, I also want to thank the many acquaintances—economists and others—who were kind enough to just share their thoughts in spur-of-the-moment conversations, dropping invaluable insights in the process.

This book started as my dissertation, and when it was still an unrealized potentiality with no tangible shape, I was fortunate enough to be able to count on the support of many people and institutions, including the Fulbright Program, the Harvard Department of Sociology, the Minda de Gunzburg Center for European Studies at Harvard University, the Departments of Sociology at Princeton University and the University of California at Berkeley, and the Institute of French Studies at New York University. For guiding me through the dissertation itself, my committee members deserve many of these acknowledgments. The relentless enthusiasm of my adviser, Orlando Patterson, his fundamental interest for deep, meaningful sociological questions, and the breadth and originality of his erudition have commanded my profound admiration since I met him during my first year at Harvard. I have valued enormously the respect, patience, and trust he gave me through the long gestation of this work. Theda Skocpol was, above all, a wonderful teacher. Her courses awakened my interest in comparative methods and the study of American politics, while her splendid work and methodological rigor have remained a constant source of intellectual inspiration and challenge. I also owe many thanks to Libby Schweber for her unfailing ability to spur one's mind with her insistence on the proper shape of the research question, for her careful attention to historical detail, and, beyond the dissertation, for her friendship and intellectual like-mindedness. Finally, I have very fond memories of stimulating conversations with Yasemin Soysal and Randall Collins during my years at Harvard.

At a critical point in the intellectual evolution of this project, my frequent discussions with John Meyer helped it come to maturation and gave me the confidence I needed to bring it to completion for the first time. I am very much indebted to his inspiring tutelage and generosity, which I continue to rely upon to this day. I immediately felt at home among the participants in the Stanford Comparative Systems workshop and learned a great deal from all of them. My gratefulness especially goes to my friend Evan Schofer and to Francisco Ramirez for his unstinting interest and communicative enthusiasm. At Stanford, my conversations with Mark Granovetter and Ronald Jepperson also gave me precious food for thought. Finally, many scholars whose work on the history and sociology of economics I admire kindly met or corresponded with me during this period: my appreciation goes especially to Roger Backhouse, William Barber, the late A. W. Bob Coats, Alain Desrosières, Frédéric Lebaron, Roger Middleton, Philip Mirowski, Keith Tribe, and Donald Winch.

After I moved to Princeton, I found another supportive community of students, visiting scholars, and faculty who helped me develop my thinking, repeatedly refreshed my excitement about the subject, and quite simply sustained me through their wonderful friendship. It was there, too, that the second life of this work began under the caring and inspirational guidance of Michèle Lamont, Frank Dobbin, and Viviana Zelizer, and that then sociology editor Ian Malcolm first expressed interest in the manuscript. Little did I know that it would take me another seven years to complete the revision. In the interval, many friends and colleagues read small and big parts of the manuscript as I was making my way through it—sometimes giving it up for months and then taking it up again. My deepest thanks go, first, to all my colleagues at UC Berkeley, who provided an incredibly supportive and intellectually stimulating environment to finish up this project. For their many thought-provoking conversations with me over the last few years, for their friendship and support, and for their inspiration, I am also indebted to George Akerlof, Elizabeth Armstrong, Sarah Babb, Nina Bandelj, Patrick Bolton, Vicki Bonnell, Michael Burawoy, Julian Dierkes, Paul DiMaggio, Ross Emmett, Peter Evans, Gil Eyal, Claude Fischer, Neil Fligstein, Cybelle Fox, Tom Gieryn, Heather Haveman, Kieran Healy, Rakesh Khurana, Michèle Lamont, Grégoire Mallard, John Martin, Sophie Meunier, Virag Mólnar, Veronica Montecinos, Kimberly Morgan, Ann Morning, Trond Petersen, Michael Reich, Ailsa Roell, Abigail Saguy, Marc Schneiberg, Brian Steensland, Ann Swidler, Pedro Teixeira, Kees Van Rees, Kim Voss, Loïc Wacquant, Margaret Weir, Robb Willer, Eric Wright, Viviana Zelizer, Nick Ziegler, Dirk Zorn, and John Zysman.

My (then) junior colleagues at Berkeley read several parts of the manuscript in our fabled junior faculty seminar. Irene Bloemraad, Jennifer Johnson-Hanks, Dawne Moon, Dylan Riley, Sandra Smith, and Cihan Tugal all had a different perspective on this work, but what each of them had to say was always remarkably pertinent, as well as incredibly thought-provoking. Leo Goodman deserves my most special acknowledgments for kindly sharing treasured memories from Chicago and Princeton every time he met me in the hallway. I am immensely grateful to six graduate students—Daniel Buch, Brian Lande, Roi Livne, Damon Mayrl, Sarah Quinn, and Benjamin Moodie—for their able research and editorial assistance, and for everything I learned from them. As for the remainder of the Berkeley sociology community, I must thank it as a whole, for giving me so much to discover and keeping me on my intellectual toes these last few years—or so I hope. The energy I have felt since I came to this department in the summer of 2003 has been one of the most exhilarating experiences of my life and has nourished this project and my person more than I will ever be able to acknowledge.

Last but not least, George Akerlof, Roger Backhouse, Patrick Bolton, Vicki Bonnell, Michael Burawoy, Frank Dobbin, Claude Fischer, Neil Fligstein, Philippe Fontaine, Régine Fourcade, Mauro Guillén, Kieran Healy, Philip Mirowski, Benjamin Moodie, and Yuval Yonay were brave enough to read and comment on large chunks of the manuscript, sometimes all of it and sometimes more than once. Some sat with me for hours to discuss "the book" while I took frantic notes; others e-mailed embarrassingly long memos, which I pored over for days; yet others filled up the pages of the copy I had provided with detailed annotations. Whatever their style, each of them deserves my most profound gratitude, even though I am well aware that I may never rise to their writing or analytical standards.

Choosing a publisher can be one of the most difficult decisions that come with the writing of a book. In my case, it was easy, and a pleasure from the start. For this experience and their steadfast support for the project I am deeply grateful to Peter Dougherty, Ian Malcolm, Chuck Myers, Eric Schwartz, and Tim Sullivan. My appreciation also extends to Nathan Carr's extraordinary work at coordinating the production of this book, and to Susan Ecklund for her sharp editorial eye.

In the end I come home. On the personal front, so many people helped in big and small ways that I am afraid I may forget to thank them all. I am grateful to all those who helped me access important documentation, welcomed me into their homes during periods of work in Europe, and sustained my excitement for the project through their conversations: Stéphanie Bonnet, François Calori, Jacques Delpla, Régine Fourcade, Marc Gurgand and Valérie Gendreau, Jérôme Gautié, Cécile Lefèvre and Frédéric Boccara, Lucile Olier and Denis Fougères, and Richard Portes. My beloved parents, Andrette and Christian Fourcade, provided more than their share of babysitting and emotional support, and so did Jean-Pierre and Josiane Gourinchas. They will always have my fondest affection. I have missed my brothers, Pierre and Benoît, and their families, and my sister-in-law, Fabienne, and her family so much since I moved to this country that I will not pass on such a golden opportunity to express my love to them, too. My dear daughters, Julie and Magda, have lived with this project for much too long, and they are, to be sure, happier than anyone to see me finally let go of it—with a last tender thought for them. Yet it is probably my husband, Pierre-Olivier, who may feel most relieved that my meticulous scrutiny of his world is finally over, though I can assure him that my fascination for it (which started when he was still interested mainly in physics) will never leave me. As an economist, he accepted his implicit objectification in this book with imperturbable serenity and grace, and turned himself into my most devoted supporter and helpful critic in the process. My love and admiration for his person and work made this research all the more attractive, and his genuine interest for, and deep knowledge of, the subject made the process all the more spirited. No one deserves this dedication more than he.

List of Abbreviations

AEA	U.S.: American Economic Association
AEI	U.S.: American Enterprise Institute
AFEDE	France: Association Française des Économistes d'entreprise (French Association of Business Economists)
AFSE	France: Association Française de Sciences Économiques (French Economic Association)
AUTE	U.K.: Association of University Teachers of Economics
BIPE	France: Bureau d'Information et de Prévisions Économiques (Economic Information and Forecasting Bureau)
BLS	U.S: Bureau of Labor Statistics
CBO	U.S: Congressional Budget Office
CEA	U.S.: Council of Economic Advisers
CED	U.S.: Committee on Economic Development
CEE	France: Centre d'Études de l'Emploi (Center for the Study of Employment)
CEPE	France: Centre d'Étude des Programmes Économiques (Center for the Study of Economic Programs)
CEPII	France: Centre d'Études Prospectives et d'Informations Internationales
CEPR	Europe (headquartered in the U.K.): Center for Economic Policy Research
CEPREMAP	France: Centre pour la Recherche Économique et Ses Applications (Center for Applied Economic Research, replaced the CERMAP)
CERC	France: Centre d'Études des Revenus et des Coûts (Research Center on Income and Cost of Living)
CERMAP	France: Centre d'Études et de Recherches Mathématiques Appliquées à la Planification (Center of Mathematical Research Applied to Planning)
CGP	France: Commissariat Général au Plan (Planning Commissariat)
CNRS	France: Centre National de la Recherche Scientifique (National Center for Scientific Research)
COE	France: Comité d'Observation Économique (Economic Observatory)

CORDES	France: Comité de Coordination et d'Orientation des Recherches sur le Développement Économique et Social (Committee for the Coordination and Orientation of Research on Economic and Social Development)
CREDOC	France: Centre de Recherche pour l'Étude et l'Observation des Conditions de Vie (Research Center on Living Conditions)
DEA	U.K.: Department of Economic Affairs
DP	France: Direction de la Prévision (Direction of Forecasting, replaced SEEF)
ENA	France: École Nationale d'Administration (National School of Administration)
ENSAE	France: École Nationale de la Statistique et de l'Administration Économique (National School of Statistics and Economic Administration)
ESRC	U.K.: Economic and Social Research Council
FCC	U.S.: Federal Communications Commission
GES	U.K.: Government Economic Service
IEA	U.K.: Institute of Economic Affairs
IFS	U.K.: Institute for Fiscal Studies
IMF	International Monetary Fund
INSEAD	France: European Institute of Business Administration
INSEE	France: Institut National de la Statistique et des Études Économiques (National Institute of Statistics and Economic Studies)
IPECODE	France: Institut de Prévisions Économiques et Financières pour le Développement des Entreprises (later merged with REXECO to form REXECODE)
IRES	France: Institut de Recherches Économiques et Sociales (Institute of Economic and Social Research)
ISEA (later ISMEA)	France: Institut de Science Économique Appliquée (Institute of Applied Economic Science), later Institut des Sciences Mathématiques et Économiques Appliquées (Institute of Applied Mathematics and Economics)
ISRES	France: Institut Scientifique de Recherches Économiques et Sociales (Scientific Institute of Economic and Social Research)
LSE	U.K.: London School of Economics and Political Science
NABE	U.S.: National Association of Business Economists
NBER	U.S.: National Bureau of Economic Research
NEDC	U.K.: National Economic Development Council
NEDO	U.K.: National Economic Development Office

NIESR	U.K.: National Institute of Economic and Social Research
NSF	U.S.: National Science Foundation
OECD	International (headquartered in Paris): Organization for Economic Cooperation and Development
OFCE	France: Observatoire Français des Conjonctures Économiques (French Observatory of the Business Cycle)
OMB	U.S.: Office of Management and Budget
PEP	U.K.: Political and Economic Planning
PPE	U.K.: Politics, Philosophy and Economics (Oxford teaching program)
RES	U.K.: Royal Economic Society
REXECO	France: Centre de Recherche pour l'Expansion de l'Économie et le Développement des Entreprises (Research Center for Economic Expansion and Business Development)
SBE	U.K.: Society of Business Economists
Sciences-Po	France: École Libre des Sciences Politiques (French Private School of Political Science)
SEDEIS	France: Société d'Études et de Documentation Économique, Industrielle et Sociale.
SEEF	France: Service des Études Économiques et Financières (Statistical Service of the Ministry of Finance
SEP	France: Société d'Économie Politique (Political Economy Society)
SSRC	U.K.: Social Science Research Council
SSRC	U.S.: Social Science Research Council
X	France: École Polytechnique

Economists and Societies

Economics and Society

> The sociology of knowledge should seek to investigate the conditions under which problems and disciplines come into being and pass away. The sociologist in the long run must be able to do better than to attribute the emergence and solutions of problems of a given time and place to the mere existence of certain talented individuals. The existence of and the complex interrelationship between the problems of a given time and place must be viewed and understood against the background of the structure of the society in which they occur, although this may not always give us an understanding of every detail. . . . If the sociology of knowledge should have any measure of success in this type of analysis, many problems, which hitherto, as regards their origins at least, have been unsolved, would be cleared up. Such a development would also enable us to see why sociology and economics are of such recent birth and why they advanced in one country and were retarded and beset by many obstacles in others."
> (Karl Mannheim, *Ideology and Utopia*, [1936] 1985, 109–10)

ECONOMISTS ARE EVERYWHERE. They manage monetary policy, measure the value of government programs to the last dollar, and routinely offer expert testimony in political hearings and in the courts. They also consult for companies, divining the future of industrial competition, calculating the costs and benefits associated with different courses of action, designing legal standards or the nuts and bolts of financial markets. From their vantage point in the media they comment authoritatively on economic ups and downs, housing booms and dot-com busts, global competition and exchange rate movements. And they can be found on best-seller lists, too, arguing that the subject matter of economics and the applicability of its analytical tool kit reach much further into everyday life than we ever imagined.

This book could be told largely as a global story—the story of how a new form of expertise has emerged, gaining influence throughout the world. Since the end of the nineteenth century, economists have developed increasingly distinctive discourses, credentials, and professional ambitions. In most countries the discipline of economics has become a legitimate, and a highly technical, field of scientific study and practice. It has secured a position within the higher educational system and has expanded its authority within a wide range of social institutions, including governments, corporations, and international organizations. As economic technologies and policy recipes have become inescapable features of the expert tool kits of modern social institutions, economic vocabulary and images saturate our culture.

To simplify, we can identify three major phases in this long-term trajectory of economics. The period from the late nineteenth century to the 1920s was dominated by methodological debates and the autonomization of economics from neighboring fields and scholarly enterprises. In this process of "academicization" or "disciplinarization," economics migrated from salons and learned societies to universities and other higher education establishments. The 1930s through 1960s witnessed its emergence as a technique of government (symbolized by the twin innovations of national accounting and macroeconometric modeling) and, more generally, as a tool for the exercise of public expertise. Alongside academic institutions, public administrations and their associated research units turned into important producers of economic knowledge. Government at all levels became the main purveyor of resources for the social sciences, which it channeled toward uses associated with new modes of social and economic regulation. Finally, since the end of the "Fordist" era, we have witnessed a massive expansion of the business applications of economics, coupled with the emergence of what Rose and Miller (1992) call neoliberal governmentality. The rise of finance and microeconomics, on the one hand, and the market liberalization of economies, on the other, have opened up new jurisdictions in the private world, turning economic knowledge into a successful corporate activity.[1]

Parallel to these global trends of what Abbott (1988) calls "jurisdictional expansion" (i.e., the increasingly tight control over specific work areas) is a fairly general movement toward the international diffusion and standardization of economic knowledge. Over the course of the twentieth century, the practice and discourse of economics have become increasingly technical through, first, the formalization of theoretical work, which has gradually incorporated analytical progress in mathematics and the natural sciences; and, second, the growing sophistication of empirical work, which has been transformed by the advent of complex statistical methodologies, high-speed computers, and large databases.[2] Economics, however, is far from unique in this regard. Most professional enterprises have, in fact, experienced the increased formalization of their rules of operation and substantive knowledge, a transformation generally equated with the increased authority of science in the modern world.[3]

Scholars of science have repeatedly found modern economics to be the most coherent and well-bounded scholarly enterprise in the social scientific field. Certainly, the dominant intellectual form in economic science (largely derived from the Anglo-Saxon tradition) generally presents itself as a universalistic paradigm. A commonly held view within the profession is that economists in various countries and various occupations (academics, administration, business) agree widely on what constitutes an economic problem, and on the appropriate tools to handle it. In addition, most economists in the world today consider that they work within an international field, which sets the intellectual and scientific standards for their national professions.[4]

The international story is essential, but it is incomplete. Economics arose everywhere. But everywhere it was distinctive. If we look back just a few decades, we see that the institutionalization of economic expertise in science, policy, or business took different routes across nations. Scientific and practical knowledge about the economy was conceptualized and institutionalized in different ways in different places, and for identifiable reasons.

It all started early, of course. Biernacki's (1995) brilliant comparison of the conceptualization of "labor" by political economists in Britain and Germany suggests that in spite of using the same term, writers in the two societies attributed profoundly different meanings to it, which were rooted in the divergent cultural contexts in which they formulated their theories. Biernacki finds that these differences (between the concepts of "labor" and "labor power") originated in the everyday practices of British and German workers and employers: in British textile mills, workers were being paid for finished cloths, whereas in German mills the wage rate was calculated on the basis of the number of shots of the weaving shuttle. These practical conceptions, which derived from the material context of industrialization in each country, tended then to crystallize into full-fledged cultural systems, which eventually became codified in writing. Having been socialized in different economic worlds, political economists and other intellectuals came to talk about "the economy" in different ways.

Closer to us, social scientists have documented the tremendous variability in the national understandings and implementation of such international economic paradigms as "Keynesianism," "monetarism," or the "Washington consensus," and have linked such disparities in economic vocabulary and practice to differences in the professional backgrounds and institutional location of the experts in charge of these policies. This suggests that being an economist still has different meanings and evokes quite diverse jurisdictional domains in different cultures and societies— as it does in different institutional locations within these societies.[5]

The United States, France, and Britain offer important illustrations of such differences. As is well known, writers from all three nations were historically central to the development of a tradition of political economy and its evolution into modern economic analysis. Table 0-1 records the proportion of citizens and residents from four nations in the population of "eminent" dead and living economists as established by Blaug and Sturges in their *Who's Who in Economics?* (1986; also Blaug 1999). The table confirms the pivotal place of these three countries (plus Germany) in the early history of economic thought. It also reveals America's extraordinary supremacy in the modern era and suggests that it is partly due to the country's remarkable success at attracting foreign scholars.

Most histories of economic thought treat the evolution of economics from the preclassical to the neoclassical era in a chronological fashion. This has the advantage of reconstructing a coherent disciplinary history by connecting individuals across nations, but it obscures the extent to which the same individuals may link up to other intellectual networks, political

TABLE 0-1
Representation of Countries in the Population of Dead and Living Economists, 1770–1996 (in percent)

	France	*Germany*	*United Kingdom*	*United States*
	Place of Birth			
1986				
"dead" economists	11.2	12	36.2	10.5
1999				
"dead" economists	9.4	10.8	27.6	18
1986				
living economists	2.3	3.7	11.6	58.7
1999				
living economists	2.7	3.5	16.0	50.1
	Place of Residence			
1986				
living economists	3.5	2	8.3	76
1999				
living economists	2.3	1.9	15.4	65.4

Source: Blaug and Sturges 1986; Blaug 1999.
Living economists: record based on citations in economic journals included in SSCI.
"Dead" economists: record based on citations in major histories of economic thought.

configurations, and organizations in their own country. How does the fact that Augustin Cournot was French and John Stuart Mill British matter for understanding their intellectual contribution? Do the vast cross-country differences in institutions and cultural perceptions shape how economists approach various problems of public policy? Surveys of opinion among professional economists conducted in the 1980s have shown, for instance, that American and French practitioners were situated at nearly polar opposites regarding many important economic policy recommendations, with British and German economists standing somewhere in the middle (Table 0-2). Americans always displayed a much higher level of general consensus on a number of standard economic propositions and were significantly more favorable to economic ideas based on free trade and market competition. The French, on the other hand, stood out for their distrust of the price system and their support for political control of economic institutions, such as the central bank or the exchange rate.[6]

Not only do economists in different countries generally support different ideas and policy positions, but their claims to expertise about the economy are justified in very different ways. Thus while American and, albeit to a lesser extent, British economists see themselves mainly as academics, continental European economists emphasize a much broader view of their function, which includes permanent administrative and political positions. Some of the internationally best-known French economic scholars, for instance, have not been primarily academics, as in the United States, but high-level civil servants: hence, in the postwar period, the cases of Edmond Malinvaud at the Ministry of Finance or Marcel Boiteux at the national electricity monopoly. Economics professors in Germany (e.g., Ludwig Erhard, Helmut Schmidt), the Netherlands (R.F.M. Lubbers), France (Raymond Barre), and Italy (Romano Prodi) have held some of the highest political appointments in their respective countries (e.g., as prime ministers, council presidents, or chancellors).[7]

In spite of a certain degree of convergence in the professional and disciplinary forms of economics around the world, and the fact that a great number of economists subjectively orient themselves toward a putative "international" disciplinary field, then, considerable variations remain regarding who is an "economist" and what "economic knowledge" means across societies. But can we describe these differences systematically? And how should we account for them? It is the purpose of this book to provide answers to both of these questions. Anticipating my reply to the first one, in the following pages I present a brief outline of the historical trajectories of economics in the United States, Britain, and France over the course of the twentieth century. I develop my answer to the second question subsequently.

TABLE 0-2

Opinion Surveys of Economists in Different Nations: Support for "Textbook" Propositions by American and European Economists (selected statements)

	U.S.* 1979 N=211	Fr.[†] 1981 N=162	U.K.** 1990 N=981	Sw. 1984 N=199	W.G. 1984 N=273	Aus. 1984 N=91	Can.[††] 1984 N=443
Tariffs and quotas reduce welfare							
Agree	95	70	84	87	94	86	96
Disagree	3	27	15	10	6	13	4
Cash payments are better than in-kind transfers							
Agree	89	70		68	72	78	
Disagree	8	19		22	21	19	
Flexible exchange rates are effective							
Agree	94	49		91	92	84	
Disagree	5	44		8	5	17	
Minimum wage increases unemployment among young and unskilled workers							
Agree	88	38	76	66	69	64	85
Disagree	10	60	24	32	30	35	15
The government should restructure the welfare state along the lines of a negative income tax							
Agree	90	50	69	45	47	48	
Disagree	8	43	15	54	46	43	
A ceiling on rents reduces the quantity and quality of housing available							
Agree	96	52	85	79	93	89	95
Disagree	2	44	14	20	6	11	5
The central bank should be instructed to increase the money supply at a fixed rate							
Agree	38	61	17	80	36	30	
Disagree	48	27	55	21	62	68	
Reducing the influence of regulatory authorities (e.g., in air traffic) would improve the efficiency of the economy							
Agree	75	37		62	75	56	
Disagree	21	56		36	23	43	

Sources: Derived from *Kearl et al. 1979 (United States); [†]Bobe and Etchegoyen 1981 (France); Frey et al. 1984 (West Germany, Austria, and Switzerland); [††] Block and Walker 1988 (Canada); ** Ricketts and Shoesmith, 1990 (United Kingdom).

THREE TRAJECTORIES

Consider, for instance, how three contemporaries, an American institutionalist (Wesley C. Mitchell, 1874–1948), a Cambridge don (John Maynard Keynes, 1883–1946), and a French engineer (François Divisia, 1889–1964), described the nature of the economist's role in society as they envisioned it toward the middle of the twentieth century:

In recent years many members of our Association have come to fear that economics may disintegrate into a number of specialties. This danger they combat by insisting that every young economist must receive a "thorough grounding in theory." The remedy seems inefficient, because the qualitative theory, in which we are commonly grounded, plays so small a role in our work as specialists in public finance and banking, in accountancy and transportation, in economic history and insurance, in business cycles, marketing, and labor problems. As economics becomes the study of objective behavior, this breach between theory and the "practical" subjects will be narrowed. (Mitchell 1925, 6)

The master economist must possess a rare combination of gifts. He must reach a high standard in several different directions and must combine talents not often found together. He must be mathematician, statesman, historian, philosopher—in some degree. He must understand symbols and speak in terms of the general, and touch abstract and concrete in the same flight of thought. He must study the present in light of the past for the purpose of the future. (Keynes 1924, 322)

It is absolutely crucial to insist on the point that, among the moral sciences, economics is by far the one that is best suited to the methods of the other advanced sciences; and to show that, because its elements can be measured, we may apply to it the most refined form of scientific reasoning, I mean by that mathematical reasoning. (Divisia 1928, 15)[8]

Certainly Mitchell, Keynes, and Divisia share a lot. They all describe economic competence as distinctive, and all emphasize the proper use of quantitative techniques as the hallmark of the economist's contribution to the common good. Yet in their own way, these quotations, of which we can find equivalents in both earlier and later periods, encapsulate some of the most interesting differences in the purpose and nature of economic knowledge among the three countries. Mitchell defines the economist first and foremost as a scientist, whose professional technique can be put to use for the resolution of practical problems. Keynes provides a very different picture—elitist, cultivated, scientific, and expert, certainly—but in a more high-minded way. Divisia, finally, comes to economics from another perspective still—that of the mathematician, who finds the discipline particularly well suited to the application of his specific talent as an engineer. Reflecting on the division, well established in France, between literary and mathematical approaches to economics, Divisia's mentor, Clément Colson, insists on the legitimacy of the latter in the book preface: "Mr. Divisia's book offers a striking example of the constant meeting of philosophical and juridical ideas ... with the scientific training of the Engineer" (1928, xxiv). While these statements are, ultimately, the product of individual authors and cannot be expected to characterize entire national fields, each of them illustrates some elements of the different understandings of economic knowledge production I analyze in this book: American "scientific and commercial professionalism," British "public-minded elitism," and French "statist divisions."

The United States: Merchant Professionals

I argue in this book that it is the centrality of market institutions to U.S. political culture and institutional makeup that has given the practice of economics in this country its particular character. American economists derive their legitimacy and social authority from their qualification, which is both based on the possession of distinctive skills (especially technical and quantitative ones) and revealed in their "market performance" outside of academia, that is, by their ability to penetrate new work domains in a competitive environment.

First, in the opening decades of the twentieth century, public officials in American administrative institutions at the local, state, and federal levels created demand for unpoliticized, technical expertise mostly drawn from the academic professions. In the absence of an elite of public technocrats, and in part out of sheer reluctance to internalize a form of research that might be perceived as biased if emanating from government, they explicitly relied on academic economists to carry out technical tasks, such as administrative rationalization, the mobilization of a war economy, military planning, and the expansion of the welfare state. This created a strong institutional basis for an economics profession that is profoundly rooted in the academic world, and in the imperatives of empirical relevance and scientific quantification. A small elite of professors within top universities exerts efficient control over the rest of the field and defines the boundaries of what constitutes acceptable economic expertise. Commanding widespread respect (both nationally and internationally) from the lower strata of the field, it also holds institutionalized access to prestigious appointments in government and international organizations. The centrality of formal markers of worth (such as a PhD from a top graduate school) to professional definitions, the fact that capabilities are usually defined in highly technical terms, according to the standards prevalent in the scientific sphere, and the economists' close identification with the principle of market efficiency reinforce a pattern that might be defined as "scientific professionalism."

Second, by defining competitive markets as the single most important principle of economic governance, American political institutions shaped both the cognitive categories with which economic writers would think about their object, and the immediate organizational ecology in which the practice of economics is embedded.[9] The combination of the definition of the economist by a technical, measurable form of competence, of a certain consumer orientation within academic institutions, and of institutionalized competition among professions has produced a situation where economic knowledge has been more "market-oriented," both cognitively and professionally, in this country than elsewhere. Throughout the course of the twentieth century, the inscription of American economics in the market system has served as a basis for a gradual expansion of the profession's jurisdictional claims, through the commercialization of economic ideas and tools. Thus, on the one hand, economics has produced a vast array of practical instruments that are widely used in policy and business (in finance and law, for instance). On the other hand, economic knowledge is routinely mobilized as a marketable political commodity that helps different groups with public claims fight one another, a process that accelerated markedly with the rapid expansion of the public policy industry after the 1960s. Finally, this market orientation of American economic knowledge production, in turn, feeds back into the intellectual process itself, by fostering a form of "intellectual imperialism" whereby any social object becomes available for an economic analysis.

The United Kingdom: Public-Minded Elites

In Britain, the identity of economists has been historically shaped by a political culture centered on small, tightly knit elite societies that traditionally enjoy great authority in producing public discourse and conducting the affairs of the nation, and by the nonprofessional, gentry tradition of the public service. This has produced a scientific field that is organized around the authority of elite institutions and personalities, but where the ability to communicate economic ideas in plain and eloquent language (through personal networks and contributions oriented toward the general public, for instance) is also highly valued.

Professions in the United Kingdom have been generally much less closely identified with such impersonal signs of competence as formal credentials than those in the United States. Professionals' authority in Britain emerged in the context of a socially dominant neo-aristocratic culture, which deliberately expressed its distance from, and distaste for, vocational or technical self-understandings.[10] Economic knowledge was also much more diffuse in the general culture. As a result, the world of economic discourse long remained the province of skilled amateurs from politics, the civil service, business, finance, or journalism, alongside more academically grounded economic writers, all closely associated through personal connections.

The world of British economics has thus been centered on this elite, public-minded society, whose maintenance has required much less boundary activity to demarcate laymen from experts. Since their legitimacy and social authority stemmed from their relationship to the institutions of power in British society (in particular, social class and passage through an elite educational institution), British economists did not need to rely as much as their American counterparts on organized professionalism and formal definitions of competence. While lacking the formal channels of access to the policy-making arena that can be found in the United States (due to the closed nature of the civil service and the Treasury's jealous defense of its prerogatives), the core personalities of the field (i.e., from Oxbridge and London) remained closely involved in policy through interpersonal networks, where they belonged automatically as members of a narrow and tightly bound upper secondary and higher education system.

This "public-minded elitism" was especially well developed during the interwar and early postwar periods—the figures of Beveridge, Keynes, Meade, or Kaldor perhaps exemplify it best. It has tended to fade away somewhat as the disciplinary focus in economics has become more ivory-tower and more narrowly professionalized. I identify two main reasons for this: first was the massive expansion of British higher education, which has allowed newly created institutions to use international channels of academic recognition to challenge the traditional supremacy of Oxbridge in both economic science and policy. Second was the anti-intellectual mood of the Thatcher era, particularly her extreme dislike of Keynesian economics (dominant in the United Kingdom at that time), which badly battered the social authority and resources of universities and contributed—at least for a time—to severing them from their traditional role.

France: Statist Divisions

The French economics profession derives its characteristics from a national political culture and institutional makeup centered on the administrative exercise of public power. The concentration of resources and legitimacy around technocratic functions and institutions divided the production of economic discourse between bureaucratic and academic trajectories, with strong differences in training and intellectual orientation between the two. In a country where political authority is essentially vested in the technocracy, economic discourse (which had mainly emerged as the product of a liberal and decentralized vision of society, and of a commitment to free trade and laissez-faire) long came into conflict with the centralizing and rationalizing nature of the public bureaucracy. As a result, the legitimation of economics as an autonomous "discipline" worthy of a separate curriculum, and as a form of expertise relevant to the state administration, was a late phenomenon, which only crystallized in the postwar period: faced with the task of reconstructing and modernizing their country's economy after the combined devastation of World War II and the Great Depression, French public officials responded by consciously designing a specially trained elite of public economic managers and technicians. A new generation of institutions for technocratic training was established to supply experts to the new administrative organizations (e.g., the Planning Commissariat, the economic and financial studies division of the Ministry of Finance) that were intended to lead France on the path to recovery. This "statist" pattern, which had its heyday between the late 1940s and the late 1970s (but had antecedents as far back as the nineteenth century), profoundly influenced the organization and intellectual identity of the field as a whole. Originating in the tradition of the state engineers, the experts trained through these means developed their own interests and approaches to economic questions, becoming a powerful medium for the formalization of economic research—a disposition that partly conflicted with the more literary and juridical style of university-based economic practitioners. The centralization of material resources (e.g., data, research funds) and decision-making authority around administrative institutions also helped define the production of economic knowledge largely as a "public"—as opposed to a "private"—prerogative. This understanding, which is widely accepted in French society today, also explains why the development of a jurisdiction for economics in the corporate world has remained quite limited (with the notable exception of large public or quasi-public monopolies).

CRITICAL ORGANIZED COMPARISONS

This rapid outline of the three national cases provides a sense of the themes developed in this book. The rushed reader may pause here and resume her reading in chapter 2, which begins the exposition of the cases. Between here and there is a rather long, but necessary, exposé of the comparative structure that lies behind the project as a whole. Indeed, this book involves definite methodological choices about the procedures of the comparison that correspond to clearly defined theoretical goals—all of which must be made explicit. Certainly, the very exercise of sociological comparison offers considerable analytical leverage: through the constant dialogue with "things different," we can understand what is so peculiar (or not) about each country, each scientific field, each school of thought, and so on. Yet the question of *how different things are* is not a simple, hard empirical "fact": it is an intellectual construct that has to be produced through particular methodological, analytical, and narrative strategies.

Qualitative comparative methods tend to fall into two main traditions: variable-oriented and case-oriented.[11] The first method, which entertains an affinity with quantitative methods, compares terms, which are constructed as similar across countries, and deduces outcomes from the joint presence or absence of those terms and from their *combination* with each other. The second method is interpretive in spirit. It proceeds from a more relativist perspective, which, in its purest form (as practiced, for instance, by anthropologists) considers that cases only make sense in their sheer uniqueness.

The problem with the first method is that the "variables" that organize the comparison are highly contextual themselves. The term "state" (*État* in French), for instance, refers to very different realities in the United States and in France: it is not so much that the French and American "states" have different structures, as Evans, Rueschemeyer, and Skocpol (1985) famously pointed out, but that the very idea and exercise of public power are constructed and carried out in a very different manner—state structure being just one indicator of this difference. What is true of institutional structures like the state also applies to ideas. Conceptual histories have shown that terms such as "free trade," "labor," or "civil society" elicited very different understandings at different times and in different places.[12] Comparative research must thus start from this spatial and temporal *variability in the analytical categories that organize the narrative*—and account both for the variable local meanings taken by an object we theoretically construct as similar, and for the ways in which objects we categorize differently across countries might serve, in fact, a similar purpose.

The second, "interpretive," method is highly attentive to the contingent nature of categories and the dilemma posed by the impossibility of stepping out of language. Yet by emphasizing the irreducibility of differences, and sometimes the irrelevance of categorization itself, interpretation runs the risk of falling into pure relativism. Such a posture might thus defeat the purpose of the comparison as an analytical tool by hardly allowing for any theory building. Stefan Collini perhaps best captured this dilemma: "There is . . . a fundamental difficulty to be faced in all attempts to undertake comparative studies in intellectual and cultural history: the units which are to be compared, whether they be ideas and concepts or identities and roles, are very largely constituted by the terms in which they are described. But any description is in one natural language and not others, and each language slices reality in partly different ways" (2006, 202).

This methodological impasse makes necessary both a critical analysis of the categories used in the comparison *and* a discussion of how these terms combine into fairly coherent constellations. We must recognize the legitimacy of categorizing as a way to manage a complex reality and authorize a dialogue between cases. Yet we must also approach the terms that organize the comparison with a critical mind—not as "variables" but as contingent, culturally defined categories. But how should we go about this in practice? One solution, I suggest, is to replace descriptive categories (e.g., academia, state, economy) that take structures for granted with analytical ones that focus on processes and mechanisms.[13] Under which intellectual and institutional conditions did economic knowledge establish its place in the realm of higher learning? How do economic knowledge and expertise enter the way in which public power comes to be defined and exercised? How are both articulated with other professions and other forms of expert (and nonexpert) knowledge?

For lack of a better phrase, I call this approach "critical organized comparison." It becomes clear that in this perspective, not even the category of "economist" can be taken for granted. On the contrary, it becomes *the* central problem of the study, and prompts the main research question to be framed in a fairly agnostic manner as: "What does it mean to be an economist in the United States (Britain, France)?" Rather than treating the concepts of "economist" and "economics" as a given of the analysis, then, we should try to understand what "unities they form" (Foucault 1972, 26), why they are perceived as continuous, individualized objects, and according to which rules their continuity and individualizability varies across nations. In short, we want to *examine the historical conditions that helped crystallize the very idea of what economics is*, and attend closely to changing local classifications and representations of this idea over time.

This position, which takes into account the complex ways people in different countries categorize themselves and others, has a number of important methodological implications. First, no answer to the questions raised here can be produced without turning the horizontal (comparative) exercise into a vertical (historical) one—that is, without simultaneously analyzing critically how each of these understandings came to be. How the production of economic knowledge was first organized, then, appears to be of great importance to understand long-term trajectories. In this regard, the end of the nineteenth century deserves special attention, for it is only around the 1880s–90s that a distinct occupational practice started to crystallize around the labels of political economy, then "economics," in Europe and America. The second methodological imperative is that local definitions, representations, and ideas—as found, for instance, in the popular press, in official classifications, or collected in interviews—must be taken seriously. It appears thus highly relevant for this study that in France, the category of "economist" does not exist as a valid occupational title (not even in the civil service), whereas in the United States and Britain, I was able to find detailed data recording the number of "economists" in government or business since about World War II, and sometimes earlier. On the other hand, it is not uncommon for a *nonspecialist* in France to sign a newspaper article by identifying himself as an "economist," something that is much more rare in the other two countries.[14] We cannot dismiss such details by arguing that French technocrats simply are not economists and are just acting preposterously when they use the label. The fact is, instead, highly relevant, and, properly contextualized and explained, it should enter the comparative exercise of demonstrating how (and why) being an economist in France means something different than it does in other countries.

Studying what I call the "identity" of economics across nations thus means analyzing the ideas, professional roles, and institutional locations associated with the making of economic knowledge and expertise claims in different contexts. Practically, it means producing, for each country, a distinct account of the long-term *modalities* of the embeddedness of the field of economics in national history, culture, and institutions. But it also means showing how such institutional and cultural patterns come to shape the social trajectories and dispositions of *individual* economists—that is, their modes of being, thinking, acting, or what Pierre Bourdieu would call their "habitus." Against the standard assumption of economics that individuals respond more or less rationally to a set of incentives and environmental constraints, then, this book starts from the radically different premise that *different societies create different types of individuals.*

By treating nations as culturally constituted (and constitutive) sets of institutional arrangements, I am thus firmly grounding this study in a macrosociology of culture that has rather fallen out of fashion. Suffering from a long association with psychological reductionism, and from the decisively microsociological stance of the cultural turn in the social sciences, the idea of "national culture" has indeed become somewhat disreputable.[15] Part of this work can be read as an attempt to revive this concept—captured, at the simplest level, through the particular subjective and objective entanglements that people find themselves in—and show its relevance to understanding the sociological character of economics in different places.

NATIONAL CONSTELLATIONS

What, as a first approximation, structures the historical trajectories of economic knowledge as well as the vocabularies, practical logics, and forms of explanation of economics across nations are culturally situated conceptualizations for imagining the social order and their associated institutionally embedded practices.[16] In short, people making knowledge claims about the economy in France, the United States, and Britain act on the basis of different understandings of their intellectual mission, their professional position, and their role in the larger society, but also on the basis of the tacit knowledge—be it social, political, or economic— they acquire as members of that particular society and state. The substantive meaning of "economist" and "economics" in each country is thus constituted psychologically and socially through formal and informal socialization—and most prominently (but not exclusively) professional socialization

This implies that we have to explain not just one but several outcomes at once, from the forms of institutionalization and jurisdictional locations of economics to its intellectual paths. We should thus strive to bind together institutions and ideas, modes of being and modes of acting and seek to analyze "styles of reasoning" (Hacking 2004) and their associated "constellations of practices" (Biernacki 1995, 474) in the same movement. We cannot get a grasp of ideational elements in economics without also analyzing the jurisdictions upon which the profession claims control; nor can we account for the discipline's social and scientific authority without also appreciating the broader dynamics at play in each society's intellectual and political fields.[17] In the case of French economics, for instance, we must seek to understand how the delayed progress of disciplinary institutionalization relates to the peculiarities of economics' jurisdiction within the state and the universities,

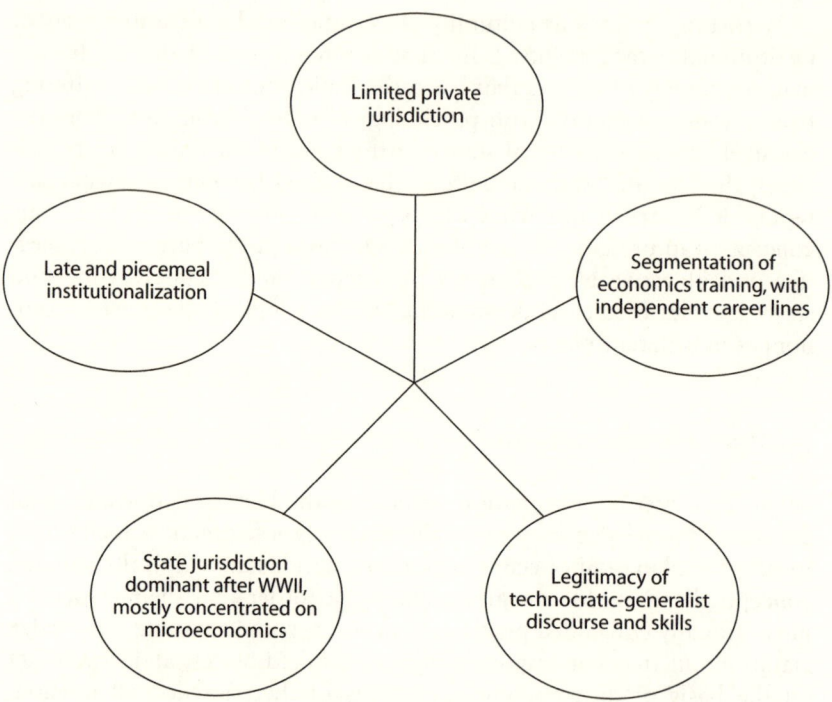

Figure 0-1. Example: the French constellation

as well as to its near absence in the corporate world. To capture this complexity, Figure 0-1 offers a schematic representation of the themes I develop in my analysis of the French constellation.

This inherently "dense" analytical focus on national *clusters* of outcomes and practices, to be studied both longitudinally and comparatively, is thus a self-conscious theoretical choice. By looking at the multiplicity of causes and consequences, such an approach rejects simplistic forms of causality and seeks to capture, instead, the depth of cultural forces. In doing so, it necessarily relies on a conception of culture as eminently *constitutive* rather than simply causally efficacious and likewise treats institutions as cultural, or ontological, forms rather than acultural variables that only serve to channel separate causal mechanisms.[18] The explanatory factor, then, is no less dense than the object to be explained.

What do we mean, then, when we say that economics is a product of culture? We may think about three main ways to conceptualize this connection. First, at the broadest analytical level, is the basic notion that any discourse on the economy is predicated upon preexisting conceptions of the political order, with which it entertains some form of "elective affinity" and which are themselves institutionalized within national organizations and political arrangements. Second, the existence of such "affinities" calls for a middle-range examination of the means whereby they are produced and reproduced—in short, for an analysis of the empirical mechanisms that sustain the distinctive "trajectories" of economic knowledge in each country. Culture, naturally, enters this second analytical level too, since (as we just dicussed) national institutional arrangements are themselves partly endogenously defined.[19] Third, we can push the preceding arguments further into the terrain of the sociology of knowledge by showing that the *context* of economic knowledge production also directly structures the substantive *content* of economics, encouraging the use of certain research orientations, technical tools, styles of reasoning, and theoretical schemes and preventing others from being seen as relevant or appropriate. Furthermore, when these objects are used to "act upon" the "economy," or "act" in economic markets and other locations in society, they also contribute to produce (and reproduce) cultural representations. I will now examine each of these three arguments in turn.

On the Political Roots of Economics

A number of authors have suggested that political culture and institutions shape the general categories available for the production of knowledge. In *Democracy in America* ([1835–40] 2000), for instance, Tocqueville argued that democratic and aristocratic political cultures lead to very different ways of organizing intellectual and scientific life. "Men living in democratic societies," he wrote, "give themselves over to meditation with difficulty, but they naturally have little esteem for it" (435). Democracy, by contrast, encourages a pragmatic orientation toward knowledge: "Every new method that leads to wealth by a shorter path, every machine that shortens work, every instrument that diminishes costs of production, every discovery that facilitates pleasures and augments them seems to be the most magnificent effort of human intelligence. It is principally in this way that democratic peoples apply themselves to the sciences, understand them, and honor them" (436–37). At the same time, the belief in equality on which democracy is built looks at the sciences as a democratic, rather than elitist, pursuit and thereby "increases immensely the number of those who cultivate them" (437).

On the other hand, "in aristocratic societies the class that directs opinion and leads affairs, placed in a permanent and hereditary manner above the crowd, naturally conceives a high-minded idea of itself and of man" (436). In those societies the sciences are practiced mainly by a small social elite, which competes mainly by means of intellectual brilliance.

"The learned are therefore carried along toward theory" and often "conceive an inconsiderate scorn for practice" (436).

Tocqueville makes his point almost casually. He also reduces the fundamental question of how a society's political culture connects empirically to the organization of its scientific and intellectual life to psychosocial mechanisms that lead individual minds toward speculation in one case and toward practical application in another. Since Tocqueville, others have pursued this general intuition, identifying distinctive national ways of understanding the world and formulating arguments, and connecting them to broader cultural patterns and modes of social organization. Galtung (1981), for instance, sketches out a mapping of four national intellectual styles, which he relates to three organizing dimensions of the social structure.[20] Jepperson and Meyer (1991) show that national patterns of formal organizing and organizational theory tend to follow closely patterns of polity organization. In his comparative study of industrial policy, Dobbin (1994) develops the argument that ideas about economic order are formed in a manner that is isomorphic to ideas about political order. Lamont and Thévenot (2000) suggest that intellectual repertoires for passing judgment and justifying intellectual positions are structured differently in France and the United States.[21] Porter (1987), Hacking (1987), and Schweber (2006) show how political culture shaped the way in which nineteenth-century French, British, and Prussian statisticians thought about statistics. Finally, Jasanoff (2005) relates the different framing of biotechnology debates and policies in the United States, Britain, and Germany to the organization of democratic representation, participation, and deliberation in each country.

There are several ways we can apply this general set of theoretical preoccupations concerning the relationship between political culture and the formation of knowledge to the development of economics. First, knowledge about the economy derives, broadly speaking, from political organization—a notion that both the original English term for "economics," "political economy" (économie politique in French) and the German one (Nationalökonomie) capture well. Preclassical (mercantilist) economics, for instance, was very much about strengthening kingdoms by means of organized policies—the promotion of production and exports, the manipulation of interest rates, and the limitation of imports. Similarly, historical connections between the emergence of classical political economy and new conceptions of society as a collection of autonomous, self-conscious individuals—in short, between economic and political liberalism—are well established.[22] In today's world, for instance, parallel liberal political ideologies seem to sustain both the recent enthusiasm about the role of civil society in organizing social life and the dominant economic consensus that so forcefully embraces markets as the best mechanism for regulating economic life. These two frameworks can be seen as different but interrelated ways to celebrate a culture where individual initiative ought to be sovereign.

Second, political governance practices produce distinctive understandings of how the economy is organized, operates, and ought to be managed, if at all—however partial, inadequate, and embryonic these understandings may appear from today's vantage point. Economic discourses partly build on this record: as a matter of fact, important traditions of economic governance were often forged *prior* to the emergence of organized, let alone professionalized, economic discourse. For instance, the policies of Colbert in seventeeth-century France, which inaugurated a tradition of active state involvement, preceded the emergence of political economy as a special domain of intellectual speculation (Colbert's critics, the Physiocrats, were the first individuals to be publicly recognized as *économistes*).[23] Similarly, the development of classical economics in eighteenth-century Britain has been widely understood as a by-product of the Industrial Revolution—whether directly through the interest spurred by the distinctively new nature of economic activities or indirectly through its impact on the political field. Polanyi ([1944] 1957) also famously described the doctrine of laissez-faire as both a cause and a post-hoc rationalization of the free market society which matured after the reform of the Poor Laws in 1834. And naturally, one cannot understand the development of free-trade theory in nineteenth-century England apart from the institution of British imperialism, as well as from diffuse moral conceptions that valued it as being tied to "national liberty, social justice and international peace."[24] This suggests that we should think of disciplinary representations of the economy as partially naturalized accounts of the working of the economy (or polity) from which they emerge.

Third, the expansion of self-conscious economic discourse is closely connected with the construction of the nation-state as a legitimate actor in governing social and economic life. As they organized around the political model of a sovereign state in the eighteenth and nineteenth centuries, emerging political units sought to construct their societies as "legitimate" economies or, to offer a twist on Benedict Anderson's phrase, as *imagined economic communities*—turning their territories into distinct and self-contained economic spaces, by creating separate economic instruments (currencies, tariffs, exchange controls, a fiscal system) and institutions (central banks, stock exchanges, ministries of economics and finance, development and planning agencies). The social construction of national economic territories authorized the emergence of a class of economic writers, later economic experts, who could both produce a discourse about these imagined economic communities and also define legitimate courses of action upon them. In some cases, for instance, in the German states, the institutionalization of university training in *Nationalökonomie* was sponsored directly by political authorities in order to assist the state in its administrative management and revenue-raising tasks.[25]

This discussion suggests quite clearly that ideas about the economy are likely to be formed in a manner that is highly dependent upon characteristics of "the nation" as a political unit. Economic knowledge is constructed upon, but also contributes to produce, representations about social organization, legitimate governance practices, and understandings of national identity. But how are these interrelationships constructed in practice? How do we go from these broad "affinities" to explain the specific features of the construction and functioning of the field of economics across countries?

The Cultural Dimension of Institutions

For the most part, the literature has left unanswered the question of the sociological *processes* whereby political culture shapes the substance and orientation of knowledge. One crucial problem is that culture is a particularly difficult concept to work with at the macrosociological level. As Sewell (1999) reminds us, empirical studies have repeatedly challenged the idea of culture as a "concretely bounded systems of beliefs and practices" à la Ruth Benedict. They have shown that cultures are eminently contradictory, loosely integrated, contested, subject to constant change, and weakly bounded. Should we, then, abandon any idea of coherence in favor of a purely decentralized vision of culture as a resource that actors mobilize and craft—whether strategically or expressively? Not necessarily. "It is important," warns Sewell, "to remember that much cultural practice is concentrated in and around powerful institutional nodes—including religions, communications, media, business corporations, *and, most spectacularly, states*. These institutions, which tend to be relatively large in scale, centralized, and wealthy, are all cultural actors; their agents make continuous use of their considerable resources in efforts to order meanings" (1999, 55–56).

The synthesis offered in this passage has two important theoretical implications. First, it suggests that culture exists only to the extent that individuals work (consciously or unconsciously) at producing and reproducing relatively stable institutions. A long tradition of social phenomenology has taught us that people, through practice, continuously re-create what is merely "thinkable," "doable," or "sayable," for them and for others, and in doing so stabilize (or "institutionalize") their social world, but also contribute to change it.[26] From this point of view, cultural analysis cannot excuse itself from studying *the practical involvement of actors within institutions.* It is from this necessarily messy world that social regularities, institutional designs, and discourses will emerge. The second implication, then, is that this messy world has a certain "cultural gravity," because we have formalized it through rules, fixed it through language, reproduced it through historical narrative and the invention of traditions. Understood in this manner, institutions are thus a good place to study how culture "anchors" practices, to use Ann Swidler's (2001) phrase, and how practices relentlessly (re-)create culture. They are the places where culture is inevitably both "at work" and "being worked out."[27]

It is against such an institutional backdrop that any attempt at connecting political culture to economic knowledge must be constructed. Rather than proceeding from the top down (by relying on a priori or essentialist views of political culture) or from the bottom up (by relying on decentralized, contradictory, and contested individual meanings), I will thus ground my study in a heuristically driven, historical analysis of the key institutional *processes* that have shaped the development of economic knowledge over the last century. Ultimately my task as an analyst will be, as Desrosières (1999) puts it, to show how the patterns observed "hold together" (or do not) in each of the three countries observed (as well as across them).

The processes singled out for detailed study here are (1) the modes of incorporation of economic knowledge into higher education, scientific research, and disciplinary organization (what I call later the "order of learning"); (2) the modes of construction and incorporation of economic knowledge through policy making and policy advice (which I refer to as the "administrative order"); and finally, (3) the place of economic technologies in the broader system of economic relations (the "economic order"). Both the experience of fieldwork and a critical analysis of the existing academic literature inspired these choices.[28] The scholarship on the rise of the social sciences emphasizes the emergence and consolidation of modern *universities* and *states* during the nineteenth and early twentieth centuries as a primary explanation for the birth and institutionalization of the social sciences, economics among them. The sociology of professions, on the other hand, points toward market competition as the driving mechanism of professional development (this dimension, which is unfortunately almost always ignored in sociological analyses of *disciplines*, turns out to be of crucial importance in the case of economics). Of course, this three-point framework does not preclude discussions of additional loci of interest (newspapers, for instance) whenever relevant.

Presumably, as the preceding discussion suggests, the three processes are all tightly coupled together in nationally specific ways, which essentially reflect the different manners in which public power is constructed and exercised across countries. Let us, again, take France as an illustration.[29] There, a public-driven political logic, whose roots can be traced back to the old regime, can be identified in (1) an *academic system* dominated by elite schools and research departments that are closely linked to the public administration; (2) a specific status for non-specialized *administrative expertise*, where economic knowledge plays a relatively large role; (3) an *economy* organized around the planning of key industries, in which public engineers assume important responsibilities (and are thereby led to develop economic capabilities). How these three institutions operate appears to be informed by a common, endogenous logic, which is rooted in the deep, durable political structure of the French public bureaucracy.[30] But it is not that some unique system of representations, or the state as an external force, would *cause* institutions to be shaped in a particular way. Rather, institutions themselves (through the individuals who carry out their logics) are precisely what gives the very idea of political culture any reality, that is, any "thinkability." In this conception, the French system of *grandes écoles* and *grands corps* (which is simultaneously an educational, an administrative, and an economic institution), is not merely a *consequence* of French political culture; rather, the very existence of an administrative elite separated from society by merit and status is *part and parcel* of what French political culture is about.

The political logic exemplified by the French model therefore does not exist in and of itself (and here my view may differ somewhat from Dobbin's [1994]): it does not have any materiality outside of its empirical *realization* in institutions. I look at it, therefore, not as an a priori cause of anything but as a scientific reconstruction a posteriori from the detailed empirical analysis of the logics at work in the institutions that are relevant for the case at hand: here the order of learning, the administrative order, and the economic order. From a methodological standpoint, these three processes are purely heuristic devices that allow me to *organize critically* (in the manner discussed earlier) the comparison between three national fields of economic knowledge. From a theoretical standpoint, the analysis demonstrates empirically the necessity to ground any claim about cultural meaning, or cultural coherence and incoherence, in the concrete analysis of institutions—rather than deriving institutions from culture.

THE ORDER OF LEARNING

The structure of the academic system and the place of economics education and research within it are particularly relevant to understanding the nature of economic knowledge production in each country. As an academically organized form of knowledge, and a training ground for a vast array of business and administrative professions, economics is shaped by broader research and higher education ecologies. The literature on the "prehistory" of disciplines, for instance, reveals that intellectual affinities and divisions are highly contingent upon local social arrangements.[31] Following this line of analysis, any account of the development of knowledge must especially question how educational institutions create further boundaries that will "lock" intellectual enterprises into certain scholastic relations by legitimating some alliances and styles of thought and repudiating others.[32] For instance, by locating the first economics chairs within the faculties of law, and the first sociology ones within philosophy, French public officials in the Ministry of Education made choices that had profound consequences for the long-term orientation of each field, and for its relationship with other intellectual enterprises.[33]

The French academic field has been studied extensively in the work of Pierre Bourdieu (e.g., 1984, 1988). Bourdieu found that the social sciences occupy a very peculiar position among all scientific fields in that external factors play an especially important part in determining these fields' internal stratification and structure of authority. Professors in the "law/political science/economics" colleges and universities are proportionally better endowed with "economic capital" than those situated in institutions devoted to the "humanities," whose capital is more heavily "cultural." Within each disciplinary field, the subjective (i.e., agentic) and objective (i.e., structural) positions of individuals are "homologous": in other words, the polar opposition between "economic" and "cultural" capital is replicated at the field's level, and mirrors the orthodoxy/heterodoxy divide. Applying Bourdieu's framework to French economics, Lebaron (1997, 2000) finds that the splitting of positions between the two dimensions of the volume and structure of capital also characterizes this particular field's internal structure. Thus top civil servants, business executives, and certain political leaders rank high on the "volume of capital" scale (as opposed to professionals in less prestigious positions). The "structure of capital" variable, on the other hand, opposes researchers (with proportionally more cultural capital) to CEOs of large private enterprises (with proportionally more economic capital), with higher civil servants being in a relatively intermediate position (Lebaron 1997, 126).

One may object that the conceptual framework developed in *Homo Academicus* and in *The State Nobility* rests on an empirical analysis of French higher education during the 1980s and is thus irrelevant to the task at hand. But this would be completely missing the point: if the *specific* findings relative to the organization of the French intellectual field at that time do not travel easily to other countries and other periods, this is not the case of the general arguments that (1) every intellectual field is stratified according to the nature of the competition that takes place within it, and that (2) these internal struggles are related to external struggles in society as a whole, and particularly in what Bourdieu calls the "field of power."

The production and organization of intellectual knowledge, then, must be studied from the point of view of the distribution of power and authority, either across disciplines within a larger field (e.g., the "social sciences") or within each disciplinary tradition. How do we translate this argument into a comparative analysis? From a comparative point of view, the concept of "field" remains extremely useful, but it must be modified to account for national differences in the social bases of authority. Hence it will not be the same institutions that confer "capital" and status, or sustain authoritative and legitimate positions in different countries. Thus in the United States, the market has provided a central reference not only for understanding the economy but also for organizing the entire higher education domain (e.g., intellectual stars, particularly in economics, can be identified by the high salaries that they command). Yet in spite of (or, as we will see, perhaps *because of*) this relatively competitive institutional framework, powerful mechanisms of academic and political control have sustained a broad harmonization of intellectual practices within the field of economics. In Britain, on the other hand, a class-divided society has produced a more stratified profession, dominated by centers of intellectual authority and societal power in Cambridge, Oxford, and, increasingly, London. Finally, in France, relative closeness to administrative power constitutes the main factor of stratification within the field of economics.

THE ADMINISTRATIVE ORDER

How economics gets entangled with and defined as "policy" in different national contexts constitutes a second obvious research site. Political and administrative institutions are important vehicles of legitimation for the disciplinary and professional projects of the various social sciences, also shaping how they form, expand, and change. Since the end of World War II, modern polities have formally committed themselves to a particular role in the economy and increasingly acknowledged the special place of economic information and expertise within government structures and administrations. Thus the *White Paper on Full Employment* in the United Kingdom (1944), the Employment Act in the United States (1946), and the Préambule to the 1946 Constitution in France all officially recognized (to varying degrees) the state's duty to ensure economic growth and welfare for its citizens.[34] The United Nations charter proclaims protection against unemployment as a fundamental human right.[35]

The structure and operation of administrative and political institutions play an important role in defining the social sciences' academic and professional space. Gieryn's (1999) investigation of the establishment of the National Science Foundation in the United States, for instance, provides a nice, concrete illustration of how disciplinary boundaries (in this case, the demarcation between the natural and social sciences) get socially constructed through political struggle. More generally, comparative-historical scholars have pointed out the importance of administrative institutions in determining the emergence of modern social-scientific discourses. In an effort to account for the successful (or failed) institutionalization of particular public policy ideas in different countries, some of these analyses have shown how local political institutions shape both the modes of access of social scientists and experts to the political realm and the substantive content of the knowledge they produce. Thus Hall (1989, 1992, 1993), Weir and Skocpol (1985), Weir (1989), and Blyth (2002) have studied extensively the institutional conditions under which economic policy paradigms either gain acceptance or get dismissed and replaced, showing that policy innovation is greatly affected by the way economic experts are incorporated in the governmental machinery. Campbell (1998) and Prasad (2006) show how political movements and economic interests help certain policy programs rise to the fore. As Skocpol and Rueschemeyer argue, "The social composition, ideas, and favored modes of research and argument of knowledge-bearing groups are profoundly influenced by the social status arrangements and the political institutions of their respective societies. In turn, these larger contexts influence whether and how policy-oriented intellectuals can have influence within national politics" (1996, 10).

Administrative institutions shape the trajectory of economics in many other ways, however. As pointed out earlier, institutions are cultural objects that produce meaning—not simply organizational arrangements that filter access. By defining the terms under which economic knowledge is incorporated into public policy, public administrations have implicitly contributed to *construct* the professional role of the economist—not simply how much influence he or she may have. In the United States, for instance, economists came to be incorporated into the state and federal bureaucracy as professionals with specific skills that were deemed relevant to the execution of certain public functions. In France, it is the administrative profession itself that was defined and reconstructed to accommodate the expansion of the state's role in the economy, with powerful effects on the production of knowledge.

In both cases, obviously, the state stimulated the knowledge orientations that suited its own political projects. The nature of economic knowledge in different countries is thus closely connected to the nature of administrative demands and to institutionalized representations about the exercise of public power. The key question, then, is not just one of the amount of state intervention, but one of its kind. The research practices of economists are partly constructed upon cultural assumptions regarding the state's economic prerogative and build upon specific understandings about the legitimate domains of application of this prerogative. In this perspective, French engineer-economists' fundamental contributions concerning the management, planning, and pricing of public goods appear closely related to the French state's early leadership in orchestrating industrial activities.[36] The British tradition of welfare economics inaugurated by Marshall and pursued by a long line of scholars (e.g., Pigou, Hicks, Meade, Sen) ought to be tied to a relatively hands-off and liberal state nonetheless obsessed with its moral commitment to the less fortunate members of society.

THE ECONOMIC ORDER

The relation of economic knowledge to its very own object—the economy—provides a third type of process through which we can understand how the economics profession has been constructed in different countries. How is economic knowledge incorporated within what Andrew Abbott (1988) calls the "system of professions"? What is its economic base? This line of investigation comes from the fundamental insight that economics is not only a discursive form—a knowledge, a discipline. It is, essentially, a profession. Not a well-bounded one, like medicine or law, which have strict barriers to entry and certification mechanisms. Anyone who wishes can claim to be an economist. And this is a common job title indeed. In the United States, surveys by the National Science Foundation have found considerable numbers of self-identified "economists"—who are mainly located in the business sector and the majority of whom hold nothing but a BA in the discipline. In France, by contrast, many public technocrats—*énarques*, members of the *grands corps*—might present themselves as such.

Economics is a profession in the sense that Abbott gives to this word: a "group with common work" (1988, 20). If one accepts the idea that there exists such a thing as "economic work"—that is, a relatively homogeneous body of knowledge and technique pertaining to the analysis of, and action upon markets, corporations or the economy as a whole—then the question: "Who performs economic work across countries?" becomes critical to any understanding of national variations in the jurisdictional domain of economics. In the United States especially, and Britain to a lesser extent, jurisdiction over "economic work" has tended to be claimed by people who are recognizably (for instance, through educational diploma) specialists. Naturally such "economists" exist in France too, but a significant part of "economic work," including important contributions to economic theory, has also been, for a long time, accomplished by different social groups—public administrators and engineers.

Where economic work is performed matters a lot, too. In the United States, economic concepts and instruments are embedded in the market to an extent that is unparalleled elsewhere. Academically certified economists can be found performing distinctive functions in lawyers' offices and courts, political staffs and lobbies, marketing departments, or consulting firms. This ubiquity of economic knowledge in America, and its relevance to a large number of occupations, corresponds to the greater market orientation of the "system of professions" at large: professions exist in an interactive ecology, which is structured by groups with competing jurisdictional claims. This means that considerable activity will take place around the definition of ever more specific jurisdictions. In this perspective, the "system of professions" becomes highly differentiated, with sometimes extremely narrow and overlapping professional niches.

Yet the systematic exercise of competition in the professional domain also means—and this is an implicit consequence of Abbott's model which has often been overlooked—that professions will be quite intimately *linked* to one another through this very exercise of competition. This will tend to produce a system of what I call "nested jurisdictions," whereby some professions get incorporated within the jurisdiction of other professions. One of the best examples of such a process is the role of scientists in the legal domain. The prominent place of science "at the bar" is not the result of a competition between science and the law: rather, it should be understood as a mutually reinforcing relationship, whereby the law uses science to expand its jurisdictional claims, and science finds in the law a means to assert its authority in society more broadly (and also to improve its financial position).[37]

This pattern is especially characteristic of the American professional landscape, where market competition is institutionalized as the legitimate way to organize the economy. In many countries, however, administrative regulation or corporatist arrangements limit the competition over jurisdictions. For instance, until recently in France, several professions still reproduced themselves through the sale of state-controlled *charges* inherited from the old regime.[38] More important, perhaps, a model of economic organization centered on the state tends to fundamentally affect the modalities of existence of the "system of professions." To the extent that such interlocking occurs, the jurisdictions of economics in such a system would tend to be "built" into the state profession itself, as opposed to "nested" within other professions in the market. Fundamental differences in the organization of the economy, then, affect whether and how professions formulate claims vis-à-vis a particular jurisdiction, or vis-à-vis each other—in sum, they affect the nature of jurisdictions ("nested" or "built-in") and their location. From this point of view, the jurisdiction of economics in France is almost the reverse image of its counterpart in the United States: since the nineteenth century, economics has constituted an important part of the identity of French public administrators—both generalist and technical ones—yet economists have played a quite limited role vis-à-vis the corporate world.

The Dialectical Relationship between Culture and Economics

One of the central tenets of the sociology of knowledge, as stated in Mannheim's classic essay ([1936] 1985), is that any form of thought, whether mundane or scientific, is politically informed by the social location of the individuals and groups who produce it. The recent sociology of science has given a much more agonistic twist to this insight. First, scientific fields have come to be regarded as fields of social struggle (Bourdieu 1975; Gieryn 1995) where the broader social interests of agents shape the scientific theories they produce and determine the strategies through which they seek to assert their authority (see also, for instance MacKenzie's [1981] analysis of British statisticians' relation to the eugenics movement or Latour's [1987] development of the concept of "translation"). Second, broader physical or institutional arrangements matter in shaping the outcome of these struggles.[39] Richard Whitley (1984) and Knorr-Cetina (1999), respectively, have shown that disciplines vary significantly in social structure and epistemic culture, depending on their system of work organization and control or even their physical organization. In an important review, Camic and Gross (2001) see this rejection of the internal (intellectual) versus external (social) divide in the analysis of knowledge as the main common ground in what they call the "new sociology of ideas."

A proper sociology of economic knowledge must thus examine the articulation between professional and intellectual forms in economics. In doing so, I will seek to avoid two common blind spots. The first one is that of essentialist conceptions of knowledge, which tend to dissociate discourses from the professional practices they are embedded in, and to focus on disciplinary development as a matter of pure intellectual genealogy. The second bias complements the first one and concerns a sociology of professions that remains un-preoccupied with the substantive forms of the knowledge produced by its "objects" (be they individuals, groups, or organizations). Instead, we should think about the substantive styles of scientific investigation and the practice of economics as coevolving within a space of possibilities defined by the broader institutional makeup of their society. Methodologically, this research thus provides a strong argument for the combined treatment of intellectual *and* jurisdictional forms of knowledge, but also for a proper account of the latter's inscription in their broader social environment.

For instance, what I call the "imperialism" of American economics, that is, its ability to produce tools for a large variety of applications (including commercial ones), cannot be understood without referring to the general embeddedness of expertise in the institutional form of the market in the United States. By contrast, French economics, whose jurisdiction is more closely bound to the realm of the state, has been much less prone to professionalize along such "marketable" lines and has remained more theoretical (at the university, for instance), or associated with a tradition of public economics and theoretical econometrics. Also interesting are the subtle cross-national differences in attitudes toward mathematics and formalization, a point I develop at some length in the case studies.

One important implication of this account, then, is to contest the "naturalness" or "taken-for-grantedness" of intellectual and professional development in modern economics. Our task will be to trace the institutional and cultural factors that have been constitutive of the economists' attitudes toward their own professional jurisdiction, as well as of their intellectual attitudes vis-à-vis particular analytical frameworks. The point is not to veer toward overdetermination but to empirically demonstrate that economic theories are themselves situated knowledge, deeply embedded in nationally specific contexts of economic, administrative, and scholarly *practice*. This means that much of the work in this book will be directed toward the substantive analysis, or the how and why, of these differences.

Thus far, I have described the analytical path that leads from political culture/institutions to knowledge forms. But this is not the whole story. After all, the relationship between culture and economics is not one-directional but dialectical: by their very nature, economic knowledge and expertise also participate in the production/reproduction of state forms and economic forms. This is true at two levels. First, economic ideas give rise to certain types of societal projects, such as the transformation of state structures and capacities.[40] But at a broader level, economic ideas and theories contribute to the production of economic culture and institutions themselves. To use Callon's phrase, the distinctiveness of economics as a science is its fundamentally "performative" character. "Economics, in the broad sense of the term, performs, shapes and formats the economy" (1998a, 2). Sociologists, then, should turn their attention toward the "embeddedness of markets in economics"—and study how economic ideas and analytical tools are routinely made to construct and transform the way economies work.

The idea of economics' performativity is both elegant and powerful. But it can easily lead to an implicit exclusion of national variations in economic knowledge from analytical purview. Is it possible, then, to reconcile performativity with the framework presented here? I argue that it is. From a comparative point of view, the interesting question has precisely to do with the articulation between economic knowledge and economic culture—with the *degree of performativity* allowed to economic theories in different nations, or with the *substantive direction taken by the performance* itself. To put it simply, different economic theories across nations might contribute to "performing" different economies, and universalized economic ideas and tools (such as the Black-Scholes formula studied by MacKenzie [2006]), once available, may not format *all* financial markets similarly. As the next chapters will show, the real-world imperialism of American economics, and its ability to shape and format the economy, is quite unique in its depth and predicated on specific institutional conditions. By contrast, economics in France has had more difficulty establishing the legitimacy of its position, both as an institutionalized enterprise and as a performative one. Furthermore, it has helped shape a quite different economy.

The task of a comparative cultural analysis of economics is to understand such discrepancies. It is to comprehend how economists and economic ideas "fit," in the deepest sense, within the different national cultures in which they emerge and operate, and how they contribute to (re)producing these cultures. It is in this dual sense—of being both culturally constructed and culturally efficacious—that this book will analyze economics as a cultural form.

CHAPTER ONE

Institutional Logics in Comparative Perspective

As SUGGESTED in the introduction, the long-term development of economics exhibits several interrelated trends that cut across national boundaries: economics attained autonomy as a discipline; it became more formal in its presentation; it expanded its influence into both the administrative and the corporate domains; and it partly converged in scientific form and method. These trends, however, evolved unevenly in the United States, Britain, and France: marketization has been much less pronounced in France than in America, for instance. Furthermore, we may trace similar trends back to different institutional mechanisms and groups of actors. The reason, this book contends, has to do with what I called earlier the definition and exercise of public power and its concrete articulation in the educational, administrative and economic domains, which shapes the *practical worlds* that people who claim expertise and knowledge about the economy inhabit. To understand how national contexts shaped the trajectory of economics, then, we must understand, through institutional analysis, how different social systems constitute certain types of actors as legitimate—whether the PhD-holding professional in the United States, the genteel scholar in the United Kingdom, or the public administrator in France. We must then show how these taken-for-granted social types imply particular modes of economic knowledge production.

The present chapter broadly defines the cultural-institutional boundaries within which these practical worlds emerged in the three countries. Before dealing with the subject of economics proper, I devote the next pages to describing the fairly stable differences in polity organization among the three nations that have persisted above and beyond any longitudinal transformations. My purpose in this endeavor is to give some depth to the notion of national "context" and to identify the variations that are relevant from a *comparative* point of view—the distinctive configurations in political, economic, and academic organization that took shape in each country and unfolded over time. Following Spillman (2004), the expository logic in this chapter will be interpretive (trying to penetrate the categories that are relevant in each social system) and "colligatory" rather than merely causal: the purpose is to "[colligate] the various happenings concerned under a single appropriation" (Walsh cited in Spillman 2004, 225) by drawing attention to the common ideas that underlie particular historical processes. In this particular case, however, the joining together of various patterns into a colligatory concept will be located at the national rather than at the temporal level.

FEDERAL CONSTITUTIONALISM IN AMERICA

Tocqueville ([1835] 2000) and even more Lipset (1963a) argued that a nation's moment of political emergence shapes its "habits of heart," or what we often call its "culture." American society, they argued, was forged by the flight from religious oppression, the experience of the frontier, and Puritanism; these historical experiences were also institutionalized through narratives Americans told themselves about themselves. In these accounts, Americans also developed a strong dislike of privileges and centralized power and became jealously protective of citizens' rights. They also cultivated a particular version of egalitarianism understood not as redistributive justice but as "equality of opportunity." The founders of the American Republic designed institutions, mainly legal ones, that sought to guarantee the "sovereignty of the people" against the assertion of central power in its various forms. The American constitutional system, which was designed to restrain federal authority by protecting the autonomy of individual states and to restrain state and federal governments' powers in order to protect individuals from unwanted interference in their affairs, translated these ideas into a series of institutional devices to safeguard the principle of community self-rule. In the political domain, this decentralized and individualistic logic has produced a political and administrative system where power is spread among federal, state, and local authorities, as well as among the different branches of government. The cultural legitimacy of this form of political organization is mainly articulated in terms of service to the interests of the public (or society) rather than the service of the state. In the economic domain, it encouraged the development of institutions that bar the government from direct economic activity except to bolster market processes against "illegitimate" (understood as "unfair") behavior by corporate actors (including unions). Finally, in the academic domain, the same decentralized logic prevailed, leading to the creation of a competitive higher education field populated by private establishments, as well as public ones with considerable institutional autonomy. The end result of this process was the entrenchment of a strong disciplinary system at the heart of American universities and a stratification of knowledge that is tightly linked to competition for students, funds, and ideas.

The "Rational State" in America

One common view among commentators on American political history is that the most important explanation for the character of the modern U.S. political structure is the absence of a feudal past. In his classic 1955 assessment, Hartz argued that contrary to European countries, where modern state structures emerged out of social conflict among competing power holders, American political culture was forged through the experience of self-government—that is, without the organizing and authoritative pressure of a central power. The advent of democracy in local communities, which Tocqueville ([1835] 2000) immortalized in his description of the New England township, preceded the growth of a true national state. As a result, the federal governing structure, which emerged after the Revolution, continued to preserve the local autonomy of political subunits such as municipalities and states. Until the Civil War and its aftermath, nation-building in the United States was largely a bottom-up process—in sharp contrast with France, where the state asserted its authority by crushing regional powers, or with England, where the monarchy brokered a deal with the landed aristocracy in order to maintain its existence.[1]

As in Britain, American public life tends to confer high public standing to individuals. The British version of individualism, however, is also combined with a strong class system topped by a sovereign and a social elite (or establishment), which traditionally occupies a leading role in politics and administration. By contrast, American individualism is more explicitly rooted in the common person and what Tocqueville called the "equality of conditions." It emphasizes self-reliance, initiative, and personal work ethic and celebrates individual success over any other type of achievement. Hence the American reverence for the "self-made man" contrasts quite sharply with the British respect for the "gentleman," whose distinction of status, but also education and manners, gives him moral authority and also responsibility vis-à-vis the rest of society.[2]

A political consequence of this reification of individual actorhood is that the development of central government authority in America has always been subject to suspicion, if not outright hostility. Consequently, Americans were particularly careful to design administrative and political institutions that guaranteed the dispersion of political authority among the many branches of government and also enabled social interests to permeate state structures and participate in the conduct of government.[3] In fact, such characteristics of the American political structure have persisted in spite of and above the massive expansion of the federal government's capacities during Reconstruction and then in the twentieth century.

The United States, like Britain, was thus slow to develop a professionalized civil service. Public officialdom in America was traditionally dominated by party patronage. Tocqueville noted during his travels that its quality was poor ([1835] 2000, 223–24). This contrasted markedly with the more formalized rules for entering government service in continental Europe and the quasi-aristocratic status conferred by that function. Hence, while France and Prussia already had well-institutionalized public bureaucracies in the seventeenth century, the modern boundaries of the American public bureaucracy were forged much later, during the Progressive period. Factionalism, incoherence, and instability characterized public service throughout the nineteenth century, at a time when the American government was rapidly expanding its capacities. Thus when bureaucratic reform was introduced in the 1880s, its main achievement was, to use Skowronek's (1982) expression, to "patch up" a state on the brink of unmanageability.

The basic structure of the civil service emerged between the creation of the merit system by the Pendleton Act in 1883 and the formalization of the role structure by the Personnel Classification Act in 1923.[4] The first reform established the principle of special examinations as a basis for access to lower-level civil service positions, and that of merit evaluations as a basis for promotion, but it laid down no career lines or tenure rules. The U.S. civil service thus did not emerge as a specialized profession or elite *corps* (as in continental Europe); neither did it ever imply long-term and rather predictable career trajectories (as in Britain). Rather, the administrative structure was organized around "positions" identified with certain skills. Individuals applied to these positions on the basis of their training and specialization, rather than their seniority or belonging to a particular class of administrators. As such, the structure remained potentially open to outsiders at every level, provided they possessed the required qualifications. The second reform, in 1923, confirmed this orientation by formalizing job classifications and hierarchies.

The upshot of these two reform bills was a twofold modification of the so-called spoils system. First, the provisions that sought to isolate the regular civil service from politics resulted in its de facto close association with executive (rather than legislative) authority. Second, whereas civil service reform succeeded in cutting lower bureaucratic positions off from political influences, patronage continued to operate at the top, especially in positions involving direct oversight of policy making. In the 1920s and 1930s, about one-third of civil service positions—including the vast majority of senior administrative offices—remained patronage positions.[5] By the early 1980s, politically controlled appointments still represented about 10 percent of all senior executive service positions.[6] As Chandler puts it, "When the President leaves office, so do approximately 200,000 senior bureaucrats" (2000, 206).

Born in a democratically mobilized polity, the American administrative system has remained less independent of political forces than its counterparts in Europe, many of which evolved out of autocratic political structures. No distinct body of administrative law protects the state bureaucracy in the United States (this is also the case in the United Kingdom). Public administration in America is also far less elitist than in what Tocqueville called the "aristocratic societies" of the Old World. The training of public officials is only loosely specialized. In a situation where "the line between the inside and the outside of government is extremely difficult to draw," public policy diplomas are not exclusively associated with public careers but serve as entry tickets into a much larger set of occupations.[7]

Both in law and in practice, public administration in the United States thus does not represent a separate order conferring special social standing. Rather, it relies on skills that are already recognized as the province of a particular profession that typically originates *outside the public realm*.[8] Silberman, for instance, notes that the American public service is "oriented toward the utilization of individual skills, without much regard to whether they were acquired outside or inside the organization."[9] This situation means that occupational identification among civil servants tends to be more firmly rooted in their respective professions than in their public status.

Markets as the Law

The American political distrust of centralized political power has a natural corollary in the celebration of the market. First, in *comparative terms*, the United States is probably the Western country where the free-enterprise system (meant literally) rules most naturally—witness, for instance, the remarkable ease with which private endeavors of any kind (corporations, associations, churches) can acquire legal corporate status.[10] Second, Americans see competition and freedom of enterprise as more than just the ingredients of good institutional design; these concepts have real moral force being inextricably linked to a vision of the good society that goes back to the early days of the American Republic.[11] As Theodore Lowi puts it, the commitment to economic laissez-faire has historically "made a happy fit with the native American fear of political power" (1969, 5). It is also legitimated by a Puritan tradition that valorizes individual effort and personal initiative.[12] Finally, the failure of socialism in the United States meant that Americans could look to no practical example of an alternative to capitalism in their historical experience.[13]

Yet as many scholars have shown, the early industrial development of the United States was shaped in important ways by quasi-public corporations, which were formed by local and state governments eager to encourage economic growth in their region. This pattern was especially common in the infrastructure and transportation sectors (e.g., with turnpikes, canals, and, albeit to a lesser extent, railroads), where a quasi-developmentalist paradigm prevailed for a good part of the nineteenth century. By the 1840s and 1850s, however, attacks on these public agencies (often based on corruption charges) had led most American governments to retreat from economic activism and to privatize most public corporations, giving way to the pattern that still characterizes much of the country's industrial structure. In this policy reversal, emergent private firms, especially large ones, received considerable privileges in order to fulfill their role as "engines of growth":

> No other country in the modern world ever granted such princely favors to private business to foster the rapid growth of industry as did the United States in the nineteenth century. Witness the general land policy, grants to railroad and bounties to other private enterprises, special favors in taxation, corporate privileges conferring public rights and functions upon banks and other undertakings, and the most general and generous eleemosynary tariff ever known. This complex system of public favors to private industry was in full force by 1870 *before there was any considerable body of economic doctrine developed on our soil.* (Fetter 1925, 18, emphasis mine)

At the same time, though, the advantageous conditions enjoyed by businesses raised fears of a concentration of power in the hands of market place winners. Under public pressure, late nineteenth-century governments passed laws and established regulatory institutions designed to enforce price competition, prevent "unfair" trade practices, and oversee various sectors of the economy.[14] As Dobbin (1994) and others have shown, the creation of the first regulatory agency in 1887 and the Sherman Antitrust Act in 1891 created the institutional conditions for what might be called the "rule of markets" in America.[15] The Sherman Act, says Letwin,

> is a peculiarly American institution, emerging from a legal tradition which, though not unique in the United States, is one of the great foundations of American civilization, and expressing a policy that has nowhere been followed so long and consistently as in the United States. If not the most powerful instrument of economic policy in the United States, the Sherman Act is the most characteristic. (1965, 3)

The Sherman Act implied that markets are not simply the *structure* of the American economy: they are its *law*. Markets are not only the best mechanism, but really the only *legally admissible* mechanism for promoting economic growth and efficiency. Two points, however, are worth emphasizing concerning the substantive content of the law of markets in the United States. First, the Sherman Antitrust Act was applied chiefly to loose networks or pools of firms but tolerated tight combinations of firms or mergers. The irony is that while U.S. antitrust law was designed to prevent collusion, it ended up giving birth to the large, concentrated corporation by forcing small firms to sell out to big ones or face the consequences of merciless price competition. It thereby legitimized the idea that, properly enforced, the oligopoly is the most reasonable and realistic approximation of the ideal of perfect competition. From the 1950s and 1960s on, these conceptions then fed into more extreme legal arguments that recommended that most market situations—even those characterized by large concentrations of power in practice—be sanctioned as inherently "competitive."

The other notable point is that the economic paradigm that emerged at the end of the nineteenth century also gave rise to some of the most unique aspects of the American administrative structure in economic matters, sharpening the role of the judiciary and creating the model of the "independent regulatory agency" that contrasts so remarkably with the more direct management style of—for instance—the French state. In Shonfield's words, the American state is best understood not as an uninvolved spectator of markets, as laissez-faire ideology would suggest, but rather as a muscular "referee," an arbiter and protector of market competition (1965, 330). Independent agencies seek to ensure compliance primarily through the mobilization of industry self-restraint and voluntary agreement with a set of negotiated ground rules; if these are deemed insufficient, however, they may go to great lengths in manipulating property rights and engaging in policies that are adversarial to business interests or practices.[16]

This is not to say that the United States has used only regulatory as opposed to administrative forms of political control over the economy. After all, the United States was one of the first countries to experiment with price controls and rationing during World War II.[17] National economic planning was explicitly embraced during the war, and industrial policy was seriously debated during the late 1970s through the early 1980s, when public trust in corporate America was at a low point.[18] Many industries (e.g., the pharmaceutical industry, the nuclear industry, the internet, and even the railroads back in the nineteenth century) arose out of active financial inducements by state and federal agencies. Finally, the United States continues to have quasi-corporatist arrangements in many key areas (the most prominent of these may be agriculture, defense, aerospace, and housing).[19] Still, even the most extreme of these interventions (for instance, government bailouts) almost never imply direct state management: American public agencies have generally rejected administrative mechanisms as a means to promote the development of specific sectors, opting instead to encourage market creation. In contrast with Europe, utilities in America are more likely to be in private hands or to have been privatized after initially being publicly owned.[20] The pension system and the health care system have always been partially private. Large parts of the American educational sector and the prison system are private or have been privatized, which has not occurred elsewhere.[21]

Academic Professionalism and the American University

These basic patterns of decentralized institutional development also hold true for America's system of higher education. In contrast with French and German public bureaucracies' minute planning of their national systems of post-secondary education, the first American colleges and universities developed as formally independent entities that were largely controlled by local trustees and administrators. After the landmark "Dartmouth College" case in 1819, private educational institutions in the United States also received legal protection from government interference.[22]

Between the Civil War and World War I, the modern university took shape in the United States. Part of this "educational revolution," as many scholars term it, was quantitative in character. Between 1870 and 1928, the number of students enrolled in institutions of higher education went from 62,000 to close to 1.2 million.[23] Not only was the expansion rapid, but it was also remarkably early by international standards. By the late nineteenth century the United States was already a world leader in terms of university attendance rates, and this advance persisted through much of the twentieth century.

The educational revolution was also qualitative. Until the middle of the nineteenth century, American colleges and universities were relatively modest establishments, often controlled by clerics, which combined classical education with moral and religious instruction. After the 1860s, however, two major developments profoundly transformed the relationship between education and society in the United States. First, the passage of land-grant legislation in 1862 and 1890 (the Morrill Acts) allocated federal funds to states for the purpose of setting up public institutions of higher education. Through these universities and their attention to agriculture, the mechanical arts, and applied sciences, the federal government sought to promote a model of advanced training geared toward practical uses. Second, philanthropic industrialists also gratified their interest in higher education by founding a group of wealthy private universities. Johns Hopkins endowed the first of these new institutions on the German research university model in 1876, and Leland Stanford, Jonas Clark, Commodore Vanderbilt, and John D. Rockefeller (University of Chicago) followed suit soon thereafter.[24]

In contrast to the older American colleges, which sought primarily to initiate students into generalist "culture," and to the practical orientation of the land-grant establishments, the new universities organized themselves around the transmission of specialized knowledge. Institutions supported by private wealth thus promoted research as the center of the academic vocation, turning it into a full-time occupation that made the production of knowledge itself the basis of interinstitutional competition. This commitment triggered a movement toward academic specialization, which also entailed the secularization of the curriculum and its expansion along scientific lines, the institutionalization of the departmental structure (following the University of Chicago's leadership), and the establishment of the PhD as the main certificate of academic competence. Finally, Charles Eliot, who served as president of Harvard from 1869 to 1909, inaugurated the free elective system whereby students chose their studies from among a set academic fields of formally equal value. This approach quickly spread, installing a consumer orientation at the center of American higher education and signaling the determination of its leaders to let the system be governed by the demands of society at large.

Burton Bledstein argues that the early institutionalization of a consumer orientation and the existence of a class of specialized university administrators separate from the academic body represent unique characteristics of the American academic context. At the turn of the century, this situation contrasted sharply with other systems of higher education where state bureaucracies (continental Europe) or elite professors (England) retained a considerable influence on the definition of curricula and the evaluation of intellectual "needs." In the United States, which lacked both a centralizing state and powerful academic guilds, the market was at the heart of academic culture from the very beginning. Competitive mechanisms came to govern many aspects of the university's internal economy, from funding sources and the recruitment of students and faculty to the development of programs of study, as well as its relations to the network of similar institutions.[25]

The graduate school and later the professional school[26] became the cornerstones of a culture of specialization that was directed at identifiable audiences. As the main providers of high-level credentials, the universities supported the rise of new professions and the expansion of old ones (e.g., medicine, law), at the same time that they were legitimated by them. Abbott makes the point that American professions used the universities as allies in internal jurisdictional conflicts over the division of labor, turning the academic scene into an arena of interprofessional competition (1988, 207–8). For instance, universities often became sites for the development of professional organizations. The expansion of graduate schools thus coincided with the foundation of specialized journals and the proliferation of national specialist associations that controlled and regulated the new professions.[27]

Chief among these groups with new professional claims were the academic disciplines, which rapidly established themselves as the fundamental social structure for organizing higher learning. Abbott (2000, 125–28) suggests that the prodigious growth and strength of the academic disciplines in the American context can be traced to two fundamental sources: first, the market-based, interuniversity organization of the production and circulation of academic labor; and, second, the intrauniversity market for undergraduate majors, which was established at the turn of the century by introducing an element of specialization into the elective system. The department and the college major are the two institutional structures from which the disciplinary system has drawn its strength and persistence over the long run.

The durability of the American university department can be traced, in turn, to its dual role as a teaching unit and as the main site for the production of academic research. In contrast to France, where research came to be organized in separate institutions and academies, or to England, where it was long practiced in clubs and learned societies, in the United States, academic research came to be firmly institutionalized in the graduate school. During the first half of the twentieth century, doctorate-granting activity progressively became the primary vehicle for the consolidation and expansion of research resources in American universities.[28] This "research university" pattern has remained profoundly stable over the course of the twentieth century despite many transformations in the regulation and funding base of the research economy. These include the rise of philanthropic foundations during the interwar period, the shift to a largely federally financed system after World War II, and the later move to private funding sources that began in the last quarter of the twentieth century. These changes dramatically affected the magnitude of the research effort and often its substantive orientations. Nevertheless, they did not fundamentally alter the *organization* of research and intellectual work more broadly, which continued to be centered in the institutions of the university and the disciplinary system.[29]

The Rise and Fall of British Elitism

The British polity has often been described as a "weak state."[30] In justifying this terminology, some scholars go all the way back to the time of the Magna Carta (1215), when the domination of the landed class over the monarchy was first established. The 1688 revolution then confirmed and expanded the sovereignty of the Parliament against that of the Crown. Both factors—early parliamentary rule and the extraordinary concentration of wealth and economic power in the hands of the British landed and mercantile elite—ensured the relative independence of wealthy individuals and their representatives from the Crown and institutionalized a political system that was heavily rooted in local estates and the constituencies they represented.

The social and political legitimacy of the landed class and its appendages (e.g., industrialists) thus extended well beyond parliamentary control. In the nineteenth century, members of the gentry also occupied local offices and ran local governments with considerable autonomy from the state. Whereas in France such functions were accomplished by paid bureaucrats who were accountable to the state only, in England they were regarded as the benevolent privilege of the wealthy and educated. As we will see, this same genteel culture extended partly to the practice of science and the conduct of central government affairs.

British nineteenth-century political culture thus looked to responsible gentlemen to take the initiative in public affairs.[31] The British were wary of the state, "which existed mainly to serve the convenience and protect the rights of individuals in private life" (Harris 1990b, 67). Against central government, the local institutions of "civil society" (philanthropies, mutual aid societies, clubs, trade unions) were "the rightful locus of public life." Charities of all kinds offered a buffer against the deficiencies of liberal capitalism. The centralization of policy under state authority in the twentieth century was accepted only as an "occasional but regrettable economic necessity" (69) prompted by democratization and the need to provide for the poor. Still, the move was significant, and the rationalization it brought about had dramatic repercussions for British scientific and administrative culture.

The Contradictions of the British Administrative System

The political patterns I have described here partly explain why central state authority in Britain long remained institutionally underdeveloped. The bureaucracy was small, in both size and influence. At the turn of the century, England possessed only 116,000 state employees (compared with around 400,000 in France and Prussia).[32] Until the rationalization of the civil service in 1871, which institutionalized competitive examinations for recruitment into the bureaucracy, administrative appointments were dominated by parliamentary patronage, and there were no formal requirements of competence. But the reforms themselves were not meant to erase privilege by raising competent administrators out of the masses. It was well understood that privilege remained the best preparation for a career in public administration. As Gladstone put it, the existence of the civil service would "strengthen and multiply the ties between the higher classes and the possession of administrative power" by selecting those who were "gentlemen by birth or training" (cited in Cain 1997, 96).

These nonprofessional and gentry origins of public functions in England explain one of the distinctive traits of British administrative culture throughout history—its (hailed or reviled) "amateur" character. Still today, the British higher education system offers little formal administrative training. In contrast with the French or even American situation, the discipline of public administration never fully established itself at British universities (with, however, the significant exception of colonial administration). Indeed, for much of the twentieth century, the traditional path into the British civil service was a humanities curriculum at Oxford (primarily) or Cambridge.

In the 1960s and 1970s, critiques of this "classical" training of civil servants mounted as the performance of the British economy rapidly fell behind its main competitors.[33] Decisive steps toward the professionalization of the civil service were taken, including the recruitment of specialists (such as economists), the wider use of consultation in administrative processes, and the encouragement of vocational training for civil servants.[34] These efforts, however, did not succeed in completely dismantling long-entrenched practices. If anything, the predominance of Oxford and Cambridge graduates in the highest positions (known for a while as the "administrative class") grew stronger: they represented "62.7% of all Permanent Secretaries in 1900–1919 and 75% in 1965–86."[35]

The highest ranks of the civil service have been described by detractors as a closed, secret world, isolated from the rest of society, though supporters regard this isolation as a guarantee of impartiality. What appears quite undisputed, however, is that top administrative functions rarely serve as instruments for elite recruitment into other sectors (such as business or politics), as they do in France, the United States, or Japan. Higher civil servants, as a matter of fact, usually accomplish their entire career in the bureaucracy.[36] This stability contributes in no small part to the unitary character of the higher British civil service and to its wariness of outsiders. Heclo and Wildavsky (1974) famously described the British government community as a "village" in which people "trust" each other, and the Treasury in particular as a "nuclear family."

British bureaucratic culture and knowledge are thus forged mainly through on-the-job training and long tenure in administrative positions. Consequently, administrative departments generally have well-formed and long-lasting "views," into which their staff is socialized early on.[37]

During the 1930s, for instance, the fiscally orthodox "Treasury view" was a decisive impediment to the diffusion of Keynesian ideas. The Treasury offered the same resistance to monetarism during the 1980s, and to the question of U.K. membership in the European Monetary Union today. But these views remain largely implicit and are rarely articulated publicly: there exists, for instance, no true British (or French, for that matter) equivalent of the U.S. *Economic Report of the President,* a document that sums up the achievements and goals of the government's economic policy.

How do these characteristics affect the operation of government? Some have argued that the absence of a tradition of specialized administrative expertise in Britain perhaps explains the "reactive" nature of British public officialdom in comparison with the confident voluntarism of the French or Swedish bureaucracy.[38] In addition, British administrators work in a dual and highly competitive political environment where activism under one government may become a liability under a different one, a pattern that sometimes motivates a preference for the status quo. As a result, British governments typically deal with new problems and controversial issues by convening large public inquiries outside the structure of government itself—for example, a temporary Committee of Inquiry or a Royal Commission. These organizations represent perhaps the most well-institutionalized British version of impartial advice and generally include notable personalities from across the political spectrum, as well as experts and members of the business elite.

All in all, then, Britain's liberal political culture and institutions have evolved to mitigate both the expansion of central government and the involvement of the general public by leaving private elites in charge to depoliticize issues. Because the idea of a rational, autonomous, and efficient state seems inconceivable without raising the specter of its capture by sectional interests, the British ideal of government prescribes diffusing authority to a multiplicity of independent advisory and consultative bodies, which have great legitimacy but limited enforcement powers. Paradoxically, these organizations have also had the effect of pressing the sectors they oversee toward administrative accountability and highly managerial forms of governance.

MORAL SENSE AND THE MACROECONOMY

After this brief examination of the structure of the state in Britain, what do we have to say about its culture? To address this question we must go back to examine nineteenth century British political institutions and their relationship to society. The Victorian Age in England is often described as "the age of laissez faire." But, as historians (e.g. Evans 1978) have shown, the British state's generally non-interventionist position in economic matters was always accompanied by a heavy dose of activity in social matters. By the mid-nineteenth century, Britain already had a dense network of private charities and an elaborate system of public relief unlike anything existing in other countries; Parliament grants to support the education of the poor; and public health standards. To be sure, these interventions remained limited, as even their supporters feared they would encourage idleness and dissolute morals. For the most part they were also locally managed. Thus the particular means of British state intervention reflected the ambiguities of a political culture that combined individualism and a strong defiance against central government power with a willingness to encourage benevolence as the highest moral virtue and to regard the welfare of all as the true test of a civilized society.[39] Over the course of the next century, the same dilemma at the heart of utilitarian moral philosophy would be played out, alternatively sustaining collective interventions and laissez-faire ones, and never going as far as fostering a too generous system that could thwart private initiative.

We can see these ambiguities in the economic and social policies of the postwar period. Writing in the 1960s, Shonfield famously characterized postwar economic management in Britain as an example of "arm's length government" (1965, 88). Indeed, while postwar British and French economic and social policies often looked similar from the outside, they relied upon vastly different procedures and instruments of government intervention. For instance, the British notion of the "managed economy" referred mainly to the use of macroeconomic management tools in the pursuit of national welfare. As laid out by Labour governments, the conduct of economic policy (until 1979) centered mainly on the active use of fiscal instruments, in connection with a social program of full employment, redistributive justice, and enhanced welfare provision. Simultaneously, however, incomes policies were also used in an effort to slow wage growth, repeatedly provoking confrontations with labor unions.

British governments also intervened in the industrial domain, most notably through the private-public transfers of the late 1940s. But British nationalizations, unlike their French counterparts, were not integrated into a larger program of industrial policy; nor was the management of the new public companies significantly altered.[40] The nationalization of the Bank of England in 1946 did not produce a major change in policy. Bankers, not government officials, continued to rule the institution. (The reverse is true in France: even private companies are often managed by people who started their career in the civil service.) And we should not forget that the same Labour government that carried out these nationalizations also created the Monopolies and Restrictive Practices Commission in 1949.

Planning policies provide yet another example of the difference in attitudes toward government intervention between France and Britain. In France, the higher civil service took the lead in developing and promoting economic planning in the postwar era. In Britain, by contrast, the Treasury promoted Keynesian management partly as a way to avoid the more radical alternative of planning, which had emerged among Labour circles during the 1930s.[41] Thus, when planning was finally implemented with the creation of the National Economic Development Council (NEDC) in 1961,[42] it was much weaker than its French counterpart and model. The NEDC and its sectoral offshoots, the "little neddies," operated mainly as tripartite consultative organizations focused on long-term economic coordination, which involved in equal measure government, business, and trade union officials and experts. It was, as John Eatwell recalls, "carefully placed outside the apparatus of government and its main instruments were exchange of information and moral persuasion" (1985, 69). Hampered by both the liberal aspiration to represent *all* interests and a long-standing distrust of state interference in collective bargaining, and lacking any links to a system of long-term finance to promote growth (as the French *Commissariat Général au Plan* had through its close association with the Ministry of Finance), the NEDC possessed little authority, even to establish growth targets.[43] But it played an important social role by organizing a space in which officials could work to change business and labor mentalities on specific issues.[44]

The Weight of the City

History has shaped the governance of the British economy and British economic culture in characteristic ways. Peter Hall, for instance, traces several distinctive institutional features of British markets back to the combined experiences of early industrialization and empire (1986, 41–45). First, unlike its continental European counterparts, British industry relies heavily on the stock market for finance rather than on the banking system, which, early on, found it more profitable to invest in overseas markets. This historical role of the City, or London's financial district, as the banker of the empire, and then its revival as "international financial entrepôt" since the 1960s, have led to the structural domination of financial over industrial capital in Britain, and to the City's considerable influence over decisions of economic policy throughout the twentieth century. Economic historians, for instance, have long stigmatized British chancellors' (including Labour ones) obsession with defending the sterling as one of the main reason for Britain's long-term economic decline. This preoccupation with the currency motivated not only the much-debated return to the pre–World War I gold parity of the pound in 1925 but also the "stop-go" strategies of the 1950s and 1960s, which sought to maintain the exchange rate, sometimes at the expense of industrial growth.[45] Deregulatory policies during the 1980s contributed further to the growth of the British financial sector.

Economic historians generally explain the hegemony of financial considerations in Britain by pointing to the close connections between the City, the Bank of England, and the Treasury. The Bank of England sees and interacts closely with financial institutions (high positions there have been traditionally staffed by bankers). It also maintains an intimate relationship (based on voluntary collaboration rather than outright dependence, as was the case in France before 1994) with the Treasury. As a result, the Bank enjoys a position of go-between between the center of government and the highly concentrated network of clearing banks constituting the City, and acts as a mediator of their political influence in Whitehall. "The basic tenet of the Treasury position," Green writes, "has been that the City's earnings have been either a mark of underlying prosperity or the means to achieve prosperity. In this respect the Treasury's definition of what actually constitutes a healthy economy has, over the long run, constantly foregrounded the role of Britain's financial sector."[46]

The segmented nature of the British industrial structure further compounds this dominance of financial over industrial interests. As Hall argues, "Britain left the industrial revolution still a nation of small firms" (1986, 42). The Confederation of British Industry emerged quite late and has had chronic difficulty drawing together dispersed and fragmented industrial interests. Finally, the same decentralized pattern has characterized the British labor movement, which is made up of a multiplicity of competing craft associations that the central organization, the Trade Union Congress, controls only partially.[47]

The British University from College to Mass Education

British academic culture was forged at a time when neither the state nor the market was a powerful force. For most of its history, higher education in Britain was a private affair managed privately, by academic guilds or communities of learned men.[48] British universities thus developed in a relatively insular fashion, adapting slowly to changes in their social environment. The oldest institutions, Oxford and Cambridge, which dominated higher education in Victorian Britain and provided a model for the "new" establishments to come, were thus self-regulating communities, jealous of their elite status and their autonomy from state control. Institutions created in the nineteenth century—first the University of London and later the "Redbrick" universities established in industrial towns—followed a similar pattern and began as private corporations.

The historical reluctance of the British state to get involved in educational affairs contributed to these patterns. In the area of higher education, state support was sporadic until 1919, when the government established the University Grants Committee to subsidize universities or help them expand.[49] Even after public money started flowing into university education, however, authorities continued to encourage the search for alternative sources of funds, and in any case refrained from getting involved in the supervision of curricula, examinations, or appointments (in sharp contrast with the French system, for instance).[50]

Though Britain's secondary school system was long much more socially progressive than that of its continental European counterparts (including France and Germany), higher education remained very selective. For much of the nineteenth and twentieth centuries, Britain had lower rates of university-level enrollments than its industrialized counterparts.[51] The dominant universities, Oxford and Cambridge, promoted an aristocratic conception of education, permeated by references to classical antiquity. They drew their students heavily from the most elite institutions of the upper secondary system, the "public" (or independent) schools and the (initially free but selective) grammar schools. In turn, they provided recruits for the governing class, as they had, in earlier years, for the clergy as well. Their principal social mission was less to produce and disseminate "useful" knowledge than to mold the minds, character, and social graces of the nation's future leaders. In practice, this meant emphasizing humanistic erudition and intellectual virtuosity, or subjects such as classics and mathematics at the expense of more vocational knowledge, including professional or specialized academic training.

The "old" academic system relied on a particular, quite intimate organizational form: the *college*. Individual tutorials within colleges valorized personal, close working relationships between students and the teaching staff, a pattern that contrasted with the more impersonal and larger classes common in continental European universities. In the British system, the education function (associated with the college) thus took priority over both the research and the credentialing functions of the university. Being almost exclusively focused on undergraduate education, British universities gave only limited recognition to advanced credentials and developed graduate schools much later than their American and German counterparts. In sharp contrast to these more professionalized academic systems, then, university appointments in Britain did not (until recently) require a doctorate.[52] Instead, recruitment for academic positions often relied upon social connections and intellectual prestige; for instance, undergraduates at Oxford and Cambridge who were brilliant enough to receive a first-class honors degree might be invited to stay on as faculty members.

These social characteristics of the older universities made them poorly equipped to train the children of the middle class and the bourgeoisie, which had emerged from the Industrial Revolution. It was only with the establishment of the "civic" (or "Redbrick") colleges and universities at the turn of the century that a more practical orientation to education, deemed more suitable for the business classes, gained some influence. Unsurprisingly, these new universities were closely tied to local industrial communities for financial support and sought primarily to meet local labor market needs. But business's suspicion of university graduates remained, and the preference for more practice-oriented, on-the-job forms of training continues to be a characteristic feature of industry and the professions in Britain.[53]

Since the 1960s, rising public expectations about access to higher education and a democratization of recruitment have spurred a massive expansion of British higher education, putting the system's traditional institutions under considerable strain. One example is the declining role and social status of academic guilds. Educational and research organizations in Britain were traditionally self-managed by the "academic oligarchy" (rather than through centralized administrative regulation as in continental Europe).[54] Recent developments, however, have somewhat upset this tradition of academic self-government. The need to manage large-scale organizations and the state's desire to increase its control over spending have prompted the professionalization of administrative functions within universities, to the detriment of the academic faculties.[55]

Similarly, Britain's, aristocratic approach to instruction has undergone important changes in the course of the twentieth century. Like the Redbrick universities in earlier periods, the twenty-five "new" universities created in the post–World War II years were designed with an explicit vocational orientation. University enrollments expanded markedly after the 1963 Robbins report which revealed that Britons were less likely to graduate from university than the citizens of any other advanced country. During the 1960s, several colleges of technology with a heavy concentration on engineering and the applied sciences were granted university status. (Forty-four "polytechnics" followed the same route in 1992.) Unmatched by a comparable growth of financial means, however, this rapid democratization also ended up altering some of the most prestigious features of the old learning environment, like the tutorial tradition.

A second change involved the gradual erosion of the academic community's social prestige and autonomy. This trend was accelerated by the virulent anti-intellectualism of the Thatcher era and by a substantial (in relative terms) decline in university salaries after the 1970s. These were important transformations in a society where the "dons" were always tightly incorporated into the cultural and political establishment.

The overall power structure of the British higher education system has remained relatively unchanged, though somewhat diluted. The older universities (Oxford, Cambridge, and London) still top the hierarchy: they remain the main feeder institutions for the academic professions, providing the majority of Royal Society Fellows and Fellows of the British Academy (respectively, 62 percent and 76 percent in 1990).[56] But as the decline in self-recruited faculty attests (only about one-third of Oxbridge faculty was Oxbridge-educated in 1992, down from nearly four-fifths in the early 1960s), their identity and predominance are not as strong as they used to be.[57] The traditional British model of universities as purveyors of cultured education has given way somewhat to the American ideal of universities as repositories for high science and technical expertise—the transformation of Oxford University over the course of the twentieth century is a good example of these conflicting demands.[58] Competition from educational institutions of lower prestige and pressure from external funding partners (both public and private) with a stake in the practical relevance of knowledge have pushed Oxford and Cambridge further in the direction of the research university model and toward a progressive, still ongoing, incorporation of vocational education. Thus, both universities have recently introduced business studies, after decades of struggle. An MBA program opened in Cambridge in 1991, 110 years after the establishment of the Wharton School at the University of Pennsylvania and nearly 30 years after two official bodies (the National Economic Development Council and the Franks Committee) recommended enhancing business education in Britain.[59] Oxford followed in 1996 with the opening of the Saïd Business School.[60] Both transformations, however, took place amid bitter controversy that recalled older debates about whether practical studies (including economics) had a legitimate place in universities.

THE PRODUCTION OF SCIENCE, FROM INFORMALITY TO THE
PUBLIC HOUSEHOLD

The practice of science in nineteenth century Britain was primarily organized by independent societies and clubs composed of cultured gentlemen with shared interests. Some public funds were allocated to scientific activity quite early (e.g., the Parliament's grants to the Royal Society), but their management remained essentially in private hands.[61] The involvement of wealthy individuals also played an important role in furthering scientific pursuits. Although many "scientists" were university dons, scientific debates involved a broader educated public beyond these institutions' boundaries. Conversely, attempts to professionalize the research orientation at Oxford and Cambridge repeatedly faced the opposition of those who regarded the universities' cultural function as their more fundamental raison d'être. Unlike U.S. or German institutions of higher education, where the graduate school model became prominent at the end of the nineteenth century, in Britain advanced training remained an informal business much longer. It took the form of a gradual and often highly personalized process of socialization that began in the close-knit atmosphere of the college during a student's undergraduate years.

Over the course of the twentieth century, however, science increasingly became a state-supported activity located in institutions of higher education. The creation of the University Grants Committee (UGC) in 1919 progressively brought universities under public control.[62] Focused primarily on London, Oxford, and Cambridge at first (these institutions received 42 percent of all Parliamentary grants in the 1930s), the UGC began supporting all institutions of higher education in the postwar period, including the former Polytechnics by the 1980s. Public funds grew as a proportion of scientific research grants, going from 44 percent in the mid-1930s to about 57 percent in the early 1960s.[63] In typical British fashion, the disbursement of these funds was formally managed by independent boards (research councils), composed mainly of academics, which were periodically asked to justify their activities to the government. In the politically adverse climate of the 1980s and 1990s, however, public authorities began tightening research councils' budgets and increasing scrutiny on the outcomes and usefulness of funded projects, which prompted a shift back toward private sources of research funding.

THE TRANSFORMATIONS OF FRENCH STATISM

Many historical commentators since Tocqueville have agreed with his observation that the emergence of the centralized state in France preceded that of the nation as a coherent community of individuals. From the inception of absolutist rule, French society (including the nobility and the court) has been managed authoritatively from above. A large and devoted bureaucracy established a tight control over civil society and sought to unify the country around its ruler by undermining all local and corporate allegiances.[64] After the Revolution especially, political elites regarded society with suspicion, seeing it as a locus of unbridled individualism, and hence of factionalism and chaos. From Napoleonic administrative centralization to the institutionalization of compulsory primary school education under the Third Republic (1881–82), nineteenth-century political regimes saw themselves as managing a society of individuals that was always on the brink of social decomposition. The figure of the autonomous central state (whether absolutist, liberal, or technocratic) made sense against the imagined backdrop of a politically unruly and irresponsible society—an attitude which Rosanvallon characterizes as the "State as the 'teacher' of civil society."[65] As J. P. Nettl remarked, "It is significant that the word *l'État* in French should be the only one normally beginning with a capital letter" (1968, 567).

L'État in French Political Culture

The central administration in France traditionally exemplifies and ensures the "continuity of institutions" against political instability. In contrast with the American government, where political appointees are found at all levels of the federal and state administrations, in France only the heads of ministries and cabinet members are subject to change when there is a renewal of political leadership.

Policy is primarily the responsibility of the government, assisted by the technocratic apparatus; the Parliament's role, especially in the economic domain, remains limited.[66] The French technocracy derives its legitimacy from this stability and from an ideology of neutrality that proclaims its independence from both political and social influences. In the postwar years, newly established schools and state agencies helped unify administrative practice around an activist, modernist stance that promised to turn the state into the principal agent of economic growth. The technical competence of the higher civil service—rather than the market—was trusted with ensuring both the impartiality of the policy process and the performance of the economy.[67]

The French approach, which consciously constructs a ruling elite through a public educational monopoly, has no equivalent in Europe. Common recruitment and training at the ENA and the *grands corps de l'État* (which compose the majority of the senior civil service) guarantee homogeneity in the administrative apparatus. Top technocrats receive a fairly generalist instruction and are expected to transfer their skills to a large variety of administrative settings, as well as other societal domains, such as business or politics. In the French system, being selected into one of the elite civil service bodies is a mark of personal quality and distinction; receiving proper training therein is a guarantee of competence.

THE RISE AND FALL OF NEO-COLBERTISM

Since the absolute monarchs, who inaugurated a form of top-down economic management for the purpose of military expansion, the French state has also exercised economic sovereignty. As Richard Kuisel remarks, despite the dominance of *liberal* economic ideology during the long nineteenth century, "the state was never *léger* in France" (1981, 9). Since the Old Regime, it controlled "manufactures," protected agriculture, and closely monitored the development of transports and the process of industrialization. For instance, in spite of important private initiative, technocrats and engineers at the Ministry of Public Works largely orchestrated railway policy from above, and the same is true for the development of canals and roads. Similarly, the state used public works programs fairly early as a device to counter unemployment, from the "national workshops" of 1848 to the various ventures of the 1930s.[68]

It was mainly after 1944, however, that the state administration began comprehensively and self-consciously to manage the national economy, thereby inaugurating the French model of state-administered growth. Intellectually, the shift toward the widespread acceptance of the French version of the managed economy took place between the 1930s and the 1950s. Under the Popular Front government, several partisans of planning gained access to political and administrative positions.[69] They led the establishment of a short-lived Ministry of National Economy,[70] and important institutions, most notably the Bank of France and the railways, came under state control through partial nationalization. Such measures announced the emergence of a political consensus on the role of the state in the promotion of economic expansion, which was to take shape during the Vichy regime,[71] and institutionalize fully after the war with the reform of the economic administration.

The new political leadership that emerged from the Resistance was determined not only to reconstruct the country but also to modernize it. The order of the day, as public officials saw it, was to transform the country into a first-rank industrial power by shaking off the rigidities of the economy. This meant rationalizing economic development by placing vital sectors under centralized management. The Bank of France was fully nationalized in 1945[72] and its management placed under state control. Postwar goverments also nationalized other banks as well as utilities and large industrial corporations.

The key institutions in this scheme were the Ministry of Finance and the Planning Commissariat (Commissariat Général au Plan). The former traditionally sits at the top of the central administration and recruits almost exclusively from the country's top schools, most prominently from the Inspection des Finances[73] and the École Nationale d'Administration. A great deal of the ministry's authority comes from its long-established function as a banker of the state. The end of World War II marked a watershed in the ministry's outlook and role. From being a watchdog of liberal orthodoxy, it became "a superministry and the center of economic management."[74] After 1947, it took over de facto supervision of the Ministry of National Economy and, through its most powerful division, the Treasury, oversaw a constellation of administrative agencies and organizations.

The Treasury's supremacy in the postwar period was also rooted in the particular structure of the French financial system, where industrial expansion was financed primarily through a government-maintained credit market and a state-dominated banking system, rather than through the stock market. In particular, the Treasury cooperated with the Fonds de Développement Economique et Social and the Caisse des Dépôts et Consignations, the country's largest banking organization, to control the financing of public and private investments.[75] It played a key role in international financial negotiations through its presidency of the Club of Paris, and until 1993 was in effect responsible for monetary policy. Finally, two of the ministry's internal divisions (the Direction de la Prévision and the Direction de l'INSEE) governed the manufacture of domestic economic information and monopolized the production and analysis of economic data.

The Planning Commissariat, in charge of defining long-term development objectives and coordinating economic policy, was created in 1946 as an independent agency responsible to the prime minister. It was conceived as one of the main agents of the country's modernization—France's third way toward rational, efficient liberal capitalism. The "indicative" five-year plans typically proposed directions for the long-term allocation of public funds and encouraged coordination between various sectors and groups in the economy. The political and practical significance of planning, however, varied over time. The plan never had any financial control of any sort, as the distribution of resources remained firmly in the hands of the Ministry of Finance. Only during the Gaullist period did the plan formally serve to set budgetary parameters. The institution then withered away after the election of Valery Giscard d'Estaing to the presidency in 1974. It was somewhat revived under the socialist administration, during the 1980s, but to little effect. Although it is today but a shadow of its former self, the Planning Commissariat remains an important forum where experts and corporate leaders prepare future policy reforms.[76]

The rest of the system has only partially survived into the post-1970s "neoliberal" era. First, the centrally managed, credit-based economy was by nature inflationary and hardly tenable over the long run. The Treasury always found it difficult to reject demands for financing, which became a clear liability in the post-oil-shock context. After an important reform in 1986, firms were redirected toward the stock market for their financing needs. Second, the process of European integration slowly removed monetary policy and exchange rate policy from the hands of the state. The Bank of France became independent in 1993, and control over monetary policy moved to the European Central Bank in 1999. Third, industrial policy lost traction when the commercial banks and a number of large industrial corporations were privatized during the second half of the 1980s and the 1990s.[77]

The weakening of the institutional architecture of the postwar neo-Colbertist state should not mask a strong continuity in governance practices, however. In particular, the long history of intimacy between the state and business was not to be easily undone.[78] Economic historians have repeatedly argued that unlike their British counterparts, the French are ambivalent toward private entrepreneurship. Both popular discourse about private enterprise in France and scholarly interpretations of nineteenth-century French industrialization have offered a (somewhat prejudiced) description of the typical French entrepreneur as conservative, afraid of innovation, and "[looking] at the government as a sort of father in whose arms he could always find shelter and consolation."[79] While this portrait is certainly somewhat exaggerated, the idea that ensuring the economic well-being of the nation, including its private industries, falls largely upon the shoulders of the state remains a well-publicized theme in France. The quote below, by President of France Général De Gaulle in 1962 encapsulates nicely this philosophy of guarded, statist, liberalism: "The market has some good points. It keeps people on their toes, it rewards the best. But at the same time it creates injustices, establishes monopolies, favors cheaters. So don't be blind to the market. You mustn't imagine that it alone will solve all problems. The market isn't above the nation and above the state. It's up to the state, the nation, to *keep an eye on the market.*"[80]

Hence while the *goals* of state intervention have indubitably changed, there has been considerable continuity in the process of state intervention. As Amable and Hancke argue, the retreat from statism was largely state-directed: "The state, somewhat paradoxically, used its power to give more independence and responsibility to large companies, while it was itself gradually reducing its involvement in the economy" (2001, 131).[81] Crucially, management positions in the newly privatized firms still fell into the hands of graduates of the *grandes écoles* and members of the *grand corps*. Not that there was anything new to this: as Suleiman (1978) and others have shown, the *grands corps* and *grandes écoles* have routinely used their prestige within the public sector to claim jurisdiction over positions in business and industry since the middle of the nineteenth century. With the institutionalization of the *économie dirigée* after 1945, the trend accelerated, and the frontier between public and private management became increasingly blurred.[82]

State-directed professional training in France has been traditionally regarded as a public good for the nation as a whole. Most of the *grandes écoles* (except a few of them which, like École Centrale, are purely private sector creations) have two tracks: an "administrative" one, whose graduates are expected to proceed into top-level administrative positions, and a "civil" one, for all other positions. But a significant proportion of the graduates of the administrative tracks ultimately make the transition to the private sector as well, often after spending years in the civil service. For instance, a 1993 study found that 47 percent of the heads of the 125 largest French companies came from the civil service.[83] The privatizations of the 1990s have further strengthened this hegemony: ENA graduates, most of them also members of the top administrative corps, went from heading 20 percent (in 1990) to almost 65 percent (in 2000) of all French stock market capitalization, displacing the Polytechniciens.[84] Parallel to these trends, the curriculum at some of the most elite institutions has developed an increasing emphasis on business issues. While this business orientation of elite higher education had always characterized the specialist schools like École des Mines de Paris or École des Ponts et Chaussées,[85] its recent permeation of more generalist institutions like Polytechnique or the École Nationale d'Administration has proceeded to the point where critics periodically denounce the "private drift" of these institutions.[86]

The "State Nobility"

The French system of higher education took shape during the Old Regime and Revolution and was consolidated under the consulate and empire. Napoléon reorganized the central administration around the new *corps de l'État*. These are administrative bodies that assist the government in preparing reforms and managing the state finances, such as the Conseil d'État (1799), the Cour des Comptes (1807), and the Inspection des Finances (formally established in 1816, though its roots go back to the imperial period). Napoléon also restructured and strengthened the system of "elite professional education institutions" that were intended to provide technical expertise (mostly engineering) to the nation.[87] These bodies fixed the framework within which the system was to evolve and provided the large and culturally distinctive bureaucratic apparatus that gives the French polity its particular character.

Applicants to these institutions had to pass a highly competitive *concours* (examination) before being channeled to a career in the central administration. The law faculties provided most of the members of the administrative *grands corps,* while members of the technical *corps* had their own vocational schools, each of which came under the jurisdiction of a particular ministry. Thus the École des Ponts et Chaussées (1747) (literally, "school of bridges and highways"), which focused on construction methods, and the École des Mines (1783), which trained engineers for the mining sector, were controlled by the Ministry of Commerce and Public Works.[88] The Ministry of War, later renamed Ministry of Defense, administered the École Polytechnique (1794) which soon became the most important of all these institutions. Established a few decades later, the (originally private) École Centrale (1829) came under the control of the Ministry of Commerce around the middle of the nineteenth century.[89] Other less technical institutions also came to enjoy considerable prestige. The École Normale Supérieure depended on the Ministry of Public Instruction and trained future high school teachers at a time when the *lycées* served a very small percentage of the population. Later in the century, comparable ventures established a basis for higher training in commercial affairs.[90] As Fox and Weisz remark, "Every time the need for a new kind of specialist was felt, it was met by the creation of another *grande école*" (1980, 3).

Throughout the nineteenth century, the *grandes écoles* and *grands corps* thus progressively became the main channels of entry into high-level administrative positions as well as "gateways to higher careers in the army and in the industry."[91] The top students at the École Polytechnique (and after World War II, at the École Nationale d'Administration) also held a monopoly on the prestigious *corps de l'État,* which gave access to lifetime civil service employment and constituted the high point of the administrative apparatus empowered by Napoléon.[92] Finally, six university faculties—medicine, pharmacy, law, theology, letters, and sciences—completed the system of higher training. In 1808, Napoléon reorganized the university system as a single, hierarchical institution, the Imperial University of France, which allowed no local control over chairs or curricula and which central authorities directed in a bureaucratic-military manner.[93] Although the system expanded and individual institutions gained some autonomy in the 1890s, the French university was run like any other government department until the decentralizing reforms of 1968. In contrast to the situation in the Anglo-Saxon world, where universities largely governed themselves, French curricula and programs were subject to approval from official bodies, and each higher education diploma had to fit within a centrally defined national curriculum. To this day, the Ministry of Education determines the number of appointments allowed to each university. As a result, the organization of university courses in France has responded more to administrative demands and requirements than to the intellectual interests of professors. Indeed, scholarly research did not emerge as a fundamental dimension of the university's mission until quite late and is probably still less developed than in other countries.

In spite of the expansion of the university (or perhaps because of it), the French higher education system continues to be profoundly biased in favor of the *grandes écoles*. During the twentieth century, the divide between the two institutions persisted, if not deepened. The creation of the

École Nationale d'Administration and the nationalization of the École Libre des Sciences Politiques (renamed Institut d'Études Politiques) in 1945 further established the hegemony of elite vocational schools over the higher civil service. Under the Fifth Republic, these institutions also came to play a decisive role in the recruitment of the political body, and government ministers in particular.[94] These developments of the administrative educational apparatus were supplemented by parallel innovations in the technical apparatus of the engineering schools (for instance, the creation of another specialized school, the École Nationale de la Statistique et de l'Administration Économiques,[95] for economic and statistical training), as well as the gradual expansion of elite business schools.[96]

As Bourdieu demonstrated, the supposedly meritocratic system of competitive examinations notwithstanding, the *grandes écoles* amount to a sort of "state nobility," recruiting primarily among the upper classes—whose sons and daughters accounted for more than 60 percent of the students admitted at the École Normale Supérieure, École Polytechnique, and École Nationale d'Administration in the 1970s.[97] By contrast, the universities, especially after the rapid educational expansion of the 1960s, were increasingly understood as an instrument of education for the masses, and were treated with neglect by public authorities. In fact, in the postwar period, France has consistently ranked at the bottom of the hierarchy of Western industrialized countries in terms of public expenditures per student in higher education.[98] Between 1960 and 1977, student enrollments multiplied almost fourfold, to nearly 20 percent of nineteen- to twenty-three-year-olds in 1977 from less than 8 percent of this group in 1960. The budget for higher education, however, did not match this growth: in constant francs, it increased only threefold over the same period.[99] This decline in selectivity and resources contributed to an overall deterioration of the university's status. The value of university credentials declined, as did the prestige of its teaching body. By contrast, the *grandes écoles* remained untouched and well protected in their privilege. In fact, during the same period when university enrollments were soaring, the student body at the top *grandes écoles* remained virtually constant. Consequently, entry into the elite schools became increasingly competitive, and their diplomas' "social value" continued to grow.[100]

The Separate Realm of Research?

Like education, scientific research in France has long been the object of central state interests. Beginning at the end of the seventeenth century, the French state established a network of special institutions devoted exclusively to scientific production: the Collège de France, the Musée d'Histoire Naturelle, the Observatoire de Paris, the Académie des Sciences, and later (in 1868) the École Pratique des Hautes Études focused on academic research training.[101]

In contrast with England, where much of the research activity was located in scholarly societies, and Germany, where university seminars and institutes served a similar function, France's scientific networks fell increasingly under the aegis of the state with only a few exceptions, like the Pasteur Institute. During the nineteenth century, growing financial patronage from the ministries progressively displaced scientific authority from the *sociétés savantes* toward official state bodies. Although some research was always carried out in institutions of higher education, in part out of an effort to compete with the Germans, whose "research universities" were admired throughout the world, this was never their primary purpose. The French, Gilpin (1968) notes, never considered scientific research to be the true vocation of the university professor, who was long regarded as a "man of knowledge" rather than as a "scientist," a generalist rather than a specialist. As for the *grandes écoles*, although they provided excellent technical training and attracted the best students, they had no established linkage with research institutions and instead prioritized their relationship with the administrative world. The French system was thus characterized by a relative disconnection between the activities of research, teaching, and elite training.

In the twentieth century, research policy came even more explicitly under centralized state control. First, the promotion of research as a separate activity received additional impetus in 1939 with the creation of the Centre National de la Recherche Scientifique (CNRS), a multidisciplinary organization designed to provide institutional and financial support to full-time scientists (mainly physicists) outside universities. Presiding over a wide array of new research laboratories, the CNRS was designed to provide the institutional infrastructure that French science lacked and did succeed at accelerating the professionalization of scientific careers. Scientists typically performed their work in research teams and were, at least in theory, sheltered from the pressures of the educational and the private sectors.[102] These policies, combined with the comparatively lower academic profile of the university and the focus of the *grandes écoles* on professional training, have perpetuated the divide between teaching and research. In fact, the two domains have been governed by different ministries (education and research) for much of their history.

The second pillar of French research policy, established during and after World War II, was the creation of "mission-oriented" institutions in virtually every domain (including economics). Large amounts of money were lavished on these organizations during the 1960s.[103] Formally, their function was to generate knowledge relevant to their ministerial sponsors and respond to specific government commissions, notably from the Planning Commissariat. This approach was intended to enable closer state control over the management of science and to provide an explicit link between scientific and economic development. Indeed, the Fifth Republic established the principle of the "central planning" of scientific production, which it sought to integrate within the general framework of the social and economic development plan.[104]

Although the main contours of the system remain formally in place, it has partially lost its policy significance since the 1980s, as Mustar and Larédo (2002) point out. Funding for large programs has dropped precipitously as military spending has ebbed and as the privatization of some industries has moved them outside of direct state supervision. The institutional separation between research and teaching has given way to partnerships between universities, *grandes écoles,* and the CNRS, which have considerably blurred the boundaries between the three institutions.[105] Moreover, the "mission-oriented" organizations of France's second research pillar have developed their own interests, beyond the administrative goals for which they were founded. Still, the culture they embody and the institutional fragmentation they have created continue to have lasting effects.

INSTITUTIONAL COMPLEMENTARITIES AND THE COHERENCE OF SOCIAL LIFE

The three political logics outlined in this chapter—American federal constitutionalism, British public-minded elitism, and French statism—are here used mainly as heuristic tools. They make sense only when understood as patterns that are *produced, and reproduced* through the particular institutional relations, processes, and purposes (for instance, in education and science, public administration, and economic practice) that constitute the grammar of social life in each particular society. But it is through concrete processes of socialization within these institutional complexes that what it means to be an economist gets defined, negotiated, and transformed over time. In other words, the different institutional constellations of the United States, Britain, and France make different sorts of economists by shaping the occupational worlds they inhabit, the social roles they fulfill, and also the scientific styles and intellectual orientations they adopt. Conversely, it is only through the mediation of individual experiences and strategies that the institutional complementarities we just observed are achieved, performed, and reproduced in practice and that we, as observers, can identify any logic in them. It is for the next chapters, then, to demonstrate the types of regularities produced by these institutional constellations in each country—that is, to explain *how* they mattered empirically, for economists and economics, in both expected and unexpected ways.

CHAPTER TWO

The United States: Merchant Professionals

> To be an economist in the United States, you have to believe
> that the market works most of the time. The situation in which
> markets don't work, or cannot be made to work, is really quite
> exceptional, and not all that interesting to study. . . . [And] you
> need a doctorate, preferably from a first-rank university. And
> to be influential in the profession, you need an appointment at
> a prestigious university. But the boundaries of who is consid-
> ered mainstream, and who is not, are enforced quite fiercely.
> (Economic journalist, phone interview, May 1999)

AMERICAN ECONOMICS arose in the context of the broad institutional
patterns described in the preceding chapter—the fragmented and profes-
sionally-oriented nature of the state bureaucracy, the regulatory emphasis on market competition, and the disciplinary organization of higher
learning. As will be shown throughout this chapter, professionalized social science in the United States emerged simultaneously with professionalized civil service. Consequently, economics was not much constrained
by the process of state-building; rather, it was part of it. In America, administrative institutions helped define economics as a specialized professional undertaking based on a skill monopoly. They did so, first, by
seeking to anchor their own authority in the ideology of professionalism,
and second by bringing professionals into the public domain through a
market for policy. As a result, the identity of American economics has
remained firmly located within universities, which alone could endow
economists with essential skills, credentials and legitimacy; and the academic discipline of economics has retained a considerable degree of intellectual autonomy. In contrast to continental Europe, where economics
was incorporated into a generalist form of technocratic expertise dominated by law, American economics developed largely as a technical and
self-referential intellectual enterprise, which ultimately gave rise to the
strong scientific program that persists today.

Paradoxically, the insulated "ivory tower" character of the disciplinary
work of economics in the U.S. context has proved remarkably compatible with a very significant penetration of the world by economic tools
and methodologies. In his 1961 presidential address to the American

Economic Association, Paul Samuelson captured this dualism well: "Not for us the limelight and the applause. But that does not mean the game is not worth the candle or that we do not in the end win the game. In the long run, the economic scholar works for the only coin worth having— our own applause" (1962, 18).

Being primarily based in universities, American economists were relatively isolated, and mainly talked with each other. When brought into the midst of political contention (through policy debates, for instance), they were compelled to emphasize their separate status and build up those technical abilities that sustained their legitimacy and impartiality in the eyes of political audiences. The forging of disciplinary strength within academia has supported the profession's jurisdictional power outside of academia and its penetration of society. Part of this influence goes unnoticed: simple economic concepts such as optimization, opportunity cost, or efficiency participate in a form of calculative rationality that has become taken for granted in the various institutions that organize social and economic life. Part of it, however, is much more visible: complex economic tools such as macroeconometric forecasting, financial products, auction designs, and various forms of economic valuation have been turned into large and often profitable industries serving both public and private clients. Hence, contrary to postwar France, where economics' main jurisdiction came to be located within the state, the commercial element in American economics is remarkably well developed, turning many of the discipline's instruments and technical innovations into marketable forms of knowledge. If in France economic knowledge was largely entrenched *within* the state apparatus, in America knowledge cultivated outside of the state would in turn be marketed *toward* it.

This combination of the scientific and the mercantile in modern American economics may seem odd, especially when seen in comparative perspective. The strangeness, however, fades away when the point of comparison switches from "economics elsewhere in the world" to "other professions in the United States." First, as Abbott (1988) has shown, American professions display both a high degree of formalism in their knowledge base and a strong competitive dimension in their mode of operation. This suggests a symbiotic relationship between the strength of the professional system and the strength of the disciplinary system in the American context (just as the weaknesses of both are also symbiotically related in the French context). Second, the commercial dimension of American professionalism is not a given but is partly the product of a historical evolution: according to Steven Brint (1994), the twentieth century was characterized by a movement away from "social trustee professionalism" toward a form of "expert professionalism" closely connected to the business enterprise. Although this trend in economics has been a global one, it is this chapter's contention that, *in comparative terms*, it has taken place particularly early and has been much more pronounced in the United States.

FORMS OF ACADEMIC ENTRENCHMENT

American economics is both an extremely large field and an internationally hegemonic one. From 1969 to 2008, fifty-two out of sixty-three Nobel Prize winners (82.5 percent) have been American, and another seven of the non-American Nobel laureates have taught in the United States for long periods.[1] This pattern of international domination is even stronger today than in the prize's early years. Since 1980 (until 2007), thirty-eight out of forty-four awards (86 percent) were given to U.S.-based professors (though a significant proportion of these were foreign-born). In what looks like a powerful feedback loop, top American economics departments produce the vast majority of the discipline's authoritative work, which further legitimates their hegemony over the rest of the field worldwide.

The relative intellectual homogeneity of American economics itself partly explains this remarkable position. The field is more consensual and cohesive than its neighbors in the social sciences and humanities—among the latter, only philosophy comes close—as well as many hard sciences. Compared with other disciplines, the job market, access to resources, and publication process in economics are also tightly controlled by powerful departments—and increasingly so in recent decades—with sometimes very high levels of self-reproduction.[2] There is little differentiation among graduate programs: a European observer recently said admiringly that "major graduate departments in the United States operate like factories, with production processes reminiscent of assembly lines, with well-defined standards of quality control" (Drèze 2001, 4). Correlatively, the boundaries of what constitutes serious work in economics are fairly explicit, widely shared, and clearly enforced. Technical sophistication—whether in terms of mathematical theory or statistical and econometric work—is a necessary condition for academic excellence, so much so that knowledge of tools generally takes precedence over knowledge of the economy in graduate teaching.[3] Consensus on best scientific practice also extends to substantive matters. As we saw earlier, American economists tend to agree more widely than their colleagues in other countries on fundamental principles, notably free trade, the economic benefits of technology, and the efficiency of the price system. (This is true even though important differences may persist in opinions about the ultimate goals and effects of specific economic policies.)[4] In all, a striving for a certain "moral purity" seems to permeate the ideology of American economics, which may take many different forms, such as the exclusion of laymen, the boundary against practical education, the defensive attitude toward politics, and a homogeneous intellectual and methodological stance.

The reasons for this character are institutional, political, and cultural. They relate to the competitive organization and geographical dispersion of the American university system and its articulation with other institutions in American society. Historically, they also relate to the power of business elites, to the fear of political radicalism, and to the religiously inspired cultural tension between the worthy and the unworthy that finds its resolution in a culture of calculability where everything and everyone can be measured (and thereby compared).[5] If American economics harbors many churches and is filled with plenty of fierce theoretical and policy struggles, it has one dominant religion—what I later call "applied quantification."

The American University and the Rise of Economics

It is, however, with a different kind of religious foundation that we will begin this narrative. By and large, the purpose of higher education in pre–Civil War America was to teach religious piety and discipline. The vast majority of faculty were involved in preaching and missionary work. Introduced in 1817 in the northeastern colleges, political economy was regarded as nothing more than a minor branch of moral philosophy. The first American economics textbooks were written by clergymen,[6] and a religious understanding of economic activity was pervasive. Capitalism and the laws of political economy were thought to be in harmony with the laws of God and consistent with the higher purpose of moral elevation.[7]

The creation in 1865 of the American Social Science Association (ASSA) "by a group of New England gentlemen educators and men of affairs who wished to study and find solutions to various social problems" (Coats 1993b, 353) marked the first step toward the assertion of a new model of authority, as Haskell (1977) has beautifully shown. The study of society moved away from religion and toward the systematic collection and evaluation of factual information, mainly for the purpose of social reform. Through its association with public commissions and civil service reform, the ASSA served as an institutional vehicle for the aspirations of rising professional groups—doctors, lawyers, and college teachers—seeking to extend their competence, as well as local notables trying to achieve social prestige and recognition.[8] In both form and content, the ASSA was thus a "predisciplinary" organization. Even though one of its divisions was called Economy, Trade and Finance, the community of inquiry it represented remained loose and did not yet possess a distinctive disciplinary identity.[9]

Within the narrow but growing community of teachers, American economic discourse did not gain much coherence (aside from a generally uncompromising commitment to laissez-faire) until the end of the nineteenth century.[10] Homegrown theory was virtually nonexistent—in economics as elsewhere (Tocqueville had already noted a certain distaste for abstract thought among Americans). The small size and geographical dispersion of American colleges were certainly major factors in this localism and "sectionalism" of American academic culture, in economics as in every other field.[11] Between the 1850s and the 1890s, Americans seeking advanced training went to Germany for their doctoral education; there they were exposed both to the historicist stream of thought prevalent in German social science and to a model of academic training centered on the research seminar. Upon their return to the United States, these "economists" became actively involved in higher education reform and in establishing an institutional base for the field of political economy. The recent creation of universities and graduate schools (like that of the other modern subjects that were to become the social sciences) and their open and as of yet unsettled internal structure constituted a unique opportunity for the incorporation of the new discipline. The number of specialized teaching posts in political economy expanded rapidly, from three chairs in 1880 to fifty-one in 1900.[12]

With the rise of the research-oriented university, the ASSA gentry-dominated model of advancing knowledge came to face the growing challenge of a younger generation of practitioners who were operating from purely academic bases, and it began to decay rapidly. In contrast with their European counterparts whose elite situation was a given, grounded in history, class, and state patronage, American university professors had to achieve their own legitimacy and social standing in a culture that had never been strongly deferential to intellectual authority.[13] They relied on professionalization to accomplish that goal. The creation of specialized disciplinary associations such as the American Historical Association (1884) and the American Economic Association (AEA; 1885), which both emerged from a split of the ASSA, marked the advent of a different approach to the nature and role of the social sciences. While initially retaining the reformist orientation of the ASSA (a point I discuss at some length later), the new organizations were strongly committed to "redefin[ing] social science as a university-based, research-oriented enterprise" (Haskell 1977, 166). As disciplinary organizations, they were designed to protect and further the interests of the new *academic* professionals against the all-encompassing claims of traditional elites represented by the ASSA. For instance, the yearly meetings of the American Economic Association soon turned into a forum for the presentation and discussion of academic papers. Professional publications, often linked to particular universities, followed almost immediately: in 1886, Charles Dunbar at Harvard launched the *Quarterly Journal of Economics,* and in 1892, J. Lawrence Laughlin at Chicago founded the *Journal of Political Economy*. In 1911, the American Economic Association started an in-house journal, the *American Economic Review*. Within the time span of a few decades, disciplinary economics was born in America.

The expansion of the American university system thus created an opening for the rapid institutionalization of economics and its transformation into a full-fledged scholarly enterprise. Certainly the university revolution in England, which led to the establishment of the London School of Economics and the commercial faculties at Birmingham and Manchester at the end of the nineteenth century, bore some resemblance to the American situation. Yet the existence of an already entrenched institutional hierarchy dominated by Oxbridge and the small size of the British university system at the time meant that economics still had to fight its way against established academic guilds and colleges in order to win a position. By contrast, in the American context, the social sciences were at the vanguard of the revolution in higher education and were thought to embody the highest moral purpose on which the new academic institutions claimed to be built. University leaders (presidents and boards alike) often favored them as "secular substitutes for religion" and saw in them a continuation of the old courses in moral philosophy.[14] The "moral" potential of economics and other social sciences thus made them a privileged medium for the assertion of Progressive principles—and indeed, institutionalist economists were often deeply involved in the moralizing enterprises characteristic of the Progressive period (such as anticorruption, the campaign against child labor, and Prohibition) in addition to the more familiar promotion of expertise. From the point of view of universities, and, later, foundations, social scientists would not only provide leadership in solving the various problems of American society but also serve to establish the (moral) reputation of their institution. Economists were thus prominently involved in the creation of graduate schools and schools of commerce, and in the transformation of universities into research institutions. They were also at the forefront of the movement to establish the American Association of University Professors in the early part of the twentieth century.[15]

American economics had thus become mainly a by-product of the professorial function before World War I. By the 1920s, however, the involvement of capitalist foundations concerned about "intelligent social control," as the director of the Laura Spelman Rockefeller Memorial once put it, prompted the creation of research organizations specializing in the methodical production of empirical knowledge. In 1916, William Willoughby, a Princeton professor, started the Institute for Government Research—one of three organizations that were later consolidated into the Brookings Institution—with the aim to bring to Washington economic studies and data relevant for the conduct of policy.[16] In 1920, Columbia professor Wesley Clair Mitchell presided over the founding of the National Bureau of Economic Research (NBER), a fact-finding body whose attention was concentrated on the study of the business cycle. The Carnegie Corporation and the Laura Spelman Rockefeller Memorial played especially critical roles as funders of these organizations and also helped secure influential appointments for social scientists in policy circles during the interwar period.[17]

To anticipate a bit, the financial base of economic research and training continued to expand in the postwar period. First, a number of newcomers in the philanthropic field (the Ford Foundation and the Alfred P. Sloan Foundation in particular) threw their support and vast resources behind the discipline. But the most significant change came from a vast increase in federal support, through the National Science Foundation's social sciences program and the systematic contractual use of economic research by military and civilian agencies. Both of these forms of support reached their peak during the 1960s and 1970s, in the wake of the Sputnik shock and the social programs of the Great Society.[18] Although this financial base weakened substantially during the more adverse political and economic climate of the 1980s, economists have consistently retained more federal and nonfederal resources than other social scientists, as figure 2-1a and 2-1b show, though they have fared less well relative to other science and engineering fields. As we will see later, the marked preference for economics over the other social sciences, which is general across private funding organizations both large and small, must be interpreted in relation to the discipline's greater ability to distance itself from accusations of political bias—an ability it owes, in part, to its more extensive reliance on formal mathematics—as well as its more intimate relationship to the business world, a topic to which I now turn.[19]

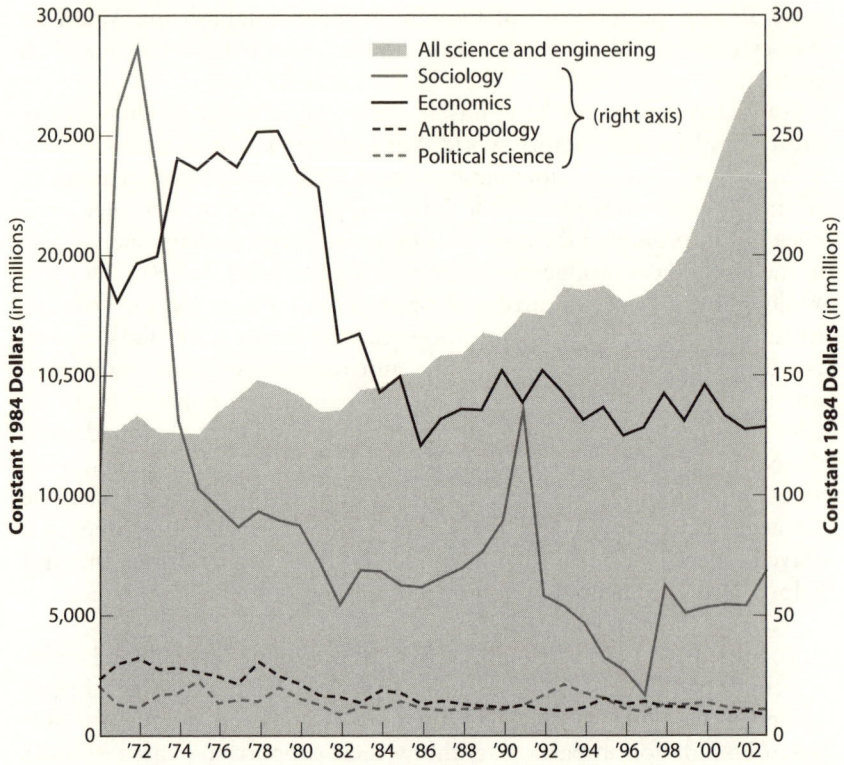

Figure 2-1a. Federal obligations for total research, 1970–2003.

Source: National Science Foundation, *Federal Obligations for Research by Agency and Detailed Field of Science and Engineering* (2004); *Academic Research and Development Expenditures* (2006); Census Bureau (for Consumer Price Index).

The Ambivalent Relationship to Business

Figure 2-2 reports trends in the number of bachelor's degrees in economics granted by American universities since World War II, in comparison with the same statistics for the neighboring fields of sociology, political science, and business. The data show that while economics has experienced nearly continuous growth throughout the twentieth century, the pace has been modest and does not even match the general expansion in undergraduate enrollments.[20] Part of this trend, however, is largely offset by the dramatic upsurge of business degrees, whose share of all bachelor's degrees awarded in the United States grew from 3 percent in 1920 to about 14 percent in 1960 and more than 20 percent today.[21]

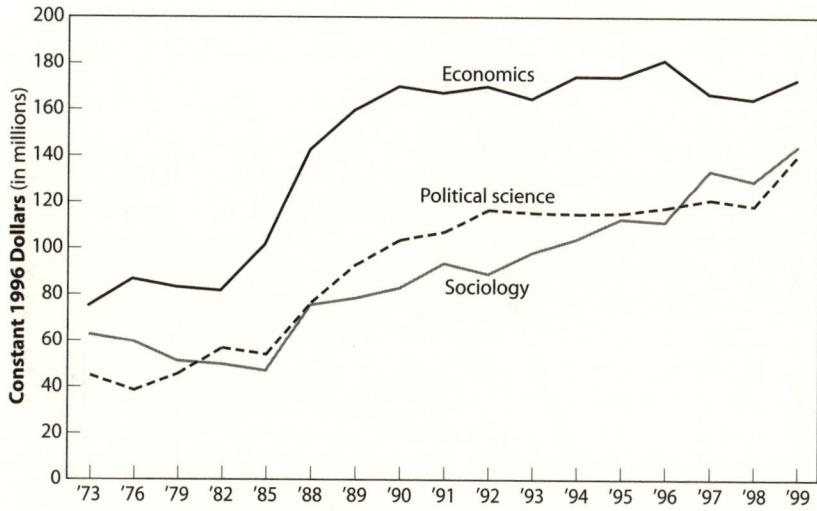

Figure 2-1b. Nonfederal expenditures for academic research, 1973–99.
Source: National Science Foundation, *Science and Engineering Indicators* series.

This suggests that in the United States, the expansion of economics as a field has been largely tied to its close connection to business. The pattern is certainly not new. In the early stages of the academicization process, the business orientation within economics was strong. Nonacademic audiences played an important role within the institutionalized channels of economic science, whether as members of the AEA or participants in outlets of scholarly production.[22] Between 1900 and 1914, more than 25 percent of the authors of articles in the main American journals were listed with a nonacademic occupation—although these percentages drop precipitously after World War I. During this early period, it was also not unheard of to have businesspeople serve as reviewers for journal articles.[23]

To a certain extent, this practical orientation could be found within economics departments as well. In fact, in a number of cases the impulse for business education came from within the economics department itself: for instance, founding deans for the schools of business at the University of Pennsylvania (Edmund James, Simon Patten), Harvard University (Edwin Gay), the University of Chicago (J. Lawrence Laughlin, Leon Marshall), and the University of Michigan (Edmund Day), were all economists. As early as the 1920s, the economics faculty in business schools was one of the largest, second only to the accounting

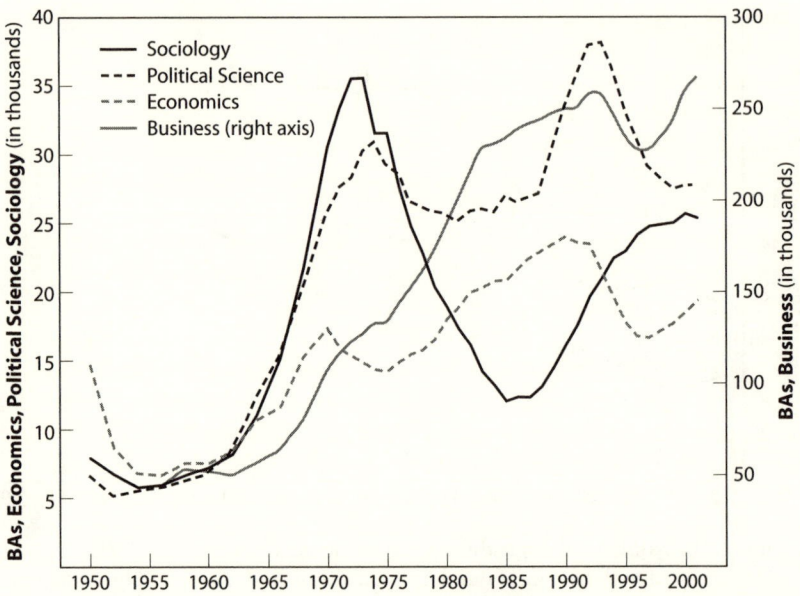

Figure 2-2. Bachelor's degrees: Selected social sciences and business, 1950–2002. *Source:* U.S. Department of Education, National Center for Education Statistics.

faculty.[24] By 1959, when the Carnegie and Ford foundations published their influential reports on business education, two semesters of economics were a basic requirement in all U.S. business schools. In about half of universities and colleges, the department of economics was located *inside* the business school.[25] Finally, although practitioners continued to dominate teaching in business schools (only about 40 percent of their full-time faculty members held a PhD in 1959), more than half of these doctorates were in economics—and the proportion was significantly higher among senior professorial ranks and in PhD-granting institutions.[26] The foundations' reports, both of which were authored by economics professors, urged business schools to increase the "advanced economics" content of business training and to trust "economic theorists" rather than "business economists" for such instruction.[27] Although the two highly influential studies were advocating a general "scientization" of business education, it is quite remarkable, but not all that surprising, that they both singled out economics as the discipline most able to provide the rigorous intellectual foundation they called for. The philanthropic organizations that had called for the reports endorsed their conclusions, throwing their considerable resources and authority behind the reform of business training. The result was a rapid diffusion of economic approaches throughout the business curriculum—including in domains that were not traditionally the province of economics, such as accounting or marketing. This is also when the transformation of finance into "financial economics" began.[28]

Yet the evolution of the fields of business and economics reveals a fundamental tension between, on the one hand, the desire of business schools to develop their own "practical" identity by developing ties with business organizations and professionalizing the field of management and, on the other hand, the scientific project within academic economics itself.[29] Hence, when economists started to reclaim a place in the business curriculum on *scientific* (rather than practical) grounds in the 1950s, they did so while forcefully reasserting the need for maintaining the institutional separation between economics and business and the intellectual *primacy* of the economics curriculum. At the University of Pennsylvania, for instance, the economics department split off from the business school in 1974. In many cases, business courses were newly confined to the postgraduate level.[30] These strategies probably allowed economists to maintain—and sometimes establish—a secure place in the undergraduate curriculum without fear of being overtaken by the more popular business program. Indeed, economics' position at or close to the top of the academic hierarchy in PhD-granting institutions has remained relatively unchallenged throughout the twentieth century. In 1926, more students at Stanford majored in economics than in any other subject; at Harvard and Berkeley, economics was the second most popular concentration; at Yale it was the third most popular choice.[31] In 2000, Harvard still awarded around 11 percent of its undergraduate degrees to economics majors, higher than the percentage for any other field, including political science (the most popular choice in 1926). Recent trends at Princeton are similar.[32]

The relationship between economics and business in the United States is both more secure than elsewhere, but still ambivalent, if not schizophrenic. On the one hand, the persistence of an institutional separation at elite schools means that economics departments can both maintain the discipline's scientific standing against the "pollution" of practical programs and guard its professional unity through its largely monopolistic control of the professional schools' job market. On the other hand, the demands generated by the business and policy worlds constitute a formidable source of institutional strength by connecting economics to the practical functions of the university and to vast nonacademic markets. Thus even though the proportion of business faculty with an economics PhD has not increased significantly since the high point of the 1970s,[33] the continued rapid growth of business schools has had a dramatic impact on the field of economics: in 2003–4, for instance, there were 549 economics PhDs teaching in the top twenty U.S. business schools, as compared with 637 in the top twenty economics departments. The absorption of increasingly large contingents of economics PhDs has turned business schools into formidable players within economic science itself—a transformation that is attested by the remarkable string of Nobel Prizes in economic science awarded to business school scholars since 1990.[34]

Boundaries: The PhD and Gatekeeping

At the heart of American economists' establishment of broad jurisdictional rights over the business and other professional schools' market is an educational monopoly. This monopoly, however, was never natural. Rather, it was the result of specific institutional processes that rewarded credentialed, disciplinary scholars and purported to keep legions of alleged dilettantes at bay. Economic questions have always had broad public appeal, partly because of their inevitable connection with politics; some of the most original minds in America tried their hand at economic writing, with more or less success. One of the best-read economic writers in all of American history was the single-tax enthusiast Henry George, a self-taught journalist who made no mystery of his aversion for the established teaching of political economy.[35] Although George's writings were immensely popular, and he became a sort of folk hero who converted many to socialism, political economists never engaged him seriously. In fact, the world of professional economics came to establish itself in part against those lay practitioners who threatened its integrity—whether maverick theorists like George, practitioners of all stripes located outside of academia, or scholars from other disciplines.

The main element in the process of professionalization of American economics was the redefinition of the PhD, an *academic* credential providing evidence of specialized *scholarly* competence, as the primary mechanism for certifying expertise in both scientific and practical matters. Partly following the German model, the PhD had emerged early as the critical device whereby the American academic profession would reproduce itself.[36] With the institutionalization of disciplines and the departmentalization of universities, however, a PhD "in something" became the basis for the development of academic specialization. In contrast to Germany, where doctorates were only loosely connected to disciplines, the professional project within American academia came to be organized around more exclusive intellectual communities.[37]

To understand the specific role of the PhD in American academic professionalism in general, and in American economics in particular, we have to remember that specialized, academic credentials is not the only way a profession may establish what Starr (1982) calls its "cultural authority." In the United Kingdom, the PhD was regarded as a Continental oddity well into the 1950s. Recruitment was controlled by informal networks, so much so that at least until the 1970s the brightest people went into teaching positions straight from their undergraduate degree. In France, where the educational system is much more differentiated, there is (or was, until recently) little consensus on which credentials may signal expertise in *economics* per se, and university professorships were obtained through an idiosyncratic examination, the *agrégation*. By contrast, the openness, size, and competitiveness of the American academic labor market provided a social structure that encouraged reliance on impersonal criteria of performance. An analysis of one of the first AEA membership directories containing detailed biographical information reveals that the majority of academic members (over 60 percent) and half the government members in 1938 had a PhD (*American Economic Review* 1938). This pattern, however, did not apply to members coming from the business world (only 20 percent had a PhD).This discrepancy was, in fact, of great concern to the association and led to the circulation of a number of proposals to restrict membership to "properly qualified" members.[38] By 1969, the percentage of PhDs among university-employed members of the AEA had grown to 79 percent, and 34 percent for business members. [39]

American economics exemplifies, in many ways, the ideal type of successful academic professionalism. Economics departments deliver a greater proportion of PhDs relative to other degrees than any other social-scientific field, a feature that has persisted throughout the postwar period.[40] PhD production is concentrated among a small number of departments: between 1904 and 1939, Columbia alone represented 21 percent of all students working on an economics PhDs, Chicago 13 percent, and Harvard 9 percent.[41] By the early 1970s, these figures had come down significantly, and Harvard had replaced Columbia as the dominant school. Still, the top twenty departments continued to produce more than half of all economics doctorates, a figure that has remained fairly stable until the present day.[42] Graduate training tends to be homogeneous across higher education institutions, even though differences in style are clearly perceptible. As a result, an economics doctorate is a general certification mechanism for academic as well as nonacademic jobs. Thus the annual convention of the American Economics Association, where PhD graduates annually sell their skills to potential buyers, attracts a diverse pool of employers, including many businesses, government agencies, and international institutions. As figure 2-3 shows, in 2001 only about 56 percent of economics PhDs were employed in educational institutions (a figure close to pre–World War II patterns) compared with more than 81 percent in 1970—and a large part of this change is due to a massive shift of graduates toward the business world: employment of PhD economists in business and industry has grown from 11 percent to 24 percent of the total over the same period. The PhD has thus gained currency well outside the boundaries of academia, which, in

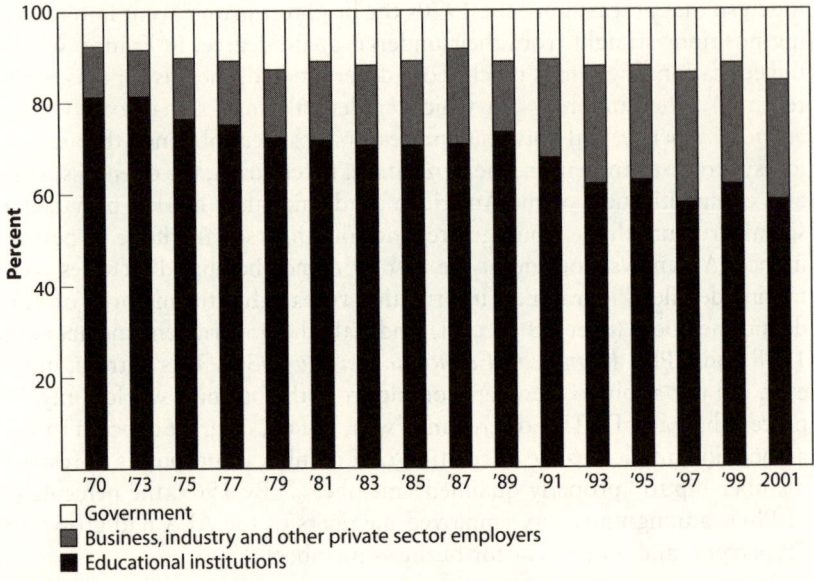

Figure 2-3. Employment sector of doctoral economists, 1970–2001.

Source: National Science Foundation, *Characteristics of Doctoral Scientists and Engineers* (for 1975, 1987, 1991); *Characteristics of Science and Engineering Doctorate Recipients: Selected Trend Tables* (for 1993, 1995, and 1997); and *Characteristics of Doctoral Scientists and Engineers in the United States* (for 1999, 2001). The category "other" was uncertain and thus removed. I am grateful to John Tsapogas of the National Science Foundation for his help in completing the data series.

turn, has fueled the process of professionalization.[43] Thus, figure 2-4a shows the dramatic expansion of economics doctoral degrees starting in the 1960s, and figure 2-4b documents the parallel growth of the American Economic Association.

If the centrality of the PhD as an institution is fundamentally rooted in the competitive structure of the academic market, the forms of incorporation of economic expertise outside of academia have only reinforced it. As will be suggested throughout this chapter, American public administrations have largely relied on the institutions of university-based professionalism as a basis for their own recruitment processes, particularly in the higher positions. Consequently, the (rare) appointment of "nonspecialists" to top-level "economic" positions has sometimes triggered bitter gatekeeping or jurisdictional struggles. The case of Leon Keyserling (vice-chairman and then chairman in the first and second Council of Economic Advisers [CEA; 1946–48, 1948–50]) is emblematic of the issues at stake. A lawyer who had done graduate work in economics,

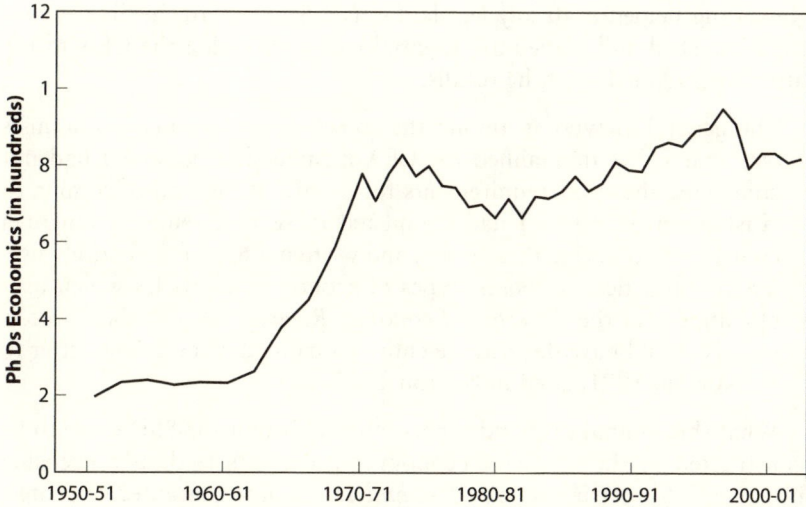

Figure 2-4a. Annual number of PhDs in economics granted at American universities, 1949–2002.

Source: U.S. Department of Education, National Center for Education Statistics.

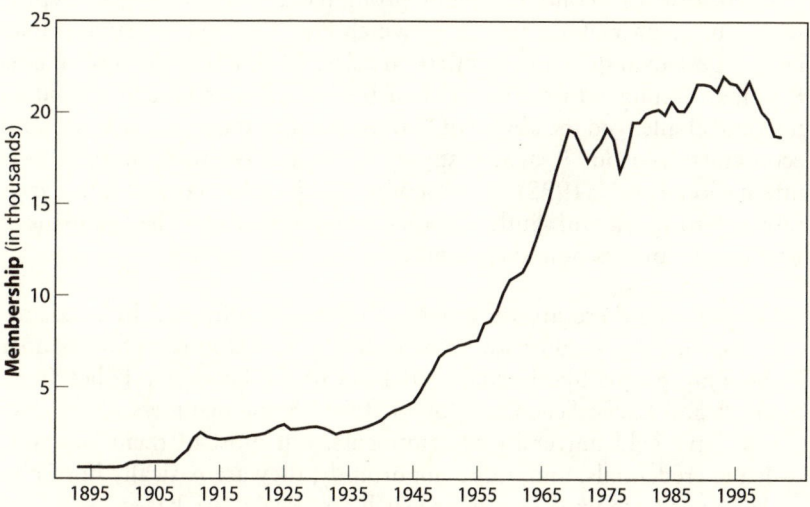

Figure 2-4b. American Economic Association Membership, 1893–2002.
Source: American Economic Association.

Keyserling helped draft key legislation as a Senate staff member during the New Deal and played an essential role in bringing the CEA to life after World War II. Yet, he recalls,

> The general viewpoint among the so-called professional economists was that I was unqualified for CEA membership because I had not completed the essay requirements for a PhD! If, instead of coming to Washington in 1933, I had completed these requirements, taught a course or two during these years, and written a few of the entirely useless (for practical purposes) types of econometric articles which usually appear in the *American Economic Review*, the so-called professionals would have deemed me entirely qualified. (Keyserling, letter to H. Norton, 1971, cited in Norton 1977, 115)[44]

What this liminal case and others indicate is that the PhD came to be constructed by the academic economics profession both as a licensing instrument for certifying expertise *and* as a moral guarantee of professional impartiality. As the interview quote at the onset of this chapter suggests, the personal narratives I collected confirm the continued centrality of the doctorate to the boundary work of American economists against the jurisdictional claims of nonspecialists. During the early years of the Reagan administration, for instance, in a dramatic contest over scientific authority, a group of journalists, think tank ideologues, businessmen, and politicians helped bring about a dramatic transformation in economic discourse—the supply-side revolution.[45] This heavy politicization of economic issues prompted a revival of gatekeeping work on the part of academics, of which Paul Krugman's activism may be the best example. In countless articles, books, and opinion pieces Krugman impugned the authority of people without academic credentials and challenged the ability of "political entrepreneurs" and "pseudo-economists"—from Reagan's supply-siders (1994) to Clinton's "pop internationalists" (1998) and George W. Bush's tax revolutionaries (2003)—to speak with authority on economic issues.[46] The following is an example of this boundary work:

> On one side there are those whose views are informed by academic economics, the kind of stuff that is taught in textbooks. On the other there are people like Kuttner, Jeff Faux of the Economic Policy Institute[47] and Labor Secretary Robert Reich. Some members of this faction have held university appointments. But most of them lack academic credentials, and, more importantly, they are basically hostile to the kind of economics on which such credentials are based. . . .
>
> There are important ideas in (economics) that can be expressed in plain English, and there are plenty of fools doing fancy mathematical

models. But there are other important ideas that are crystal clear if you can stand algebra, and very difficult to grasp if you can't. (Krugman 1996a)

The last paragraph of the quotation suggests two points. First, economists define their skill mainly through the mastery of mathematical tools, acquired in graduate school. The PhD thus serves as a key instrument of both professional standardization vis-à-vis outside markets *and* disciplinary, intellectual standardization inside.[48] The belief that professional standing depends on economics' ability to cohere around a "strong" scientific program was articulated quite early, for instance, in the AEA's effort to homogenize economics instruction in the early 1950s. Hence the so-called Bowen report of the AEA recommended that all economists "should have a sufficient orientation to mathematical ideas, symbols and modes of thought to make economic theory and statistics more intelligible" and implicitly suggested that "mathematical economists"—people with "a command of mathematical skills at the most stratospheric level"—should dominate the professional hierarchy.[49]

The second point is that the use of mathematics is extremely codified, too. As McCloskey (1985) has shown, economic model-building has become a tightly controlled process, guided by, first, the methodological imperative to make—following Friedman's (1953) recommendation— "valid and meaningful predictions about phenomena not yet observed" and, second, by the rhetorical imperative of parsimony and elegance. What binds American economists together, then, is a common set of *practical* rules, normalized through PhD training, regarding the proper way to "do" economic science. These rules apply both to theoretical work (models), where conclusions have to be derived in a strictly deductive manner from a limited set of *acceptable* assumptions, and to empirical work, with its fetishist emphasis on causality. But how did this character of American economics develop historically? What are the factors that influenced the field's intellectual trajectory? And how different is it from economics as it is practiced in Britain and in France?

The Meaning of Science in American Economics

To understand the intellectual trajectory of American economics, we have to return to the period when academic research as a whole got institutionalized in America. For economics, the critical historical juncture took place between 1885 and 1914. This was the time when economists, through their negative and positive interactions with university administrators, public institutions, and business corporations, came to define both their place in American society and the intellectual boundaries of their scholarly enterprise.

The Defense against Politics and the Rise of Scientism

No one took as much to heart the missionary and progressive nature of the "new" social sciences as did the founders of the American Economic Association, many of whom (like Richard T. Ely, John Bates Clark, Henry Carter Adams) combined their scientific aspirations with Christian commitments[50] and sought to reform society by mobilizing popular support for their progressive views. Rapid economic growth had brought irreversible changes to American society, most notably the emergence of a large population of impoverished industrial laborers, whose radical actions attracted the sympathy of a number of young historical economists. Under the leadership of Richard T. Ely, a prominent figure in the Social Gospel movement, the American Economic Association adopted a progressive platform at its inaugural meeting. The ambitions laid out in the document were not unlike those of the AEA's German counterpart, the Verein für Sozialpolitik: to serve as an enlightened society of experts with an avowed social reform purpose.[51] Most spectacularly, it embraced the view that rational administration was the key to social and economic progress:

> We regard the state as an agency whose positive assistance is one of the indispensable conditions of human progress.
>
> We believe that political economy as a science is still in an early stage of development. While we appreciate the work of former economists, we look not so much to speculation as to historical and statistical study of actual conditions of economic life for the satisfactory accomplishment of that development.
>
> We hold that the conflict of labor and capital has brought into prominence a vast number of social problems whose solution requires the united effort, each in its own sphere, of the church, of the state, and of science.[52]

The Christian socialist and anti-laissez-faire stance expressed in the platform was controversial from the beginning. Reflecting both the more radical social orientations of midwestern teachers and their professional desire to keep the doctrinal views of nonacademics (businessmen in particular) at bay from serious economics, these positions initially deterred the most orthodox economists. Hence while General Francis Amasa Walker, an apologist of industrialism who was famous for his theoretical justification of profit, was chosen as president of the AEA, other important conservative figures such as J. Laughlin (founder of the Political Economy Club) and the mathematician Simon New-comb initially declined to join the organization. As the AEA experienced a rapid influx of members from around the country, most of whom endorsed a laissez-faire position, political tensions increased to the point where the "westerners" envisioned a split.[53] In the end, however, they relented to the pressure. In 1887, the organization purged contentious references from its platform and from then on defined itself in exclusively scientific terms.[54] Positions on matters of public policy continued to divide the academic social sciences, however. During the wave of academic freedom cases that spanned from the 1890s to the 1910s, many economists came under sharp public attack for promoting views that offended powerful constituencies in matters as varied as the labor movement, free silver coinage, public utility franchises, or fiscal policy. E. Bemis was dismissed from the University of Chicago, E. Ross from Stanford, and H. C. Adams from Cornell. John Commons had to temporarily retire from academic life after the state legislature came down upon the University of Indiana, and university trustees at Syracuse (his next appointment) decided to discontinue his chair in sociology.[55] Richard Ely was tried at Wisconsin for favoring strikes, after which he gave up much of his political engagement.[56] At Wharton, Scott Nearing was sacked in 1915, presumably because of his activism against child labor and the war; the school's first two deans, Edmund James and Simon Patten, who were active in various progressive causes, also ran into difficulties.[57] The list continues.

As Furner (1975) has shown in her well-known study of these cases, the switch from "advocacy" to "objectivity" constitutes a key turning point in the history of American social science. As knowledge production became increasingly accountable to external control (such as boards of trustees and university administrators, or state legislatures in the case of public universities), reformist activism in the United States came to be represented as incompatible with the academic vocation. The turn-of-the-century political attacks against progressive social scientists set the limits of acceptable behavior and drove them to confine their scholarship to "safe" intellectual ground. In the case of economics (but the pattern is similar in other social sciences), these pressures encouraged a retreat to a more narrowly "scientific" discourse, which protected scholarship from easy vilification. Hence, not only did these cases help transform the social role of academics, who went from openly supporting social reform to a form of politically hands-off professionalism channeled through research bodies and expert commissions; they also had powerful intellectual consequences. In a context of political incertitude and relative lack of autonomy of the intellectual sphere, marginal analysis came to be regarded as a safe and attractive research strategy by American economists, especially by the younger generations who had to create a position for themselves.[58]

The other reason for the shift has to do with the structure of the intellectual field and the nature of intellectual authority in American society. In contrast with the German Verein für Sozialpolitik and the French Société d'Économie Politique, which represented currents that were dominant, if not hegemonic, in their respective countries (historicism on the one hand, *libéralisme* on the other), or even the British Royal Economic Society, which in many ways was Alfred Marshall's personal achievement, the AEA toward the end of the nineteenth century already regarded itself as an umbrella organization for a diverse and regionally fragmented field. In this context, economists soon realized that the public display of their own internal disagreements could damage their credibility. Lacking the hierarchical controls and intellectual authority of its European counterparts, the American economics profession sought to find common ground by neutralizing the political element in political economy.

At the same time that it allowed the AEA to reconcile the variety of opinions of its members, the turn to scientific professionalism also helped legitimize social scientists' claims to relevance vis-à-vis potential users in government and business, thereby redefining "science" as the most promising strategy to influence policy.[59] On the demand side, the Progressives' crusades against political corruption, waste, and inefficiency rapidly pulled the new academic experts into the public domain. As Furner puts it, "Direct appeal to the public on controversial social questions was retained as a theoretical right, but economists were expected to channel most of their efforts through government agencies or private organizations where scholars could serve inconspicuously as technical experts, after the political decisions had been made, rather than as reformers with a new vision of society" (1975, 257–59).

By the 1920s, a whole set of institutions articulated the language of the objective, impartial knowledge of facts as the necessary precondition to the resolution of the social and economic problems of an advanced industrial society. Closely associated with this was the notion that the new scientific methods and procedures of marginal analysis and statistics were the best defense against the perceived evils of radical political partisanship. Being contentious by nature and, as we have seen, quite contested in practice, the modern social science disciplines thus saw academic institutions as the best guarantee of their moral authority.

Philanthropic foundations, which also emerged during this period, came to embody this cultural attitude about the effectiveness of rational knowledge and its potential use for societal betterment through their support of applied, quantitative studies produced in academic settings.

The (discursive, at least) imperative of relevance and the problem-solving orientation also came from the close relationship these organizations entertained with government and business.[60] Here, too, relevance was coupled with an explicit rejection of openly political positions, as well as the curbing of scholars' involvement in social reform, both of which were accused of threatening the organizations' legitimacy in the eyes of those wealthy audiences they sought to appeal to.[61] One way out of this dilemma was to equate the idea of socially useful knowledge with the collection of factual data. Hence, the foundations helped guide the development of an entire research economy that prioritized applied, quantitative studies and fostered a detailed, applied orientation among American social scientists. It is under this particular institutional regime that the economic school of thought best known as American institutionalism flourished.

THE "POSITIVE" CHARACTER OF AMERICAN INSTITUTIONALISM

American economics at the turn of the century was a diverse intellectual field, shaped by different European influences and by a decentralized university system. American students returning from German universities in the middle to late nineteenth century promoted the study of social and economic institutions as the core mission of political economy, and managed to entrench their approach in places such as Johns Hopkins (around Richard T. Ely), Wisconsin (around John R. Commons, Edwin Witte, and Selig Perlman) and later Columbia (around Wesley C. Mitchell). Harvard and Chicago, on the other hand, remained traditional neoclassical power bases, closer to the Marshallian tradition in Britain.[62]

Whether geographically or intellectually, the boundaries between "institutionalism" and neoclassicism were far from clear-cut, however. American institutionalist thought brought together a fairly diverse crowd of practitioners. In an attempt to reconcile their scientific aspirations with their awareness of social change, a fair number of people found themselves in a position of intellectual compromise between both approaches: of the earlier generations, many liberal historicists (such as E.R.A. Seligman) also embraced marginalism.[63] Some institutionalists went further and converted fully to the neoclassical orthodoxy (a good example was John Bates Clark's spectacular turnabout). Studies of interwar economics have confirmed the persistence of such an intellectual continuum from institutionalism to neoclassical economics during that period, with a number of prominent figures (Allyn Young, for instance) holding intermediary positions.[64] Yonay's (1998) work in fact suggests that in their aspirations to control the "soul of economics," American institutionalists were no less scientist than their neoclassical counterparts.

They relied on positivist rhetoric, sought to build intellectual legitimacy by likening their work process to that of the natural sciences (particularly biology), and presented themselves as the "true" heirs of Alfred Marshall in their methodological exchanges with the Marshallian orthodoxy. Furthermore, their aspirations to shape and control the economy were far more ambitious than those of the neoclassicals, who remained much more wedded to laissez-faire ideas and therefore tended to have less impact on policy.

To the extent that an institutionalist school ever existed as a relatively organized body of thought, its distinctiveness came more from its attitude toward economic research than from the existence of a unified paradigm or even a common political stance. Its principal intellectual characteristics were an inductive, empirical approach to the study of the economy, and a faith in government policy and institutional reform as a way to engineer social transformation. Both features of institutionalist thought stemmed from the strong belief in the usefulness of economic knowledge for human and societal betterment, and both have continued to inform the development of American economics to the present day.

The intellectual characteristics of American institutionalism are particularly interesting to analyze in comparative perspective.[65] First, while the American movement shared with its German precursor a taste for induction and the close observation of facts, it differed quite substantially from it (and to a certain extent from the English historical school as well) in the importance it came to give to history. As Ross remarked, by the 1920s, one of the school's "striking features was that, for the most part it did not study institutions and thus did not fully engage with history" (1979, 417). Rather, American institutionalism (especially in its later versions at the National Bureau of Economic Research) remains more closely associated with the systematic collection and analysis of data on current economic conditions than with historical work in the German mold. One of the movement's main figures during the interwar period, W. C. Mitchell, sought first and foremost to identify empirical regularities through the close quantitative observation of facts; he is best remembered for his monumental work on the business cycle.[66] In his 1924 presidential address to the American Economic Association, Mitchell laid out a "quantitative" future for economics dominated by questions of measurement, not only of physical and monetary quantities but also of human behavior through the development of the experimental method—a prescient statement. This purely inductive approach, he argued, would make the mathematical sophistication of pure economic *theory*, as envisioned by Marshall or Jevons, irrelevant. In fact, he predicted, "our whole apparatus of reasoning on the basis of utilities and disutilities, or motives, or choices" will become obsolete. "Motives will not be disregarded, but they will be treated as problems requiring study" (1925, 5).

Little did Mitchell realize that economic quantification in America would ultimately follow *both* of these routes. Mitchell's esteemed colleague at Columbia, Henry L. Moore, had pioneered the statistical estimation of the laws of neoclassical economics. During the interwar period, Moore's students' at Chicago—Henry Schultz (who headed a statistical laboratory funded by the Social Science Research Council) and Paul Douglas—pursued his program of establishing the validity of the neoclassical intellectual apparatus on a purely *statistical* basis, by estimating some of its key concepts (e.g., demand curves, elasticity) from actual empirical markets, mainly agricultural product markets. "What we have to do to make our discipline an experimental science," Schultz wrote, "is to examine our concepts or laws from an operational point of view." (1928, 647).

The language is strikingly similar to Mitchell's. It is often not well appreciated by sociologists how much the intellectual programs of institutional and neoclassical economics in fact *overlapped*, not least in their common reliance on statistics. Certainly Mitchell, in his emphasis on an inductive exploration of the economy through measurement alone, had little faith in Moore's efforts to statistically specify neoclassical concepts. But he applauded Moore's patient collection of data and his careful work with it. It is also important to point out how much *this* research program seems to have been at odds with the interests of British economists at the time. Anticipating Keynes's reaction to econometrics later on, Marshall and Edgeworth disdained Moore's efforts.[67] It is not that British economists were mathematically illiterate or uneducated about the state of the real economy (they certainly were not), but theory for them always had a much higher status. In the United States, one would have to await the Samuelsonian revolution after World War II for such a clear hierarchy to establish itself, and even then, it was never complete and has arguably lost part of its appeal. By the 1980s, indeed, an inductive, atheoretical research program in economics started to come back with a vengeance, both on intellectual grounds (e.g., Sims 1980) and in response to outside demands from business and government.

From this broader perspective, institutionalism ceases to be a sort of parenthesis in American intellectual history. The institutionalist research program's loss of intellectual ground after the 1930s and its rapid demise after 1945 become understandable in light of the specific trajectory of quantification in America: the modern history of American economics is fundamentally a history about "rival ideals of quantification," as Porter (1994) put it, rather than rival ideals of economic analysis (as is arguably the case with French economics). American institutionalism was displaced because its model of quantification was made obsolete by the combined rise of mathematical economics and econometrics, which associated empiricism with the explicit formulation and testing of economic theories. The quantitative bent of economics, however, persisted under new forms and continued to rely on America's deep cultural reverence for numbers and facts as the only means to achieve relevance and scientific legitimacy. Its institutional bases—in universities, foundations, and government agencies—also continued to inspire and insist upon this view.

The Postwar Mathematization of American Economics

In the 1930s, the use of mathematics for the advancement of economic analysis was familiar to American economists, yet by and large pioneering work in this area had failed to leave an imprint. Among the forerunners, Simon Newcomb was a mathematician and astronomer whose interest in economics had emerged almost accidentally and his *Principles of Economics* was virulently attacked by important institutionalist figures. Schumpeter notes that the publication of Irving Fisher's *Mathematical Investigations* (1892) "passed practically unnoticed"([1954] 1994, 873). Empirical work, on the other hand, was generally descriptive, with the notable exception of agricultural economics (e.g., Moore, later Ezekiel), where the unique availability of agricultural data and the proactive attitude of the Department of Agriculture toward economic research had stimulated the early development of applied econometrics. Other pioneers in mathematical economics and econometrics were mainly European, from France, England, and Austria. U.S. academia, however, rapidly closed the gap with Europe in the 1930s and 1940s, thereby taking over scientific leadership in the field. Three events played a critical role in this evolution: the birth of macroeconomics, the connection with military research, and McCarthyism.

THE NEOCLASSICAL SYNTHESIS AND THE ECONOMETRIC REVOLUTION

As an analytical framework focused on aggregate variables, macroeconomics lent itself quite naturally to mathematical formulation. The English economist John Hicks (1937) pioneered a mathematical representation of macroeconomic relations, which was later expanded upon by Franco Modigliani in the United States (1944).[68] However, it was probably not until Samuelson's *Foundations of Economic Analysis* (1947) and his textbook *Economics* (1948) were published that mathematical modeling crystallized as the aspiring dominant method for economics. While Hicks was shy about his mathematics, pushing them into the appendix, Samuelson had no such qualms. *Au contraire*: he made it very clear that mathematics ought to be embraced as the natural language of economics. In the opening pages of the *Foundations*, Samuelson defined his approach as

> the method of comparative statics, meaning by this the investigation of changes in a system from one position of equilibrium to another without regard to the transitional process involved in the adjustment. . . . This method of comparative statics is but one special application of the more general practice of scientific deduction in which the behavior of a system (possibly through time) is defined in terms of a given set of functional equations and initial conditions. (Samuelson 1947, 7–8)

In short, economics should emulate theoretical physics: at the macro level, it should describe the economy with a minimum set of equations; at the micro level, it should rely on the methodology of constrained optimization. Samuelson's textbook popularized these distinctions and rules as the basic method of economic theory and set out, with considerable confidence in the engineering skills of economists, the main themes of Keynesian macroeconomic policy. Currently in its eighteenth edition, it has been a considerable editorial success, both in the United States and worldwide.[69] From the point of view of his impact on the *style* of economic analysis (even leaving aside his properly *theoretical* contributions), Samuelson was probably right when he immodestly stated: "I can claim that in talking about modern economics, I am talking about me."[70]

The revolution was sweeping: by 1960, nearly 80 percent of *theory* articles in the three main U.S. economics journals used algebra, up from about 20 percent in 1930.[71] The *Foundations* convinced a new generation of economists that, as Robert Lucas put it, "mathematical analysis is not one of many ways of doing economic theory: It is the only way. Economic theory is mathematical analysis. Everything else is just pictures and talk" (Robert Lucas, cited in Walsh 2006, 168). The turn to modeling gave economics both a lofty scientific status and a high moral ground; armed with their macroeconomic models, economists now claimed to be able to deliver economic growth and full employment. The economy had been turned into a "thing" whose behavior could be described (through national accounts), modeled into equations, tested, predicted, and acted upon.[72] "The heyday of Keynesian economics," Solow writes, "provides a wonderful example of the interplay among theory, the availability of data, and the econometric method" (1998, 65).

Indeed, the mathematical revolution had an empirical counterpart. Unsurprisingly, the intellectual trajectory in the handling of economic data parallels the trend toward structural equations in economic theory. By the 1940s, the so-called econometric approach, which promoted the use of probability theory to "find the correct choice of model for the observed data," was on the rise, posing a serious challenge to the descriptive statistical research program of the NBER.[73] From a largely inductive style based on the identification of empirical regularities, economics moved to a structural approach where theoretical models were fitted to data. In the United States, the "measurement without theory" debate gave a somewhat dramatic flair to the transition, with one of the leaders of the new approach attacking Mitchell and Burns for the lack of theoretical grounding in their 1946 volume, *Measuring Business Cycles*.[74] Said Koopmans: "Fuller utilization of the concepts and hypotheses of economic theory *as a part of the process of observation and measurement* promises to be a shorter road, perhaps the only possible road, to the understanding of cyclical fluctuations" (1947, 162). With this, the era of descriptive statistics was judged to be intellectually obsolete, although in practice it persisted somewhat longer, notably at the NBER. Ronald Coase reportedly said of institutionalism: "Without a theory, they had nothing to pass on except a mass of descriptive material awaiting a theory or a fire."[75]

What gave mathematical economics a new impetus in the twentieth century were convergent intellectual and organizational developments. It is indeed not irrelevant that by the time Koopmans published his review, he was a member of, and about to head, a strange new institution: the Cowles Commission for Economic Research. The watershed had come in 1930, when a small network of like-minded European and American scholars with a serious background in mathematics joined forces to create the Econometric Society. Almost immediately thereafter, a wealthy Colorado banker named Alfred Cowles III gratified his interest in the scientific production of economic forecasts by providing financial backing for the precarious association and its journal, *Econometrica*.[76] With Cowles's underwriting, the Econometric Society grew rapidly, going from only 16 members at the time of its founding in 1930 to 163 members in 1933 and 671 by 1939.[77] Meanwhile, the Cowles Commission (later Foundation) for Economic Research, which acted as a sponsor to these organizations, also provided a stable research base for a number of refugee scholars with nonstandard affiliations (some of whom may have otherwise had difficulty finding regular jobs in the American academic system). In addition to their varied national origins (many Cowles members came from continental Europe), several also held noneconomics degrees in fields such as physics (Tinbergen, Koopmans), mathematical statistics (Frisch, Wald), and mathematics (Roos, Davis, Debreu).[78]

In 1939 the organization moved from its peripheral location in Colorado Springs to the University of Chicago, a decisive step toward incorporation into the core of the American academic system.[79] Further recognition came in 1942, when the commission began receiving funds

from the Rockefeller Foundation, as well as small amounts from the
National Bureau of Economic Research. Under the leadership of Jacob
Marschak, the commission's research program began focusing on modeling the economy as a system of simultaneous economic equations with
random variables. In the process, Cowles scholars also devised statistical
methods to estimate economic models' parameters from observational
data. If the Cowles Commission did not invent the language of modern
economics, it certainly played a key role in making the "model construction–statistical estimation" sequence part of the disciplinary vulgate. Ultimately, Cowles would become the main center for the development of
large-scale macroeconometric models, later moving to more abstract
work in linear programming and Walrasian general equilibrium analysis.[80] To realize the organization's immense impact, one need only mention that fully a third of the recipients of the Nobel Prize in economics
between 1969 and 1990 had been formally associated with it.[81]

WAR AND COLD WAR

World War II was the second important event in the mathematical
evolution of American economics. Its conduct brought to the fore the
need for planning, forecasts, and resource allocation strategies, and federal agencies tapped quantitative abilities where they existed, primarily
among statistically inclined scientists and social scientists. Hence work
conducted under federal government auspices led to the development of
output analysis, statistical estimation, national accounts, resource allocation, and linear programming techniques.[82]

The outbreak of the cold war created an even larger market for skills
that seemed most attractive to the federal government in a highly uncertain international context, such as game theory, allocative programming,
and operations research. The Department of Defense, notably the U.S.
Navy and the U.S. Air Force, actively supported these lines of analysis,
which "seemed to have potential value for the missions of the national
defense and security establishment."[83] The technical demands of the war
economy under its various forms (declared or latent) from the 1940s to
the 1960s, and the reorganization of scientific research around a "national security state" investing massively in engineering and the physical
sciences, exerted a powerful "pull" effect on economics.

As Mirowski and others have shown, the government's intensive investment in national defense explains much of the intellectual reorientation of
American economics in the postwar period.[84] Military funding introduced
economists (but also philosophers and psychologists) to engineering-based
techniques of operation research and cybernetics, new computational
tools, and new technical challenges (the "missile gap"). The new institutional configuration helped push economics into previously uncharted

intellectual terrains such as game theory and artificial intelligence, and contributed to an extensive redefinition of its place in society. Economics was now becoming the "general" science of rational decision making.[85]

The second, perhaps less obvious, effect of military funding is that it sheltered the most technical segment of the profession from the intellectual demands of university economics at the time, as well as from the need for direct policy relevance. The latter had dominated debates about the place of economics in the early part of the century and was a central concern of financial sponsors like the Rockefeller Foundation. The evolution of the Cowles Commission after 1948 is a good case in point. By the 1950s, the organization switched patrons and became a beneficiary of the quite lavish funding of the RAND Corporation (a postwar military think tank turned nonprofit organization) and the U.S. Office of Naval Research. Under the attractive label of "decision theory," and with Tjalling Koopmans now at the helm, Cowles's research program started evolving in a much more abstract direction.[86] The effect was to launch economics on the path of mathematical formalism for at least two decades, a development some regard as profoundly un-American—a sort of historical aberration in a mostly pragmatic intellectual path.[87] Indeed, the crowning achievement of this program, the Arrow-Debreu (1954) proof of the existence of general equilibrium, drew much of its inspiration from the French mathematical collective "Bourbaki" and its taste for rigorous axiomatization.[88]

It was partly the increasing abstraction of the work at Cowles that caused some important quarters of the profession to doubt the value of the scientific program being carried on there. As Mirowski and Hand (1998) have argued, with the Columbia-Wisconsin institutionalist pole virtually wiped out, the postwar intellectual landscape in American economics centered on three powerful poles: MIT (Samuelson), Cowles (econometrics/general equilibrium), and the University of Chicago. Of these, Chicago was probably least receptive to the influence of the other poles. Indeed, despite the commission's being housed there from 1939 to 1955, there was much about Cowles that Chicago economists disliked. Milton Friedman and Frank Knight in particular objected to Cowles's Walrasian, formalist method, its interest in computer simulations, and, not the least, its sympathies for socialist planning and government intervention, with which Cowles's characteristic systems of structural equations had an explicit affinity.[89]

WITCH HUNTS

And it was, obviously, not an opportune time to show such sympathies. The cold war had begun, and public and private patrons were nervous about the ideological implications of the research they supported. In

1952 and 1954 two successive congressional committees launched investigations into the activities of the major foundations on the suspicion that they helped spread radical ideas.[90] Similarly, the social sciences were first excluded from the National Science Foundation at its creation in 1950 on the grounds that their messy politics might "compromise the perceived ethical neutrality and taken-for-granted disengagement of natural scientists" (Gieryn, 1999, 97). Finally, many insidious campaigns targeted individual scholars. Frederic Lee suggests that "at least twenty-seven economists" were explicitly harassed, or worse, during the McCarthy era (2004, 180). Red-baiters made life at Stanford miserable for Paul Baran.[91] Paul Sweezy at the University of New Hampshire was prosecuted for refusing to answer a state legislative committee's questions about his political activities. A particularly nasty episode unfolded at the University of Illinois in 1950–1951, soon after the economics department started to recruit scholars from Cowles; the dean who oversaw the hiring process, Harold Bowen, was forcibly removed from his position.[92] Others (like future Nobel Prize winner Lawrence Klein) could not find a job because of their sympathies for Marxism or even progressive Keynesian views. Indeed Samuelson reports that "'Keynesianism' was a naughty word politically long after the war," frequently associated with Marxism in right-wing circles.[93] Some institutionalists who had been involved with the early policy experiments of the New Deal also appeared suspect of political partiality and liberalism, if not outright radicalism.[94]

Faced with these attacks, the profession kept a low profile and avoided direct involvement: the American Economic Association created the Exploratory Committee on the Status of the Profession in 1952 but it did not empower it to investigate specific academic freedom cases.[95] The result of the witchhunts was that Marxian economics was effectively muted for more than a decade within U.S. academia, even though the *Monthly Review* (which Paul Sweezy had founded in 1949 with journalist Leo Huberman) managed to carry on its operations and continued to command remarkable prestige among left-wing intellectuals worldwide. But one would have to await the rise of the New Left in the wake of the civil rights movement and the anti-Vietnam War mobilization for the movement (now renamed radical economics) to regain some legitimacy and experience a revival under the banner of the Union of Radical Political Economists.[96]

The other revolution was quieter, but no less powerful in its consequences. With the scientific competition with the Soviet Union accelerating, dominant institutions in the research economy (from the Ford Foundation to government-sponsored agencies) increasingly embraced the formal methods' promise of efficiency, accuracy and mastery of the social and economic world. When the social science program of the National

Science Foundation was finally born in the late 1950s, for instance, its administrators were extremely careful to assert its legitimacy by emphasizing the similarity of methods with the natural sciences, and by mainly supporting highly technical research (including pure mathematical theory).[97] A review of funding patterns by the National Science Foundation over the 1958–79 period shows its heavy involvement in quantitative research and econometrics, notably in the areas of productivity and large-scale modeling (for instance at the Cowles Foundation during the 1960s and 1970s). Furthermore, the best funded scholar over this period, Mordecai Kurz, was supported as head of the Institute for Mathematical Studies at Stanford University, where he coordinated an international network of mathematical economists around Kenneth Arrow.[98]

By the 1960s, economics departments increasingly educated students in developments in neoclassical theory and econometric techniques. U.S. academic economics as it developed through the intellectual medium of what came to be known as the "neo-classical synthesis"[99] (which relegated Keynesianism to the status of a special case of general equilibrium theory) was much less challenging in its policy implications than earlier stagnationist forms, which assumed that the economy was subject to chronic underemployment of capacities and thereby justified a much more active spending policy.[100] Now rekindled as "growth theory," American macroeconomics claimed to deliver the tools to outrun the Soviet Union in the competition for global economic power. Hence the key institutions in the U.S. research economy concentrated their support on those aspects of economics that were antagonistic neither to the interests of the United States nor to those of American capitalism.[101] It is quite remarkable that the only study of Marxian theory ever supported by the National Science Foundation was entrusted to the father of postwar orthodoxy, none other than Paul Samuelson.[102]

Economic Imperialism

The centrality of mathematics in economics is by no means unique to the United States, of course. As we will see in the following chapters, British economists, as well as a large segment of the French economics profession, are also very comfortable with mathematics as a theory-building tool. However, the intellectual and institutional trajectories leading to the mathematization of economics, and its implications for the broader shape of economic science, bear some unique characteristics in each of the three countries. The endless competition over technique in the United States, whether empirical or formalist, is largely grounded in a historically evolved professional culture that identifies such methods with objectivity and the pursuit of efficiency. It also plays a crucial role in the regulation of the academic market itself. In a competitive and largely self-referential academic environment which is itself partly a product of that same boundary work against direct political involvement, the development of sophisticated mathematical tools, or the creative manipulation or application of established ones, has proved to be crucial in ensuring distinction and professional stature. Consequently, being able to master the right mathematical and statistical technology often takes the form of a strict moral imperative. This was strikingly formulated by one of my interviewees, a prominent academic economist who summed up the modus operandi of the discipline in the United States as follows:

> You are only supposed to follow certain rules. If you don't follow certain rules, you're not an economist. If you don't do it right, you're not *pukka*. . . . *Pukka* is the opposite of *kuchcha*. *Pukka* is brick, and *kuchcha* is dirt. *Pukka* is brahmin, *kuchcha* is outcast. *Pukka* means "high caste" in Urdu. So that means you should derive the way people behave from strict maximization theory; where people are maximizing economic art, that's *pukka*. *Kuchcha* . . . would be adding odd things to your argument, things that you have, the noneconomic arguments. So considering an argument where fairness played a role, for instance. Of course, there are people who do fairness in a *pukka* way. By being axiomatic. "I'm going to make these five axioms and then I'm going to derive how the world is." The opposite would be arguing by example. You're not allowed to do that, I know you're not allowed to do that. There's a word for it. People say, "That's anecdotal." That's the end of you if people have said you're anecdotal. . . . [Another thing is] what modern people say . . . The modern thing is: "it's not identified." Your causality is not identified. God, when your causality is not identified, that's the end of you. (professor, University of California, Berkeley, November 2003)

Characteristically, all the great scientific revolutions in postwar American economics relied extensively on the success of new formalizing technologies, which made the previous set of rules obsolete and fostered the image of cumulative scientific progress. The Samuelsonian revolution generalized the use of mathematical metaphors and the technique of economic modeling. The formalist revolution (Arrow-Debreu) imposed strict axiomatization. The rational expectations revolution drew on the rigorous modeling style of general equilibrium theory to require macroeconomics to rely on strict microeconomic foundations and the hypothesis of perfectly competitive markets.[103] By contrast, important intellectual challenges in postwar British (post-Keynesianism) or French (the regulation school) economics were based on new substantive frameworks rather than on technical virtuosity. The regulation school, for instance, used very little, if any, mathematics, in spite of its "authors" coming almost exclusively from arguably the best mathematical college in the country (Polytechnique). We may contrast this with the fact that unorthodox approaches in the United States were obliged to conform to mainstream methodological and formalist standards.[104] Influential currents in American Marxist thought, such as John Roemer's work, use the tools of game theory and the analytical methodology of neoclassical economics to investigate classic Marxist questions.[105] In a world where training is homogeneous and scientific rules are fairly rigid, the only way to establish some form of legitimacy is by following the same methodological standards as the dominant group. Reflecting on the trajectory of American Marxism, McCloskey notes:

> The new analytic Marxists have produced an impressive literature doing MIT neoclassical economics as well as or better than the MIT neoclassicals. The plan is to argue in terms that the neoclassicals appreciate, as in Stephen Marglin's *Growth, Distribution and Prices* (1984). Rhetorically speaking the plan is admirable. We are not going to make progress in economics until we discover how to talk to each other. (1994, 155)

One consequence of this implicit consensus is that the different subfields of economics—which before World War II were organized around local and rather independent intellectual subcultures, from industrial organization to money and finance—have been unified by the common language of constrained optimization. The unification of this language has in turn motivated the expansion of economics into new and increasingly remote fields.[106] The discipline's ability to expand its range of empirical investigation has also been assisted by the greater availability of ever more detailed data, technological revolutions in computer power, and the explosion of social demands for economic expertise, as I discuss in detail later. Hence formalism and abstraction have enabled modern economics to evolve into an internally unified science capable of seizing opportunities to spread to a wide range of intellectual domains.

This imperialist expansion of modern economics is largely an American development, however. The European mainstream has been less eager to apply economic methodology to such a large variety of objects. It is, for instance, remarkable that the economic approach to human and social behavior was developed in the United States (Becker 1976), as were the school of public choice for the analysis of political behavior and the program to apply economic theory to the design of legal rules, which has gone by the name of "law and economics." In each of these cases, the theoretical innovation relied on extending the paradigm of the rational economic actor (i.e., optimizing under constraint) to individuals and situations that were previously exempted from it: e.g. state actors, intimate relationships, and crime.[107]

These examples tend to vindicate Abbott's (2000, 144) argument that the formulation of "totalizing claims" is part of the nature of disciplinary development. Still, nothing in that argument enables us to understand the particular, substantive direction that totalizing claims have taken in American economics, namely, the derivation of *everyone's* behavior from constrained optimization rather than (for instance) the building of comprehensive frameworks (as in various forms of structuralism, which have been more common in Europe). The imperialism of American economics is rooted in a deep moral belief that no one stands outside of economic rationality and that, furthermore, money is the primary medium through which economic rationality expresses itself.

"Intelligent Conservatives"

The single most important reason for this imperialistic development of American economics is what we can loosely call the Chicago school. It is among Chicago economists that the search for neoclassical purity has reached its peak, both at the level of the single individual and at the level of the entire economy. First, *every* individual is a rational, self-interested (even rent-seeking) actor: public officials, elected politicians, husbands and wives, or criminals are no exception. The work of Gary Becker, George Stigler, James Buchanan, and Richard Posner finds its roots in this basic assumption. Second, the economy operates as the competitive model assumes: "Markets clear, decision makers optimize, money illusion is absent" (Reder 1982, 19). There are no rigidities; there is no market power.

An article Milton Friedman published in 1953, which is still today one of the most debated articles on economic methodology, perhaps best epitomizes both of these commitments. In "The Methodology of Positive Economics," Friedman formulated the controversial claim that economic theory should be judged not by the realism of its hypotheses but solely on its ability to correctly predict observable outcomes—as if the hypotheses were correct. Characterized as "instrumentalist" by Boland (1979), this position made the clarification of practical problems of policy making the relevant yardstick by which all "positive" economics should be evaluated.[108] Many commentators have concentrated on the "as if" methodological statement,[109] seeing it (quite erroneously, I think) as a general license for the kind of economic formalism that came to redefine the field in the 1950s and 1960s. This interpretation is doubly misleading. First, it casts Friedman as an economic formalist. But the association with institutionalism was, after all, quite prominent in Friedman's training (as well as in the training of other leading Chicago economists such as Gary Becker).[110] Consider: his mentor at Rutgers, Arthur F. Burns, was an institutionalist economist. Friedman started his career working closely with Mitchell at the NBER before being hired by the National Resources Committee as a statistician during the New Deal. And one of his best-known empirical works, *A Monetary History of the United States* (which Friedman published with Anna Schwartz in 1963), was written in an arguably institutionalist vein.

Second, this interpretation misreads the particular intellectual context in which Friedman formulated his claim. To some extent, the emphasis on predictive accuracy can be read instead as a license for a certain form of *empiricism* directed against econometrics, as I argue later. More important, Friedman's argument was explicitly intended as a defense of laissez-faire economics against what he saw as two threatening tendencies developing in neoclassical economics: first, the claim, common since the 1930s, that "monopolistic competition" was widespread in the economy, and, second, any attempt to conceive of behavior as deviating from constrained optimization. Friedman deployed the criterion of predictive accuracy essentially as an argument for preserving these two central assumptions.

Friedman legitimated holding on to both of these hypotheses on the grounds that they were more parsimonious, less confusing, and yielded real-world predictions that were just as good. But convenience was not all there was to it. At stake were beliefs about economic reality itself, not simply about the *epistemological relationship* of economics to economic reality. The assumption that people behave rationally was not seriously challenged until the recent emergence of behavioral economics—but even that view remains marginal in economics today. To a large extent, the same applies to the hypothesis of perfect competition. Postwar Chicago economists (Director, Stigler, Posner, Friedman, Hayek, Becker) played a key role in legitimating the representation of the real economy as naturally competitive and downplaying various forms of economic concentration as efficient responses to market conditions that do not seriously threaten competition. (Importantly, these views were endorsed by conservative foundations, such as the Volker Foundation, or the Walgreen Foundation, which bankrolled some of the research done at Chicago, as well as Chicago scholars' more political pamphlets).[111] So successful was this line of argument that when John Kenneth Galbraith raised serious critiques against it in his best seller *The New Industrial State* [1967], his description was vehemently rejected, including by the then largely Keynesian economics mainstream.[112] Few economists were willing to entertain the idea that Galbraith's emphasis on the power of large corporations was a good characterization of the structure of the U.S. economy.

The effects of this naturalization of the competitive model as *the* world were far-reaching for macroeconomics. Not only was the perfect competition hypothesis largely accepted at face value, but it was also never subjected to rigorous econometric testing.[113] One prominent economics professor whom I interviewed lamented:

> The reason why we lost is that we sold ourselves to that methodology. You see, in economics you test hypotheses. But if the null is that the world is perfectly competitive, the data is always too weak to reject it. It is almost impossible to refute the null. Summers wrote an article for the *Journal of Finance* where he showed that it takes 5,000 years worth of data to reject the null of efficient markets. (professor, West Coast university, November 4, 2003)[114]

Friedman's instrumentalist epistemology has thus served to legitimate the preservation of a rigid version of price theory (in which nominal price or wage rigidities do not exist, for instance), which is perhaps paradoxical given the tendency of some to interpret his work as "anything goes" when it comes to hypotheses. It is precisely the point that anything does not go. In practice, Chicago's reluctance to accept empirical evidence or theoretical innovations that represented a threat for the competitive markets hypothesis was remarkably successful at both establishing perfect competition as the obligatory reference point and fostering a generally critical, if not dismissive, attitude toward econometrics.[115] Empirically, Chicago disciples in macroeconomics typically privilege more inductive studies of correlations associated with the method of "calibration"—an approach to parameter estimation that *starts from the assumption that the model is correct* and, in a typical Friedmanian fashion, is supposed to explain regularities documented by empirical studies. (This stands in contrast with the standard approach in econometrics, where a model is always *tested* against some alternative.)[116] The Chicago method is thus a strange mix of a quite dogmatic form of neoclassical economic theory with an empirical approach based on stylized facts and detailed microeconomic studies. Ironically, the latter are not dissimilar to the kinds of quantitative work that used to be carried out by many institutionalists. Hence the technique melded a then unparalleled mathematical prowess with the two perhaps most powerful and enduring ideals in American economics: the virtues of free markets and applied quantification.[117]

What has been uniting Chicago economists across generations in the postwar period (the interwar period was a much more diverse terrain) is the firm conviction, reproduced in model assumptions and modeling techniques as well as in the refusal to engage in econometric debates, that—on the macro front—competitive markets should, essentially, remain the baseline, "irrespective," as one interviewee said, "of what your eyes and ears tell you." Or maybe it is that "what your eyes and ears tell you" has been different at Chicago than what it has been elsewhere. In the traditional neoclassical view, the competitive markets hypothesis was an unattainable ideal, against which the necessarily imperfect economic reality could be measured. If necessary, markets could be brought in line by means of active government intervention. In this view, natural economic reality was the world of imperfect competition.[118] This allowed economists to legitimate a certain role (both macro and micro) for the state as a protector against the market (in the case of externalities, for instance) *and* as an institution that was also in the business of fostering competition (hence the support for antitrust policies). In the postwar Chicago tradition, by contrast, the distinction between reality and ideal made much less sense—what comes out of Chicago writings (for instance, by Friedman or Stigler, both influenced by Aaron Director) was a much more *pragmatic* definition of the competitive markets hypothesis, in which none but the most egregious business practices posed a serious threat to the competitive system. This understanding made it easier for real markets to meet the competitive market standard *and* came to sustain a minimalist interpretation of antitrust policy as well as a strong antiregulatory streak.[119] Chicago *saw* (sees) the world in a very distinctive manner: natural economic reality *is* the world of perfect competition.

How can we explain sociologically the intellectual distinctiveness of Chicago economics within the broader U.S. field? Some have emphasized the university's position relative to state power–in this case, its relatively peripheral situation both with respect to the policy process and even within the city of Chicago itself. Being less involved in government, Chicago economists were less supportive of it, which further contributed to their isolation from it. Indeed, similar patterns could be observed with respect to both the Institut de France and, to a lesser extent, the French University, as well as for the Manchester school in England during the nineteenth century. But the equation between distance from political power (whether geographical or institutional) and political position is far from perfect. Ultimately, Chicago's distinctiveness may have had more to do with the lesser importance of foreigners in the department, the intellectual legacies of influential teachers with extremely long tenures (Knight, Friedman, Stigler, Becker), as well as with consistent patterns of recruitment and socialization through core courses in price theory, rigorous qualifying exams, and a workshop system designed to mold students into reliable adherents of the Chicago approach—"intelligent conservatives," as Richard Posner once put it.[120]

The Academic Roots of Public Expertise

We have seen that American political institutions and culture have played a constitutive role in structuring the jurisdictional and scientific orientations of American economics. Yet *administrative* mechanisms have also helped articulate distinctive conceptions about the exercise of public power and correlatively distinctive understandings about the nature of economic expertise and the role of economic experts.

Since the end of the nineteenth century, American officials have relied on institutions devoted to higher education and research to certify the quality of the economic experts whom they employ. This is true at all levels of the civil service: At the higher end, economists recruited from academia on a temporary basis usually occupy specific positions in a wide range of agencies, the Council of Economic Advisers being the most visible. At the lower levels of the civil service, public administrations have given formal recognition to the institutions of university-based professionalism as a basis for their own recruitment processes, classifying and matching candidates to administrative positions according to their specialized skills. The most remarkable application of this academic credentialism may be found in some of the independent agencies, such as the Federal Reserve or the Antitrust Division of the Department of Justice, where a PhD from a highly ranked department is a sine qua non for obtaining a position. In 1996, the thirteen branches of the Federal Reserve System employed more than 250 PhD economists, likely the highest concentration anywhere in the country.[121] Finally, governmental administrative agencies have come to routinely purchase expertise through a market for technical advice in which suppliers are generally located outside of state agencies—in universities mainly, but also in think tanks and private consulting bodies.

The Making of the Economic Expert

In a well-known paper about the role of economists in American policy making, Robert Nelson identified the Progressive Era as the period when a distinctive set of dispositions (in Bourdieu's terminology, an *habitus*) vis-à-vis the place of the economic expert in American government was forged. It was during that time that the economist, he argues, came to be regarded as "a professional expert who advises government in technical and scientific matters and takes social values and political preferences as given. Once these values and preferences have been expressed by political leaders, economic expertise can be applied to make the governing process work as efficiently and as effectively as possible" (1987, 53–54).

Whether Nelson's characterization represents a reliable analysis of the relationship between economists and the political realm, or whether it should more likely be read as an instance of the ideology that underlines it, does not really matter for our purpose, since our argument is that both are closely intertwined anyway. More interesting, perhaps, are the historical conditions under which such an understanding developed. As suggested earlier, the "professional ideal" took shape around the turn of the century during the coincidence of, on the one hand, academics' search for insulation from political controversy and, on the other hand, an emerging institutional niche for economic expertise within government and business. We thus have good sociological reasons to think that the attitudes Nelson identifies as characteristic of the relationship between economists and government are not sui generis to the practice of economics, in a manner analogous to Merton's (1973) ethos of science, for instance. Rather, they have been forged in the context of the dynamic and highly peculiar interaction between academic science and policy in the United States.

During the Progressive period, which extended roughly from the mid-1880s to World War I, social movements sought to assert the autonomy of governments at all levels (municipal, county, state, federal) by promoting a class of public servants that would be immune to political patronage. In this major political transformation, members of the then emerging professions were incorporated into various public bodies as governments engaged in a deliberate attempt to "remove various economic and social problems from the political arena" (Silberman, 1993, 276). For instance, the creation of independent regulatory commissions as well as federal institutions for data collection relied extensively on the new professional associations (American Economic Association, American Statistical Association) for expertise and guidance. A large number of academic economists took up temporary positions in such institutions, which also served as important training grounds for the younger generations of researchers.

In some cases economists were more directly involved in policy design. Perhaps the most radical of the Progressive civil service reform laws was drafted by John Commons, then at the University of Wisconsin, and enacted under La Follette's governorship of that state. Commons, along with several of his academic colleagues, was appointed to various state commissions, prompting the critique that in Wisconsin the university governed the state. Yet, as Commons wrote in his autobiography:

> I could never see it that way. I was never called in except by Progressives, and only when they wanted me. I never initiated anything. I came only on request of legislators, of executives, or committees of the legislature. The same was true of many other members of the faculty. . . . [Each professor] can furnish only technical details and then only when he is wanted by politicians who really govern the state. So with the "brain trust" at Washington. [Commons is writing during the New Deal.] I see individuals coming and going according to whether or not they furnish the President with what he wants. (1963, 110)[122]

Commons presents public involvement as the outcome of a competitive political process. In his account, the pattern in Wisconsin was not a government of experts, as critics would have it. It was, at most, a government that relied on external expertise to govern. There was thus nothing essentially technocratic about Commons's involvement—it was, rather, understood as the purchase, by state agencies and reform organizations, of a set of discrete technical services that could be revoked or stopped at any point in time (as they indeed were with the change of administration in Wisconsin in 1914).[123] In this instrumental relation, it was the university, and not the state, which "functioned as a permanent professional base from which [Commons] asserted claims to expertise, established policy connections and made temporary forays into the world of policy research and influence" (Schweber 1996, 173).[124]

As in Wisconsin, administrative rationalization in other states and at the federal level also relied extensively on the emerging professional communities rooted in the universities, albeit to a somewhat lesser extent. Certainly, the pattern was not entirely new,[125] nor did it all come from the demand side, as Commons suggests. As historian Daniel Rodgers (1998) has shown, German-trained economists had brought the model of expert-staffed public inquiry commissions back from Germany and used these commissions to influence state and federal policy after new academic norms made more open activism taboo. The AEA aggressively sought to make itself relevant to the federal government by lobbying for the establishment of standards for statistical and economic work in federal agencies, particularly in the Department of Agriculture. A decisive push for the formalization of professional standards came during World War I when the U.S. Civil Service Commission officially asked the AEA to examine and classify "some 900 cards filled in by economists and statisticians who had expressed their willingness to serve the government." The AEA obliged and in 1918 complemented this task by creating several specialized committees to channel economic experts into public service.[126] No fewer than sixteen major AEA figures, among them Frank Taussig (U.S. Tariff Commission and Foreign Trade Committee), Mitchell (War Industries Board), and Edwin Gay (Central Bureau of Planning and Statistics) ended up working in federal war agencies.[127]

Successive American governments drew upon professional organizations and institutions (which, in this period, were almost exclusively academic) to build up their own capacities in the economic domain. In the Progressive conception, the new forms of expertise on which governments had to rely remained socially defined and validated *outside* the political system (not *by* it as in France or Germany). Through the formal involvement of academic institutions and actors, public administrations implicitly recognized the economic expert as an academic whose value lies in the possession of a specific competence. As I will show later, such understandings have continued to shape the relationship between economists and the state throughout the twentieth century—the institutionalization of the Council of Economic Advisers and other public advisory bodies (for instance, the Congressional Budget Office) being among the most conspicuous aspects of this administrative regime.

Conversely, the early and formal acknowledgment by political institutions of the "usefulness" and technocratic capability of academic economists has shaped the latter's identity in powerful ways. Andrew Abbott (2005) describes this codependent pattern as the "linked ecologies" of states and professions. It encouraged academic institutions to "professionalize" along technocratic lines and to embrace the attitudes that are usually required of the regular civil service. Through the "demands for expertise" placed upon the academic sector, American state administrations participated in the structuring of the academic profession itself, in the shaping of its substantive orientations, and in the construction of particular professional roles and attitudes among American economists. By relying on academic disciplines to establish their own job classifications and recruitment criteria, public institutions fostered disciplinary specialization and the establishment of strict certification mechanisms.

American Foundations and the Public Purpose of Social Scientists

Although the practice of associating university economists with the political and policymaking processes in the United States became fairly habitual during the Progressive Era, only a few government agencies made use of *permanent* economic experts before the New Deal. The two major exceptions were the Federal Reserve Board, where economists had been present from the institution's creation in 1913 (having helped design it), and the Department of Agriculture, where a practice of using economic research to inform the design of policy had led to the formation of a specialized research unit in 1921, the Bureau of Agricultural Economics.[128]

The 1920s represent an interesting transitional period between the progressive drive for efficiency and faith in rational knowledge, on the one hand, and the activism of the New Deal and World War II, on the other, when economists poured into government service. The experience of World War I had already changed both the practice of economic policy making and the government's willingness to intervene in the economy. Emergency government during the conflict had a considerable impact in legitimating activist approaches to economic policy, in bringing economic experts into contact with government, and in developing awareness among public sector officials and businessmen about the necessity of improving economic and statistical information.

In many ways, however, it was capitalist foundations that epitomized and promoted this new conception of the role of certified social-scientific knowledge in bringing about ordered and controlled social progress. During the interwar period, an institutional nexus centered around the Carnegie Corporation and the Laura Spelman Rockefeller Memorial Fund served as a sort of interface between universities and government agencies and helped promote the view that factual knowledge should be the primary guide of government action. In Washington, Herbert Hoover contributed to enhance the relationships between government departments and the extra-governmental research economy that was then developing among philanthropic foundations and research organizations. During his terms as secretary of commerce (from 1921 to 1927) and then as president of the United States (from 1928 to 1932), his administrations routinely commissioned work from academics, "sponsored scholarly studies, called conferences, enlarged statistical services, and assembled and used a large battery of expert advisers" (Lyons 1969, 50). Mitchell's National Bureau of Economic Research, for instance, worked almost exclusively on projects commissioned by the Secretariat of Commerce and financed by philanthropic money.[129]

This economic research sector remained largely external to the state, however.[130] Rather than looking at expert knowledge as a technocratic arm of the state itself, Hoover understood it as facilitating the public involvement of private actors. The Committee on Recent Economic Changes, for instance, was intended primarily to help inform the decisions of the new managerial elites of American capitalism, and much less to serve as a guide for active policy reform.[131] Indeed, the Hoover administration remained highly suspicious of government economic intervention—even after the outbreak of the Great Depression and in spite of the more ambitious proposals of some of his own economic advisers.[132]

Still, the Hooverites' attitude toward the rational use of social-scientific research reflected a certain technocratic pragmatism, which would soon come to characterize the New Deal. Yet whereas much of the social-scientific research encouraged by Hoover had been financially sponsored by private organizations (primarily the Social Science Research Council [SSRC] and the Carnegie and Rockefeller foundations), the Roosevelt administration created a momentum for building up research capabilities *within* the structure of government itself, sometimes by relying on the very same personnel. For instance, two key personalities in Hoover's system, Wesley C. Mitchell and Charles E. Merriam (a political scientist, former head of the SSRC), were appointed at the head of the National Planning Board, a research organization within the Public Works Administration, which would soon become a key source of economic advice for the White House, acting as a think tank for long-term economic issues and (in later years) postwar planning.

The incorporation of economists in government during the New Deal relied on two complementary trends on the supply and demand sides of the labor market. On the supply side, there were simply no academic jobs to absorb the flow of young economics graduates who came freshly out of academia in those years. Government employment thus served as a safety valve in an academic labor market devastated by the Great Depression.[133] In addition, the shocking context of the Depression spurred the cohort of "young Turks" to see new opportunities to exercise their knowledge for the public good and promote their expertise.[134] On the demand side, the new administration's unprecedented activism in the face of the slump created numerous agencies, all of which immediately sought to enlist specialists drawn from academia.[135] Isador Lubin, who acted as commissioner of the Bureau of Labor Statistics, commented: "During the early days of the present administration virtually every university in the country was combed by the various federal agencies for competent economists" (Lubin 1937, 216).

The decades of the 1930s and 1940s thus represented a double watershed for economics, both an institutional and an intellectual one. On the one hand, Roosevelt's massive resort to university-educated manpower secured the rise of experts in the administrative machinery. It also established the principle of the "academic in government," which would later lead to the creation of permanent and academically grounded economic advice institutions, among which the Council of Economic Advisers figures most prominently. On the other hand, the bitterness of economic policy debates during that era and the ultimate failure of the most radical economic ideas and policy schemes to get securely entrenched also signaled the limits of the academics' influence in the political domain.

As many scholars have shown, the economic logic underlying the first New Deal was proto-Keynesian in some of its elements, but the well-known British economist (who had yet to publish his *General Theory*) had little to do with it. Roosevelt in 1932 had campaigned against Hoover's failure to balance the budget, and fiscal conservatives occupied prominent positions in his administration.[136] The earliest measures of active government involvement, such as the public works programs and the attempt at industrial planning, were framed as a series of pragmatic responses and emergency measures, rather than as a comprehensive, "paradigmatic" policy strategy inspired by a brand-new theory.[137] In fact, the early New Deal measures drew mainly on indigenous ideas in vogue since the 1920s. Innovations in labor and agricultural legislation, social security, public utility regulation, or corporatism were influenced by institutionalist economic thinking (many students of which had been recruited by the new agencies) and local policy experiments, such as John Commons's earlier activities in Wisconsin.[138] The renewed emphasis on the necessity of increased business regulation and planning had also been popularized by Adolf Berle (a Columbia law professor) and his student Gardiner Means in their successful book *The Modern Corporation and Private Property* (1932) and various other works. By 1935, Means, who had in the meantime become one of the most prominent economic advisers of the early New Deal, further elaborated the theoretical rationale for his structural policy approach: the present lack of market adjustment, he argued in a government report, was due to industrial concentration and the propensity of large corporations to "administer prices." This was a far cry from Keynes's "animal spirits" and the deficiencies of effective demand but consistent with the long-standing American policy focus on large corporations' penchant for manipulating the price system.

Roosevelt's brain trusters soon found themselves the object of relentless attacks on the grounds that they exercised powers way beyond their formal positions. Columbia institutionalist economist Rexford Tugwell,[139] who with Means was one of the chief proponents of planning, became a "favorite target for conservative critics of the New Deal" (Hofstadter 1963a, 215). As a result of this contestation, some of the most prominent institutional innovations of the New Deal, particularly those that ran counter to traditional economic strategies, failed to secure a durable impact on government policy. The comprehensive industrial planning experiment initiated by the National Industrial Recovery Act was short-lived, struck down by the Supreme Court in 1935 in the midst of widespread dissatisfaction. Stryker's work on the New Deal has shown that another "radical" institution, the economics research section of the National Labor Relations Board, did not succeed better in creating a niche and was ultimately dismantled by Congress in 1940. The National Resources Planning Board survived longer but ultimately suffered the same fate in 1943. Its advocacy of welfare programs, full employment policies, and planning was perceived to be socialist in inspiration; the organization, which had reached a staff of nearly three hundred people in 1943, fell because of the charge that it promoted irresponsible government spending and government interference in business activity. On the other hand, agencies whose economists defended a more orthodox approach based on competition-enhancing mechanisms, like the Social Security Administration and the Treasury, flourished.[140]

While planning ultimately failed to mobilize a wide constituency as a strategy to restore growth, the case for unbalanced budgets gradually gained support through the 1930s as a more acceptable alternative, not only among economists but also among other public officials and political

actors. The second New Deal saw the first self-conscious adoption of explicitly expansionist budgets. The persistence of the Depression and the
administration's failure at keeping the budget in balance opened a win-
dow of opportunity for the promoters of a different approach to macroeconomic management.[141] In part, the idea of "compensatory spending"
by the government during recessions was not unfamiliar in the United
States and had been advocated by Chicago economists since the beginning of the slump.[142] But of greater importance to this shift was the conversion of a number of academics and high-ranking officials to the
Keynesian analytical framework around 1936, the year Keynes published
the *General Theory*. By the end of the 1930s, deficit spending was advocated by a small network of personalities in key governmental positions,
including at the Federal Reserve Board, the National Resources Planning
Board, and the Department of Commerce.[143] A clique of young Keynesian
converts around Alvin Hansen at Harvard carried the message in academia.[144] It is ultimately this disparate constellation of people which
helped win the budget battle in 1938. Even then, it took considerable lobbying and public activism to turn it into a policy strategy. Ultimately, the
war may have been more important in legitimating both the new economics and the new role for economists.

Institutionalization: Macro and Micro

In comparative perspective, the wartime involvement of academic economists with the American federal government is quite remarkable. The
proportion of authors of economic articles in the main academic journals who held government appointments jumped from 2.7 percent in
1932–33 to 16.8 percent in 1942–43.[145] By contrast, in the United Kingdom the incorporation of economists in the government machine during
the wartime, while unprecedented, was more modest in quantitative
terms. The British war government relied on a small number of elite
professors, with the traditional, generalist civil service continuing to provide for the main positions. In France, top-level technocrats essentially
ran the war and the Vichy government (although many of them developed some form of economic expertise during the 1930s).

In America, the massive influx of economists into federal service raised
the question of professional standards with particular acuity. Public administrations wanted to make sure they were hiring qualified people.
The National Resources Planning Board, reproducing on a larger scale a
process familiar since World War I, sought the cooperation of the American Economic Association for classifying its members by field of expertise and evaluating their credentials.[146] Academics, on the other hand,
worried that expansion without certification would devalue economic

research altogether. One proposal to counter the perceived threat of weakened standards called for the development of nationally administered "initiation procedures" for the economics profession (Copeland 1941).

Samuelson has referred to World War II as the "economists' war." Certainly, the knowledge of quantitative measurement techniques of all sorts appeared critical to the effort to mobilize productive capacities and allocate resources. Economists, especially the younger generations, who had had more technical exposure, possessed skills that were not available elsewhere. As one interviewee who worked in the Bureau of Labor Statistics during the war told me: "In the entire Bureau I was the only one to know how to use a slide rule."[147]

The necessity of planning for the military effort, a need that continued as the nation gradually demobilized after the end of hostilities, brought about an extraordinary overhaul of the federal administrative structure, which helped transform both the role of economic expertise and the nature of economics itself. As we have seen, the bankruptcy of the prewar economic order (both national and international) had already convinced large numbers of politicians and high government officials of the necessity to reform the institutional bases of capitalist economies. The war provided further legitimation for these changes: economic planning, which had been advocated and attempted rather unsuccessfully during the New Deal, was finally undertaken out of military necessity. Pump priming could not be avoided, given the scale of the war effort, and provoked little controversy. Even prices were brought under federal control.

The "suspension and reshaping of expectations" during the military conflict, as Hirschman (1989) described it, created the conditions for a unique level of expert involvement. The new institutions brought together young economics graduates, some of whom would later rise to scientific fame: the young Milton Friedman and Paul Samuelson served at the National Resources Planning Board; Simon Kuznets and Robert Nathan at the War Production Board worked on military planning using the national income accounting techniques they had developed at the Commerce Department; John Kenneth Galbraith was "price czar" at the Office of Price Administration. As Mirowski (2002b) has shown, economists were also recruited by military agencies, which brought them into contact with mathematicians, physicists, and the new field of operations research. The Dutch physicist Tjalling Koopmans, for instance, developed a model of optimal shipping routes and shipping convoy sizes while employed by the British Merchant Shipping Mission in Washington and shortly after the war became heavily involved in linear programming through his connections with operation researchers working at the Department of Defense (particularly George Dantzig). The influence of experts was especially powerful in the international domain, where a transgovernmental alliance of economists at Bretton Woods—both American (Jacob Viner, Alvin Hansen, Harry Dexter White) and British (John Maynard Keynes, James Meade, Lionel Robbins)—was given extraordinary autonomy to forge the postwar liberal international economic order.[148]

The position gained by economists during the conflict provided a strong argument for acknowledging formally their specific role in government, both as highly skilled technicians within the administrative structure and as aides to decision making.[149] This resulted, first, in continued reflection on the professional requirements for the employment of economists in government service and, consequently, increased reliance on advanced degrees. A second consequence was the creation, by the 1946 Employment Act, of the Council of Economic Advisers in the White House and the Joint Economic Committee in Congress. The main argument in favor of the CEA was that it would provide the president with professional economic advice. But in contrast with its most immediate and vocal predecessor, the National Resources Planning Board, the CEA was a small and purely advisory structure with no practical authority. As such, it offered only a limited challenge to Congress and other powerful executive branch economic agencies such as the Treasury and the Bureau of Budget.

THE PLACE OF THE CEA

The Council of Economic Advisers consists of three principal members and relies on a small (twelve- to twenty-member) staff of professional economists, who are generally drawn from academia on temporary rotations. Out of twenty-three CEA chairmen since the beginning of the institution, all but four were academics, and all but two held an economics PhD.[150] Academics have also become dominant among CEA staff. While less common during the Truman administration, academic staffers became routine under the chairmanship of Arthur Burns (1953–56) and even more under Walter Heller (1961–64). This evolution has led some commentators (for instance, De Long 1996, 42) to describe the institutionalization of a strong academic core in American economic policy making as a historical accident. Yet such an explanation overlooks an important fact about the structure of American political institutions. As pointed out in the analysis of the New Deal earlier in this chapter, reliance on academic institutions has long appeared a normal course in a country that has traditionally filled its top civil service positions with outsiders. In fact, academic economic expertise has not been confined to the CEA but has gained prominence in other administrative bodies since the war, with (among other trends) the institutionalization of chief economist positions at the top of each federal department and agency.

Many observers have interpreted the sheer existence of the CEA as a de facto "advocacy group for mainstream economics" within government, and so see the institution as a powerful agent for the routine incorporation of economic arguments into policy discourse.[151] The agency provides highly visible government positions that are available to the academic elite and employs dozens of credentialed economics PhDs. On the other hand, this situation does not by itself guarantee the institution a powerful influence on policy. Rather, the latter depends almost exclusively on how seriously the president, who has many other sources of advice, not least a personal assistant for economic affairs, takes its recommendations.[152] Historically, the CEA did not gain the upper hand in economic matters until the Kennedy administration, when the agency's commitment to full employment, encapsulated in the 1962 *Economic Report to the President* and implemented with the Johnson-Kennedy tax cut of 1964 (which CEA chairman Walter Heller forcefully lobbied for), signaled a confident, technocratic, Keynesian turn in macroeconomics. Enthusiastically supported by the vast majority of the profession, the tax cut is often regarded as the golden age of economists' influence on American policy.[153] Two of the authors of the 1962 report were future Nobel Prize winners (Robert Solow and James Tobin). Paul Samuelson and John Kenneth Galbraith were close advisers to Kennedy himself. The economists' influence extended beyond the CEA: the director of the Bureau of the Budget and the undersecretaries of the Treasury were all economists.

Still, this golden age looks like a rather short-lived episode when placed in historical perspective. Part of the CEA's authority in the 1960s relied on Kennedy's atypical openness to academics and on the agency's relative monopoly over technical economic expertise, particularly the use of new conceptual tools such as the full employment budget or the notion of "potential output" of the economy. After the heyday of the mid-1960s, however, economic expertise diffused rapidly to other government agencies, which could then argue more effectively with the CEA and inevitably mitigated the council's technical authority:

CEA cannot blow people out of the water with the depth of its analysis like it could do it in the 1960s. Few people understood what the term "multiplier" meant in the 1960s, much less were able to argue with the CEA's argument about a tax policy to stimulate the economy. When CEA said that the effect of a specific tax action on investment was such-and-such there wasn't any other agency doing its own empirical work to argue with it. But now, Treasury may say: "No, it's Y." And Labor, "It's Z." (quoted in Porter 1983, 414–15)

More fundamentally, no single government agency was ever able to dominate the definition of American macroeconomic policy, and the CEA is no exception. Policy orientations in the macroeconomic domain result from a power interplay among administrative institutions (including the Federal Reserve), as well as from a complex and competitive political process between the presidency and Congress. As institutionalist scholars have shown, new economic ideas in the United States benefit from the large number of points of entry to penetrate the administrative apparatus, especially when traditional policy paradigms are being challenged by an economic crisis, and expert consensus is low. Yet the same balkanization also affects their institutionalization in the long run, since political actors, administrative departments, and interest groups compete with one another for influence. All the major paradigmatic shifts in macroeconomic policy—the New Deal, the 1960s turn to Keynesianism, and the supply-side revolution in the 1980s—have exemplified this pattern. New Deal administrations were divided between institutionalist/pro-planning agencies (National Recovery Administration, National Labor Relations Board), "Keynesian" agencies (Federal Reserve Board, Department of Commerce), and traditional neoclassical agencies (Treasury, State Department).[154] In the 1960s, the CEA's strategy of what Lekachman (1966, 287) has termed "commercial Keynesianism" (or a preference for business tax cuts), won out against the alternative of more aggressive fiscal policies promoted by the Labor Department and over the opposition of the Federal Reserve.[155] And the first Reagan administration pitted a traditional neoclassical Council of Economic Advisers against a monetarist Federal Reserve and a supply-side Treasury.[156] In fact, when the CEA chairman, Harvard professor Martin Feldstein, publicly aired his disagreement with the president on the economic implications of massive federal budget deficits, he had to resign from his position.

THE ECONOMICIZATION OF SOCIAL POLICY

Since the CEA's creation, its autonomy has been severely curtailed by its political dependency on the White House and by the sharing of competences with other economic agencies. Relatively cautious conceptions of the fiscal instrument, which privilege "automatic stabilizers" (e.g., transfers and taxes) over discretionary policies, as well as the progressive evisceration of these automatic stabilizers since the 1970s, have also limited the government's margin of maneuver in *macroeconomic* affairs.[157] Yet this does not mean that the CEA should be dismissed as irrelevant. Instead, we should expect to find the influence of this highly placed staff of economists in areas other than macroeconomic stabilization. We should search for evidence of the diffusion of an "economist's view of the world" which has turned *microeconomic* tools and concepts (e.g., efficiency, opportunity, cost-benefit trade-offs and incentives) into the standard language of public policy.[158]

The postwar institutionalization of economic expertise in government was indeed also very much about the increasingly routine use of technical, microeconomic tools to evaluate and transform a myriad of micropolicies in fields such as education, health care, social policy, environmental policy, and market regulation. Much of this transformation involved the consolidation of a new professional role: the "government economist," now recognized as a separate occupational specialization. Many of the economic experts recruited into government during the 1930s and World War II were temporary appointees. Starting in the late 1940s, however, economic expertise became a more enduring element of the civil service. Viewed over the course of the century, the federal government's in-house capacities in the economic domain expanded considerably. Figures from the Office of Personnel show that the number of federal employees listed as "economists" grew from about seven hundred[159] in the late 1920s to a little over five thousand in 1997, with a peak toward the end of the 1970s. Figures 2-5a and 2-5b show this dramatic buildup of economic capacities in the 1960s and 1970s, particularly in newer and smaller agencies such as the Environmental Protection Agency and the Department of Energy (this also holds true for many departments not included in the graph, including Transportation, Education, and Justice). The figures also illustrate the reinforcement of economists in traditional centers, most prominently the Treasury and the Department of Labor.[160]

With expansion came an increased formalization of how to define an economist, according to both functional professional domain and level of skill; as we have seen before, this formalization was achieved through the combined mobilization of bureaucratic and professional resources. In the 1950s the AEA proposed, through the voice of its Committee on Economists in Public Service, that "a substantial piece of competent, independent economic research" be required for the recruitment of government economists in the higher grades.[161] The formal position classification standard adopted in 1963 called for "the full understanding and competent application of the basic tools of the profession" for people in "economist" positions.[162] Interviews I conducted in various governmental offices (Congressional Budget Office, Small Business Administration) suggest that the PhD has become an implicit requirement for many specialist positions.[163]

By and large, the work of government economists is not associated with macroeconomic stabilization (though the design of national accounts and macroeconometric models did at one point employ legions of

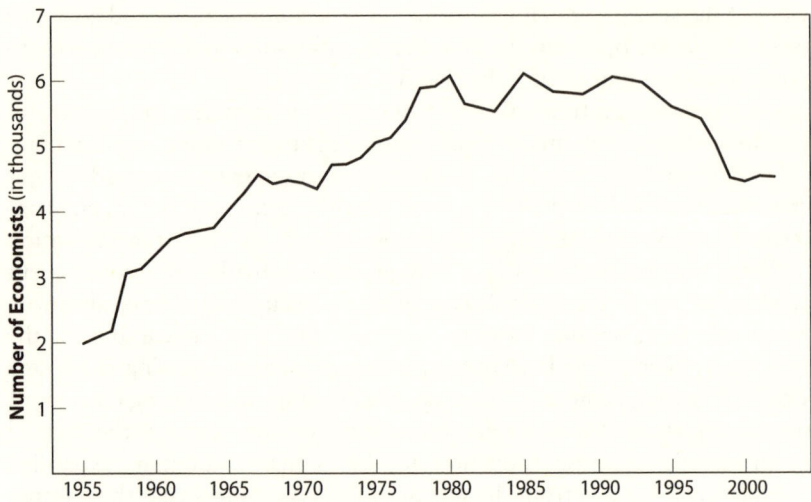

Figure 2-5a. Total number of economists in American federal government, excluding Congress and Federal Reserve, 1955–2002.
Source: U.S. Office of Personnel Management, *Occupations of Federal White and Blue-Collar Workers,* 1955–2002.

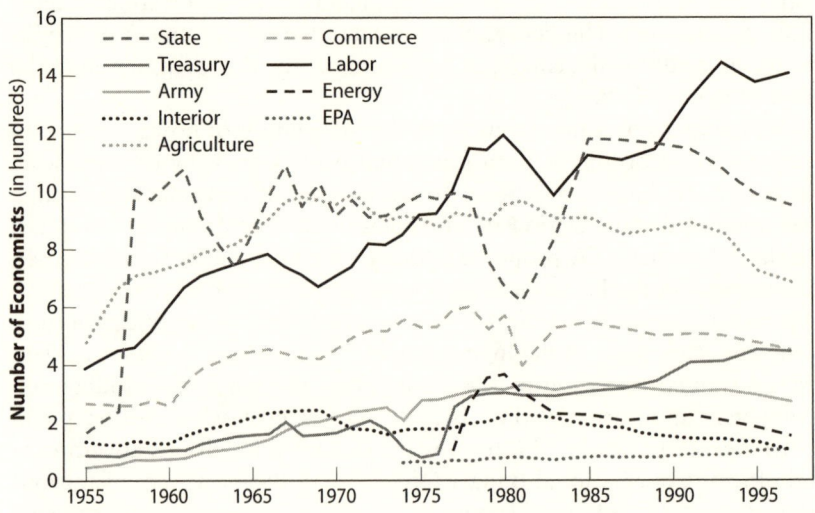

Figure 2-5b. Number of economists in selected federal government departments, 1955–98
Source: U.S. Office of Personnel Management, *Occupations of Federal White and Blue-Collar Workers,* 1955–98.

economists and statisticians), but instead involves the use of microeconomic tools and concepts to evaluate social programs, design regulatory rules, or manage externalities. Theodore Porter has shown that cost-benefit analysis in the United States emerged among military engineers and was taken over by economists only after World War II. From the Department of Defense, cost-benefit analyses "spread to all kinds of government expenditures, and later even to regulatory activities," as well as to the assessment of public goods such as education or health (1995, 188). The technique of program budgeting (institutionalized as the Program Planning and Budgeting System [PPBS]), for instance, began as a formalization of bureaucratic routines associated with wartime controls and planning. It grew by adding capacities related to the management of an ever-expanding welfare economy and by taking advantage of the emergence of new academic specialties among economists.[164] In 1965, the vogue of these ideas was encapsulated in President Lyndon Johnson's decision to establish a "special staff of experts who, using the most modern methods of program analysis, will define the goals of their department for the coming year. And once these goals are established this system will permit us to find the most effective and the least costly alternative to achieving American goals" (quoted in Novick and Alesh 1970, 11).

Although PPBS did not survive very long as a management technique, it did have important long-term effects in securing a large and organized presence of economists in government service and more generally in public policy research at both rank-and-file and management levels. In particular, it established the principle of a core staff of economic experts within each government agency that could systematically evaluate departmental proposals from an economic point of view. In 1974, the Congressional Budget Office (CBO) was created with the mission of investigating the government's budget proposals and their potential alternatives.[165] Since then, any piece of legislation must *by law* be accompanied by cost estimates from the CBO. Outside government, the Brookings Institution conducts further checks on the budgetary process.

Certainly, microeconomic questions are just as politically controversial as macroeconomic ones. Johnson's last chairman of the CEA, Arthur Okun, noted rather bitterly:

On the micro front the CEA is flying in the face of all of the political pressures. . . . The one eye-opener to me as a young man from academia coming to Washington was the intensity of these producer interest group pressures on all sorts of micro economic decisions. . . . Almost invariably these producers' interests are contrary to the special interests of economic rationality. That's a big uphill climb. (quoted in Hargrove and Morley 1984, 297)

Relative professional consensus (as exists on many microeconomic issues) is never a sufficient condition for policy change. Still, the diffusion of microeconomic approaches certainly transformed the culture of policy analysis, as economists brought with them a general inclination to organize socially desirable outcomes (environmental protection, poverty reduction, public health, occupational safety, etc.) through the use of incentives and the price system, and to regard direct government interventions as generally impairing the efficiency of the economy.[166]

Political critiques, both from the left (government action is insufficient and biased toward big business) and from the right (government action is inefficient), also sustained this transformation in the aftermath of the War on Poverty, fueling the effort to subject all public policies to a rigorous economic evaluation. Executive branch agencies, congressional bodies, and public policy research organizations found themselves under pressure to incorporate economic tools and approaches into the evaluation of economic and social policies, budgetary operations, as well as legal rules, and to encourage the development of economic methodologies best suited to their role.[167] By the mid-1980s, many government organizations—for instance, the Environmental Protection Agency, Antitrust Division at the Department of Justice, the Office of Policy Analysis at the Department Interior—were in fact required to properly train their staff in economic methods. And so the revolution in the use of applied microeconomics for policy purposes covered a broad spectrum, from industrial regulation to social policy.

THE EXPERIMENTAL LOGIC IN AMERICAN PUBLIC POLICY RESEARCH

Referring to the social science explosion that accompanied the expansion of social programs in the wake of the War on Poverty, one interviewee said that "this was a sort of peak for what officials in politics and public policy expected out of economic research." People were confident that "with enough research you could solve almost any probem" (senior fellow, Brookings Institution, August 12, 1999). One particularly interesting development in this respect, and a good illustration of the remarkable political logic at play here, was the vogue of social experiments. As a method, social experiments take inspiration from controlled trials in medicine, using random assignments of applicants to a social program (e.g., in skill training, education, housing, health) to compare policy outcomes in the recipient (or "treatment") group to those in the control group. One of the first large-scale social experiments, grown out of an MIT economics dissertation, was carried out for the Office of Economic

Opportunity as the New Jersey Income Maintenance Experiment in the mid-1960s (to evaluate whether a guaranteed minimum income would be feasible without causing the labor force to shrink). In the following years income maintenance experiments were initiated through multicity projects. Other federal agencies adopted the technique, which in this way spread to other domains, including housing, vocational training, education, and welfare reform (Orr 1999). By the end of the 1990s, about ten major social experiments were still initiated each year, financed primarily by the federal government, state governments (increasingly), and the Ford Foundation.[168]

The comparison with other countries is instructive here. It suggests that in both scale and character, much of this research is a distinctively American specialty. The number of large natural experiments exploded during the 1970s at the same time that controversy over the legacies of the Great Society policy agenda mounted, and social policy analysis decisively veered toward economists.[169] Yet this development may be more than a simple, natural consequence of state expansion itself (otherwise we would observe a similar trend elsewhere). Rather, it is deeply embedded in the nature of American welfare politics, with its deep moral and practical concerns about the effects of social policy on individual behavior. In a country Esping-Andersen (1990) identifies as the archetypal "liberal" welfare state, government-sponsored social programs were suspicious enough that they had to be subjected to systematic policy evaluation. Social experimentation can thus be interpreted as another "technology of distance" from politics (Porter 1995, ix). As Harold Wilensky (2005) has suggested, however, the narrow conception of policy effectiveness embodied in experimental and quasi-experimental methods has helped overdetermine the finding of many experiments that policy has no impact, thereby vindicating the original suspicion and fueling the lack of support for program development and follow-through.

The dramatic reorganization of public policy research around an experimental logic is also tied to the country's federal structure, which provides a natural setting for the exercise of experimental, as well as pseudoexperimental (or "microeconometric") methods.[170] As the policy reforms undertaken during the Reagan presidency turned initiative in social policy matters over to lower levels of government, states became testing grounds for a variety of social programs, and cross-state variations were seen as increasingly relevant to social-scientific methods.[171] One observer of this transformation described it in the following way:

We've managed to convince the government that to understand how politics affects anything they should do random precise, controlled experiments. Some workers should get the training and some should not. We can see whether the training has any effect.[172] That's tough for governments to do that obviously. Partly because the U.S. is so big, with lots of states, we managed to do that. (professor, Ivy League university, May 1999)

The initiative, then, did not come entirely from politics. Economists themselves played a role in actively promoting their new research methods vis-à-vis their funding sources in public policy and in the foundations, putting the administration of policy itself at the service of research in the process. And it is in this process of interaction between policy demands, the greater availability of microeconomic (individual-level) data that derived from them, and the evolution of tools (e.g. the reformulation of Cowles's econometric method by microeconomists) that both public policy and economics got transformed. These characteristics, however, are predicated on specific representations about the legitimate scope and nature of state action in America, as well as the need for public agencies to justify their actions—and do so according to market criteria to boot. As Samuel Bowles wrote in an insightful piece, in practice cost-benefit analyses and other public expenditures criteria "tend to reintroduce in veiled form the very same market criteria which govern resource allocation in the private sector" (1974, 130).

The Economics Industry

It should be clear by now that much of the policy-relevant economic research in the United States is not conducted directly by government agencies themselves but is routinely externalized to an "economics industry" (the term is from Stein [1986]) of outside contractors working in close connection with academics. American distrust for the federal government prerogative thus goes beyond a suspicion of its intervention in social and economic affairs; it also extends to the government's competence when carrying out policy-relevant research.[173] A senior economist from the Congressional Budget Office thus lamented to me that

the research orientation (in government) is pretty low. When you have to address daily policy needs, you cannot do research. At CBO, for instance, demands from Congress come constantly, either from congresspeople directly, or from their staff members. . . . On the other hand, it's very easy to get money for contracts. You see, having more staff positions in government does not get you more votes. It gets you less. Voters do not like to have more people on the payrolls. So Congress is extremely reluctant to create such positions. Spending money on contracts, on the other hand, looks like government is doing something for the people. So we end up paying money on consultants for research that would have been much cheaper if done by the staff. There are many private firms and nonprofit organizations that specialize in government contracts, and they often subcontract those to academics. (senior economist, Small Business Administration, August 1999)

As an illustration, the overwhelming majority (over 90 percent) of the large government-sponsored social experiments completed between 1962 and 1996 were contracted out to private firms and academics.[174] But this is simply part of a larger pattern of intellectual symbiosis between government and economic professionals. Many of the methodological, and some theoretical, innovations produced in applied microeconomics were by-products of similar contracts with local, state, and federal agencies in need of practical tools that were usually mediated by the economic research industry of semipublic (e.g., RAND) or entirely private (e.g., Charles River Associates) consultants, and sometimes even in close connection with the interested businesses themselves. The characteristically fragmented and multilayered nature of American government discussed in chapter 1 prompts each administrative unit to sponsor the methodological developments that help it carry out its functions and, by the same token, help it justify its existence and jurisdictional claims. In addition, competition between administrative institutions and the involvement of external constituencies through lobbying almost ensures that methodological settlements will result from negotiated processes between the different parties at work. An interview I conducted at the Congressional Budget Office described this complex knot of relationships between academics, federal agencies, and corporations on the occasion of new auctions of usage rights to the government-controlled radio spectrum.[175]

[Some academics] worked for us and [some] we talked a lot to. There was a great conference at Princeton on radio spectrum auctions. Everybody came. . . . [Then] this "smart guy" at the FCC wrote the proposed rule-making for auctions. They [i.e., the FCC] were given the authority to auction spectrum, and they had to figure out auction rules, and he wrote up: "This is what we know about it; this is what we're thinking; now you can comment." And writing about it, in the footnotes to the "Notice of Proposed Rulemaking," [were] references to all the articles by all the academic auction theorists. Well, all the telecommunications companies immediately hired all the academics. . . . And then these guys developed, really pushed auction theory forward by huge leaps, under contract. They were being paid by these telecoms, so they got a lot of good publications out of it too. (Senior economist, Congressional Budget Office, August 13, 1999)

By now we can see that this pattern of scientific innovation in economics is not new. From national accounts to game theory to auction theory, government action has been intertwined with the development of economic theory and methodology. While this pattern is not exclusive to the United States—there are clear equivalents in France and in the United Kingdom as well—two features are characteristic of the American context. First, this work in the United States has continuously involved academics drawn from universities and consulting firm experts, whereas in France it was mostly the province of a somewhat different breed of scientists, namely engineers working in public administration or national enterprises. Second, the French (or even British) economic contexts have been less conducive to such "technological" work overall. The regulatory and legal (as opposed to administrative) mode of economic governance in the United States, its characteristic back-and-forth movement between government agencies and outside constituencies, and, above all, the greater willingness of American public powers to rely on price mechanisms to manage the economy and society have all opened up important jurisdictions for economics in the marketplace itself. These jurisdictions also promise lucrative rewards for those with economic expertise. In short, economics has become a real business.

Economics in the Marketplace

Historically, the story of the entanglement between economics and the corporate world is not all new, of course. First, we have already discussed the unique proximity between economics and business education in this country. Second, the profession of "business economist" institutionalized earlier in the American industrial sector than elsewhere. Third, economic experts from academia and government have been particularly prone to turn their knowledge into a marketable asset. There is widespread evidence of a comparatively early and substantial establishment of the economic consulting market in the United States, and its application to a large variety of areas, from pollution control to crime to, very prominently, finance. Fourth, the business world (as well as other interest groups) makes great use of economic research in its routine lobbying and political activities, a point I develop later with a short discussion on think tanks.

According to National Science Foundation surveys, the majority of self-identified "economists" are employed in business.[176] The private, for profit sector also employs a substantial share of doctoral economists: 22 percent.[177] The "business economics" profession is itself quite well organized: the National Association of Business Economists (est. 1959) currently lists about 4,500 members, half of them with economics PhDs.[178] This is also congruent with the fact that close to 15 percent of the

American Economic Association membership is still located in the business sector (1997 data). Other indicators of the close relationship between academic economics and business might include the large proportion of CEOs with a degree in economics, or the general "economicization" of business education since the 1960s, discussed earlier.[179] One interviewee described this comfortable position of economics in the business world with considerable assurance:

> Lately I've been doing some consulting that has had me speaking with corporate executives, and the thing that's astonishing to me is that everybody out there running a company really knows their economics. I mean, Jorgensen's "User Cost of Capital," for example. It's a formula that describes what opportunity cost of funds a firm should use when deciding whether to invest. That formula is etched in the skull of CFOs at all the top companies now. And I think one of the reasons why we've had the economic success that we've had is that the business schools have taught the people who are running their companies good sound economics. And I think there's been a feedback into the profession in the sense that there's been almost a clinical trial of economics by having people out there using economic principles to run their companies, and then succeeding, and then teaching us that we were right, and sort of reinforcing research in a specific area. (senior fellow, American Enterprise Institute, August 1999)

This assessment, as we will see later, contrasts remarkably with the angry disillusionment I encountered among the few French academics who have been trying to make their expertise available to the private sector.

THE BUSINESS OF ECONOMICS

Statistical and econometric techniques provided one of the first areas of commercial involvement of economists, and academics often led the way in the commercialization of research to outside constituencies. Before World War II, in the absence of strong government involvement, prominent academic and research institutions authored and marketed most statistical indices, analyses, and forecasts. In 1917, for instance, a group of Harvard economists and statisticians established a commercial venture for the collection of statistical data and the development of the first barometers of business activity. Throughout the 1920s, the Harvard Economic Service offered forecasts based on its analysis of three indices of economic activity,[180] a methodology that was widely imitated around the world. Another prominent interwar example was Irving Fisher, an eminent economics professor at Yale who organized his own consulting and advisory business in the form of a competitor forecasting service. Both organizations were quite successful in their activities, at least until their failure to predict the 1929 stock market crash and the subsequent deepening of the Depression seriously damaged their credibility.[181]

The list of academic economists who have set up shop in the private sector is very long, and there is no point being exhaustive here. Suffice to say that market mechanisms, the reluctance of government to internalize research, and the decentralization of political, administrative, and corporate decision making in the United States all provided a niche for the widespread commercialization of academic skills. I develop these points in the following sections by analyzing two particularly interesting examples of such activities: econometric forecasting and legal advice.

An Example: Econometric Models. The econometric model industry provides a good example of the processes whereby economic knowledge is readily commodified for private uses in the United States. As pointed out earlier, the first econometric models originally emerged within the framework of academic research institutions. The Cowles Commission, as well as several universities (including the University of Michigan and the Wharton School, where Lawrence Klein later obtained a job), played an important role in supporting these early efforts. The first large-scale model of the American economy was then developed at Brookings around 1959, in association with the Social Science Research Council. Involving large teams of researchers, it played a pivotal role in shaping applied econometric practice throughout the world.

Government agencies in the United States have been much less conspicuous in the history of macroeconometric model building than in France, or even in Britain, where the Treasury used to run the most advanced enterprise in this area. For the most part (but with the notable exception of the Federal Reserve), American models were developed *outside* government departments, and then bought and used by bureaucratic administrations. This pattern reflects a distrust of direct political meddling with model construction, a suspicion that is reinforced by the existence of parallel—and mutually critical—budgeting offices in the legislative and executive branches.[182] A prominent academic economist who had served as a high-ranking official at the Congressional Budget Office thus saw in the agency's lack of an internally produced model "a defense against criticisms that the model is biased."[183]

The commercialization of macroeconomic models was encouraged by the emergence of demand (notably from the public sector) and the diminishing returns of macroeconometrics from a scientific point of view. After the first pioneering efforts, it had become increasingly difficult for academics to legitimate their involvement in an intellectual activity that was not "at the frontier" anymore.[184] Between the early 1940s to the late 1970s, the practice of macroeconometric model-building evolved from a traditional research enterprise sponsored by foundations and universities into a purely commercial venture, exemplified by the emergence of three large private economic forecasting firms, all of them founded by academics.[185] Wharton Econometric Forecasting Associates (WEFA), which sold a business application of the Wharton model, was formed by Lawrence Klein and others to support the economics department at the University of Pennsylvania. Data Resources Inc. (DRI) and Chase Econometrics, also the children of academics (Harvard professor Otto Eckstein in the former case and Michael Evans in the latter), were created in the late 1960s as forecasting and consulting firms more explicitly geared toward corporate uses.[186]

Another Example: The Legal Jurisdiction.   Another interesting illustration of economic jurisdiction in the business world concerns the codependent relationship between economics and law.[187] As we will see, such a relationship is natural in continental Europe, where economics was generally institutionalized as a component in the (primarily legal) training of civil servants. Part of the history of economics in these countries (and this is especially obvious in France) has to do with the latter's slow dissociation and autonomization from the legal realm.

In the United States, however, the economics profession took an almost opposite trajectory. Economics there had its intellectual origins in moral philosophy, and by the 1890s was already constituted as a strong and independent disciplinary project. In contrast with France, where law was constitutive of the economics profession as it institutionalized in the early part of the twentieth century, in this country law was a separate realm that could potentially become an object of professional investment. American courts took an early interest in economic questions and occupied themselves with market regulation at a time when economists were generally hostile to it.[188]

The law, thus, has been constitutive of the market patterns that emerged in early twentieth-century America and has played a considerable role in shaping the universe within which firms (public or private) operate. Furthermore, legal and administrative rules are the object of constant formal and informal negotiation. American corporations are thus faced with a constantly evolving and ambiguous regulatory environment where their economic actions, while set within a defined legal framework, may nonetheless be interpreted in widely different ways. In this situation of high uncertainty, firms, courts, and government offices all resort to economic professionals to provide quantifiable standards to evaluate the impact of regulations and the realm of possible actions, as well as eventually to argue, prosecute, or defend their behavior in court.[189]

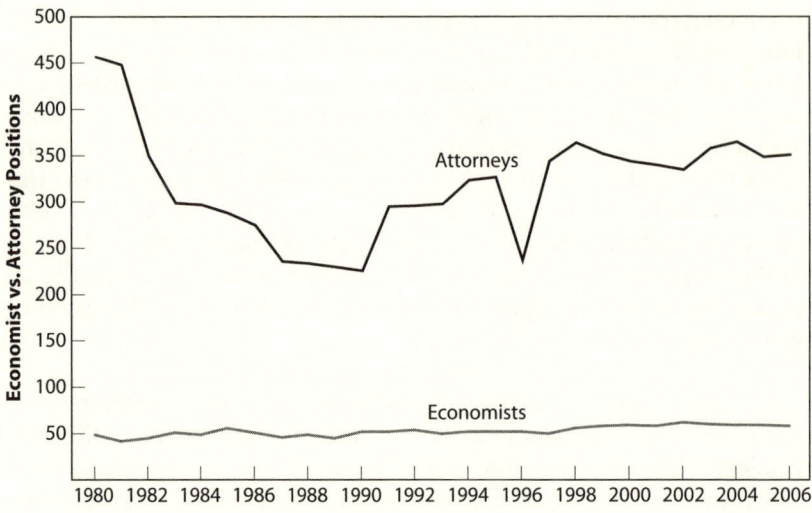

Figure 2-6. Economist versus attorney positions, Antitrust Division of the Department of Justice, 1980–2006.
Source: Antitrust Division, Department of Justice.

Antitrust and other regulatory laws (e.g., environment, health, and safety) provide nice examples of how the extent, complexities, and ambiguities of the regulatory framework create a de facto niche for economists in the legal arena. Since the 1960s, judicial processes have become increasingly subject to the imperatives identified by economic theory.[190] Correlatively, the influence of economists in government agencies traditionally dominated by attorneys grew markedly during the 1970s and 1980s.[191] At the Antitrust Division of the Department of Justice, for instance, the share of economists in the top professional positions went from about 8 to 9 percent to 17 to 18 percent over the course of the 1980s; it has since stabilized at around 13 to 14 percent as documented in figure 2-6. These figures, however, do not fully capture the rising importance of economic reasoning, which must also be related to the deep "economicization" of lawyers' training itself over the same period (both in law schools and in government) and to the increasingly central place of economists in legal decisions and actions. As Eisner and Meier put it in their analysis of the evolution of antitrust institutions, "Economists went from a secondary position as members of a support staff to being equal partners in the policy process"(1990, 277).

A related development is the emergence of a substantial market for economic consultants in the legal sector, both as inside experts within law firms and corporations and as outside providers of professional testimony (e.g., NERA economic consulting, or Charles River Associates, which fought a famous antitrust case for IBM).[192] In recent decades, the neoliberalization of the economy and, in particular, the weakening of the regulatory environment (partly under the influence of the "law and economics" movement within academia), as well as the reliance on increasingly complex techniques to assess the legal or illegal character of economic actions, have tremendously benefited economists. The *Wall Street Journal* recently summed up the evolution of antitrust the following way: "Traditionally, trust-busters focused on blatantly illegal behavior, such as price-fixing, leaving little leeway for an economist's interpretation once the facts were established. . . . More recent cases, such as the one against Microsoft Corp. in the late 1990s, have involved tricky calculations of how much consumers might be damaged by a company's market domination" (Anders 2007, A1). Indeed, in the preliminary case of the federal government against the Microsoft Corporation (1999), both parties relied heavily on the expertise of teams of economists, each of them led by a well-known MIT professor.[193]

One of my interviewees summed up this growing entanglement between law and economics in the following way:

> The laws affecting business have increasingly been based on economic theory. Economists now teach in the law schools. Many lawyers now have PhDs in economics as well. And so both the laws affecting business firms and the regulations, telephones, electricity, railroads, etc. are directly based on what economics teaches. And naturally when there is a dispute, they turn to economists as their experts. And this has become a very big business in itself. (professor, New York University, October 1999)

The rise of economics in the legal arena thus reflects a successful movement of jurisdictional expansion in Abbott's sense. We may—as a first approximation—understand this tendency of American academic discourses and professions to enter new jurisdictional domains as a structural consequence of the fragmented and competitive makeup of social institutions (particularly the legal and political systems), which produces a tendency to rely on formal rationalization and expertise, as Jasanoff (2005) has demonstrated. But these structural conditions are only necessary, not sufficient, explanatory factors. The invasion of the legal domain by economic science has relied on a vast scholarly movement ("law and economics"), which extends its roots back into the interwar period but organized as an academic force in the 1960s. We must thus understand the development of analytical tools making economic expertise relevant to the legal jurisdiction in relation to the specific conflicts and dynamics within the academic fields of economics and law. "Many economists,"

Medema argues, "saw the application of economic tools to legal theory as a natural extension of the economic paradigm, a precedent for which already existed in public choice analysis" (1998, 217).

Abbott (1988) argues that professional communities routinely use academic knowledge to enhance their professional status and legitimate their entry into new jurisdictions, and understands the former as a key element in the making of American professionalism. We can see the logic of Abbott's argument at work in the FCC auctions, which economists constructed as a successful "application" of game theory, obscuring the complex interplay of interests at work and winning a lucrative market for auction theorists in the process.[194] The case of "law and economics" (as well as a number of other fields, such as finance, or auction theory)[195] also suggests a complementary dynamic whereby academics' entry into "private" jurisdictions also helps strengthen their scientific claims. This, of course, does not necessarily mean that the *logic* of action behind such moves should be interpreted as the result of rational calculation. Rather, it suggests the operation of what Bourdieu (e.g., 1988) calls a "habitus," that is, a practical disposition developed in the context of legitimacy struggles within the fields of economics, policy expertise, or business education, all of which coincide rather well with the objective interests of their bearers.

Obviously, control over practical jurisdictions *always* and *everywhere* constitutes a central element in the construction of scientific boundaries and the formulation of scientific claims. In Bourdieu's terminology, it is a form of "capital." What is remarkable about the American case, however, is the fact that the country's economic culture and organization seem so naturally to lend legitimacy to the very broad jurisdictional claims of economists. We will see that this is not necessarily the case elsewhere.

Think Tanks and the Politicization of Economics

One group of institutions—the think tanks—occupies a quite unique place in the American political landscape, at the crossroads between politics, business, and universities. Initially conceived as external checks on the federal budgetary process (this was the impetus behind the creation of the first major think tank, the Brookings Institution), or as coordinators and sponsors of empirical economic studies by academics (NBER), think tanks have progressively evolved into a field of relatively autonomous, sometimes aggressive purveyors of ready-made research for political staffs. Until World War II, such organizations rarely sought to play an active part in the processes whereby *specific* policy proposals enter the agenda. The NBER was always strongly opposed to the formulation of specific policy recommendations. The Brookings Institution's famous criticisms of the New Deal budgets in the 1930s were presented as an exercise in expertise from the point of view of mainstream economics. Since then, most of the activity at Brookings has centered on the evaluation and analysis of existing governmental decisions, though the organization became more proactive after the 1960s.

The development of think tanks can be understood as part of a general logic in American politics that centers on the incorporation of private interests in the political process itself, on the one hand, and on the place of science in constructing authority to gain the upper hand within this very process, on the other. The internal heterogeneity and porous boundaries of political parties in the United States means that they rarely serve as the vehicle for the articulation of strong economic views—unlike the British parties. Instead, such articulation tends to take place in a more decentralized manner and involve consulting for individual politicians.

More specifically, the instrumentalization of economic knowledge within American politics may be traced to the transformation of the purpose and scope of interest group politics following the growing economic involvement of government in the 1930s–40s. The new centrality of fiscal policy (even with the limitations of the U.S. case) changed the context in which private groups could legitimately enter the policy process and prompted them to articulate their own policy views around explicitly scientific rationales supported by economic research. One of the first organizations to act on such a basis was the Committee on Economic Development (CED), a business think tank created in 1942 with a staff recruited among University of Chicago economics faculty and PhDs (Theodore Yntema was its first director of research). The work of R. M. Collins (1978, 1981) and Weir and Skocpol (1985) has amply demonstrated the role of the CED and its predecessor organizations in making compensatory fiscal policy acceptable to Roosevelt in 1938, as well as pushing the American postwar economic order in the direction of commercial Keynesianism. They also showed that the CED continued to influence that consensus as it evolved toward the acceptance of a more discretionary use of fiscal policy in the 1960s.[196]

As economic expertise became an important political currency, ideological competitors in the policy arena increasingly decided they needed their own sources of economic expertise. This was illustrated by the creation of a new generation of ideological research organizations (the Heritage Foundation and the Cato Institute stand as examples).[197] The revival of corporate class consciousness during the 1970s gave rise to a massive increase in financial support for congenial bases of political action and technical expertise.[198] By the 1980s, an abundance of more openly ideological institutes sought to produce "relatively sophisticated and well-documented analyses of the economic effects of specific government policies on business, and criticisms of the scientific basis of health and safety regulations."[199] These organizations served to launch a number of public campaigns in favor of specific economic reforms (e.g., tax cuts, deregulation), which were later popularized by Ronald Reagan.[200] Many of Reagan's closest advisers and political appointees came from this sector, as well as from journalism, congressional staff positions, and consulting firms, all described by Krugman as the "fringes of economics."[201]

Social control over open partisanship in academia has not prevented the emergence of a large research sector at the margins of academia, using the same professional rhetoric but for more partisan purposes and with potentially much greater influence on the policy process. The following quotation, from the same American Enterprise Institute economist who earlier marveled at the penetration of economic knowledge into the business world, illustrates the ambiguities of the techno-political philosophy that inspires the members of some of these organizations (and in this case one of the most academically "respectable" of them):

The American Enterprise Institute [AEI] is really one of the focal points, of connecting academic work to the press in a way that the press can understand. So I'm on television a lot, I write for popular journals a lot now, and popular magazines. And that stuff is, I guess, the core responsibility of the institute. That makes it, I think, sort of an important component of the mechanism that makes the economy work. We talked earlier about how MBAs learned economics from economics professors and then start running their companies better. Well, I think that places like AEI teach people true lessons so that the lessons stick—propaganda doesn't stick; propaganda can win an election for a candidate but it doesn't change things fundamentally, at the low frequency, it's not going to last forever. Spreading the truth does. And I think that one of the functions that AEI tries to have is take the things that the frontier economists are teaching us, and make them digestible for the masses. And yeah, I'd have to say that for me, I take that responsibility with almost religious zeal, that I think it's one of *the* most important things I could do, as an economist, that I could help people—if people just understood supply and demand, if voters understood supply and demand, the world would be a much better place. So the challenge is daunting but the game is potentially [very high stakes], in terms of really making a difference in how the world works for the good of everybody. I think that it's one of those places where you can have a very big effect if you can succeed at getting the lessons across. So that's what AEI's about, really. (senior fellow, American Enterprise Institute, August 1999)

Within the think tanks field, claims of economic expertise have tended to get entrenched in institutions that are close to the business community and its interests, often in a libertarian vein. A survey of Day's *Think Tanks: An International Directory* (1993) shows that among the organizations dealing specifically (though rarely exclusively) with economic matters, a large majority (more than 80 percent) officially proclaimed their commitment to the promotion and defense of free-market ideas, often against the involvement of the state. Such institutions are not only much more numerous; they also far outstrip liberal ones in the size of their financial base. In 1992, for instance, the budget for the liberal Economic Policy Institute (EPI) was a mere $1.3 million, a far cry from the Heritage Foundation's $18 million, or even the $3.5 million of the Cato Institute. In 2004, the discrepancy was just as large, with, respectively, $5.5 million for EPI, $34 million for Heritage, and $14.9 million for Cato (figures 2-7a and 2-7b).

Some of these institutions—particularly the more ideological ones— entertain a complex, often antagonistic relationship to mainstream academia, being in a dominated position from the point of view of the scientific and educational capital of their members. Conversely, for academics, the existence of these organizations makes the kind of gatekeeping work discussed at the beginning of this chapter all the more urgent. Certainly the "heteronomous" nature of the economics field, its pervasive vulnerability to social demands, and the absence of exclusive professional controls explain much of this boundary work in the United States as elsewhere. But it is never as necessary to affirm the existence and proper character of a boundary as when it is fuzzy and porous. Evolving in an open, decentralized polity where the provision of policy advice and ideas is organized on a competitive basis rather than through elite networks, whether formal (France) or "old-boys" (United Kingdom), American economists have to continually evaluate their (and others') claims to legitimacy and defend themselves through status symbols (the PhD) and the constant reaffirmation of scientific boundaries.

AMERICAN ECONOMISTS, FROM PROFESSIONAL SCIENTISM TO SCIENTIFIC PROFESSIONALISM

Economics is always and everywhere a political endeavor. To the extent that they involve choices about the structure of society (even if it is to leave society unchanged) and furnish arguments to be used in political struggles, economic methods inevitably have political underpinnings and political implications. That point was clear from the beginning among

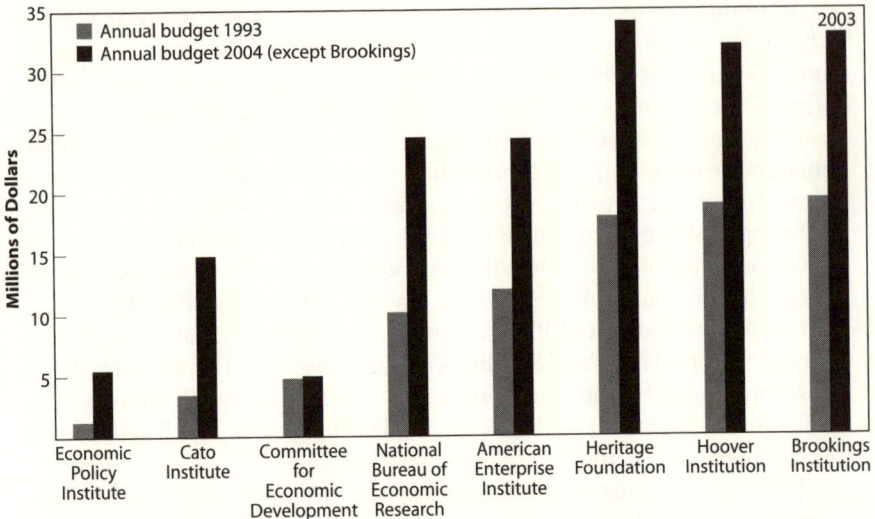

Figure 2-7a. U.S. think tanks: annual income (1992 and 2004 data; Brookings data, 2003).
Source: Day 1993 for 1992 income; and individual organizations' annual reports for 2004 income.

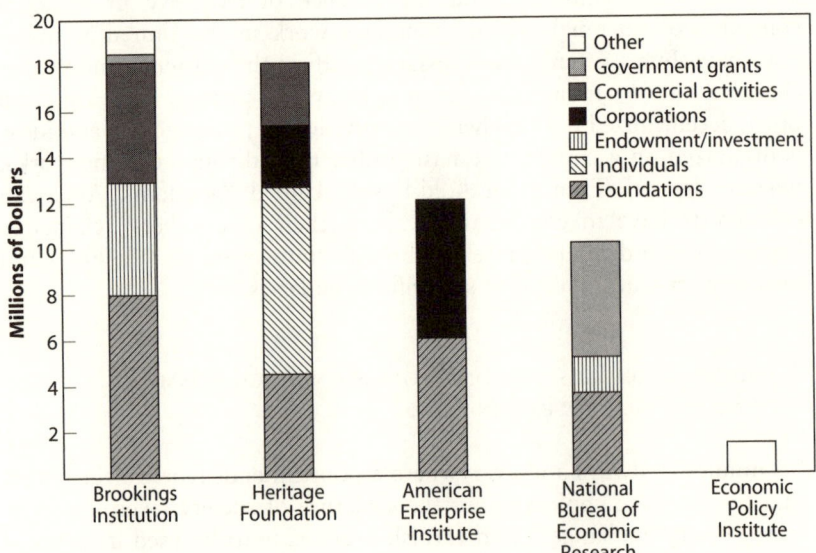

Figure 2-7b. U.S. think tanks, budget composition, 1992.
Source: Day 1993.

American economists. At the discipline's very inception, political entanglements with reform threatened the legitimacy of the disciplinary enterprise they had set out to build. During the early part of the twentieth century, as well as in other periods that were highly charged ideologically, such as the New Deal and the years immediately after World War II, the various "patrons" of economic science, whether private or public, expressed considerable concern about the ideological underpinnings of social scientific knowledge and actively encouraged approaches they saw as "scientific" and less prone to arbitrariness in their dealings with academic communities. One such approach was the reliance on numbers as a means to eschew political differences. There is no equivalent to the extraordinary amount of data production and analysis that went on in American social science throughout the interwar period, and still goes on today. Porter summarizes the point nicely:

> It is no accident that the move towards the almost universal quantification of social and applied disciplines was led by the United States, and succeeded most fully there. The push for rigor in the disciplines derived in part from the same distrust of unarticulated expert knowledge and the same suspicion of arbitrariness and discretion that shaped political culture so profoundly in the same period. Some of this suspicion came from within the disciplines it affected, but in every case it was at least reinforced by vulnerability to the suspicions of outsiders, often expressed in an explicitly political arena. It was felt most intensely in fields treating matters of public interest, and in many cases quantitative methods were initially worked out by applied sub-disciplines, migrating only later to the more "basic" ones. (1995, 199)

The emergence of mathematical economics and econometrics after the 1930s—much of which was accelerated by an influx of European scholars into U.S. academia—led to a reinterpretation of the agenda of scientism, however.[202] Economics was closely integrated into a new, more activist conception of the state through its emphasis on engineering economic growth, rationalizing decision making, and making policy efficient within the context of a free-market economy. But these goals were clearly bounded. Contrary to England, distributive issues never held center stage. Contrary to France, neither did industrial ones.

With the virtual disappearance of institutionalism in the early postwar decades, these intellectual commitments became the mold in which new generations of scholars were socialized, and the construction of a highly organized, and highly promiscuous, intellectual edifice took on a life of its own. In other words, the rapid entrenchment of applied quantification in American academia cannot be dissociated from broader aspects of the country's political culture, mode of economic organization, and particular historical trajectory. We may understand this character of American economics through two metaphors. The first is what I called "professional scientism" at the onset of this chapter. In other words, scientism came to be identified with a "professional outlook," in the sense of a claim to objectivity, a focus on analytical capabilities, and a high degree of collective organization and regulation. The latter refers to the strong jurisdictional control maintained through the role of educational criteria, the PhD in particular, as well as to the policing of field members through well-established "rules of economic method."

The second metaphor is that of "scientific professionalism." The intervention of economists in public and private arenas has been shaped not only by their own "scientific" capabilities but also by particular expectations emanating from the institutions that requested such expertise in the first place. All government bureaucracies appeal to the technical skills of economists. Yet not all of them have relied on academia to the same extent, or in the same way, as the U.S. government. The lack of an established *class* of top administrators in America has brought academia closer to the world of technical public expertise. It is on the basis of their ability to fulfill this role that academic economists have been incorporated at the highest levels of the state apparatus. Also, the institutionalized competition within government, and between government and social groups, has created a strong institutional basis for an economic expertise that seeks to locate itself in the unassailable realm of "science"—with all the difficult gate keeping work such a position entails.

We may make a similar point about the economists' jurisdiction in the American corporate world. Economists in business put their technical abilities in the service of the organization by streamlining decision making or lobbying government. Here again, this is not specific to the United States. Yet I have argued that the nature of economic organization—the greater reliance on market mechanisms, the permanently unsettled nature of the law, as well as the structure of the interprofessional ecology whereby professions appear "relevant" to one another—also tends to create a form of "nesting" of economic knowledge within various other occupations and institutional locations. For this reason, economic concepts and tools become an integral part of the processes whereby social objects are routinely constructed and evaluated. Economists define not only the practical standards according to which such conceptual objects as "monopolies" and "competition" are being judged; they also have authority to craft definitions of "discrimination," "pollution," and "welfare."[203] It is in this greater "colonization of the lifeworld," to use Habermas's (1984) phrase, that we may perhaps best characterize the influence of economists in modern America.

CHAPTER THREE

Britain: Public-Minded Elites

> Everything is very mixed up. All the people I can think of have
> a lot of academic friends, and meet academics and meet politi-
> cians. They are a bit of intermediaries, I guess, so that's—yes. I
> think comparing it with the U.S., I think just the fact of it being
> so much smaller a society here is—so that we all know a lot of
> academics. We all know a lot of journalists, a lot of media peo-
> ple, a lot of politicians. I don't think that is so much so of my
> friends in America who are academics. And they don't seem to
> know journalists, and they don't seem to know politicians.
> They seem to be much more isolated in academia, whereas I
> think Oxford is such a small society and we all know lots of
> them and they are all much more mixed up here.
>
> (professor, Oxford University, June 1997)

PERHAPS MORE than anywhere else, economic concerns and knowledge
are part and parcel of British public culture. The country is famous for
the level and quality of economic reporting in the generalist press, as
well as for its specialized financial and economic publications, such as
the *Economist* or the *Financial Times*, which have been around for well
over a century (the former since 1843, the latter since 1888) and are
widely read both at home and worldwide. Many commentators would
argue that this public interest for economics has been partly nourished
by a century-long debate about the causes of Britain's long-run economic
decline—"very few other countries have been quite so introspective
[about their economy]," one economic columnist told me (June 1997).
At the end of the nineteenth century, Britain was still the world's leading
industrial power. Between 1913 and 1979, its ranking in terms of GDP
per capita "deteriorated from third to eleventh amongst the OECD-16
nations" (Middleton 1996, 16). This slow economic weakening, reversed
only in the 1990s, has kept economic questions, and the search for solutions, at the fore of the public agenda.

The long-term trajectory of British economics seems to mirror the
country's general economic path. The end of the nineteenth century saw
the publication of Marshall's *Principles of Economics* and the successful
professionalization of the discipline. During the interwar period, England

(and particularly Cambridge) was the site of major intellectual developments such as monopolistic competition and Keynesian macroeconomics.[1] By the 1990s, however, not only had British economics lost its intellectual preeminence to the United States, but the future of the profession itself seemed so uncertain that the Royal Economic Society and the Economic and Social Research Council (ESRC) had to commission special reports about it.[2] One after the other, these studies confirmed that the dismal science was in a rather dismal state and warned of the impending death of the "British economist." Growing salary differentials with the private sector were causing new generations of economics students and professors to switch to nonacademic careers in finance and economic consulting.[3] British graduate economics programs were filling up thanks only to an incoming flow of foreign students; they attracted a very small proportion of nationals. As the authors of the ESRC report commented, "It should probably be made clear to parents that, within the foreseeable future, their children and grandchildren will not be taught at university by U.K.-born economists" (Machin and Oswald 2000, 347).

Critics identified economists' lagging salaries as the main cause of the discipline's woes. Yet the wage crisis was itself an indicator of a deeper problem: the unraveling of a particular model of expert control. The transformation of disciplinary organization imposed from without through the scientific domination of American economics and from within through an increasingly results-oriented national research policy seemed to find itself somewhat at odds with British traditions of hands-off training and informal channels of authority.

The fact is that British economics was not much of a formalized enterprise for a good part of its history. Authority in the field flowed from peer recognition within tightly knit social networks, often based in elite institutions, rather than through credentials or scientific publications. In contrast to France, where the very notion of economic competency was an object of competition between public officials and academic actors, or even to the United States, where such a capacity came to be more firmly rooted in the possession of a specialized university degree, in Britain, the boundaries of economic expertise were more fluid and informally defined. An economist, in the British context, was essentially someone who possessed a socially validated experience with economic writing, commentary, or policy. Such a conception might include civil servants, journalists, politicians, financiers or businesspeople, although the center of gravity of this world resided primarily among those Oxbridge-London academics who were also involved in public debates, informal advice, and shadow politics.

British economists often deny having any influence on policy and compare their position unfavorably to that of their American counterparts, who possess institutionalized channels of entry into the political process in the form of the Council of Economic Advisers and high-profile positions in various government agencies. However, there is reason to think that such a view is partly misleading, being based on a confusion between formal access and influence. Against this conception, I will argue that elite academic establishments in Britain have in fact maintained quite intimate connections with the administrative world—with the possible exception of the Thatcher years—as well as with an active public sphere where ideas circulate more through informal channels and political organizations than on the basis of formal appointments and functions. In this sense, economics exemplifies the "clerisy ideal" that prevails throughout the British intellectual world. As scholars have described it, this ideal envisages the mobilization of educated elites to offer political guidance, change mentalities, and generally take part in the affairs of the nation. In this view, authority does not derive primarily from the possession of specials skills, but from the moral superiority conferred by a certain social trajectory, which gives one the right and duty to uphold true British culture.[4]

A Late but Extensive Institutionalization

The history of the development of economics within the British higher education context starts with a paradox. Notwithstanding the far-reaching influence of British and Scottish authors in shaping the intellectual landscape of economic writing worldwide from the eighteenth century on, the academic institutionalization of the discipline was slower in England than in other advanced countries.[5] In the early part of the nineteenth century, economic writers rarely held professorial appointments, with the exception of in Scotland. A few chairs in political economy were created in the 1820s,[6] but little expansion followed. By the end of the nineteenth century, economics classes represented a small part of the general training in history (e.g., at Oxford) or moral science (e.g., at Cambridge). Political economy was still regarded as a practical subject whose place in the elite university tradition remained controversial; the fact that economics had most successfully established itself in university extension classes designed for a popular audience certainly seemed to confirm the discipline's inferior status.[7]

Even as a practical subject, economics did not fare terribly well, however. British universities traditionally excluded professional education, which was handled primarily by occupational groups themselves. The commercial professions did not deem political economy to be a useful subject until the 1890s at least. Nor did the British civil service, which was dominated by people educated in the humanities, do much to legitimate economic knowledge. Political economy became a required subject of civil service examinations after 1871, but it carried far less weight than the classical subjects. The latter fact stands in marked contrast to the German model of the cameralistic sciences, or even the French École Libre des Sciences Politiques, both of which, as Donald Winch remarks, embodied more technocratic conceptions of the state.[8]

Despite its relative neglect by universities in nineteeth-century England, political economy was a hot topic in popular reviews, learned societies, and clubs. Didactic tracts written for the general public, such as Mrs. Marcet's *Conversations on Political Economy* (1816) and Harriet Martineau's *Illustrations of Political Economy* (1832), enjoyed immense success. Serious economic debates took place in general-purpose publications such as the *Edinburgh Review*, the *Quarterly Review,* or the *Westminster Review*. But even in these media, "the great majority of economic articles were written by part-time journalists, whose major occupation was most commonly politics" (Stigler 1965, 43). Indeed, when the scholarly *Economic Journal* first appeared in 1891, the more polemical *Economist* had already been around for almost five decades championing and diffusing liberal economic ideas under the editorial leadership of Manchester school journalist Walter Bagehot.[9]

The practitioners of political economy during this period of British history were mostly leisured gentlemen, enlightened businessmen, intellectuals, journalists, statesmen, and civil servants. They gathered in learned societies such as the powerful British Association for the Advancement of Science (whose Section F covered economics and statistics), the National Association for the Promotion of Social Science, and the more scientifically minded London Statistical Society, or in elite clubs such as the Political Economy Club of London.[10]

Economics and the Modernization of British Higher Education

Political economy started to equip itself with the attributes of a more professorialized (and professionalized) field toward the end of the nineteenth century. The British Economic Association (later Royal Economic Society) was created in 1890, following the American model of a scientific organization. The *Economic Journal* followed almost immediately, providing the new body with an outlet. In 1894 the publication of *Palgrave's Dictionary of Political Economy* gave more coherence to the increasingly recognized and separate domain of knowledge. Critical steps were taken to make political economy a subject for full-time study. But in contrast to the national curricular change implemented in the French university in the last quarter of the nineteenth century, the institutionalization of economics in Britain reflected the intense localism of higher education and the specific social conditions faced by each university.

At the turn of the century, several key developments helped economics take root in the British University System. They were the foundation of the London School of Economics and Political Science in 1895, the creation of the faculties of commerce at Birmingham and Manchester in 1900 and 1903, and curricular reform at the University of Cambridge, where Alfred Marshall succeeded in establishing a separate "tripos" in "economics and political science" in 1903. Though these institutions were established within a decade of one another, they originated in very different motivations and views about the role and mission of political economy. The first three were entirely new, and their curricula reflected the priorities of local financial backers; the latter, by contrast, represented the evolution of an older institution that was mainly regulated internally. (Oxford was a similar case, though there the fate of economics was not resolved until the 1920s.)

Fabian Society leaders Sidney and Beatrice Webb[11] established the London School of Economics (LSE) as a vocationally oriented school that they partly modeled after the French École Libre des Sciences Politiques to train experts for government service (who, it was hoped, would also hold modern, socialist views). The Webbs, however, envisioned the LSE's orientation as much more applied and empirical. Echoing the inclinations of the German historical school and institutionalist economics across the Atlantic, they aimed to ground the work of the new school in factual knowledge of industrial life. The financial involvement of the City and the London Chamber of Commerce in the project supported this problem-solving orientation, though it also encouraged an evolution of the school toward the managerial interests of the business sector, away from the founders' original socialist plans—indeed, one of the school's most successful programs was a course on railway economics.[12]

In both Birmingham and Manchester, the faculties of commerce were even more explicitly initiatives from the business community, and their organization thus reflected the concerns and desires of that powerful constituency. Economics at Birmingham was granted a fairly limited place among a host of other business-relevant subjects designed for industry-bound graduates. The Manchester Faculty of Commerce and Administration had a similarly vocational orientation in its curriculum design, though it allowed more flexibility to specialize in economics: hence the school's later influence as a center of economics training. The work that came out of Manchester was mainly empirical, however, focusing on the problems of the Lancashire industrial area.[13]

These developments differed quite markedly from the institutionalization of the Cambridge economics program, which created a theoretical powerhouse that was to dominate the English field of economics for the next half century. The principal architect of the reform, Alfred Marshall (1842–1924), faced the different challenge of having to demonstrate the intellectual relevance of the subject at a venerable institution that saw itself as the sanctuary of the classical tradition. Marshall thus sought to advance the cause of economics as a distinct theoretical and scientific enterprise, even though he emphasized the importance of practical uses for economics and took care to enlist broad social support in his negotiations with the university. But the Marshallian enterprise was first of all an academic initiative that aspired to be more "scientific" than the ventures in London and the industrial towns. The deliberate exclusion, by Marshall, of the subject of accountancy from the Cambridge tripos made this orientation clear.[14]

Following Cambridge's leadership, all major British universities established chairs in political economy during the 1890s and 1900s. During the interwar period, the discipline gained greater autonomy as it expanded, so that by 1945 all major institutions had also created specialized "honours schools" in economics, and the discipline was nowhere in a position subordinate to other fields. Even at Oxford, which was most wedded to the classical curriculum, curricular reorganization progressed markedly despite the hegemonic influence of the humanities in university governance. Oxford had one of the oldest chairs in economics, yet by the end of World War I, it still counted very few economics teachers among its faculty. Oxford's most influential economist, Francis Y. Edgeworth, himself regarded economics as a derivative subject for which there existed no better foundation than the classics-heavy curriculum offered in the School of Literae Humaniores. Though Oxford's economists showed little appetite for disciplinary expansion, in 1921 a group of university philosophers who took "more than a passing interest in Political Economy" and were eager to shake the hold of ancient history on their subject successfull lobbied for the creation of the Honour School of Philosophy, Politics and Economics (PPE) (Chester 1986, 30). The creation of the PPE program had a decisive effect on economics at Oxford, yielding a rapid (though somewhat haphazard) buildup of the faculty. The result of this recruitment drive was that "by 1932 the majority of [Oxford] colleges had a Fellow or a Lecturer in Economics" to provide for the new school (Chester 1986, 49). As the 1930s progressed, the university then sought the support of foundations and wealthy philanthropists to expand its infrastructure in social studies. This led to a grant from the Rockefeller Foundation establishing the Institute of Statistics and, later, to Lord Nuffield's gift founding an eponymous college devoted entirely to the social sciences.

In spite of its difficult beginnings, the PPE Honour School at Oxford was remarkably successful. By the late 1940s, it had overtaken all but the Honour School of Modern History in terms of the number of students who were reading for it; the influence of philosophy declined, and that of economics and politics increased. Indeed, by 1949–50, economics majors represented nearly a quarter of all full-time students at the universities of Oxford, Cambridge, and Manchester, and almost 60 percent of those at the London School of Economics.[15] A 1957 Civil Service Commission report lists economics (including PPE) as the third most successful subject for recruitment into the administrative class, after history and classics.[16]

In the postwar period the expansion of economics became part of a general revolution in British higher education. By the 1950s, state officials were acutely aware of the country's backwardness in access to higher education and sought to actively promote its growth, particularly by expanding subjects that were deemed modern. In keeping with the conclusions of three successive postwar commissions on education, the first two of which were headed by economists (reports by Clapham [HMSO 1946] and Robbins [HMSO 1963]; report by Heyworth [HMSO 1965]), the British government singled out the social sciences as important vehicles for the growth of the new universities in the 1960s and 1970s.[17] The number of teaching posts in economics nearly tripled between 1960 and 1969, from 679 to 1,802.[18] Figure 3-1 shows the rapid rise of economics degrees for the period after 1970, although the impossibility of gathering data on joint degrees (such as PPE) means that the figure significantly understates the general importance of economics at British universities. During this period, this growing number of graduates encountered employment and research opportunities in government departments, the private sector, and nonprofit research institutions.

By the late 1970s, however, newer subjects (e.g., sociology) and "transdisciplines" (e.g., urban planning), as well as hybrid programs with a clearer vocational orientation (e.g., business and financial studies), began to challenge the more narrowly specialized, "academic," and elitist form of training represented by economics. In its most specialized form, the discipline appeared less apt than other, more directly practical, types of degrees, to satisfy the massive student demand generated by the rapid democratization of higher education after the 1960s. Economics lost popularity among students, while business made steady gains. At the A levels (end of high school), economics dwindled from about 6 percent to 2.5 percent of all exams taken between 1991 and 2001, while business rose from about 2 percent to 4.5 percent.[19] At the university level, the growth

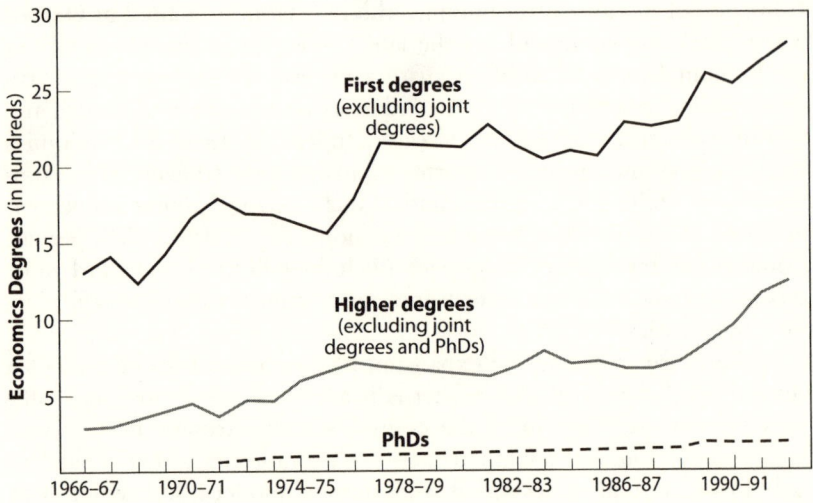

Figure 3-1. U.K. economics degrees, 1966–94 (does not include joint degrees).
   Source: HMSO, Department of Education and Science, *Education Statistics for the United Kingdom*, 1970–79; HMSO, University Grants Committee, *University Statistics*, 1980–94.

of economics enrollments stagnated during the 1980s, and by 1989, the number of economics teachers in university had dropped back to 1,332.[20] Economics enrollment began recovering only in the 1990s, whereas business and management programs expanded quickly and continuously throughout the period (figure 3-2).

   To some extent, however, these trends mask a growing affinity between economics and business studies which we have already observed in the U.S. case, though the discrepancy in enrollments between the two fields is much larger there. First, as elsewhere, the influence of economists in business schools has increased markedly. Second, the reverse is true as well; economics itself serves mainly as a preparation for business careers. As figure 3-3a shows, well over 80 percent of U.K. undergraduate economics degree holders go on to employment in commerce and industry (mainly banking, accountancy, insurance, and finance). But the same is increasingly true of economics postgraduates, for whom industry has practically overtaken education as the biggest sector of employment (figure 3-3b).[21]

   Looking back at the development of British economics over the long run, we may thus qualify the paradox first noted at the beginning of this section, namely, that the country that did so much to establish economic theory in its modern form was slow to institutionalize the subject in its

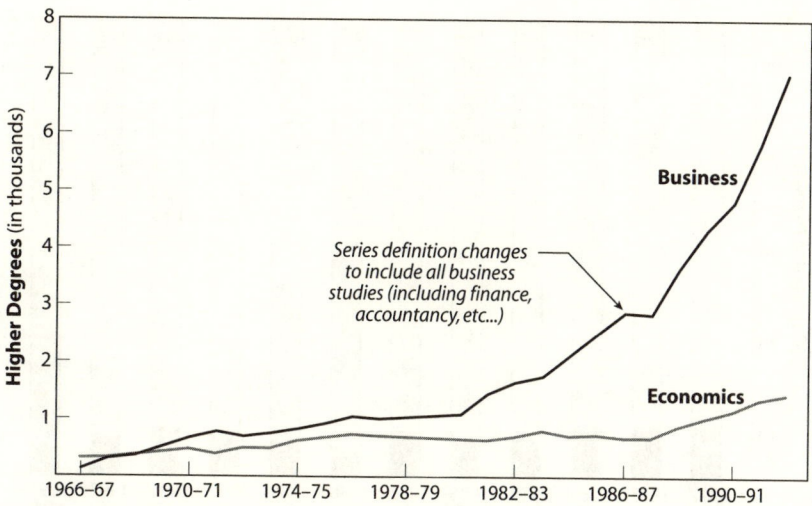

Figure 3-2. U.K. higher degrees, economics vs. business, 1971–94.

Source: HMSO, Department of Education and Science, *Education Statistics for the United Kingdom*, 1970–79; HMSO, University Grants Committee, *University Statistics: Students and Staff*, 1980–94.

universities. Once the legitimacy of economic studies was established successfully (around the turn of the century), the discipline developed into a quite powerful force within universities and public life. Figure 3-4 shows the dramatic buildup of the Royal Economic Society during the interwar period, which contrasts interestingly with the slower pace of development of the American Economic Association over the same period. The British situation also differs markedly from the French one, where the discipline remained formally under the tutelage and influence of law until well after World War II, in spite of early nineteenth-century gains such as the creation of the École Libre des Sciences Politiques and the multiplication of university chairs. In Britain, on the other hand, the self-governance of universities and the need to accommodate deeply entrenched academic interests—particularly at Oxford—were initially important barriers to academicization. Yet once these obstacles were overcome, the very same institutional features then enabled economists to maintain a strong position within universities, including the most prestigious ones.

Collectivization of the Social Sciences

This examination of the academic system in Britain would not be complete without a more detailed analysis of the structures and institutions

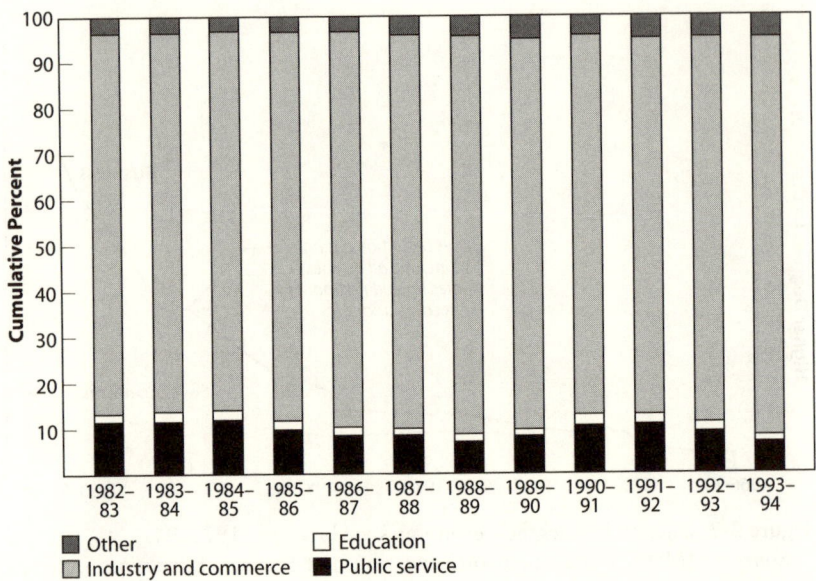

Figure 3-3a. First destination employers of economics first degree graduates in home employment by sector, 1982–94.
Source: HMSO, University Grants Committee, *University Statistics: First Destination of Leavers from Higher Education*, 1980–94.

that supported the development of an economic research infrastructure in the twentieth century. Historically, this pattern of expansion was somewhat analogous to that identified earlier for the process of academicization. An intense activity of data collection took place in England in the nineteenth century, but it was mainly focused on social and public health problems and remained somewhat decentralized. Scientific societies and reform groups, often closely associated with local governments, drove most social investigations and industrial surveys, and central administrations acted more to federate and coordinate these efforts than to direct them.[22] The Board of Trade, which collected economic data centrally, seems to have been somewhat less effective in its task than the General Register Office, which gathered data on social conditions and public health. Roger Middleton points out, that the collection of economic data in Britain tended to be hampered by the "enormous resistance to any intrusion into the affairs of wealthy individuals or businesses" (1998, 123).

Until 1945, sources of British economic statistics were famously dispersed: they included government bodies, from central administrative departments to local offices, learned societies, universities, and even

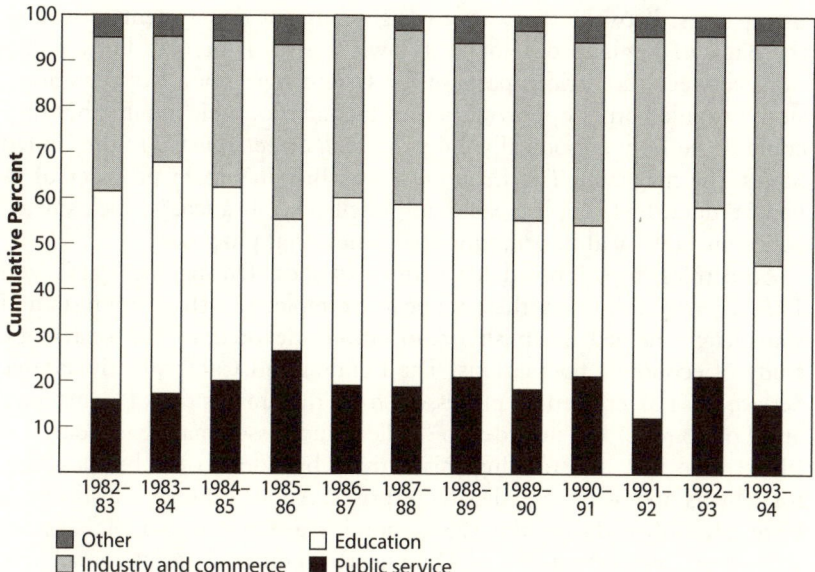

Figure 3-3b. First destination employers of U.K. economics higher degree graduates in home employment by sector, 1982–94.

Source: HMSO, University Grants Committee, *University Statistics: First Destination of Leavers from Higher Education*, 1980–94.

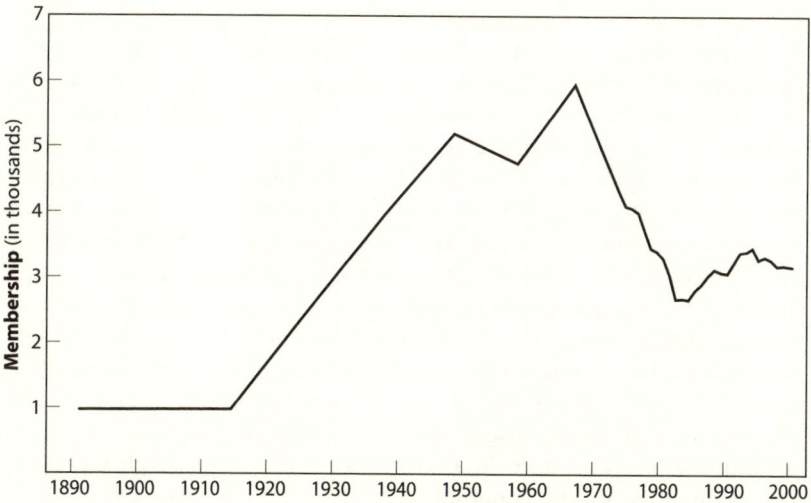

Figure 3-4. Royal Economic Society membership, 1891–2003.

Source: Coats and Coats 1973 for 1891–1969; Royal Economic Society thereafter.

newspapers. Between the wars each government department as well as the Bank of England developed its own statistical branch, but connections between the various parts of the system were poor. Royal commissions provided other opportunities for factual economic inquiry, but they could do so only episodically. Like the *Wall Street Journal* in the United States, the magazine *The Economist* was Britain's main provider of financial data. In 1926, it created an "intelligence branch," which started collecting statistical information for commercial purposes.[23]

Academics, too, lobbied for better statistics. During the 1920s and 1930s, partly following the American example, British economists and statisticians helped establish organizations devoted to the systematic study of economic fluctuations. The London and Cambridge Economic Service (LCES), created by professors from the universities of Cambridge and London in 1922 in order to "collect and disseminate basic data for [their] own use, and funding this activity by sales to the business sector,"[24] was one of these earliest enterprises. Applied research institutions were established during the 1930s, notably at Oxford and Manchester, where both intellectual tradition and nearby industrial basins contributed to an interest in empirical research. The Oxford Economists' Research Group, a collective devoted to the investigation of business decisions, was formed in 1935. A few months earlier, Jacob Marschak, recently emigrated from Germany, had helped found the new Oxford Institute of Statistics, devoted to the study of the business cycle and the conduct of industrial and labor surveys. Marschak directed the institute until he left for the Cowles Commission in 1939.[25]

Foreign linkages were indeed often crucial to the development of such endeavors. Sometimes, foreigners brought their expertise in person: for instance, Wesley C. Mitchell (founder of the NBER in the United States) spent 1931 at Oxford, where he helped orient the research program toward applied quantitative studies. More important, linkages to American philanthropic organizations were key to bankrolling social-scientific research throughout Europe, and especially Britain, both before and after World War II.[26] As Fisher remarks, "Rockefeller philanthropy (in the area of economic research) provided more funds than either Government or British philanthropy put together" (1977, 557). Nearly one-quarter of total income for the London School of Economics during the period between 1923 and 1937 came from Rockefeller sources.[27] The Rockefeller Foundation also provided the original grant for the Oxford Institute of Statistics and the Oxford Economists' Research Group, as well as moneys for the Economic Research Section at the University of Manchester (1931), the National Institute of Economic and Social Research (NIESR, created in 1938), and the Cambridge Department of Applied Economics (created in 1946 at Keynes's initiative).[28] Everywhere,

Rockefeller philanthropy aimed to promote the American-style model of applied research I described in the preceding chapter.

These institutions constituted an important organizational step for British economics. Staffed with academics, they encouraged a new conception of economic research as a collective enterprise. Empirical investigations undertaken under the new organizations' auspices contributed to the further professionalization of British academic economics, particularly by promoting a new wave of scholarly publications. For instance, the journal *Oxford Economic Papers*, created in 1938, became a receptacle for the works of Oxford-based economists and their program of grounded empiricism. Similarly, the review *Manchester School*, created in 1930, became a vehicle for the work of the Economic Research Section, conducted in close association with local industries.

The crucible of World War II led to the progressive integration of these activities into the machinery of the British state itself. While the vogue of planning ideas during the 1930s had, here as elsewhere, prepared the terrain for government centralization in many areas, including data collection and scientific research, the war was an even more important catalyst. Social scientists and statisticians were incorporated into government under the general umbrella of operations research, and the government started officially supporting economic measurement activities. Meade and Stone developed the first national income estimates while working from the Cabinet Office in 1941. (As Patinkin [1976] recalls, their predecessor in this area, Colin Clark, had never succeeded in securing governmental assistance to support his work.) In 1941, the Central Statistical Office (CSO; today renamed the Office of National Statistics) was created to federate the various British government offices, and the Government Statistical Service (a special recruitment and career path for statistical jobs) was established in 1946. The government also sponsored major activities involving social scientists to prepare for the postwar period. The *White Paper on Employment Policy* (1944), the blueprint for the development of the British welfare state, became in the words of the CSO's first director "the Gospel for the development of economic statistics afterwards" (Campion 1958, 2).

The Clapham report in 1946 stressed the need for the government to support the social sciences via public funding to universities. But it also claimed that the social sciences were not ready for the creation of a designated research council tasked with allocating research funds, similar to that which already existed for the medical and agricultural sciences. As in the United States, politics was at the core of the problem: the report warned of the "premature crystallization of spurious orthodoxies" that could ensue if such an organization were brought into existence.[29] By the 1960s, however, such a position was less tenable. Confidence in the utility of the social sciences had greatly expanded, including among public officials. British elites greatly admired American science and social science both for their growing worldwide influence and for the social consideration they seemed to enjoy, as evidenced by the substantial financial backing they received from a variety of public and private organizations. In England, calls for government funding (for both the natural and social sciences) were entangled in the debate over British national decline. Planning was on the agenda once again as an instrument of British modernization, and social scientists aggressively promoted the relevance of their work to the already favorably disposed Labour government of Harold Wilson. In 1965, the Committee on Social Studies finally recommended the establishment of the Social Science Research Council. The organization was set up immediately with the aim of funding evidence-led research that would inform government policy. By 1968, the SSRC received more funding from the British government than the Medical Research Council, and by 1976, it received twice as much.[30] As is common in British practice, but also because of persisting concerns about politicization, the SSRC was designed as a "quango," an independently managed organization funded by the government.

It is instructive to contrast the fundamental differences in the conditions of emergence and development of the SSRC and its principal counterpart in the United States, the social and behavioral sciences program at the National Science Foundation. As we have seen, within the latter the social sciences gained legitimacy only by stressing the scientific basis of their research procedures and methodologies in a context of high ideological tension. In order to secure approval from skeptical natural scientists, American social scientists were careful to erect protective boundaries between scientific work and politics by avoiding direct mentions of policy applications (see the studied "neutrality" of the NBER or the National Science Foundation, for instance) and privileging a form of research defined as "basic" (where the distinction between applied and basic research was drawn directly from the natural sciences). In the United Kingdom, suspicions of political bias were just as strong, yet they were solved in a characteristically different way. The challenge there was to demonstrate the relevance of social-scientific research to government work and policy making. In the 1980s, it was also by claiming its usefulness and reorienting its work in a more empirical direction that the SSRC was able to resist the onslaught during the Thatcher era.[31]

Small Worlds

Margaret Thatcher's hostility toward the social sciences, which was one of the causes of the SSRC's dangerous fate in the early 1980s, had roots in a popular form of anti-intellectualism, but she also had more concrete grounds for her antagonism. Thatcher and her education minister, Sir Keith Joseph, saw the social sciences as a hotbed of socialistic ideas, and economics was no exception. Indeed, the dislike was mutual. In 1981, only a few months before Lord Rothschild was appointed to conduct a study to determine the fate of the SSRC, 364 economists across forty academic institutions had signed a letter to the *Times* of London denouncing Thatcher's budget plans and warning of impending doom for the British economy if they were to proceed. A closer look at the list reveals that no fewer than 54 signatories came from one single institution, Cambridge University.[32] Given the central importance of Cambridge in the history of British economics, this merits further attention. In fact, this piece of history alerts us to one important element in the character of British economics, at least until that period: its relatively centralized character.

The pattern, in fact, goes back a long way. Cambridge already dominated British economics—as it did British intellectual life—at the end of the nineteenth century. Herbert S. Foxwell, for instance, reported that in 1888 Marshall's students controlled half the (very small number of) economics chairs in England.[33] In contrast to the United States, where the university landscape was more decentralized, more "democratic," and hence remained more diverse longer, in England, the stratified organization of higher education as a whole fostered an early concentration of intellectual authority around a limited number of extraordinarily powerful personalities and institutions. As Skidelsky states, "Most British economists before Marshall were men reared on a single book—John Stuart Mill's *Principles*. Their successors also tended to be men of a single book—Marshall's *Principles*, supplemented by oral tradition, Marshall's evidence to a couple of Royal Commissions, and privately printed fragments of the master's thought" (1994, 206). In the postwar period, the pattern was repeated with Keynes's works, which had acquired the same commanding influence.

We can point to many institutional reasons for this remarkable concentration of British intellectual life. But none is more important than the small size and remarkably hierarchical structure of British higher education that we discussed in chapter 1. In contrast to the United States, where elevation to a professorship has been part of the normal development of academic careers, in England few people ever achieved such status. Even today, many remain in inferior grades their entire lives or receive this supreme academic honor late in their career, sometimes only as they near retirement and rarely ever outside of LSE/Oxbridge. Joan Robinson, for instance, did not become a professor until the ripe age of sixty-two. And such a well-respected economist as Roy Harrod never rose higher than a readership at Nuffield College.

How academic appointments were decided was often mysterious. The absence (or great scarcity) of higher degree diplomas meant that appointments occurred very early in people's careers, sometimes immediately after college. In Cambridge, for instance, the doctorate started being given with some regularity only in the 1930s. But even then, their status was not well established. The Oxford D.Phil. (degree of doctor of philosophy, for instance, "was still viewed by many arts dons as a distasteful medium of dry Teutonic pedantry" decades after its introduction (Harris 1994, 218). Coding work based on Blaug's *Who's Who in Economics?* (1999) shows that only 47 percent of the most well-known British economists born between 1900 and 1930 (and thus coming of age between 1925 and 1955) had a doctorate.[34] Of the generation born between 1930 and 1960, 27 percent attained eminence without one such degree (and over half of the others obtained their degree in the United States).[35] If we look at the *staff in post* at British universities, the figures are even more striking: by 1970 still less than 30 percent of those teaching economics had a doctorate.[36] Finally, a sample of 150 U.K.-based Royal Economic Society members I drew from the 1994 register yields a percentage of PhDs of 42.

Even more important than the limited role of postgraduate degrees was the character of advanced training, which by all accounts remained fairly hands-off. This informality partly reflected the generally intimate nature of the British college system—the very small worlds within which students were groomed and careers were made. Appointments rested frequently on personal contacts and recommendations, and an informally shared sense of who was promising and brilliant. In his interview with Keith Tribe, Hans Singer, who came to Cambridge from Germany as a doctoral student in the 1930s, recalls that young economists (including him) were routinely designated for jobs by their powerful mentors. "Keynes' weekly seminar," he says, "was also a tremendously powerful job market because in the background there would be sitting important visitors to Cambridge" (Tribe 1997, 62). As a matter of fact, this highly personalized mode of recruitment persisted well after the war. To some extent, the job selection process today is still much more casual than in the United States and especially France, with its high reliance on *concours* (examinations) at all levels of the career process. William Baumol (from the United States) and Kevin Lancaster (from Australia), who had come to study at the LSE, were appointed to the school's faculty barely a few weeks into their postgraduate degree. Formal requirements mattered less than personal connections to the university (especially at Oxford and Cambridge, which tended to recruit their own) and signs of academic brilliance such as a first-class honors (even when obtained in subjects other than economics).[37]

My own interviews with various generations of British economists repeatedly stressed this point:

> The great thing for a long time, in Cambridge and Oxford, you took your degree, and if you got a first class, you got a fellowship straightaway. And you could stay in the college and never publish a line and read your books. (professor, University of Cambridge, June 1997)

> Well, it was a very incestuous thing when I was an undergraduate. These professors would spot some undergraduate who they thought had an enormous amount of talent and then they would do extraordinarily well and be hired for the faculty. [Name of a person], for instance, who is now director of the [name of an economics research center], he was effectively tenured, given a tenured position on the faculty as an undergraduate, before he'd taken his exam. Now there was no uncertainty about that because everybody knew that he was a great genius and was going to get a First and he would be the best thing that had ever been there. And it was terrible for him, for something like ten years, he wrote absolutely nothing because he'd never had a chance to find out what he was good at. He'd been declared a genius at birth, and it almost finished him off. (professor, U.S. East Coast university, July 1999)

In countries such as Germany and the United States, which are federalist in structure and expanded their systems of higher education early on, intellectual authority in economics was decentralized among a fairly broad network of universities of comparable prestige that competed against one another. In Britain, by contrast, intellectual capital long remained concentrated in the two elite universities of Oxford and Cambridge, along with the relative newcomers the London School of Economics and, perhaps, the University of London. These institutions also trained the largest numbers of economists, and they were centrally located around or in London, which fostered a constant stream of intellectual exchange and political connections.[38]

These features had important consequences for the nature of economic knowledge and for the consolidation of economic "styles" in each institution. The Canadian economist Harry Johnson, for instance, argues that this "centralization of professional advancement" within the Oxbridge-London network contributed to the crystallization of an orthodox Keynesian core in England and the relatively belated diffusion of the monetarist counterrevolution in academic circles (1971, 6). A visitor to Cambridge in the 1950s, he wrote cynically about the somewhat confined, insular atmosphere of the campus and the overwhelming "shadow of Keynes" (Johnson and Johnson 1978). That a large number of economists in the

1960s spent a lot of time and effort not only developing Keynes's ideas but also arguing about "what [he] really said" is an indication of the extraordinary authority his work commanded in British academia during the second and third quarters of the twentieth century.

Another factor contributing to the convergence of authority toward these centers was the persistently elitist operation of the core institutions in the British field. First, class seems to have been an important factor for securing advancement in the economics establishment, here as elsewhere in British society. Kadish (1989), for instance, suggests that the lesser class or regional origins of historical economists[39] in the nineteenth century hampered their successful incorporation into elite culture, ultimately compromising their careers. Nearly all the leading personalities in twentieth-century British economics have come from "public" schools—perhaps the most potent indicator of social class in Britain.[40] Thus, in their analysis of Royal Economic Society (RES) officers and council members between 1891 and 1960, Coats and Coats (1973) found that almost none of them attended a state school, and very few went to a (more selective) grammar school, even though a much larger proportion of the RES's membership at large (almost 40 percent in 1960) did. John Maynard Keynes, Dennis Robertson, Hubert Henderson, Richard Stone, James Meade, Richard Kahn, Ralph Hawtrey, John Hicks, and R.G.D. Allen graduated from public schools (although some had gotten access to these institutions by winning mathematical scholarships). Even Roy Harrod, who was raised in a financially struggling but highly cultivated household, had received an impeccable upper-class education at Westminster School.[41]

Social clubs, seminars, and close personal connections among elite members played a particularly central role in structuring the world of British economics. Participation in such bodies, however, was just as informally controlled as appointments were, and relied more or less on co-optation. Harry Johnson attests that student membership in the Political Economy Club of Cambridge, created by Keynes, was by invitation only.[42] Even official institutions operated under a model where belonging meant much more than paying a fee. While the Royal Economic Society was not formally a closed organization, its membership, government, and operation remained very elitist until the 1970s at least.[43] Between 1912 and 1971, the RES had only two secretaries: Keynes (1912–45) and E.A.G. Robinson (1945–71). The society's publication, the *Economic Journal*, had only three editors between 1891 and 1961 (Edgeworth [1891–1912], Keynes [1912–45] and Harrod [1945–61]).[44] Cambridge, however, was not alone in this oligarchic pattern: the *Review of Economic Studies*, which was associated with the London School of Economics, was edited by the same person (Ursula Webb [Hicks], daughter of Sidney and Beatrice Webb, wife of John Hicks, and a renowned economist herself) during its first twenty-seven years of existence, from 1933 to 1960.

Unsurprisingly, however, the cliquish nature of the Royal Economic Society and other key bodies of British economics did not always sit well with the growing community of practicing economists across England, who aspired to raise their scientific profile. In the 1960s, a challenge emerged in the form of a more "proletarian" organization (three British economists I spoke to independently chose this word to describe it)—the Association of University Teachers in Economics (AUTE).[45] More inclusive than the RES (it encouraged students to participate), the AUTE organized an annual conference (something the RES did not do at the time), brought in well-known foreign speakers, and generally expanded the involvement of economists from institutions of lesser status, such as provincial universities and polytechnics. The AUTE's conference rapidly drew in large numbers of participants, including many foreigners, so much so that in 1982, the Royal Economic Society reached out to the AUTE to combine its own annual meeting with the association's conference, ultimately leading to a merger of the two organizations. The result of these transitional years was a revival of the RES (see figure 3-4) and an incontestably democratic (and international) evolution of both the RES and the journals. Editorial and leadership authority in these institutions weakened somewhat over the last three decades of the twentieth century, and the annual conference now attracts a host of young scholars from all over Europe.[46] Still, my interviews suggest the persistence of exclusion albeit in new guises. For instance, two nonmainstream economists mentioned that they "would not even try" applying to the RES-AUTE annual conference because their papers "would be rejected" outright. Both were, by contrast, regular participants in the American ASSA conference (of which the American Economic Association is a part). One of them drew the following comparison between the British and the American institutions:

The Royal Economic Society is not an umbrella organization. It's very narrow and it doesn't try to be anything other than that. . . . Well, I've given a paper to the ASSA, under the URPE [Union of Radical Political Economists] section. Let's be clear. . . . So there is feminist economics, Marxist economics, the methodology stuff. It exists, but at such a low level. So the danger, of course, is that the American Association would say, "Oh, what a broad group we are, we allow everybody to exist." Well, they allow them to exist, but you know, it's so marginalized it gives the appearance of openness when really it isn't. (lecturer, De Montfort University, June 1997)

The interviewee had few illusions about the place of heterodox approaches in either country. The implication of the quoted passage, however, is that American economics achieves marginalization under the guise of equality and the sanction of the market, while the process in British economics has been more confidently driven by the moral superiority of the center itself. We have already examined the latter's sociological basis; we will now analyze its intellectual roots.

THE SCIENTIFIC AND MORAL TRANSFORMATION OF BRITISH ECONOMICS

The intellectual form under which British economics developed, and particularly the scientific claims formulated by Alfred Marshall and his disciples, were an important vehicle for the centralization of authority just discussed. In marked contrast with the German historicists and the American institutionalists, the leading professionalizers of British economics on the eve of World War I regarded the ability to make general statements—to "reduce processes to system," in Marshall's words—as the hallmark of the practice of economic science. As Philip Mirowski has amply demonstrated, they conceived of their intellectual mission as a primarily theoretical one, much like in the physical sciences, which they frequently invoked as models.[47]

Marshall had set the tone in his immensely influential textbook (though he was not without predecessors).[48] Published in 1890, the *Principles of Economics* helped synthetize the language of economics around marginal analysis and the partial equilibrium approach. And while Marshall himself was a broad-ranging and cautious scholar who constantly qualified his statements in footnotes and tirelessly advocated empirical work, he was unequivocal about the importance of abstract reasoning in his general approach to economics: "The modern economic organism is vertebrate; and the science which deals with it should not be invertebrate. It should have that delicacy and sensitiveness of touch which are required for enabling it to adapt itself closely to the real phenomena of the world; but none the less must it have a firm backbone of exact reasoning" (1890, 71).

Marshall's vision for the discipline of economics bears traces of his struggles against economic historians at Cambridge. For him, pure economic theory was the base upon which empirical investigations, which he called the "superstructure" of economics, ought to rely. Most of his contemporaries, and even more so those who followed him, such as his disciple and successor Arthur Cecil Pigou, agreed. In his eulogy for Marshall, John Maynard Keynes unequivocally embraced the legacy: "[Marshall was] the first great economist *pur sang* that there ever was; the first who devoted his life to building up the subject as a separate science, standing on its own foundations, with as high standards of scientific accuracy as the physical or the biological sciences" (1924, 56–57).

There are many possible explanations for the intellectual character of British economics, with its overwhelming adherence to the rational-liberal theoretical paradigm and the concomitant weakness of the historical school. On the one hand, a political culture rooted in the sovereign power of the individual partly explains the founding images and representations of the discipline in the British context. As Rosanvallon has pointed out, the form taken by British economic discourse exhibits a profound affinity with the rise of civil society as both a political concept and a new social reality. In contrast with Germany's historicism, which came about in a bureaucratic-autocratic political culture, Adam Smith's science of wealth "constructed itself on a new representation of politics." It reproduced the emergent British society's view of itself as a collection of interacting individuals.[49]

The particular configuration of the British intellectual sphere was of great importance, too. Intellectual legitimacy in nineteenth-century British elite culture was heavily vested in "classics," which included the study of the humanities but also that of mathematics. The latter, indeed, were regarded as part of a "classical heritage" going back to the Greeks. Mathematics, in fact, was deemed "the discipline most appropriate to intellectual training"[50] and throughout the nineteenth century reigned at Cambridge as a fundamental component of the prestigious tripos examinations system.[51] Many of the major figures in British economics were trained as mathematicians. Some examples include Jevons, Marshall, Keynes, Hawtrey, Hicks, Ramsey, later Champernowne or Mirrlees (even Oxford-trained Beveridge had a double first in mathematics and classics).[52]

Sanderson suggests that a number of applied subjects (physics, engineering, economics) made their way into the core university curriculum in England through their connection with mathematics.[53] The natural sciences were incorporated quite late in British university education, sometimes not until the 1880s, and in part their strategy to gain acceptance relied on their ability to demonstrate a truly "scientific" character. Economics struggled, too. In 1877 a proposal to dismiss Section F (economics and statistics) of the British Association for the Advancement of Science (on the grounds that it did not practice true science) triggered a serious crisis.[54] It was resolved by the progressive elimination of most inductive and historical elements from the core of political economy, and the concomitant ascendancy of the deductive method. Thus, although Britain, like Germany and the United States, did experience its own version of the *Methodenstreit*, including a form of "socialism of the chair" between the 1870s and the 1920s, historical approaches failed to gain a strong foothold.[55] Instead, British economists came to look toward mathematics and mathematical statistics in their quest for institutional legitimacy. Hence, at a time when the economic contributions of the great French mathematician Augustin Cournot were forgotten in his own country and another French mathematical economist, Léon Walras, whom Schumpeter later labeled "the greatest of all economists" ([1954] 1994, 827), was not even granted a teaching position at home, Jevons, Marshall, Edgeworth, or Philip Wicksteed, all of whom used mathematics in their approach to the study of the economy, stood as the most authoritative figures in the British field. Nonmathematical scholars such as Cairnes, Foxwell, and Neville Keynes "openly encouraged the development of mathematical economics."[56] Indeed, even the historical economists, who had more serious reservations, "did not hinder the study of pure economic theory, let alone the use of mathematics."[57]

By and large, the relevance of mathematics in economics was uncontroversial after Marshall set out his scientific program for the discipline. (Marshall himself had written a mathematical appendix to his *Principles of Economics*). It was admitted that, as a science and as a *technical* competence, economics required the proper use of certain instruments, and that included mathematical knowledge. British economists also firmly supported the development of statistics in their country, which they considered to be an integral part of their scientific mission. In fact, there was little demarcation between the social worlds of economists and statisticians until after 1945. Although the disciplinary boundaries between the two fields had been clear since the beginnings of Marshall's professionalizing enterprise, both groups gravitated toward the same social circles.[58]

Likewise, elementary mathematical skills were understood to be a necessary part of every economist's training, though their use remained optional in practice. In comparison with continental Europe, and even in contrast to the United States (which remained more pluralistic until after World War II), the scientific style in British economics was already fairly well developed before 1939. Even at Oxford, where a descriptive, historical, and empirical approach to economic problems had been ascendant prior to World War I, the faculty largely rallied to ahistorical, mathematical, and marginalist views by the 1930s.[59] Until 1950, the use of mathematics was more common in articles published in the *Economic Journal* than in the *American Economic Review*.[60] The *Review of Economic Studies*, started in 1933, was even more thoroughly technical.[61]

Yet some ambivalence remained. The unwritten rule was that as long as precise words could "carry the message," it was better to rely on them than on equations.[62] And though he consistently "championed the cause of better economic statistics," Keynes famously expressed skepticism at the emergence of econometrics.[63] If the use of mathematics was well accepted, it still had to bow to the exigencies of economic theory and clarity of style. For instance, such a superior mathematician as Frank Ramsey restricted the exposition of his "mathematical theory of saving" to mathematical methods familiar to economists when his own approach had been sustained by more advanced mathematics, namely, the calculus of variations.[64] In her analysis of the rhetoric of American economics, McCloskey thus compared the "embarrassed modesty with which British economics writers pushed mathematics off into the appendices" to the glorious confidence of Samuelson's *Foundations* (1985, 70). Using mathematics that was too complex or redundant amounted to an unnecessary showing off of skill and could, in fact, defeat the purpose of clarity and relevance. So even though more British articles used mathematics, their use of it remained more guarded.[65]

Lionel Robbins's presidential address to the Royal Economic Society in 1955 perhaps best illustrates this pragmatic approach to the use of mathematics: [66]

> The question of whether it is sometimes useful to put economic propositions in mathematical form has been long ago settled; it is no longer intellectually interesting. We take it for granted nowadays that, in the treatment of some parts of the subject, an occasional resort to simple mathematics is quite a normal thing.
>
> But to say this is one thing; to say that a separate division of the subject entitled mathematical economics should be compulsory on all students taking honours economics is another. . . . I think that mathematical economics is a division of the subject, which should be fostered; it deserves a place in the program of a properly articulated department. But at this stage, at any rate, where examinations are concerned, this should be the place of an option, not part of the syllabus compulsory on all candidates.
>
> In contrast to this, I would say that the opposite status should be given to a paper in economic statistics. . . . It is perhaps the chief technical qualification, which the outside world has the right to demand of any applicant for a job who comes bearing our certificate of competence. (Robbins, 1955, 590)

And, indeed, the organization of economics teaching in the early post war period seems to have reflected both of these attitudes. Thus a cross-national UNESCO survey in 1954 found that the teaching of economic statistics, mathematics for economics, and econometrics was especially strong in the United Kingdom compared with the United States, Sweden, and France. But the subfield of "mathematical economics" was for a time less well represented than in these other countries, including France, where engineers played a pioneering role in this domain. In short, mathematics and statistics were routinely integrated into the scientific *practice* of economics, but they were not singled out as a special subject within economics itself, with a few rare exceptions. [67]

This cautious attitude toward mathematics may explain the subsequent rift within British economics. As scientific leadership moved to the United States and the field evolved toward further formalization in the pursuit of the neoclassical synthesis, a whole segment of the British profession was left behind while those economists who were more comfortable with mathematical tools found themselves on the ascendancy within the disciplinary core. Some important figures—Joan Robinson, Nicholas Kaldor—found themselves on the losing end of this intellectual trend, while others owed part of their success (now essentially bestowed in the United States) to the use of complex mathematics. A good example is James Mirrlees, about whose work one U.S.-based economist commented in a conversation that "the level of formalization he used was completely uncommon in 1971. Only perhaps in finance would you find mathematics that was as sophisticated. [Mirrlees] just raised the mathematical level for everyone." In the *Economic Journal*, the percentage of articles based on "mathematical models without any data" went from 34 percent in the 1972–76 period to 50 percent in the 1977–82 period, an extraordinarily rapid transformation that also reflects the growing presence of American authors in the pages of the journal noted by Coats (1991) and Backhouse (1997).[68] From the 1970s on, mathematics became a subject of contention in a way that it had never been before. An editorial note in the *Cambridge Journal of Economics* in its 1987 volume illustrates both the growing mathematical divide within British economics and the persistence of traditional attitudes toward the issue. The editors of this publication created to defend a Cambridgian version of Keynesian economics against the neoclassical version popularized elsewhere, asked contributing authors to "use mathematics *only* when its application is a *necessary* condition for achieving the stated objective of the paper. When mathematics is used, the necessity for doing so should be explained, and the major steps in the argument and the conclusions made intelligible to a non-mathematical reader. Wherever possible, authors are encouraged to put the mathematical parts of their argument in an appendix."

"Intelligent Radicals"

> The soil in which nineteenth century British economics grew
> was liberal and utilitarian. Although utilitarianism is poten-
> tially the most authoritarian of all doctrines—no other contains

so total an injunction that the individual should sacrifice his welfare to that of the mass—, it is nonetheless linked to liberalism in that both spring from the same rationalistic roots. Being a liberal nearly always involves the belief that most people are—at least potentially—reasonable enough and the consequences of their use of reason predictable enough, to make paternalistic government intervention unnecessary. And being a utilitarian both induces and is induced by a rationalistic attitude to existing institutions; the ethical goal of the greatest happiness translates readily into a touchstone of institutional efficiency.

(Maloney 1985, 12)

One of the most important aims of this book is to specify how not just the institutional but also the intellectual framework of economics varies across nations. As part of this latter pursuit, we need to examine British economists' substantive and methodological preoccupations a bit more closely. Having explored the crystallization of British economics' scientific style, I thus turn now to the qustion of its substantive concerns. As in the other cases, we will look first and foremost at the social location and practical engagements of economists and particularly at their interactions with political institutions, in order to understand the kinds of questions that they end up engaging with, formalizing and arguing about.

One topic that received almost universal attention in the nineteenth century was the "social question," or the place of the new industrial classes in modern society. The first great social surveys (by Le Play in France, Booth in England, and the Verein für Sozialpolitik in Germany) had revealed to the middle-class public the horrendous living conditions of urban industrial workers. Concerned about the threat of class conflict, European elites (including conservative ones) found themselves at least partially aligned with burgeoning socialist movements in pushing for the adoption of a number of minimal social welfare measures. Settlement houses sprang up in England and the United States, moving educated young people to urban working-class neighborhoods to help "improve" the situation of the poor as well as society's knowledge and understanding of the poverty question.

Political economy was no stranger to these concerns and activities. In the United States many institutionalists, often following the example of their German teachers, were heavily involved in social reform. Social concerns were important in France as well, where a few prominent figures defended socialist or cooperativist views (Paul Cauwès and Léon Walras come to mind in the former case, Gide in the latter). But it was in England that these themes had the strongest appeal.

England, by then, could look back on a long tradition of poverty administration. The Elizabethan Poor Law (1601) and its successor, the Speenhamland system, had established England as the country where "compassion had become public policy" (Himmelfarb 1985, 4). The English upper classes, indeed, had come to care about poverty after wreaking havoc on much of the rural population's livelihood in the great enclosure movements.[69] But poor relief also had many detractors. Some of the most prominent classical political economists (Ricardo, Malthus, and Senior) fought it bitterly both on principle and over its particular implementation. [70] The New Poor Law of 1834, which made relief less accessible, paid less than the lowest paid and least attractive jobs on the market and imprisoned the poor in workhouses, signaled what Karl Polanyi has termed the "Great Transformation": the institutionalization of the idea of the self-regulating market in political economy and the broader society, and, consequently the scientific validation of the illegitimacy of human solidarity as a basis for social order. In England, Polanyi clearly saw, "pauperism, political economy and the discovery of society were closely interwoven" ([1944] 1957, 85).

This great evisceration, however, did not remove concerns about poverty from the center stage of British intellectual and political life. To the contrary: as Orloff and Skocpol point out, "the implementation of the New Poor Law called for administrative supervision and social planning on a national scale" and "inevitably and recurrently generated pressures for *national* debates, investigations, and policy changes" (1984, 740). These pressures intensified toward the end of the century as officials and public opinion worried that poor relief institutions dealt inadequately with the growing population of the "worthy" (i.e., working) poor.

Meanwhile, the position of political economists slowly shifted, too, partly because of the combined mobilization of factory law reformers, trade unions, and socialists of various types. One of the most famous economic writers of his age, John Stuart Mill, clearly departed from the Ricardian tradition in his attempt to "humanize" political economy. Though he stopped short of supporting a more equal distribution of income, Mill acknowledged that societies should be able to (and indeed often do) tamper with the distribution of wealth. A bit later, Alfred Marshall professed in the opening pages of his *Principles* that the question of "freeing all from the pains of poverty" is what "gives to economic studies their chief and their highest interest" (1890, 4). As a witness before the Royal Commission on the Aged Poor in 1893, he stated: "I have devoted myself for the last twenty-five years to the problem of poverty, and very little of my work has been devoted to any inquiry which does not bear upon that."[71] Marshall supported government intervention toward this goal, but argued that it should be minimal: for the most part, he believed in the ability of economic progress to eradicate poverty and stimulate "economic chivalry" among members of society (1907). His disciple Pigou started from almost the same ethical position: the beginning of economic science, he wrote, lies in "the social enthusiasm which revolts from the sordidness of mean streets and the joylessness of withered lives." ([1920] 1960, 5). Pigou, however, was braver than his mentor and ended up (following another contemporary of Marshall, Edgeworth) advocating for progressive taxation to improve the income distribution. He did so cautiously, however, because he did not trust the poor to use the money in a sensible manner.

At the root of these positions was the moral ethics of utilitarianism and its familiar dilemma, beautifully summarized by Maloney's quotation at the outset of this section. On the one hand, utilitarian arguments could support revolutionary ends, and especially redistribution, on the grounds that the "utility" of a shilling was higher for a poor person than for a rich person. They also suggested that individual welfare should be sacrificed for the sake of the mass. On the other hand, the liberal belief that only laissez-faire guarantees the maximum utility for all strongly limited the means available for achieving such ends.[72] Joan Robinson sharply criticized the Marshallian dilemma in the following terms: "Marshall, certainly, was a great moralizer but somehow the moral always came out that whatever is, is *very nearly* best. Pigou set out the argument of his *Economics of Welfare* in terms of exceptions to the rule that *laissez-faire* ensures maximum satisfaction; he did not question the rule" (1962, 74). Hence the economists' social consciousness, though alert and compassionate, would remain quiescent while capitalism chugged along unfettered.

To a large extent, the Keynesian formulation radically changed the terms of this debate. Keynes, obviously, was much more pessimistic about the ability of capitalism to deliver prosperity single-handedly. Keynes's great originality was his refusal simply to assume (as the Victorian economists had before him) that free markets would automatically deliver, save some adjustments, the highest possible welfare for the greatest number of people. For Keynes, human psychology was such that there was no guarantee that the movement of prices would allow the economic system to self-regulate. The problem of poverty thus got recast from a temporary but unavoidable condition to a systemic problem of capitalism: that of unemployment, that is, of lack of adjustment on the labor market.[73] And the reason for all this, shockingly, was that the rich might lose confidence and save too much! As Joan Robinson, again, put it: "The notion that saving is a cause of unemployment cut the root of the justification for unequal income as a source of accumulation" (1962, 75). Though he himself was not particularly outspoken on questions of redistribution, Keynes was a strong supporter of the Beveridge report (HMSO 1942), which established the foundations of the British welfare state. He was also instrumental in helping secure its approval among rather unenthusiastic Treasury officials.[74]

More important, however, Keynesian macroeconomics was the outcome of a particular ethical worldview. Since Adam Smith, British economists had been lamenting the stupefying effect of capitalism on the human mind. In that respect at least, Keynes was a true classical economist. As Skidelsky (1995) has shown, morality played a big role in his argument for securing full employment: full employment makes people happier by freeing them from material constraint and allowing them to better enjoy the true pleasures of life, such as the arts, nature, in short, leisure. (Indeed, Keynes was rather disdainful of material pleasures). One cannot understand his famous toast to the economists as "the trustees, not of civilization, but of the possibility of civilization" outside of his conception of these moral implications of macroeconomics, or outside of Keynes's confidence (no doubt socially and culturally determined) that civilization *can* be defended if the right people are in charge. We may mention Keynes's reaction to Hayek's *Road to Serfdom as a* good illustration of the latter. In a letter to Hayek following publication of the book, Keynes states that he finds himself "in a deeply moved agreement" with Hayek's depiction of a dark future should Britain proceed with a planned economy. But, he adds, "Moderate planning will be safe if those carrying it out are rightly orientated in their own minds and hearts to the moral issue. Dangerous acts can be done safely in a community which thinks and feels rightly, which would be the way to hell if they were executed by those who think and feel wrongly" (cited by Friedman 1997, 20).[75]

At just about the time when Keynes (and many of his contemporaries, such as Richard Kahn and Ralph Hawtrey) situated the terms of the ethical debate directly at the "macro" level (thereby circumventing the utilitarian problem of aggregating individual utilities), morality and economics were being disentangled in yet another way. The critique came from the London School of Economics, at the time a still young institution striving for legitimacy. Its chief architect, Lionel Robbins, was then the leading exponent of economic liberalism (though he later rallied to the Keynesian position). Robbins, who was strongly influenced by the logical positivism coming out of Austria at the time, argued that economic science should be defined so as to exclude ethical judgments.[76] As Backhouse (forthcoming) suggests, his target may have been more radical left-wing writers such as Hobson and Tawney, but his arguments against interpersonal comparisons of utilities could be used to mount a critique of the dominant Pigovian tradition. This is what a group of younger LSE faculty set out to do, claiming in the process to rebuild the subject on the basis of a new conception of utility that did not involve any interpersonal comparisons.

The idea was simple. Though utilities could not be compared, it was still possible to argue that an allocation of resources was more efficient than another if some people were better off and no one was worse off. The conditions for such an efficient allocation of resources, later named a Pareto optimum, were worked out during the early 1930s as part of the debate over whether socialist planning could be as efficient as capitalism, a debate in which Hayek was heavily involved. The problem was that the Pareto criterion was extremely weak, for changes that benefited one person would almost always make someone else worse off. So the LSE economists tried to argue that a change could still be a social improvement if those who gained could compensate the losers and still be better off.[77]

In addition to running into insurmountable technical problems, the project, known as the "new welfare economics," implied a considerable narrowing of the scope of economics. Questions of inequality could only be approached from the point of view of the efficiency (not the fairness) of the distribution of utilities. As Sen put it, a social state "can be Pareto optimal with some people in extreme misery and others rolling in luxury, so long as the miserable cannot be made better off without cutting into the utility of the rich" (1983, 32). Others were also quick to point out that the new approach threatened to completely "stultify" economics in its ability to say anything relevant to policy.[78] It also drastically reduced the space for discussions of *ethical* goals in the discipline, as Keynes, who generally disliked this literature, clearly saw.[79] This made British economists particularly pessimistic about the possibilities for the new approach, a feeling that two intellectual developments soon reinforced. The first one came out of the United States, when Kenneth Arrow established in the 1950s (while trying to work out a collective utility function for the Soviet Union at the Rand corporation) that, under a set of fairly reasonable ethical assumptions, it was impossible to derive social goals from individual goals without resorting to dictatorship. The second development was a LSE product and was more characteristically driven by the British economists' eagerness to contribute to policy debates. James Meade and two U.K.-educated economists, Richard Lipsey and Kevin Lancaster, showed in their "theory of the second best" that piecemeal reforms that caused the Pareto-optimality conditions to be satisfied in one part of the economy might reduce welfare if those conditions were violated elsewhere.[80] Given that it was easy to point to numerous violations of the Pareto-optimality conditions, this raised doubts about whether welfare economics could provide any general rules by which policies could be judged, thus vindicating a pragmatic, empirical approach to policy problems (that was also not predicated on the first-best assumption that free markets always provide the best solution).

In practice, many British economists thus continued to struggle to reconcile economic performance and efficiency with redistributive social goals. In the 1950s Kaldor justified redistribution on the grounds that wealth inequalities diminish effective demand. In the next generation, Anthony Atkinson, a Cambridge-trained economist working from within a tradition inaugurated by Hugh Dalton at the LSE during the interwar period, developed new ways to measure inequality and justified greater equality in the distribution of income as a mechanism of insurance in a world where future income is uncertain. By and large, then, practical economists continued to operate in a Marshallian world where utilities (and therefore policies) are comparable, at least partially. James Mirrlees's work on optimal taxation, a doctoral thesis in Cambridge in 1963, also derives from a straightforward utilitarian position, beginning with the question of "which feasible redistributive system yields the greatest total utility" (in this case, the best social distribution of skill).[81] My interviewees (in all countries) repeatedly singled out British economists' distinctive contribution to the study of public finance and inequality, poverty and development, and their sometimes important influence on policy in these domains (see, for instance, the role of Dalton, Kaldor and Meade).[82]

A second line of attack against the scientistic critique of welfare economics focused on reconsidering the ethical assumptions of the discipline and reaffirming the historical relationships between economics and philosophy, which had traditionally been strong at Oxford, with its undergraduate degree in philosophy, politics, and economics. The reformulation of welfare economics and social choice theory on *ethical* grounds motivated, for instance, the search for alternative criteria to economic efficiency as a metric for judging and measuring social welfare. Little's emphasis on the capacity for individual choice, Sen's "capability" approach and Dasgupta's emphasis on well-being each exemplify a distinctively British tradition, also rooted in the country's particular colonial history, that places the ethical aspects of economic problems squarely in the foreground.[83] As Deaton (2007) has recently and very succinctly argued, the recent divide between the British and American economic approaches to global warming might be just another instance of these broader cultural differences.[84]

Economics' familiar dilemma between equity and efficiency was certainly always implicit in the discipline's utilitarian DNA; but it played out, and still plays out, differently in different national contexts. Certainly moral issues were also relevant in the American case, yet they had a different object. Moral evil in American economics comes less from the concentration of income than from insufficient market competition (which leads to the concentration of *capital* and unfair practices by business). As early as 1899, John Bates Clark, for instance, declared that the distribution of income in society was controlled by the natural law of marginal productivity, which gives to each man the product of his labor. American economists eschewed a direct confrontation with the problems of poverty and inequality until the 1960s, and even then their policy positions were rather ambivalent, as Steensland (2007) has brilliantly shown. Writing about the early post–World War II period, Daniel Rodgers remains astonished at the failure of the Beveridge report to make an impact among those same American readers who had been so keen to take up the language of the Keynesian multiplier: "Their eyes fixed on the frontiers of growth, the prophets of managed aggregate demand could barely disguise their irritation with Beveridge's preoccupation with poverty" (1998, 500).[85]

British economists, by contrast, continued to see the incorporation of the lower classes as a morally and economically relevant problem, and the devastations waged by the war only strengthened this goal. James Meade, for instance, titled one of his books *The Intelligent Radical's Guide to Economic Policy* and articulated what could serve as a much more general credo for the British economics profession in the postwar period: "The intelligent radical is at heart an incurable egalitarian and is appalled by the gross inequalities which he observes in modern society. But he desires to cope with them by methods which are compatible with the maintenance of a free and an efficient economic system" (1975, 68).[86]

The claim was unambiguously one of expertise. That expertise, however, could work to address certain chosen social aims, which legitimated policy and even political involvement. Economic theory, in the British context, was always to be cultivated not for its own sake but for its ability to guide public policy in the reasoned service of certain moral ideals. Policy and politics were always very much a part of the British economist's world, even after the process of scientific "disciplining." Following Keynes's remark that economists ought to be useful people, "much like dentists," an entire generation of economists who had come of age between the world wars put a commitment to progressive policy at the center of their own "professional" vocation.[87] Keynes himself, of course, was a master at navigating policy networks. He worked through every channel available to him: press articles, government committees, club chambers and the (often unsolicited) memorandums he tirelessly dashed off to government officials and political leaders. Meade, of whom Middleton says that his "influence on policy remains unsurpassed, at home and abroad" (1998, 169), repeatedly described his "main concern in economics" to be located in the "contribution which economic analysis has to make to the solutions of problems of economic policy," and was a founding member of the U.K. Social Democratic Party.[88] Even Britain's most distinguished theorist, John Hicks, derided the "science of exchange" he had contributed to: "There is more to life than just catallactics. . . . While we can accept the help of the catallactist, we need not leave him the last word."[89]

Classics and Moderns

The authority structure of British economics started to break down as a result of two trends: first, the democratization of the higher education system, and second, the migration of intellectual leadership in the field away from England and toward the United States. This transfer of influence, which took place between the 1940s and 1960s, corresponded, on the one hand, to the rising star of the neoclassical synthesis in America against its institutionalist precursors and, on the other hand, to the leftist evolution of a number of Cantabrigian economists, which culminated in the "capital controversies" between Keynesians in Cambridge, England, and Cambridge, Massachusetts. The advent of the neoclassical synthesis not only made modeling and econometrics the cornerstone of economic literacy but also reduced the Keynesian approach to a special case of neoclassical theory. Hence although Keynes's economics was exported from Britain to the United States in the 1930s, it was then marketed back to Europe as "Keynesian economics" in the 1940s and 1950s.[90] In my interviews, I collected numerous commentaries on this critical episode in the intellectual history of the British economics profession. British economists' accounts of the rise of American authority and of the concomitant decline of British leadership in economics are replete with cynicism and resignation:

> (People in Cambridge) did not accept (the rise of American economics). . . . Somebody once said: "We thought of ourselves that Cambridge was the center of the universe, that King's College was the center of Cambridge, and Keynes the center of King's." And that persisted. There was an enormous arrogance. (professor, University of Cambridge, June 1997)

> The British attitude was to look down upon the Americans. In the United States, they met second-rate civil servants whereas they were used to the very high personal quality of the British civil service. The American civil service is more open, more fluid. I think the British did not understand American society. . . . The key shift in influence happened toward the end of the 1950s. There are some people whose rep-

utation did not really cross the Atlantic, like Joan Robinson, Nicky Kaldor, Richard Kahn—all the militant Keynesians. Those people had the feeling that Britain was the center of pathbreaking ideas. Joan Robinson told me one day: "Why have the Americans forgotten all that we taught them?" That was bastard Keynesianism for her. (professor, University of Sussex, June 1997)

The neoclassical synthesis, which had developed across the Atlantic, was now perceived by a certain segment of the British economics profession as the Trojan horse of American imperialism. Conflict crystallized around the question of how to measure capital. The British Cantabridgians argued that there is no metric that is independent of the rate of profit, which proves that neoclassical growth theory is tautological. This point, first raised by Joan Robinson, argued by the Cantabrigian economist Piero Sraffa (1960) in a short but influential book, and defended by others in countless publications, seemed for a while to constitute the definitive intellectual weapon through which some in Cambridge (England) would reassert their predominance, debunk the neoclassical theory of growth once and for all, and reclaim what they now saw as the convergent legacies of Keynes and Marx.[91] Instead, as Hodgson (1997) has shown, the controversy over the aggregation of capital was largely ignored by the mainstream, for ideological as well as practical reasons (the Cambridge proposition was impossible to model and its empirical implications could not be observed), and died out rapidly. Within Britain, however, the influence of left-wing Cantabridgians remained strong, though not undivided. Soon, old and new generations of self-identified "Cambridge economists" found themselves torn over the legacy of Keynesianism and the economic strategies to be derived from it.

With Cambridge partially marginalized, as symbolized by the *Economic Journal's* relocation from Cambridge to Oxford in 1971,[92] the London School of Economics became a pivotal force in the transformation of British economics. A relatively new and specialized school, it had always been more cosmopolitan, and had been an important center of (relative) resistance to Keynesian ideas during the 1930s and 1940s after a host of Continental scholars (among them Austrian economist Friedrich Hayek) immigrated there. Between 1945 and 1995, 40 percent of the LSE staff with a doctorate were U.S.-trained, including many Americans.[93] The school's *Review of Economic Studies* (started by a group of "young Turks" in the 1930s) epitomized this international orientation. Being elected to its editorial board, one interviewee recounted, was an "honor, it was some measure of the fact that you were one of the young people who was really doing good stuff" (professor, U.S. Ivy League University, June 1999). By the late 1970s, LSE had established a position of leadership in the social sciences that matched Oxford's dominance in the humanities and Cambridge's hegemony in the natural sciences. In a 1976 survey of British university and polytechnics teachers, 49.8 percent of respondents selected the London School of Economics as the best economics department, in the country, well ahead of Cambridge (20.3 percent) and Oxford (7 percent).[94]

The LSE also became a feeder institution for the new establishments created as part of the postwar move toward mass higher education. Richard Lipsey, for instance, a Canadian-born economist with a PhD from LSE gave up a chair at LSE to build the economics department at the University of Essex.[95] By the 1960s, American graduate schools and journals had already established their control over international prestige hierarchies in economics. Some of the new universities in Britain set up advanced programs that sought to emulate the structure of American higher degrees. Essex was the first department to introduce a "taught" MA in economics, an innovation that older schools had been resisting until then. LSE quickly followed suit. The University of Warwick opted for a similar strategy of research specialization and advanced training, while other departments such as Sussex stuck more closely to the old model of liberal education.[96]

The democratization of higher training thus made possible the emergence of new institutional niches that relied on the standards of American-style professionalism to promote their position within the field. Oxford and especially Cambridge had less incentive to follow these norms, partly because their prestige insulated them from competitive pressures. But criticism was mounting, linking Britain's flagging economic performance to its outdated higher education institutions and specifically targeting the practice of recruiting civil servants from socially privileged Oxbridge graduates with arts degrees. Change took place first at Oxford, which had not been spared by either the Robbins report (1963) or the internal Franks inquiry (1966). In 1965 a joint degree in economics and engineering was introduced, which symbolically marked the disentanglement "of technical economics from its traditional chrysalis of all-round political economy" (Harris 1994, 244). After his arrival at Oxford in 1968, James Mirrlees used his entrepreneurial skill, mathematical background, and international connections to transform the postgraduate BPhil (now renamed MPhil) into an intensive, research-oriented degree. Microeconomics at Oxford went from being qualitative and applied to being quantitative and formal. Curricular reform at Cambridge, by contrast, was delayed until the 1990s, and was implemented amid general intellectual warfare.[97]

The anti-establishment and pro-market research policies of the 1980s, to which economics as a discipline was particularly vulnerable, accelerated the challenge to traditional hierarchies and the reconstruction of the intellectual environment around a more narrowly professional model. Among the changes deserving mention is the (absolute) contraction in university budgets and available research funds and the (relative) contraction in salaries, as well as the general reorientation of funding toward knowledge defined as socially "useful." These transformations created a difficult climate within universities, and many British economists left for the United States during this period. As figure 3-4 shows, the Royal Economic Society's membership declined sharply, although admittedly the downward trend had started sometime in the early 1970s.

The introduction (in 1986) of the Research Assessment Exercises, which institutionalized competition between universities and departments by linking the provision of public funds to research output, created further tensions. In the tightly controlled field of economics, this policy seems to have furthered the marginalization of heterodox scholarship (such as post-Keynesianism), which was incapable of raising its profile in an international pecking order defined largely by the U.S.-dominated mainstream (Harley and Lee 1997; Lee and Harley 1998). What is often understood as the "Americanization" of British economics was thus deeply embedded in very specific national processes, including a dynamic of democratization within the field of higher education and transformations in the relationship between government and academia. These changes both strained the traditional patterns of academic authority and helped further the more narrowly professional logics associated with the U.S. model.

ADMINISTRATORS AND SPECIALISTS

To a large extent, changes within the state administration in Britain followed a similar institutional path. As the highbrow approach to economic science that prevailed at the beginning of the century progressively gave way to a more narrowly defined academic practice, the genteel tradition of the civil service was also profoundly transformed by the rise of economic specialists in its midst. But this change was a much more contested process than similar trends in the United States (where state institutions actively encouraged skill specialization) or even in France (where state institutions sought to produce their own specialists). The history of British administration, by contrast, is the history of the still ongoing struggle to maintain the mandarin dominion.

This struggle centered around two points of contention. First, British administrators, who were steeped in a culture that had traditionally rewarded classical erudition and communication skills, remained suspicious of the technical machinery developed by economists.[98] Second, traditional civil servants saw the practice adopted by several governments of obtaining economic advice by setting up nondepartmental structures staffed with outsiders and linked directly to the cabinet as a threat to their prerogative and impartiality. And rightly so: many of these organizational innovations were indeed aimed at contesting the Treasury's bias toward financial orthodoxy by promoting more daring approaches to policy, such as planning or incomes policy.

These strategies generally failed, however. None of the agencies created in such a fashion proved durable. Some were absorbed into the Treasury (as the Economic Section or the Central Economic Planning Staff in the 1940s and 1950s); others were simply dismantled and their responsibilities dispersed (as happened with the Department of Economic Affairs (1964–70) and the more generalist Central Policy Review Staff, the cabinet's permanent think tank from 1971 to 1983). Over the long run, then, the power of the Treasury within Whitehall has remained largely secure, but this stability in the structure of British public officialdom partly masks some significant changes in the making of public officials themselves.

The Normalization of Irregulars

Unlike the United States, Britain did not develop a permanent staff of government economists until well after World War II. Civil servants taught in the liberal tradition of Oxbridge—primarily Modern History or Greats at Oxford—often possessed little, if any, formal economic training. Economic advice came mostly from the few officials who had developed a solid expertise in economic and financial matters at the Treasury, the Bank of England, or the Board of Trade, and from powerful actors in industry, banking, and finance. (The City was always especially prominent.) Bank of England networks, for instance, are usually regarded as responsible for the disastrous decision to restore the prewar gold parity of the pound in 1925.

Prior to World War I, there is little evidence that British administrators held the "modern" conception of the economy as an entity that should be fixed and manipulated. Nevertheless, some university dons, Treasury civil servants, and businessmen had begun to consider "expertise" in economic matters as a distinct area of competence. Economists and statisticians were more vocal in their demands, too, and publicly petitioned the government to establish an economic general staff in the cabinet and to improve official statistics.[99] A small number of economic experts served in the Treasury during World War I, including Keynes, William Beveridge, and Hubert Henderson. Keynes also advised the British delegation at the Versailles treaty conference in 1919. By the end of the war, however, officials were eager to return to the prewar model of a small "watchman state" and to the more arm's-length pattern that had previously characterized British administrative culture. When they needed economic advice, officials preferred to rely upon traditional resources—personal networks of trusted people, royal commissions, and public inquiries—rather than on specialized professional staff.[100] Still, the idea of coordinating important social research through government (as was already being done in the natural sciences) had supporters, particularly in Labour circles. In 1924 a project to create a standing interdepartmental body to conduct inquiries on economic and social issues took shape by the initiative of Prime Minister Ramsay MacDonald and his Lord Chancellor, Lord Haldane. The government ultimately did not follow through on the scheme, but its conservative successor seized on the idea, shifting the emphasis toward imperial development and scientific issues. The Committee of Civil Research was formed in 1925 and instigated a number of important industrial and scientific investigations.[101]

Throughout the 1920s, Britain faced chronic unemployment problems that only intensified with the outbreak of the Great Depression. Shortly after the 1929 election, Labour prime minister Ramsay MacDonald, resurrecting his plans from 1924, assembled a small group of economists (Keynes, R. H. Tawney, and G. D. H. Cole) and industrialists in order to help his government face the deepening slump. This Economic Advisory Council (EAC; 1930–39) was the first structure concerned exclusively with the provision of economic advice at the center of British government. It was supposed to act as a true "think tank," reporting directly to the cabinet by means of special committees.[102]

In spite of its unprecedented institutional location and its rather impressive membership (subcommittees included such influential figures as Henry Clay, Hubert Henderson, Arthur Pigou, Lionel Robbins, and Dennis Robertson), the EAC ultimately failed to have a significant influence on policy. Differences in opinion among economists were a major problem. Internal divisions—between Keynes and Robbins in particular—were in fact so strong and irreconcilable that the Economic Advisory Council was incapable of formulating any policy advice during the 1931 crisis. It did not help that the traditional civil service was reluctant to grant nondepartmental organizations any measure of authority. The upshot was that British governments remained largely dependent on Treasury advice (and thus on Treasury orthodoxy regarding balanced budgets and currency stability) throughout the Great Depression, in spite of the violent criticisms of some economists, Keynes chief among them.[103]

As elsewhere, World War II dramatically changed this situation as military pressures prompted the government to undertake such interventionist expedients as manpower planning and the control of raw materi-

als and prices, sometimes against the judgment of professional economists. The ranks of the civil service swelled (the elite Administrative
Class, for instance, more than doubled during the war, to 4,900 members). The war cabinet itself housed a separate advisory body, the Central Economic Intelligence Service, which evolved into two distinct services in 1941, the Economic Section for coordinating general economic
policy, and the Central Statistical Office for data collection. These organizations relied more explicitly than their forerunners on specialized expertise, and particulary on academics. (LSE professor Lionel Robbins directed the Economic Section, which also included Alec Cairncross,
Donald MacDougall, Kit McMahon, James Meade, Richard Stone, and
Austin Robinson.) In addition to the Economic Section's novel institutional approach, economists and statisticians were also drafted into regular Whitehall departments (e.g., Keynes, Henderson, Robertson, and
Lord Catto in the Treasury). All told, Alec Cairncross suggests, "there
were at least fifty officials in Whitehall who had at one time or another
been university teachers in economics."[104]

For these reasons, Roger Middleton (1998) argues that the war and the
work of the Economic Section can be deemed the heyday of economists'
influence in government, as the "dons" were for the first time associated
with the formulation of policy at the highest levels, in the cabinet itself.
In contrast to the United States, however, where the drive to incorporate
professional expertise continued after the war with the creation of the
Council of Economic Advisers and with a vast influx of economists into
government service, Britain's wartime Economic Section soon receded in
prominence. Although the organization continued to attract young academics through the postwar years, most of the professors who had been
drawn into government service during the conflict quietly and willingly
returned to their university departments as soon as it ended.

> They wanted to get back to academic life. They had had six years
> away, and that is a long time; I think they felt: "this is all very well
> in wartime." You could really make your own way in wartime. You
> could really make your own career. But in peacetime you were going
> to be part of a solid structure, and unless you get in the right post to
> begin with you may find it very difficult. Nearly all the Economic Sec-
> tion disappeared and went back to their universities. Lionel Robbins
> wasn't going to stay on, and James Meade wasn't going to stay on. . . .
> No, it was a great problem finding anybody for any of these jobs in
> the immediate post-war period. (Sir Alec Cairncross, interview in
> Tribe 1997, 50)[105]

After the war, then, the Treasury rapidly regained its preeminence over
the cabinet in the conduct of economic policy,[106] overcoming a short-lived

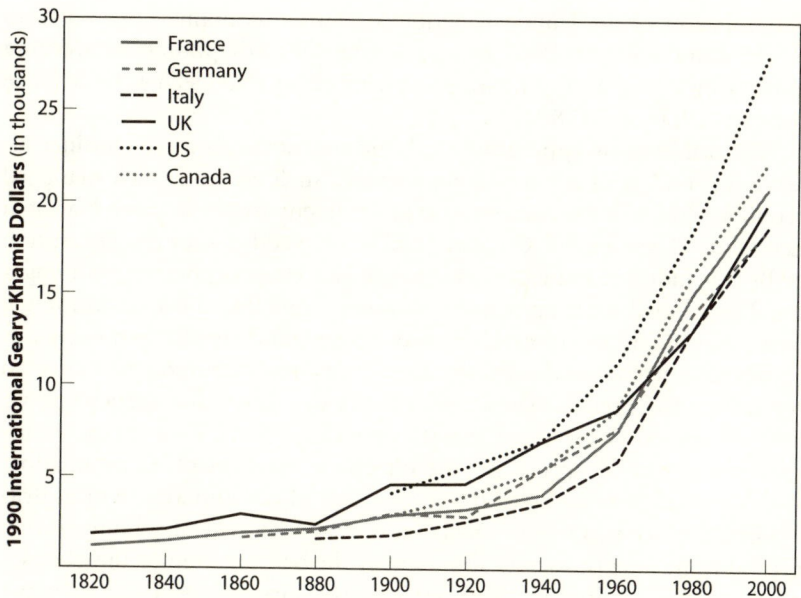

Figure 3-5. GDP per capita, selected countries, 1820–2000.
Source: Angus Maddison, *The World Economy, Historical Statistics,* 2001.

attempt by the Labour government to create a Ministry of Economic Affairs and institutionalize planning through the creation of the Central Economic Planning Staff.[107] The Economic Section lived on, although its function changed from advising the cabinet to advising the chancellor on matters of macroeconomic policy. One of its chief functions was now to prepare economic forecasts for the budget, and it was finally integrated into the Treasury in 1953. Despite continuing hostility from "generalist" public administrators against economic "specialists," there is ample evidence that this modestly sized structure and its fewer than twenty staff members contributed to the diffusion of a new economic culture in British government. Economic specialists started being recruited away to other Treasury divisions, even transferring to administrative grades.[108]

The 1960s saw intensifying public criticisms of British administrative culture as archaic and incapable of facing the challenges of modernity. This was the consequence of a seemingly inexorable relative decline in the postwar British economy as evidenced by slow growth rates and continuing weakness in manufacturing. While the British economy experienced uninterrupted growth in output during the period, its poor performance relative to some of its European neighbors and former colonies was a considerable source of dismay. Figure 3-5 illustrates the striking deterioration of the United Kingdom's relative economic position from world dominance in 1900 to one of the OECD's poorest-performing nations in 1980. As the figure shows, much of that decline took place between 1960 and 1980.

This situation prompted political and industrial elites to consider alternative models of economic governance, such as the French managed economy. In 1961 the conservative government established the National Economic Development Council (NEDC or Neddy) after the Federation of British Industry indicated its interest in giving corporatist planning a try. The council built up a large economic staff, hired on a contractual basis, commissioned research to universities, and set up committees to gather data from social partners. But it was never able to come close to replicating the French experience. On the one hand, the agency's proximity to central government threatened its legitimacy vis-à-vis the industrial world and compromised the effectiveness of its planning mission, which was already complicated by the lack of coordination within British industry itself. On the other hand, even the central administration proved to be unenthusiastic about either the organization or the philosophy that had inspired its creation. The Treasury, in particular, saw any hint of activism as a menace to its privileged position within Whitehall. This contrasts tellingly with the French Ministry of Finance, which happily used the planning agency as a vehicle for its own influence and received broad support from the industry for it.[109]

The problems of the NEDC were further compounded by the election of the Wilson government in 1964, which raised fears of *dirigisme* and also stripped Neddy of its jurisdiction over national economic development. Since the early 1960s, the Labour Party had resolved upon a renewed approach to economic management that emphasized the scientific and technical aspect of administrative practice and promoted long-term planning as a tool for achieving growth. Many members of Wilson's government were well acquainted with economics and economists. Harold Wilson himself had studied PPE at Oxford. Before starting a political career, he had been successively an Oxford fellow in economics, a member of the Economic Section, and president of the Board of Trade (1947–51).[110] PPE graduates and Oxford dons (Roy Jenkins, Donald MacDougall, Douglas Jay, Thomas Balogh) populated his administration and advising circles, and some ministers shared Wilson's enthusiasm for economists' input into policy making. Barbara Castle at the Ministry of Transport, a passionate socialist, was instrumental in raising the profile and number of economic specialists in her own administration.

One of Wilson's most ambitious administrative innovations was the centralization of all government economic expertise within the new Department of Economic Affairs in 1964. Largely the brainchild of

Wilson's special economic adviser, Oxford economist Thomas Balogh, the new institution was expected to provide a counterweight to the Treasury on long-term policy orientations and to help formulate the National Plan. Balogh, who as a young man had emigrated from Hungary, violently attacked Treasury mandarins as "dilettantes."[111] The DEA rapidly built up a staff of economists, many of them directly drawn from the National Economic Development Office (the staff base of the NEDC). Interestingly, however, the "creative tension" which the Labour government had expected to generate between the Department of Economic Affairs and the Treasury amounted to little in practice. As conflicts between the two institutions developed over the conduct of policy, it became apparent that the Treasury and the Bank of England remained the true centers of power. In 1966, they had the Plan scrapped and the deflationary measures implemented to counter a mounting sterling crisis. The DEA's economists strongly recommended a devaluation of the sterling, but this was sharply opposed by the Bank of England and key government members who did not want to be associated with the loss of value of the currency. Ultimately, devaluation could not be avoided and finally took place in 1967. That symbolic victory, however, was insufficient to save the DEA, which was folded in 1969.[112]

The failure of the DEA and the shrinking of the NEDC into little more than a discussion forum revealed not only the difficulty of challenging the preeminence of the Treasury and the Bank of England in economic matters but also the persistence, well into the "Keynesian" age, of a rather conservative economic philosophy at the center of British administration. Being a purely financial institution, not an agent of economic development (in contrast to the French postwar Ministry of Finance, for instance), the Treasury tended to focus consistently on controlling public spending and defending the pound rather than on promoting economic growth. On the eve of the Thatcher era, which swept away much of the remaining interest on this point,[113] Heclo and Wildavsky (1974) argued that the Treasury had never truly cared about economic growth.

Economizing Whitehall

It is thus elsewhere that one must turn to find the long-term legacy of the institutional changes wrought during the 1960s and 1970s. Certainly the shift toward greater specialization within the civil service—and, in particular, the further institutionalization of a core of economists within Whitehall—merits special attention. First, career civil servants began receiving training in economics and statistics. In 1963 the Center for Administrative Studies opened for this purpose, later (in 1970) becoming the Civil Service College. Second, specialist grades underwent massive

expansion. As mentioned previously, most government economic specialists during the formative years of the Economic Section were not
"career" civil servants but temporary appointees whose place and primary allegiance were rather ill defined. Their rather pejorative nickname
of "irregulars" conveyed the suspicion that they were nothing but political birds of passage. Hence, the creation in 1964 of the Government
Economic Service (GES) as a distinct civil service class providing govern-
ment-wide organization for the management of economists' careers represented an important turning point (the Government Statistical Service
had already been in existence since World War II). Now economic specialists could have a civil service career through the GES. Figure 3-6a
shows the marked expansion of the Government Economic Service over
time, particularly under Labour administrations (1964–70, 1974–79,
1997–2007); Figure 3-6b shows its diffusion throughout government
ministries. Whereas in 1964 GES members were exclusively found in the
Department of Economic Affairs and the Treasury, by the late 1960s
there were large concentrations of economic specialists in such places as

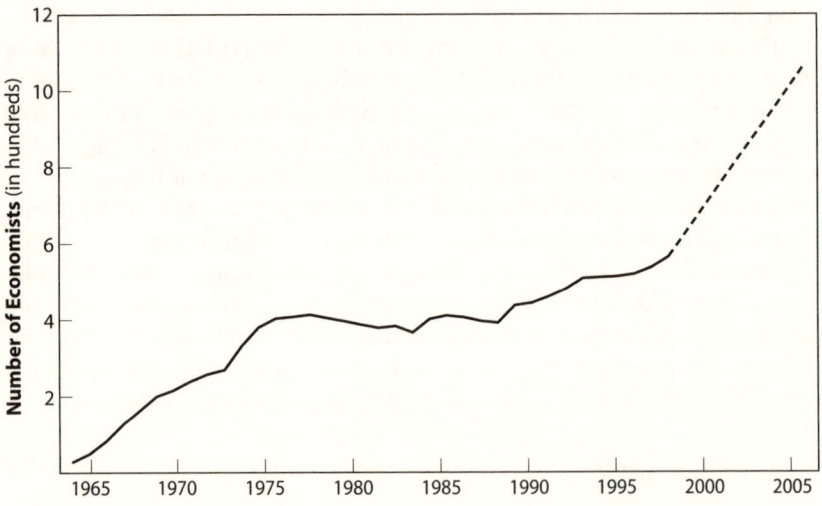

Figure 3-6a. Number of economists in the Government Economic Service,
1964–2007.
Source: Government Economic Service. Data were obtained for 1964–99, with
an update in 2007. *For presentation purposes only,* data for 2000–6 was extrap-
olated from 1999 and 2007 figures, assuming a constant growth rate over the
period. While the Government Economic Service doubled between 1998 and
2007, the civil service *as a whole* grew by only about 17 percent (data for Civil
Service staff in post obtained from the civil service online statistics).

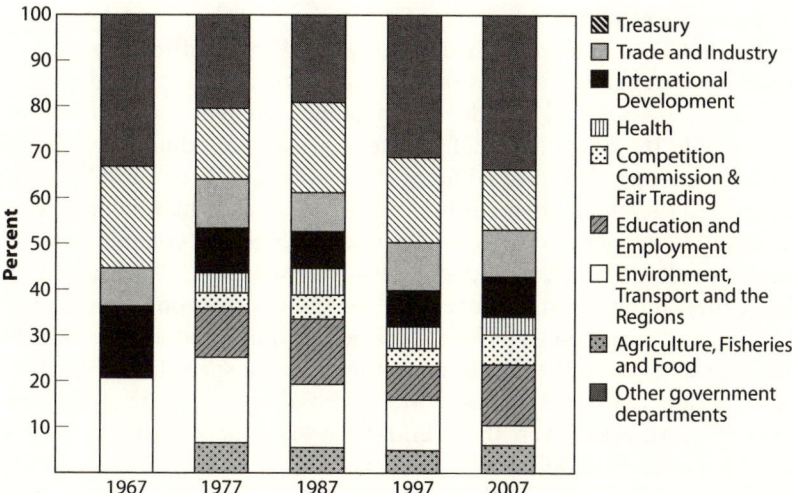

Figure 3-6b. Composition of the Government Economic Service, ten-year intervals (1967, 1977, 1987, 1997, 2007).

Source: Government Economic Service. I am deeply grateful to Tracie Humphrey at the Economist Group Management Unit (HM Treasury), and Alison Cookson-Hall (Government Economic Service), who provided me with these data.

the Departments of Education and Employment, Trade and Industry, or Transport and the Environment (the latter even had—for a while—more economists than the Treasury itself). These figures also show that the GES expanded much more slowly under conservative governments (and even shrank under Margaret Thatcher, who downsized the entire civil service), specifically in those departments not favored by the government, such as the Ministry of the Environment headed by Michael Heseltine. In fact, the GES grew fastest during the Blair premiership, nearly doubling in size between 1999 and 2007.[114]

If a flirtation with planning and liberal corporatism had been the prime reasons for the rise of government economic expertise in the 1960s, its expansion in the 1970s was driven by the diffusion of cost-benefit analysis and the campaign to rationalize government structures and operations. The Plowden report (HMSO 1961) on public expenditure control and especially the Fulton report on the Civil Service (HMSO 1968) helped launch a debate over the professionalization of administrative work. In a direct attack on the classicists who dominated the Civil Service, the Fulton committee denounced the service's amateur philosophy and acerbically advocated a "preference for relevance" in the recruitment of the administrative class, particularly for those who were to fill Treasury posts. Evidence reviewed by Geoffrey Fry (1990), however, suggests that the Fulton committee's main recommendation to hire specialists with higher degrees remained contentious both within and outside the committee. Of course, civil service administrators defended their turf. But even some of those who had been most vocal in castigating the amateurish culture of the mandarins, like Balogh, were not ready to do away with the well-rounded generalist; committee members generally felt that the existing means of selection, which relied on the quality of the institution of origin much more than on the subject of training, still managed to pick the best people quite well. Ultimately, the government rejected the idea of recruiting relevant specialists in favor of more modest steps such as post-entry remedial training in the social sciences. Nevertheless, even these initiatives, of which the Civil Service College is one instance, were by all accounts rather ineffective. Administrators continued to dominate policy making, and the management and training of government specialists remained in the hands of individual departments rather than being administered in a centralized manner. (The Civil Service Department was short-lived.) In the 1990s, government departments also began to sponsor skill upgrading among their recruits. The GES and the Bank of England were especially proactive in sending their recruits back to university so that they could meet the technical expectations of their occupational position.[115] Discussing the Department of Trade and Industry's policy of giving people the opportunity to get a MSc while drawing full pay, one of my interviewees added, "We usually prefer [to send them to] LSE or Warwick, because they are more technical" (economist, Department of Trade and Industry, June 1997).[116] Finally, at the top level, we can point to a modest "economicization" of the culture of the generalist senior civil service as economics-based programs such as PPE became a more common avenue into Whitehall, specialists proliferated in higher grades, and some of them even moved into administration.[117]

Social Closeness versus Government Closure

The Government Economic Service amounts to no more than a functional differentiation—a separate hierarchy—within the British public administration. (In that sense, it is not unlike the position of "economist" in the U.S. civil service or that of the INSEE administrator in France.) In contrast to the U.S. Council of Economic Advisers or Germany's Sachverständigenrat, however, British economic specialists rarely occupy highly visible official positions and tend to be confined to more obscure advisory roles. Nor does the administrative civil service possess the kind of institutional coherence provided by the French École Nationale d'Administration, where all generalist administrators (the *énarques*) go through a common education that includes some measure of economic training. France has public policy specialists who are deemed able to do well anywhere their competencies are applied. In Britain, being a generalist means something quite different; it refers to the broad-ranging culture people bring to the job, even when that job remains quite specialized.

From the beginning of the twentieth century, economists have been routinely called upon as members of or expert witnesses for royal commissions and committees of inquiry.[118] Although powerless to make actual decisions, these institutions had an important impact in altering the terms of debate on the issues they dealt with. The history of British economic policy is peppered with landmark blue books and commission reports bearing the name of a famous economist (the Beveridge report, the Robbins report on education, and the Meade report on taxation are notable examples). Second, as in the United States, the fact that governments need to recruit people who are not career civil servants into advisory positions has become completely taken for granted in Britain. On that basis, individual economists from academia or business have been drawn into core Whitehall departments (e.g., at the Treasury, the Board of Trade/Department of Trade and Industry, the Monopolies and Mergers Commission, the Office of Fair Trading) and at the Bank of England. All the directors of the Economic Section from 1939 to 1953 were academics. All the chief economic advisers to HMG Treasury since 1953 were former economics teachers, except for the most recent one, Ed Balls. The Treasury has consulted special academic panels on forecasting since 1976, and the Bank of England has had a Monetary Policy Committee that includes important academic figures as well as a large research department since it was granted independence in 1997. More important, perhaps, British economists have been prominently involved in policy through their role outside the regular framework of the career civil service as "special advisers" to politicians and political parties. Harold Wilson during his two governments (1964–70 and 1974–76) and Margaret Thatcher (1979–92), both of whom had their reasons to be suspicious of Treasury expertise, made especially conspicuous use of these positions.[119] And it is certainly not an exaggeration to say that several of the major British economists in the twentieth century, including John Maynard Keynes, James Meade, Hubert Henderson, Roy Harrod, and later Nicholas Kaldor, Thomas Balogh, Wyn Godley, Alan Walters, Tony Atkinson, or John Eatwell also served as lifetime political advisers. Kaldor, for instance, advised the Labour Party through the 1950s and then three Labour chancellors in the 1960s and 1970s. He was a major presence in tax policy debates not only in Britain but also throughout the developing world.

Many of the connections between academics, businessmen, civil servants, and politicians were formed during their college years, and sometimes even earlier. Due to the prominent role of Oxbridge in the training of the higher civil service, relations between these institutions are natural, and actively maintained by both. Public officials, for instance, routinely turn to their former teachers in universities for research and advice, both formally and informally. Also, in contrast to the United States, a stint in a government department such as the Treasury or the Bank of England is not uncommon as a prelude to an academic career, especially in applied fields.[120] In a situation where advanced graduate education was long barely existent, these institutions served a training purpose and conferred a great prestige. The Bank of England, in fact, has a long tradition of being an institutional bridge between academic and policy careers, with elite professors serving in top administrative and advice capacities for prolonged periods of time.[121]

Such relationships are maintained mostly through personal connections, associations, clubs, and political organizations. In its early incarnation, for instance, the Royal Economic Society provided a place of engagement and contact between the worlds of policy, science, and business. Despite its name, the RES started as much more than an academic forum. Its first president in 1892 was then chancellor of the exchequer, George Goschen, and its first four vice presidents were all members of Parliament. This contrasts markedly with the United States, where the American Economic Association was from its outset the nearly exclusive province of professors. As the studies by Coats and Coats (1970, 1973) have shown, the RES was headed by a nonacademic figure until 1928, and the practice of having prominent policy makers in the society's leadership positions continued well into the postwar period.[122] Individuals from the public and private sectors (e.g., business and banking) constituted the dominant fraction of the membership until at least the 1960s. Although this is no longer true (in 1994 academics represented more than 60 percent of the Society's membership),[123] other important organizations play a similar social role. Since its founding in 1983, for instance, the Center for Economic Policy Research, a network of several hundred academic economists worldwide (but dominated by scholars from the United Kingdom and the United States), actively seeks to animate economic and policy discussion among the "intelligent public" (as one interviewee put it, referring mostly to civil servants, influential businessmen, and journalists). Through conferences, media outreach, and projects commissioned by public and research institutions (including many associated with the European Commission), this "think net" tries to stir public debates by producing reports on the hot policy topics of the day. Again, this contrasts significantly with the more sober public stance and conscientious political neutrality of its U.S. equivalent, the NBER.[124]

ECONOMIC PERSUASION

Active engagement in political debates is hardly new to British economists. The history of the nineteenth century is filled with high-profile policy controversies involving important intellectual figures. The Ricardians of the first half of the nineteenth century were perhaps the first group to present themselves as experts on economic issues and be recognized as such by the larger public.[125] But in more recent periods, it has not been uncommon for university economists to issue public statements in the media when they felt they had something important to say, whether or not their input was solicited. Middleton, for instance, shows that out of twenty-four key British economists alive in 1914, nineteen of whom were academics, seven gave policy advice, thirteen engaged in journalism, and twelve advocated for particular policies.[126] Some, like John Hobson, were wildly successful writers. These patterns were also common during the interwar period. Keynes, Beveridge, Henderson, and Harrod, for instance, were all involved with the Liberal Party and worked actively in its committees and summer schools (Harrod later switched to the Conservative Party). Keynes was a particularly prolific pamphleteer, writing on every hot topic of the day. Outstanding examples of his broadsides include his devastating critiques of the German reparations (*The Economic Consequences of Peace*, 1919) and of Churchill's decision to return to the gold standard (*The Economic Consequences of Mr Churchill*, 1925). His *Can Lloyd George Do It?*, written with Hubert Henderson in 1929, became the textbook of the 1930 Liberal campaign.[127]

Economists of an even more leftist bent also made their voices heard in British politics. The forerunner of the Labour Party, the Fabian Society, had always associatied social reform with efficient administration seeking to make rational use of economic knowledge. This conviction had prompted the Fabians to sponsor the establishment of the London School of Economics in 1895.[128] After its creation in 1906, the Labour Party continued to entertain close relationships with academics and, in particular, relied on economists to shape its economic programs and policies. During the 1930s, labor-friendly economists set up clubs and research bureaus to generate new economic ideas and research and to advise Labour governments.[129] Together, these organizations "enlisted an impressive array of economic expertise that included, among others, Colin Clark, E.F.M. Durbin, Ernest Bevin, G.D.H. Cole, Hugh Gaitskell,

Douglas Jay, James Meade and John Strachey."[130] During the 1960s and 1970s, the list of academic economists involved in Labor Party circles was even longer. The party's left wing developed an "Alternative Economic Strategy" in close connection with a number of Cambridge dons during the 1970s. The blueprint was a mixture of Keynesian demand management, nationalization, trade protection, and planning agreements between the state and the private sector. Though widely discussed, it was never implemented. Finally, New Labour has maintained close connections with the London School of Economics.[131] This social and political rather than institutional centrality of economics professors is further evidenced by the fact that a significant number of them received knighthoods (e.g., Hicks, Robertson, Meade, Mirrlees, Dasgupta, Atkinson, Vickers, King, Portes, Ball, Peacock, Walters, Budd) or even higher titles (e.g., Keynes, Robbins, Kaldor, Balogh, Eatwell, Desai, Layard, Burns, Bauer) during the period under investigation here.

In this domain as in many others, the Thatcher years are outliers. The prime minister's distrust of consultative institutions is well known: the number of royal commissions and departmental committees of inquiry was sharply reduced during Thatcher's tenure. For advice, Thatcherites went to business people, the think tanks, and the small number of monetarists who were isolated at the periphery of the academic system: Patrick Minford at the University of Liverpool, Brian Griffith at the City University, and especially Terence Burns, Terry Ward, and later Stephen Littlechild at the London Business School. Margaret Thatcher's chief economic adviser, Alan Walters, had taught at the LSE, but characteristically his trajectory into the economics profession had started outside the center. The core of the British profession found itself largely at odds with the prime minister's policies and manifested its distrust in the manifesto mentioned earlier. The government dismissed both university and government economists outright as incorrigible Keynesians and launched a number of specific attacks on important academic (the SSRC) and administrative institutions (the Central Policy Review Staff) amid a more general retrenchment in higher education and state administration. With salaries dropping in real terms, prestige and morale in both places reached a low point during this period.[132]

Much has been made (Blyth 2002) or unmade (Prasad 2006) of the importance of think tanks in crystallizing and putting on the political agenda the economic ideas that motivated the Thatcher revolution in policy. Our interest here has to do with the place of this sector in the social organization of economic knowledge in Britain, and how it might differ from the situation both in France and in the United States. As in the United States, think tanks in Britain exist somewhat at the margin of the academic field, though important economists might be involved in them. But their main raison d'être is political. Hence one of the first important British think tanks (Political and Economic Planning or PEP later merged into the Policy Studies Institute) was established in 1931 to publicize the ideology of planning. It attracted people of different political persuasions, from the Fabians to Oswald Mosley (in that respect at least PEP was not unlike the X-Crise group we will discuss in the next chapter, though the latter was clearly more technocratic in its recruitment). The think tanks established in the early decades of the postwar period were, in turn, reacting against the pro-government ideological consensus and economic policies of the postwar Labour government that PEP had, in part, helped bring to the fore. Hence a political movement to revive classical economic liberalism crystalled in 1955 when members of the Conservative Party and captains of industry created the Institute for Economic Affairs (IEA) to serve as a vehicle for the views of the neo-liberal Mont-Pèlerin Society. During the 1960s and 1970s, the IEA published a spate of pamphlets promoting the application of free-market principles to a large variety of microeconomic problems, and helped spread monetarist views on the macroeconomy.[133] The Adam Smith Institute (founded in 1976) and the Center for Policy Studies, on the other hand, are more directly political organizations with closer linkages to the Conservative Party. One of my interviewees, an LSE professor, thus commented: "You would give a lecture at the Institute for Economic Affairs, it is a serious organization. But you would not do so at the Center for Policy Studies" (June 1997).

Because of the structure of the British state, the British research institutes, unlike their American counterparts, have a somewhat more peripheral position vis-à-vis the policy process, working mainly through interpersonal networks, political parties, and the press. In 1989, the *Economist* summarized the discrepancy between the two countries by writing that "in Washington, think tanks have large, grand offices. In London they are strictly hole-in-the-wall jobs, occupying a few town houses in Westminster." Fifteen years down the road, the situation has not changed much: in 2004, the Institute of Economic Affairs had a total staff of 12 people and a budget of about £1 million, compared with 148 staffers and $38 million for its closest equivalent in the United States the American Enterprise Institute.[134] Another contrast with the U.S. situation is that Labour-affiliated organizations, that have sprung up since the late 1980s, like the Institute for Public Policy Research and the Social Market Foundation, are financially powerful *relative* to their conservative counterparts, sometimes significantly more so. This is also true of the more academically oriented think tanks such as the Institute for Fiscal Studies (est. 1969), the older National Institute of Economic and Social Research, or the Center for Economic Policy Research, which draw much of their

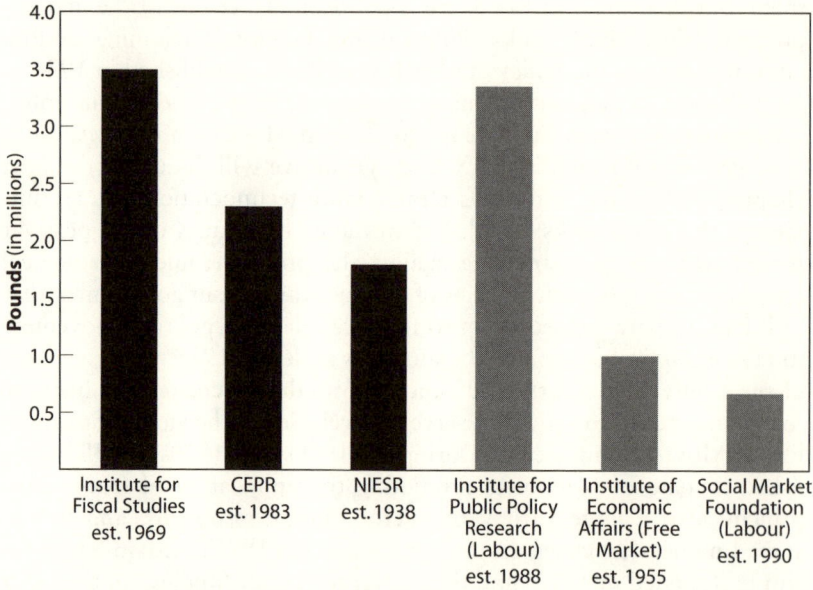

Figure 3-7. Selected U.K. think tanks, resources for fiscal year 2004.
Source: United Kingdom Charity Commission, Register of Charities.

strength from public funding and contracts with (mainly) public institutions, as well as the Europen Commission (figure 3-7).[135]

The Enduring Relevance of the Press

The economic press has long been central to the British economic debate and indeed to the very identity of the British economics profession. Specialized journalistic commentary on economic matters was already well established in the nineteenth century, both in the general press and in specialized periodicals. As Scott Gordon (1955) has shown, the *Economist* played an important role not simply as a vehicle for free-trade agitation but in the development and diffusion of the laissez-faire doctrine itself. Over the course of its long life, it has been a central element in the British (and now international) public sphere, remaining remarkably consistent in character, style, and ideological commitment.

These changes, naturally, were in part the result of the development of economics itself. In the nineteenth century, journalism was well rewarded financially, and, in the absence of other channels of diffusion, generalist reviews constituted the principal medium for the expression of economic ideas, whether theoretical or policy oriented. Nassau Senior, who occupied the first Drummond Chair at Oxford and had a marked influence on "economic policy" during the 1830s (through his participation in several government commissions and advisory activities with the Whig party), wrote regularly for the *Economist*.

Although the late nineteenth-century movement of academicization led by Marshall partly established itself in reaction against the association between economics and policy agitation, university economists continued to write frequently in the press up until at least the late 1950s. Keynes's talents as a pamphleteer and journalist are almost legendary. He edited the economic supplements of the *Manchester Guardian Commercial* and published some of his most famous pieces there. He arranged the purchase and became chairman of the board of the *Nation and Athanaeum* (later *New Statesman* after the fusion of the two periodicals), then placed its editorship in the hands of another economist, Hubert Henderson. A wonderful debater and proselytizer, Keynes wrote around three hundred newspaper articles during his lifetime.

As Parsons (1989) has shown, the Keynesian revolution in the 1930s and 1940s, like the monetarist counterrevolution in the 1970s, was carried in large measure by a group of young journalist converts: Nicholas Davenport in the columns of the *New Statesman*, Francis Williams at the *Daily Herald*, and Douglas Jay at the *Economist* and the *Daily Herald*, all of whom were active in Labour economic policy circles. "The 'Keynesian' revolution in economic theory was to bring in its wake a revolution in economic journalism which was as significant as that which had taken place during the 'Ricardian' revolution" (Parsons, 1989, 5).

There is, however, some reason to regard this mode of communication of British economists as a more structural feature that goes beyond the historical moment of the Keynesian revolution and the little world of the Cambridge converts. For instance, in his biographical essay about Roy Harrod, Phelps Brown reminds us that "already in 1951–1959 Harrod had published 356 articles, through 99 media. . . . He wrote regularly for the *Financial Times*. . . . In addition, on the first day of each month, he supplied Phillips and Drew stockbrokers with a memorandum on the current situation" (Brown 1980, 30–31). Another example is Lionel Robbins, who, while somewhat less prolific in the public place, and extremely reluctant to take "political" positions, was chairman of the *Financial Times* from 1961 to 1971.

Let us briefly mention two explanations for the centrality of economic commentary in the British public sphere, and the role of professional economists in it. The first argument, evoked earlier, refers to the structure of the British state and its relationship to society. Weir and Skocpol (1985, 149) suggest that the journalistic involvement of Keynes and his followers had a lot to do with the closed "organizational structure of the

British state in the 1920s," which, by excluding outsiders from economic policy-making positions, incited them to present their ideas directly to the public. A second explanation points toward the focal position of the City of London (and its networks within the state) not only as an all-important consumer of economic and financial news but also as a constituency seeking to broadcast its views toward the state. The *Financial Times*, for instance, emerged in the mid-1880s as a direct outgrowth of the rising international power of financial institutions. It has dominated financial journalism in Britain ever since and has influenced subsequent ventures.[136] From the 1920s to the 1990s, another set of publications, the bank reviews, also provided economic commentary. Started as "mouthpieces for the views of their proprietors," the bank reviews began in the 1930s to assume a much broader role by opening their pages to outside experts and, in particular, academic contributors, who used them as public platforms.[137]

The centrality of professors in economic commentary declined markedly after the mid-1950s, however, when the main newspapers turned to specialized, homegrown economic journalism. Since then, economics in the press has become increasingly the province of a distinguished body of specialized columnists who frequently publish books for the general public in the tradition of their great nineteenth-century predecessors—for instance Walter Bagehot. This new generation of journalists asserted itself most visibly by championing the monetarist "counterrevolution" after a virulent controversy on the "economic consequences of Lord Keynes" erupted in the *Times* in the fall of 1974. Much of the battle between Keynesians and monetarists during the 1970s was thus fought out in the economic and financial press and in the bank reviews.[138]

The emergence of a class of financial journalists should not be read too simply as a competitive displacement of academic writers from the political sphere, however. In part, it was a development of its own, motivated by the existence of a pool of elite school graduates who held on to the model of talented amateurism in economic discussion and sometimes felt ambivalent vis-à-vis the technical evolution of the discipline. One of my interviewees, a prominent economic columnist, thus reflected on his own trajectory in the following terms: "[The press] offered a job to people from the universities to develop their careers much faster than if they had gone to the university, or if they had gone to the Bank of England, for instance. It would have taken them a million years before they would have been able to give their opinion, and then it would have had to be private" (journalist, *Financial Times*, June 1997).

This successful British columnist was keenly aware of how peculiar his position seemed to observers outside the English context. "Harry Johnson," he went on, referring to the Canadian economist mentioned earlier, "was always amazed that people like us were journalists because he couldn't understand why we didn't thrive at a university." As suggested above, the career structure in universities (with every few professorships) might have been a deterrent here. But the quotation is also revealing of broader expectations—"being able to give one's opinion," indeed he also spoke later of his "evangelical desire"—upon which such careers relied and that certain social trajectories seemed to authorize. Samuel Brittan (*Financial Times*), Peter Jay (*Times*), William Hutton (*Observer*), Martin Wolf (*Financial Times*), or Diane Coyle (*Independent*) were part of the select milieu of British economics in a way nonacademic writers in the United States never could be. Brittan went to Cambridge. Jay and Coyle attended Oxford. All worked at the Treasury before starting their careers as journalists and popularizers of economic knowledge. (They also wrote popular books on economics and the economy.) Wolf (also an Oxford graduate) and Coyle served on the council of the Royal Economic Society. Rupert Pennant-Rea became deputy director of the Bank of England after his editorship at the *Economist* ended. Some of their earlier peers had made a successful passage back into academia (Andrew Shonfield) or higher administration (Peter Jay's father, Douglas). And in a world where advanced degrees carried less weight than a First at Cambridge or Oxford, most of them had impeccable records, having gone through the same key educational institutions as their academic colleagues. This was quite a different crowd, then, from either the mavericks (e.g., Jude Wanniski, George Gilder, Craig Roberts) who wrote in the *Wall Street Journal* at the time of the supply-side revolution or from the university professors and Nobel Prize winners who, as professional experts traditionally dominate economic columns in American newspapers and magazines.[139] Neither hack nor scholar, the very British figure of the newspapers columnist illustrates my assertion that we must understand economic experts in terms of the cultural categories generated by their society.[140]

Liberalization and the Privatization of British Economics

The preceding example, about the role of the economic and financial press, points toward the importance of the corporate jurisdiction for the British economics profession. As in the United States, the latter has been expanding steadily since the 1960s. But the difference is that in Britain the business world remains less interested in formal education: only 64 percent of top businessmen had a university education in 1990, as opposed to 95 percent of the French and 88 percent of the German.[141] The reverse proposition is also true: elite schools did not see themselves as having to provide for the practical occupations, leaving this task to institutions of lower prestige. As for economists, as we have seen, those who established the discipline sought mainly to further its intellectual status. They grounded the professional project of economics in a distinctive *scientific* identity, which maintained a clear distance from more practical (hence low-prestige) occupations and fields.[142] Still, the moral boundary against "management studies" did not necessarily imply a lack of social connection to the business world. Many British economists, including some of the most prominent ones, also deemed a good understanding of actual business conditions and practices to be essential to their scientific work. This orientation was explicit in Marshall's and Keynes's view of political economy, for instance; it later inspired an important tradition of qualitative business surveys that thrived at Oxford through the late 1960s, as well as in other universities located near large industrial basins.

By the 1960s, the inroad of economists in the business sector was attested by the existence of a separate professional association, the Society of Business Economists,[143] and the publication of a study on "the economist in business" (Alexander, Kemp, and Rybczynski 1967). The society's current membership data list about six hundred members, yet this represents in all likelihood only a small fraction of the number of people involved in this occupation. (In 1993, for instance, the *Economist* reported that "an estimated 400 economists work in financial research in the City" alone.)[144] Interestingly, the society's current president and vice president—respectively, Lord Burns and Sir Alan Budd—are former academics and civil servants, evincing the same pattern of social authority noted earlier.

Naturally, the rise of the financial markets after the 1960s has contributed to the rapid growth of financial employment among "business economists," in Britain as elsewhere. Recent surveys conducted by the Society of Business Economists show the enhanced weight of the financial and consultancy occupations and the declining role of the traditional "industrial" jurisdictions.[145] Yet the British situation exhibits some peculiarities thanks to the political context in the 1980s and the degradation of conditions in higher education since the 1970s. Both of these developments have caused an exodus of would be academics toward the corporate sector. In 2005, compensations in banking and finance were, on average, more than three times those in academia, and more than twice those in government. Thus advanced economics degrees are increasingly seen as points of entry into the financial professions, rather than as academic credentials. Commenting on these issues, the *Economist* noted: "The brightest Harvard economists study for Ph.D.s and end up in jobs teaching economics at university or, if they are not quite up to the mark, working for the Federal Reserve, the IMF or the World Bank. The brightest Cambridge graduates head straight for the City" (*Economist,* January 3, 1992, 69).

More generally, the political and policy developments of the 1980s have moved the center of gravity of the British economics profession toward the business sector.[146] Privatization and the transformation of the regulatory context created a demand for economic expertise that was not easily found in the academic world then. As such, they opened a niche for the consultancy market and prompted the emergence of "new" jurisdictions in the corporate world (e.g., London Economics, specialized in privatization, or Tim Congdon's Lombard Street Research) or the acquisition of new skills among old ones: "Privatization in effect forced companies to hire experts on economic regulation. [Also, as it has] spread across the world, British economists have found that expertise gained at home is highly marketable."[147] Britain thus dominates economics in Europe not only through its universities and research organizations (like the CEPR), some of which are tightly integrated into the dominant U.S. academic field, but also through its financial markets, economic press, and private consultancies.

THE WANING HIGH CULTURE OF BRITISH ECONOMICS

Authors who have reflected upon the British pattern of economic knowledge organization characterize it as a "Mid-Atlantic" model that stands halfway between the American and continental European styles of professionalization.[148] On the one hand, intellectual patterns bring the British field closest to the United States. On the other hand, the stratification of the educational field and the presence of a powerful and prestigious civil service draw it toward the continental European tradition.

The idea of a "mixed" pattern does indeed capture some important features about the British economics profession. This chapter, however, has sought to link the latter's nature and identity with more specific characteristics of the British political culture and social system. In the British "model," the identity of economists has been historically shaped by their embeddedness in the high-status, well-educated clerisy whose knowledge ought to be put to the general service of society. Economists who occupied positions at Oxbridge and (to a lesser extent) London could best draw upon this authority by virtue of the proximity to political power that comes with these institutional locations, often relayed through political parties, social clubs, and the press.

This is not to say that British economists spoke as pure "intellectuals" rather than as experts, however. Their authority on economic matters was itself firmly rooted in the scientific status and technical competence of their particular disciplinary project. But they remained reluctant to cast their role in purely technical terms, as exemplified by the cautious attitude toward mathematics, which, especially in earlier periods, they considered entirely necessary as a tool but still requiring "translation" into plain language. Indeed, it was this taint of esotericism that initially diluted their legitimacy in the eyes of nonspecialized administrative audiences. Rather, their interventions were frequently articulated in moral terms, where the nature of the curriculum emphasized economics' dependence upon moral science in general, and questions of inequality, redistribution, and well-being loomed large in their scientific preoccupations.

This model of "public-minded elitism" was especially well developed during the interwar and early postwar periods. (The figures of Beveridge, Keynes, Meade, or Kaldor perhaps exemplify it best.) It partly lost its preeminence as a result of several trends. First, the shift to a system of mass higher education has weakened the traditional supremacy of Oxbridge, which best embodied this model. Second, disciplinary growth in economics has been associated with an expansion of scientific academicism, which has prevented some of its practitioners from engaging in broader advocacy. Finally, during the Thatcher years, academics found themselves much more isolated than they had ever been, though the pattern was reversed again under the Blair government.

It is fair to ask whether such patterns constitute, in themselves, a distinctively British trait. France, too, is a medium-sized country with a very cohesive civil service that can be said to rely on social connections to a great extent. Yet the nature of the educational system in France, as we will see in the next chapter, produces a much more profound separation between the administration and the university. In this situation, French university economists have remained at the periphery of the policy world, while a particular brand of economic experts, the state administrators, monopolized economic management. It is thus to France that we now turn.

CHAPTER FOUR

France: Statist Divisions

> Among the French ruling elite, it is Finance Inspectors who
> pass as economists. That is, they are people who were trained
> at Sciences-Po and ENA, who do not know anything about
> economic theory, and who emphasize economic policy as op-
> posed to economic analysis. But they are close to political
> power. On the other hand, you have the Polytechniciens-
> ENSAE, who do mathematical economics, or even mathematics
> without economics, and those pass for another type of econo-
> mists. That is what being an economist in France means to me.
> (professor at Sciences-Po and university, July 1995)

IN LATE twentieth-century France, the field of economics was undergoing
something of a schizophrenic crisis. In 2000, a rebellion erupted among
economics students, many of them from the École Normale Supérieure,
who were denouncing the overuse of mathematics, the hegemony of
neoclassical theory, and the lack of practical relevance in the teaching of
economics.[1] The movement, which called itself *autisme-économie*,[2]
spread rapidly to the universities and soon received the support of prominent intellectuals and left-wing newspapers (such as *Le Monde Diplomatique*) and sympathetic coverage in the general media. A petition cir-
culating widely in France and abroad gathered hundreds of signatures,
including those of several prominent economic scholars. The intensity of
the movement's critique led the French government to order a special inquiry into economics teaching, whose conclusions ended up broadly cor-
roborating the students' complaints (Fitoussi 2001).

Autisme-économie grew, in part, from a well-established tradition of
economic critique in France. Echoing Marx's attack on classical political
economy, the movement held that economic science is bourgeois in essence: by presenting itself as "pure science," the professional practice of
economics conveniently ignores its moral and ideological underpinnings
and ends up serving only the interests of wealthy countries and individuals. Another charge was that the practice of economic policy is profoundly antidemocratic and that the rule of experts stifles public debate.
In fact, an earlier petition, the "Appeal of Economists to End Uniform

Thinking," had made the latter argument by sharply condemning public officials' unimaginative approach to the unemployment problem.[3]

By formulating these critiques, as well as others before them, economic teachers, intellectuals, activists, and popular writers were thus asserting the primacy of democratic discussion over and against the technocratic authority of economic ideas. And, indeed, this intellectual critique of economics and economic policy in France coincided with mounting political expressions of discontent with global capitalism. This sentiment could be seen in a spate of best sellers decrying the dehumanizing effects of the market economy[4] and, somewhat later, in the popularity of ATTAC and the antiglobalization movement.[5]

These charges are interesting because they exemplify the difficult status of economics in France. They highlight not only the challenges it faces from competing intellectual enterprises but also the ambivalence expressed by many of its own practitioners and institutional patrons. These modern characteristics are not entirely new, however: French economics was a remarkably disputed affair from the beginning. As an institutional project, it looks very different from the enterprises we have described in the United States and Britain, being quite delayed on some dimensions (e.g. university teaching) yet early on others (e.g. scientific project with disciplinary claims). Professional associations of economists, for instance, are less well established in France than in similarly sized European countries. Thus the Association Française de Sciences Économiques has only around 850 members[6] (against nearly 3,150 for the British Royal Economic Society and 3,200 for the German-speaking Verein für Sozialpolitik).[7] France also does not produce regular "surveys" of its stock of economists': employment data do not identify "economist" as a job title, nor do surveys of scientific manpower or the civil service consider it a special occupational category.

This ambiguity of status has roots in the historical structures of economics in France and, in particular, in the multiplication of career paths to economic expertise in the twentieth century. This diversity in training, in turn, has produced contradictory definitions of economic competence, which range from a set of formal skills to a technocratic status to a much broader vision of the social scientist as a generalist intellectual.

I argue in this chapter that much of the explanation for this pattern lies in French economics' relationship to the French state. The development of economic knowledge production in France has depended strongly on the involvement of, and authority conferred by, central administrative authorities. But that support came rather late. Before the late 1950s, the study of economics in France had a weak institutional basis, as a minor in law faculties and specialized schools. In the postwar era, however, the modernizing French state actively pursued the development of economic expertise. Administrative agencies became the source of an economic knowledge production that was closely coupled with the management of France's mixed economy and relied on the traditional institutional power of elite civil service training establishments, the *grandes écoles* and their associated *corps*. Concentrating both material resources and social authority, these institutions came to dominate the production of economic information, economic policy, and, perhaps unexpectedly, economic science itself. This "statist" pattern of organization also limited the development of economic knowledge (particularly quantitative knowledge) in the nonstate sector. Few were ready to challenge the state monopolies in the economic domain and, in any case, those who might have done so often lacked the material and symbolic resources to be effective.

The smaller, in relative terms, membership of the Association Française de Sciences Économiques thus does not indicate a lack of institutionalization of economic knowledge and techniques in France. Rather, it reflects a *substantively different* form of social organization from the professional model best exemplified by the U.S. case.[8] People might see themselves as members of certain *corps* and graduates of certain schools—such as the École Nationale de la Statistique et de l'Administration Économiques (ENSAE) or the École Nationale d'Administration (ENA)—before they think of themselves as "economists." In many cases, the discipline of economics makes much less sense as a source of professional identity than does a particular career trajectory.

This chapter provides an account of the conditions under which these understandings emerged and analyzes their consequences for the production of economic knowledge in France. As elsewhere, we will not assume that the boundaries between who is and who is not an economist are given a priori. Rather, we will reconstruct these boundaries in relation to the broader set of public and private institutions that organize political, scientific, and economic governance in that country. In doing so, we will also show how processes of social categorization, jurisdictional development, and intellectual struggle in France differ from those in the United States and Great Britain.

A Fragmented Academicization

Since the end of the nineteenth century, the university has been the main producer of certified economics graduates in France: as of 2007, French economics faculties churned out close to 500 economics and business doctorates every year and employed just over 1,900 economics professors of various rank.[9] Yet in spite of its numerical presence, the university has had a comparatively small influence over the fields of economic policy and research. Instead, graduates from those unique French institutions, the *grandes écoles*, have come to dominate both: since the 1960s at least, economic policy and the bulk of technical economic expertise have come under the control of a class of technocrats and engineers trained in administrative *corps* and specialized schools. Furthermore, this same technical-bureaucratic sector has become the dominant (i.e., the most legitimate) motor of scholarly research, through its command of formal tools, data collection, and analysis, as well as through its close integration with the Anglo-American scientific pole.

From Libéral Networks to Law Professors: The Slow Progress toward Disciplinary Autonomy

At the opening of the nineteenth century the production of economic discourse was not yet a professionalized affair, in France as elsewhere. Economic writings and ideas, however, were everywhere, from the productivist gospel of Henri de Saint-Simon and the socialist utopia of Charles Fourier to the laissez-faire radicalism of the Idéologues, who were occasionally armed with Frédéric Bastiat's devastating satire. The fortunes of these various networks depended very much on the political context. Although the influence of economic writers on government did at times run very high,[10] it was never sufficient to help the discipline secure a strong foothold in education. In sharp contrast to its German counterpart, the French state for the most part remained reluctant to organize a centrally administered form of training in the subject.[11] Rather, successive regimes until the Third Republic concentrated elite administrative education around technological and engineering subjects, keeping to a tradition started by the revolutionary governments and the first Napoleonic empire.

Part of the reason for the state's chilly attitude toward political economy had to do with the intellectual orientations of economic discourse itself. Laissez-faire liberalism, of a somewhat more optimistic sort than the British classical school, was by far the dominant current of thought in France. With several members established at the Académie des Sciences Morales et Politiques in the Institut de France, the very pinnacle of intellectual prestige, these Idéologues, as they called themselves, believed strongly in turning their version of political economy into popular, enlightening, "republican" knowledge.[12] Their main purposes were political, and specifically antiprotectionist and antisocialist, rather than scholarly. Many of their activities thus revolved around the popularization of liberal ideas through government lobbying and journalistic activism. In 1842 the creation of the Société d'Économie Politique[13] and its journalistic organ, the Journal des Économistes, gave impetus to these campaigns. A dense press network and a publishing house, Guillaumin, completed the apparatus by targeting educated elites.[14]

Although the *Journal* was somewhat ecumenical and functioned as a protoscientific vehicle, it remained nonetheless very much wedded to the promotion of free trade and laissez-faire. As for the Institut de France members, who by and large controlled these organizations, many continued to privilege public involvement and the discussion of legislation and policy over scholarly pursuits. In fact, the midcentury generation of Idéologues was better known as the Journalistes. Both labels continued to appropriately describe their approach to the social role of the economist throughout the second half of the century. To take one example, Paul Leroy-Beaulieu (1843–1916) founded another economic journal, *L'Économiste Français*, in 1873[15] and wrote for two of the most influential press organs of the time, the literary *Revue des Deux Mondes* and the political *Journal des Débats*.

The laissez-faire liberals were acutely aware that institutionalizing their doctrine was a political imperative, however, and they lobbied heavily for the further expansion of economics teaching in France, relying on their social and political connections to advance their cause. Through their activism, economics found a niche in the complex network of special schools, the *écoles*, which served to train the nation's elites. The first chair was created in 1819 at the Conservatoire des Arts et Métiers[16] at the request of Jean-Baptiste Say, who was also its first tenant. The July Monarchy regime (1830–1848), which was more favorable to economic liberalism, restored the Académie des Sciences Morales et Politiques in 1832 and also founded the first chair in political economy at the Collège de France (it, too, was given to Jean-Baptiste Say shortly before his death and remained in the hands of staunch liberals until the twentieth century). Another chair, also occupied by an *économiste libéral*, was created at the *École des Ponts et Chaussées* (1846). Courses in political economy were commenced at the École Supérieure de Commerce de Paris (from 1825), the École des Mines (1848), the École Centrale (1856), and the École des Hautes Études Commerciales (1881).[17] Finally, owing to the liberal sympathies of the then minister of education, Victor Duruy, the Paris law faculty created the first university chair in political economy in 1864.

To some extent, the piecemeal institutionalization of economics in the nineteenth century reflects the contradictions between the laissez-faire orientation of the emerging discipline (and of the Idéologues in particular, who controlled most established positions) and the politically centralized environment in which it was operating. In contrast to its British counterpart, the French academic system depended heavily on the state, both in the realm of research and in higher education. Significantly, the institutional development of economics during the nineteenth century mirrors almost perfectly the country's chaotic political history, expanding under *libéral* governments (e.g., the July Monarchy) and contracting under the two most centralizing regimes, the First (1804–1814) and Second (1852–70) Napoleonic Empires. Generally the science of "laissez-faire," as French political economy had come to be known, was somewhat at odds with imperial conceptions of greater state control over economic organization and with the prevailing economic sentiment of the country, which was, with a few exceptions, overwhelmingly favorable to protectionism.[18] Thus, as first consul, Napoléon I presided over the abolition of all economics teaching from the prestigious Institute of France: the Académie des Sciences Morales et Politiques was shut down in 1803.[19] Similarly, during the early years of the Second Empire, the police kept a watchful eye on political economy lectures and publications,[20] and politicians "[fought] the pretensions (of the field) to become a guide for public policy."[21] In fact, political economy raised so much distrust that successive regimes carefully barred it from training students at the prestigious École Polytechnique throughout the entire nineteenth century (Armatte 1994).

In this context, the Idéologues' most important institutional success was probably the founding of the École Libre des Sciences Politiques in 1871, a private school that sought to compete directly with the university in preparing students for civil service examinations.[22] Political economy from the beginning occupied a central place in the school's curriculum. By the end of the 1870s, the École Libre had ten teachers in the subject among its faculty.[23] An amazingly successful institution, the school helped secure the *libéraux's* connection to the politico-administrative field. By the end of the nineteenth century, it so excelled in preparing students for state examinations that soon the vast majority of those admitted to the *grands corps* were trained there. Between 1899 and 1936, 97 percent of the new recruits (by examination) to the Conseil d'Etat and Inspection des Finances, and 88 percent of those admitted to the Cour des Comptes and the Corps Diplomatique came from the École Libre.[24] And almost half of the professors in post in 1900 were themselves members of the high administration, making it de facto a major center for top bureaucratic training.[25]

In spite of these changes, the university—a key institution, given its much larger student body—long remained out of reach of liberal political economists. With the exception of the Paris chair, the *libéraux's* lobbying efforts at incorporating some regular political economy teaching into the law curriculum (which then constituted the main avenue for civil service recruitment) continued to face the combined skepticism of politicians and jurists. The discipline was finally introduced in 1877 as a compulsory subject in the law curriculum, and a chair in political economy was created in every law faculty in France. In the absence of a separate credential for economics professors, however, it fell upon jurists, whose contempt for the new field was barely hidden, to teach the required courses.

Given the tight control of the law faculties over the discipline, this was only a partial victory. Still, the reform represented a real turning point: for the first time, the teaching of economics had become a full-time job. The proportion of professors among economic writers increased sharply, weakening the connection with the higher classes and the *salon* model, which had prevailed among the Institute network.[26] Many members of the law faculties came from the middle classes, were more practical in their orientations, and were deeply suspicious of the liberals' beliefs in natural laws. Most of them had trained in law and had a poor knowledge of classical political economy. Under their influence economic discourse became more pluralistic, opening up to historicist methodology, socialist and protectionist positions, as well as foreign influences, and occasionally challenged the *libéraux's* longstanding intellectual monopoly. In 1879, for instance, Paul Cauwès, a follower of the German historical school, made a sensation with the publication of his *Précis du cours d'économie politique*, which embraced protectionism and claimed that political economy was essentially the study of national economy and legislation, denying thereby the existence of any universal laws in economics. In 1887 a group of university professors led by Charles Gide created the *Revue d'Économie Politique* in a fairly antiliberal and scholarly mold, explicitly repudiating the more political model of the Institute and the *Journal des Économistes*.[27] (The *Revue*, however, like the law faculties, would gradually be reconquered by liberals as they themselves started to gain positions within the new system.)

Meanwhile, the institutionalization of economics in higher education was proceeding gradually. A doctorate in law with an "economic and political sciences" specialization was introduced in 1895, and the *agrégation* for the law faculties acquired an "economic science" minor in 1896.[28] By the early 1900s, there were about forty professors of economics teaching in the law faculties.[29] Yet in spite of these numerical gains the subordinate academic status of economics remained a subject of constant concern. Writing in 1937, Gaétan Pirou of the Paris school of law deplored the auxiliary character of political economy in France. In contrast with both the United States and the United Kingdom (but like Germany), students did not specialize until the doctorate, which meant that "every advanced student in economics had to spend (at least) his or her first three years of college studying law."[30] The situation was not much better in the engineering schools. In spite of the introduction of new chairs at the École des Ponts et Chaussées (1901) and the École Polytechnique (1903), political economy remained marginal to the core curriculum and attracted very few students.[31]

Change came gradually after World War II, after prolonged and painful reflection (partly driven by international institutions, like UNESCO)[32] on the crisis of the French university system, and amid heated debate between opponents and partisans of the organic connection between economics and law. The curriculum of the *licence* was amended in 1955 to make room for a specialized "economics" track. Even within this new curriculum, however, only one-third of the courses during the first two years were in economics, the rest being composed of law and history teachings; economics courses predominated only during the third and fourth years.[33] Finally, the Ministry of Education established a separate *licence ès sciences économiques* in 1959.

The gradual progress toward institutional autonomy made the assertion of a stronger disciplinary project possible. In 1950, a younger, more specialized generation of university professors organized around a new scholarly outlet, the *Revue Économique*, which started to follow intellectual developments in the Anglo-American world more closely.[34] The Association Française de Sciences Économiques, created the same year, also marked the progress of a new professional model oriented toward the construction of a self-contained scientific community. Its old predecessor, the Société d'Économie Politique, was still in existence but remained more of an elite club patronized by businessmen and high-level technocrats.

Still, in contrast to contemporaneous developments in the United States, the French transformation was modest. Mathematics, for instance, had made few inroads into the law faculties. On the eve of disciplinary autonomization (in 1957), France counted sixty-nine members in the Econometric Society. Of those on whom biographical information was available (forty-two), eight had a law or economics doctorate or an *agrégation de sciences économiques*. Nearly all the rest (thirty-two) had an engineering or mathematical background. Seventeen were pursuing careers in the public administration nebulae, at the Ministry of Finance or in the national public monopolies (Electricité de France, Gaz de France, Charbonnages de France), thus far outpacing the eight members who taught in a law faculty.[35] Practically, the situation was this: only a small number of individuals (e.g., Henri Guitton in Dijon, Jean Bénard in Grenoble) teaching in the law faculties were well acquainted with formal methods and actively promoted their diffusion. But generally, the lack of competent personnel meant that these subjects were often taught by outsiders from the administrative world or from the mathematical and stastistical faculties, particularly the École Normale Supérieure (Guilbaut) and the Institut de Statistique de l'Université de Paris (Fourgeaud).

Politically, too, the situation had not changed much. During the 1950s the teaching of economics remained largely in the hands of *libéral* professors who were strictly protective of their domain. In spite of the Communist Party's popularity among French intellectuals after the war, those who shared its ideology were still unwelcome in (indeed, effectively barred from) the law faculties and often had to start their careers elsewhere.[36] Hence, by the time French universities were faced with the largest student movement in their history in 1968, the political gap separating the law faculties from the rest of the intellectual world in France was considerable. Students from the Faculté de Droit et de Sciences Économiques of Paris were among the last ones to join the strike movement. But even they deemed economics in the law faculties politically conservative, old-fashioned, and antimodern (and the relative indifference of economics professors to the question of university modernization seemed to confirm such a verdict).

Partly responding to these demands and partly extending the institutional process under way for a very long time, the *loi d'orientation* of 1968 finally endorsed an administrative separation between law and economics and replaced the old faculties with new, autonomous administrative units based (in principle) on the voluntary association of professors (the UERs).[37] The reform permitted a dramatic expansion of both economics faculty and enrollments in the 1970s, just at the time when they started to stagnate in the United States and the United Kingdom (figure 4-1).[38]

Some of the new universities created by the 1968 reforms (the most relevant case here is probably that of Paris-Dauphine) took a modernist and elitist orientation that privileged mathematical approaches (particularly in finance), professionalization through research, and connections to the business world. The dynamics at work in the British and American cases, whereby newer (and thus subordinate) institutions seek to improve their position in the field by establishing connections with the more legitimate segment of the academic profession internationally, were thus clearly at play in the French context, too.

Not everyone welcomed the transition to a more specialized disciplinary orientation, however. First, many power holders in the field still came from the old system and naturally favored the more institutional and sociolegal type of knowledge they had come to represent. (In fact, this model continued to prevail in administrative schools like Sciences-Po and the École Nationale d'Administration, where the teaching of economics remained closely associated with legal training). Second, the

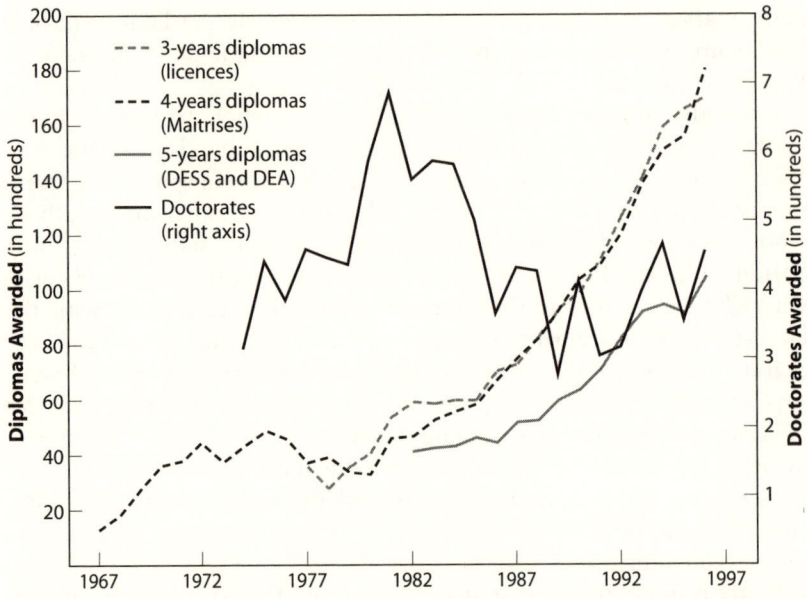

Figure 4-1. France: Three-, four-, and five-year diplomas and doctorates in eco-nomics and business (sciences économiques et sciences de gestion), 1967–96 (doctorates on right vertical axis).

Sources: Direction de l'évaluation et de la prospective, Ministry of National Education, France, INSEE, *Annuaire Statistique de la France*, 1999.

social movements and the vast educational expansion of the late 1960s and 1970s had, as elsewhere, finally brought to center stage a new gen-eration of critical scholars who favored interdisciplinary cooperation and greater political engagement on the part of social scientists.[39] In 1973, for instance, a debate erupted in the columns of the journal *Le Monde* when a left-wing group organized under the label Association pour la Critique des Sciences Économiques et Sociales denounced the discipline's pretensions to analyze and govern contemporary capitalist societies. Replies to the manifesto (broadly coming from the neoclassical segment of the field) articulated a defense of the objectivity of "science" against politics, of the usefulness of existing tools, and made reference to an international consensus.[40]

As suggested in the introduction, this debate has recurred under vari-ous forms since then and has its root in a long tradition of economists' political engagement (both on the left and the right), as well as a certain resistance, still conventional in certain segments of the university world, against mathematical technique. In order better to understand these conflicts and the stakes they raised, we need to explore in greater depth the intellectual patterns associated with the institutionalization of economics in French universities, and the specific challenges posed by the growing assertiveness of mathematicians within the discipline in this national context.

THE "SOCIOLOGICAL" TRADITION IN FRENCH ECONOMICS

Apart from the engineers (whom I discuss later), the mainstream of French economics was "literary" for a long time. Philip Mirowski's comparison of economic reviews suggests that the rapid expansion of mathematical discourse, which started in the late 1920s in the pages of the U.S.-based *Journal of Political Economy* and *Quarterly Journal of Economics*, was delayed until the 1950s in the case of the *Revue d'Économie Politique* (1991, 150). The *libéral* school of the nineteeth century was never very interested in scientific abstraction and concentrated much of its efforts on educating elites dealing with practical problems of policy. Paul Leroy-Beaulieu, for instance, dismissed the mathematical approach on the grounds that the (universal) law of substitution between subjective human needs makes mathematics "irrelevant for practical use"; they were, in his own words, "a pure delusion, a true deception."[41] The university professors shared with the liberals a general hostility toward mathematics and theory while sometimes holding quite different doctrinal views.[42] In contrast with their British counterparts (Jevons, Marshall, Edgeworth), who had built economics as a deductive science, or the engineers, who regarded formalization as a useful tool, many French economists looked down on mathematization as an unacceptable narrowing down of a discourse that they thought was as much an art as a science.[43] Instead, they held on to a conception of political economy as a moral science whose purpose is to understand, based on the close observation of facts, the laws that govern man's relationship to the material world.

The absence of mathematical capital among the *libéral* school's members partly explains their aversion to greater formalism, which had the potential to erode their quasi monopoly on the definition and practice of political economy in France. The vast majority of French economists in the nineteenth century, liberal or otherwise, were trained in classics or in law, and many were ignorant of even the most basic mathematics.[44]

The university reform of the 1870s set in motion institutional dynamics that contributed to keep mathematical approaches out of the law faculties. The most important of these was probably the method of appointment in French universities, which made access to chairs dependent on holding a national diploma, the *agrégation de sciences économiques*. A powerful instrument in the hands of university-based gatekeepers, who presided over examination boards, and thus over the definition of the skills to be rewarded, the *agrégation* long served to maintain the hegemony of the professors by failing upstart mathematical economists or other potentially undesirable candidates, who were then excluded from the possibility of teaching at the university.[45] Early on, observers had criticized the examination's bias toward general abilities and against specialized and technical knowledge.[46] In 1907, Charles Gide commented about the *agrégation*:

> The victors in this mortal struggle are not necessarily those who are the best gifted from the scientific point of view, or the deepest or most sagacious thinkers. They are oftener the most brilliant intellects or the best speakers. Nearly all the tests, or at least the decisive tests, are exclusively viva voce; written work, assuming that the young candidates have already written anything, goes for nothing in the decision. (207)

François Perroux bitterly echoed this judgment in 1945:

> The preparation for the *agrégation* is really ridiculous. One trains young men with rhetorical methods to make presentations in three parts on topics they know nothing about. No specialized personnel is available to teach them theory, statistics, nor even a modern description of institutions. They receive no encouragement to go study abroad. When they will become professors, they will have a high—sometimes very high—teaching load. They will lose precious time giving and grading exams. . . . Their libraries will be poor. If they ask for research funding, they will face administrative formalities that no one will help them overcome. And they will be told with a shrug that their main task is to prepare students for exams and that they must "respect the tradition" of the law faculties. (6–7, cited in Lamontagne 1947, 31)

We will see later that these concerns about the "generalist" nature of the *agrégation* diploma and its relative indifference to scholarly accomplishments persisted well into the second half of twentieth century and are, to some extent, still hotly debated today.[47]

Perroux's complaint, however, points toward a much broader set of issues that I have already evoked in chapter 1: the relative lack of resources of French universities compared with both their foreign counterparts and the *grandes écoles*. A further constraint in economics was the absence of any significant concentration of professors. In contrast with other countries where economics departments were already set up before World War I, the French situation was much more decentralized, with only one or two economics chairs at every law faculty. In 1946, an American foundation official traveling to France noticed that "the social sciences are weak here."[48] Since curricula were decided administratively, professors lacked any liberty in their teaching: most had to confine themselves to introductory courses, often the history of economic doctrines. This explains the very high proportion of general textbooks among French economists' publications during this period. Combined with the traditional sovereignty of academic mandarins in their own institutions, the relative isolation of university economics made it difficult to assert a bold disciplinary project and led to a form of intellectual balkanization.

Meanwhile, the persistent influence of law also continued to promote a broad understanding of political economy that included knowledge of institutions, history, and administrative practice. French university economists saw their discipline largely as a "juridical and literary" enterprise with limited theoretical ambition (Pirou 1937). As a result, the law faculties were, with one important exception (the Institut de Statistique de l'Université de Paris) slow to accommodate the intellectual breakthrough of the econometric revolution and the rise of social demands for technical economic expertise.[49] In two widely diffused textbooks, written shortly after World War II, André Marchal summed up the position of many by setting clear boundaries to the use of statistical methods and quickly dismissing mathematical economics as pretentious and largely irrelevant (Marchal 1948; 1953, 61). In the early 1960s, shortly after the separation from law, less than a quarter of the economics BA courses at the University of Paris centered on mathematical or statistical subjects (the term "econometrics" had yet to make its appearance in the university curriculum).[50]

Home to many original currents of thought, including several brands of socialism, and important individual innovators, French universities nonetheless failed to produce a distinctively "French school" of economic thought with a coherence comparable to its British and German counterparts. The general approach was to conciliate different methods and "maintain economic science within a framework of general knowledge [culture générale]," as voiced, for instance, by the president of the agrégation examination in 1950 (Noyelle 1951, 196). Hence a volume published in 1902 and ambitiously titled L'École économique française (Béchaux) comes to the strikingly modest conclusion that the main trait common to most French economists is a descriptive and humanistic orientation and a studied distance from deductive scientism. In his 1953 assessment bearing a similar title (La Pensée économique en France depuis 1945), André Marchal notices the same eclecticism but suggests that "the tendency to reintegrate economic science within a sociological framework is probably the most characteristic trait of contemporary French economic thought, at least for the 'active generation' (between

30 and 60 years old)" (1953, 75), a generation of which Marchal himself was a representative.

By pointing out the parochialism, intellectual conservatism, and relatively atheoretical style that came out of the particular institutional situation of the French universities, I do not want to imply that French contributions to economics amounted to little. In fact, it is perhaps the continued affirmation of an integrated conception of social science that constitutes the originality of the French approach during the interwar and immediate postwar periods—a conception that to some extent lives on today. The porosity of French disciplinary boundaries between economics and law, but also sociology and history, is particularly striking. To be sure, the disciplines were institutionally separate—economics being located in faculties of law, and sociology and history in faculties of letters—but they were brought together through crosscutting intellectual projects whose origin, sometimes, had preceded academic institutionalization. For instance, the Durkheimian school placed "economic sociology" at the core of its intellectual project, and economists played a key role in carrying it forward in the pages of the *Année Sociologique*.[51] François Simiand (1873–1935), one of Durkheim's most brilliant disciples, who taught political economy at the Conservatoire National des Arts et Métiers and then at the Collège de France, aspired to reconstruct economics as a special part of sociology by applying to it the same "positive method" as outlined in the *Rules of Sociological Method*. Simiand hoped to root economic generalizations in the observation of long statistical series, and he disdained both the abstract economics of the deductive school and the "historicizing historians" of the German school.[52]

While Simiand himself had few disciples, his methodological position, which was neither deductive nor descriptive, characterizes much of French thinking during the interwar period. Of course, American institutionalist scholarship held somewhat similar beliefs, but in contrast with French economic practice it was much more quantitative and less closely linked to sociological preoccupations. In the United States, economists generally looked down upon sociology. Sociology, in turn (at least in Talcott Parsons's version), built its separate disciplinary project by rejecting the institutionalist legacy and carefully acknowledging the primacy of neoclassical economics within its proper intellectual domain.[53] Such a division was unthinkable in France, partly because of Durkheim's prestige and all-encompassing project, and partly because economics did not have the same commanding position. As a result, the sociological ambition in French economics remained pervasive. For instance the *Revue Économique* at its foundation in 1950 stated a (short-lived) intention to "concentrate its efforts on organizing intellectual exchanges be-

tween the varied social disciplines and political economy, and to promote connections and joint surveys."[54] Another important review,
characteristically named *Économies et Sociétés*, was founded by François Perroux, one of the dominant personalities of the early postwar period, as part of his longstanding attempt to import "structural" considerations (i.e., references to the power of organized groups and of the
state) into economic analysis.

Another intellectual project of note, one that had important institutional implications for economics, came out of history. The *Annales*
school, which had started its ascension in French academia during the
1930s, achieved a major success with the creation of the VIth Section of
the École Pratique des Hautes Études (EPHE) in 1947, which carried out
its ambition of regrouping all the social sciences around history. With
Fernand Braudel, Charles Morazé, and Lucien Febvre at the helm, the
non-degree-granting EPHE promoted a broad, interdisciplinary approach built around economic history.[55] Unsurprisingly, members of
the VIth section were closely involved in the founding of the *Revue
Économique*.

These intellectual patterns, however, were to change quite dramatically as a consequence of two developments: the first was economics' institutional autonomization from legal studies, which, as I have already
discussed, left new departments more free to assert a stronger disciplinary project. The second was the increased assertiveness of engineers on
the academic scene, which triggered a standardization of disciplinary
practice in economics. Still, the aspiration of achieving a unified social
science persists strongly among learned French audiences.[56]

The Technical Economists and the "Economic Calculus" Tradition

While French universities have historically been the country's main centers of production of economics teachers, they were never the only ones,
even in the nineteenth century. As François Etner (1987) and Theodore
Porter (1995) have shown, a tradition of "economic calculus" had emerged
among mathematicians and engineers around the beginning of the nineteenth century. Although hailed as pioneering by modern historians of
the discipline, their work had little impact on the mainstream of French
economics. Thus the "invention" of the demand curve by the mathematician Antoine Augustin Cournot (1801–77) was largely ignored by his
contemporaries, much to Cournot's chagrin.[57] Civil engineers at the
École des Ponts et Chaussées, who were involved with the development
and management of infrastructures and utilities, also developed important approaches to resource allocation, taxation, public-good pricing,
and cost-revenue calculation. Like Cournot's *Recherches Économiques*,

however, the tradition of microeconomics developed at the Ponts et Chaussées, most notably by Jules Dupuit [1804–1866], stayed largely at the margins of the French community of economists. Although many engineers were quite actively involved in the Société d'Économie Politique and the Société Statistique de Paris, their scientific innovations generally fell outside the purpose of economics as stated by the field's dominant personalities in the Institut or, later, in the law faculties. Often, the engineers' ideas circulated through different media (e.g., the *Annales des Ponts et Chaussées*) that were relatively inconspicuous to these audiences.

Léon Walras (1834–1910) was yet another, somewhat singular, figure in this landscape. An *École des Mines* graduate who did not pursue an engineering career, he had to move to Switzerland to find a teaching position in spite of tireless attempts to establish himself in France.[58] His efforts to found "pure" (abstract) economics found little echo in France. Walras was alienated from the dominant groups for both methodological and political reasons: his socialistic positions in favor of the nationalization of the soil, in particular, were highly controversial (even among engineers, many of whom were just as *libéral* as their university colleagues). Consequently, practically minded public engineers seem not to have cared much about him either. In fact, the applied marginalism they practiced on the ground (to measure the utility of the railways, for instance) had yet to be linked with the theoretical marginalism upon which Walras was founding his general economic analysis. The connection between the two would only be made by Maurice Allais in the 1940s.

After 1910, economics professors in the engineering schools started being recruited among the body of engineers (rather than the jurists), which helped form a more coherent intellectual tradition. Two members of the Corps des Ponts et Chaussées (hereafter X-Ponts), Clément Colson and his student François Divisia, (who took over from him) both taught at the École des Ponts et Chaussées and the École Polytechnique, indeed dominating, if not monopolizing economics education in engineering schools during the interwar period.[59] As Lucette Le Van–Lemesle states, "If he ever wanted to, one single professor could train three quarters of the engineering students" (1993, 575). Colson's courses were practically oriented, but he kept them quite literary, much in line with what went on in the rest of the field at the time (the law universities still excluded all mathematical training).[60] Divisia, however, was more comfortable with his inheritance. He promoted the use of statistical methods, mathematical formulas and graphs and helped found the Econometric Society.

By the middle of the twentieth century, these engineers shared enough of a sense of the distinctiveness of their social trajectory and of their unique character as a technocratic elite to start reclaiming the original contribution of French "engineer-economists" to the development of economic science worldwide.[61] They did not constitute a well-institutionalized group, however. With the exception of a few professors, such as Divisia, engineer-economists prior to the late 1960s were not usually "professional" academic economists in the sense of being involved full-time in economic teaching and research. Many did not even see themselves *primarily* as economists. In several cases, their contributions to economic theory and applied economics were by-products of work they did within public administrations or public enterprises. This path had been set in the nineteenth century by figures like Jules Dupuit, a Polytechnicien and engineer from the École des Ponts et Chaussées, who had a distinguished engineering career in the management of water systems. Clément Colson (1853–1939) himself was director of the railways. Maurice Allais, Polytechnicien and member of the Corps des Mines (henceforth X-Mines),[62] completed his first major manuscript during his spare time while working as a Mining Administration official, although he soon obtained a permanent research position at the Centre National de la Recherche Scientifique (CNRS). Throughout his career he worked extensively on operational problems, such as peak-load pricing and the computation of marginal costs in transportation. René Roy, a Polytechnicien, member of the Corps des Ponts et Chaussées and a student of Colson, was at the Ministry of Public Works. Pierre Massé, another X-Ponts, and Marcel Boîteux, a mathematician trained at École Normale Supérieure, both occupied positions at Electricité de France (EDF), the French electricity monopoly. It was there that Massé made his early contributions to operations research and the analysis of investment policy rules and that Boîteux developed his analysis of marginal cost pricing.[63]

Porter (1995) has persuasively argued that nineteeth-century French engineers did not see themselves as quantifying experts the way members of the U.S. Army Corps of Engineers did. Like other French technocrats, they understood their role much more broadly: as general managers who had to take into consideration a wide range of factors, many of which are not quantifiable. Consequently, general knowledge and intuition were quite important in helping them reach administrative decisions. Still, these generalist administrative roles should not obscure the engineers' quite distinctive path when it came to their articulation of economic principles. Many (though not all) of them, approached economics with sophisticated mathematical skills and with an analogy to the natural sciences in the forefront of their minds. Hence the continued separation, even after World War II, of the engineers from the mainstream of the economics profession was unmistakable.

This did not mean that each side longed for a better integration with the other one: for Maurice Allais, for instance, there was no better economics training than the career path of the engineer (in the same way that studying classics remained a perfectly acceptable preparation to economics to Oxford's best mathematical economist): "We have never ceased to advise our students who want to deepen their understanding of the economy to start this process by acquiring an experience of practical life, and in particular of the concrete life of corporations, by spending a few years in industry or in an administrative position that allows them to keep in close contact with the business world. Nothing is more fake than a purely bookish knowledge of the economic world" (Allais 1954, 70). Just as the university professors were very mindful of their intellectual distinctiveness, and kept it well protected through the institutional mechanism of the *agrégation*, the Polytechniciens and other graduates from top engineering schools thought they belonged to an altogether different class of economists thanks to their superior mathematical skill (they were, rather, econometricians, or *économètres*) and more elevated social status. Consequently, they sought to keep the unworthy at bay. To cite Allais, again: "The recruitment of econometricians requires minds of the highest caliber. . . . Trying to teach the use of mathematics to students who do not have the ability to master it, as is currently done in some economic training institutions, is a complete waste of time and a probably quite dangerous thing to do" (Allais 1954, 71).

The engineers' seminars often took place outside traditional academic venues, in cafés or in mathematical centers, and included practitioners from both the public and the private sectors.[64] In the absence of formal training, these institutions played a key role in socializing the next generation of *grandes écoles* graduates interested in economics. For instance, Marcel Boîteux, Edmond Malinvaud (a Polytechnician, graduate of ENSAE and member of the Corps des Administrateurs de l'INSEE, or X-INSEE), Jacques Lesourne (X-Mines), and also Gérard Debreu (another *normalien*)[65] were all connected to Allais through the transportation seminar he organized at the École des Mines. In 1951, René Roy founded the CNRS econometrics seminar, which was taken over by Malinvaud in the 1970s, and afterward by Jean-Michel Grandmont (an X-Ponts). It was through these institutions and the international renown they attracted that the engineer-economists started to carve out the central position they now occupy in the scientific landscape. Doing so, however, took several decades and hinged on a profound transformation in institutional structures—particularly administrative structures—that took place in the postwar period. A first change was the more assertive institutionalization of an economic orientation within the public administration, which created the conditions for the production of a critical mass of nonuniversity economists. A second important step was the progressive, somewhat serendipitous, establishment of research havens for these people within administrative agencies, where many ended up devoting themselves to academic work. The final step was their penetration of traditional academic institutions—that is, the universities and the CNRS—after the 1970s.

The Nationalization of Economic Expertise

The expansion of state capacities in the postwar era had a decisive effect on the careers of the engineer-economists and on their position within the French field of economics. Here I do not mean simply to underline the importance of state development in the reshaping and growth of the social sciences. That all industrialized postwar states managed their economies by drawing on technical economic expertise (notably in the areas of national accounting, macroeconometric model-building, forecasting, planning, strategy, and others) is not a point of contention.[66] We have, for instance, already mentioned how critical state demands were for the development of economic knowledge in the United States from the 1940s through the 1960s, and how they continue to shape it today.

What is less well understood, however, are the different ways in which states came to manage their new tasks. In most countries, public administrations relied on social science inputs provided by outside institutions, universities in particular. In the United States, for instance, where the higher education system is comparatively responsive to the demands of its environment, universities adapted relatively quickly by institutionalizing technical forms of economic training. As a result, experts were often university professors on consulting contracts with various government or quasi-government agencies.

France followed a different path. The old law faculties could hardly provide the kind of specialists that the public administration had determined it needed to reconstruct the country's economy after the war. In 1945, most law faculty professors possessed few, if any, capabilities in the areas of forecasting, econometrics, and public economics. Also, the government's modernization strategy of state intervention and structural reform found itself at odds with the generally conservative approach taught in universities. After the outbreak of the Great Depression, various reformist currents within the political parties, unions, and the administration had criticized approaches to economics diffused at the law faculties as institutional, literary, and dogmatically *libéral*.[67] These critiques were for the most part born among the milieu of *grandes écoles* engineers, particularly from École Polytechnique. The X-Crise group, created in 1931 and transformed in 1933 into a research center, the Centre Polytechnicien d'Études Économiques, thus encouraged the development of new forms of economic expertise that were more technical (mathematics and statistics were routine elements in the society's bulletin), and largely favorable to the use of state intervention and planning as ways to restore production.[68] This technocratic ideology in French administration and industry fused with a certain reverence for "American" management methods, technical competence, and social science, which after the war diffused through the powerful channels of U.S. influence in Europe (e.g., American foundations and the Marshall Plan administration).[69]

It is important to understand that planning ideas in France were not necessarily understood to be antithetical to economic liberalism. Indeed, some of the most *libéral* economists could accommodate themselves quite well with the institutional apparatus that was put in place after 1944 as long as planning did not mean *dirigisme*. Jacques Rueff is a good example: Polytechnicien and *Inspecteur des finances*, professor at Sciences-Po, and a high-level civil servant, Rueff was a classical liberal who opposed Keynes on almost everything, starting with the use of public deficits. But he found himself quite at odds with the more visceral liberalism of some of the law professors and favored a role for the state in organizing the social order (and in that respect at least his ideas approached those of the German ordoliberals). Maurice Allais, whom we have already discussed, is another case. Like Rueff, he was involved in neoliberal circles (they were both members of the Mont-Pèlerin Society), but his economic work demonstrated the potential efficiency of centrally managed public utilities.[70]

Still, the modal position of the new generation of economic practitioners in the postwar period was more in tune with the rising economic fashion of the day—the macroeconomics of John Maynard Keynes.[71] Some were well aware of the policy experiments of the New Deal. Some had also read Keynes, though most economics professors had not. The first translation of the *General Theory* in French, by Jean de Largentaye, a high-level Treasury official, came out at the end of 1942. As a matter of fact, Keynes was better known in interwar France as the man who had opposed German reparations than as the promoter of a new economic policy regime. The first supporters of Keynesianism in France were, with a few exceptions (such as Perroux), not university economists but higher civil servants, government officials, and a number of personalities in leftist parties and unions, in other words, "men concerned with practical affairs."[72] Although the reform of the statistical apparatus and new forms of state intervention had begun under the Vichy government, it was really around 1946–47 that economic expansion started being envisioned in a general, "macroeconomic," conceptual framework, which remained largely foreign to most university economists until the 1960s.[73] In addition, some of the most popular policy measures (e.g., the full nationalization program proposed by the left wing of the Resistance) conflicted with the economic liberalism prevalent among university professors.

Unsurprisingly, the growth of the public sector and of the state's involvement in economic management after 1945 first benefited administrative institutions with an established financial and economic competence (most prominently the Inspection des Finances and the technical "corps" like the Corps des Mines and the Corps des Ponts et Chaussées). However, partly because of the economic conservatism of these agencies, some public officials understood the postwar situation as demanding a new class of specialists in economic and statistical matters. In keeping with the tradition of higher level expert training, the state became rapidly involved in the manufacturing of its own economic administrators. After 1945, bureaucratic control over the production of economic knowledge increased considerably as the state created training institutions for economic expertise, centralized economic research around the needs of the public administration, and enlarged the role of economic management agencies. This resulted in a massive influx of engineers, mathematicians, and young law faculty graduates with greater mathematical skills into the field of economic management and an institutionalized semiautonomous class of economic specialists, who were dependent on the state for their status and careers.[74]

New institutional structures within or closely connected with the administrative sector played a critical role in the intellectual upbringing of this generation, providing a sort of "on-the-job" training for new breeds of economic technocrats. Hence, the Institut de Sciences Économiques Appliquées (ISEA),[75] an economic research center established in 1944 by François Perroux under the patronage of public financial institutions, which was one of the main diffusers of international innovations in the French context (most prominently national accounting and the work of Keynes);[76] the Institut National de la Statistique et des Études Économiques (National Institute of Statistics and Economic Studies, or INSEE), established in 1946 as a central statistical administration for the collection and analysis of economic and social data, as well as (later) the production of economic forecasts;[77] the central planning agency (Commissariat Général au Plan), the brainchild of one of the most well-connected mediators between France and America, Jean Monnet; and, finally, the statistical and forecasting service of the Ministry of Finance, or Service des Études Économiques et Financières (SEEF),[78] which was later to evolve

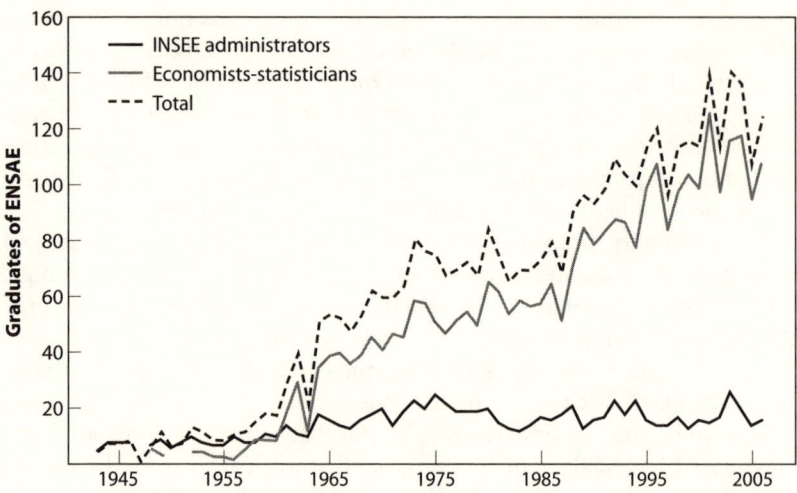

Figure 4-2. France. Graduates of École Nationale de la Statistique et de l'Administration Économiques (ENSAE), 1943–2006.

Source: Desrosières 1995; ENSAE. I am very grateful to Madame Sylviane Gastaldo, ENSAE, who provided the data to complete this series.

into the current Direction de la Prévision.[79] These organizations incubated the first national accounts and macroeconometric models in France.[80]

The real question was how to staff the new agencies. We have already seen that university graduates were not seen as suitable, in part because of inadequate technical skills and in part because of the state's tradition of grooming its own specialists within separate institutions. The Vichy government had already established a small school for the purpose of economic and statistical training in 1942, the future École Nationale de la Statistique et de l'Administration Économiques [ENSAE]. By 1946 the school had been reassigned to train some graduates of Polytechnique as a new statistical elite, some of whom would enter a new administrative *corps* managing the INSEE, while the rest would move on to jobs in the private sector. The École Nationale d'Aministration (ENA) was created in 1946 with a similar purpose in mind, though it was less focused on purely technical skills. State administration further rationalized higher level economic training by creating the Centre d'Étude des Programmes Économiques (CEPE) in 1957[81] and reorganizing the ENSAE in 1960, whose student body rapidly expanded thereafter (figure 4-2).

Thanks to these initiatives, economic administrations could now rely on specific training institutions rather than the eclectic and informal training provided within the Commissariat Général au Plan or the SEEF. The CEPE's purpose, for instance, was to provide continuing education to the technocrats and practitioners in the public administration, turning them into economists or, more specifically, economic technicians. A number of engineering school graduates followed this path before serving the public administration in an economic capacity. One of them, who trained at the CEPE during the mid-1970s, thus recalled:

> Political economy in those years was taught in the law faculties. It was not Keynesian, and not quantitative at all. A quantitative branch of economics had emerged with the establishment of national accounts. But there was still a deficit of people to occupy these posts (that is, people who would be able to do applied economics studies with a minimal Keynesian background) both in the corporate and administrative spheres. The CEPE's mission was to manufacture such people. We had to follow a very intense training that lasted one year. Naturally this does not produce people who know economics well, who have a broad culture in economics. That is a characteristic of French economists, at least the people from my generation. (research scholar, CEPII, August 1995)

These educational and training organizations, which recruited from the most mathematically skilled cohorts of engineers and university graduates, thus constituted a new pole of economic knowledge production partly autonomous from the university. Economics courses in these institutions came under the control of state administrators and engineers (e.g., Malinvaud, Roy, Jean Ullmo) rather than of university professors of political economy.[82]

The Rise of the Engineer-Economists

The engineer-economist tradition of research began to take a more consistent shape in the 1970s as a result of three converging processes. First, during the postwar years, one of their new areas of expertise, the production of economic and statistical instruments for the purpose of state-led economic management, was the research frontier in economics. Today national accounting, model-building, and forecasting are regarded as routine, unexciting tasks by economists working in government. In the 1960s and 1970s, however, they elicited much more enthusiasm. Histories of the early years of national accounting and the Planning Commissariat tell a heroic story of intellectual pioneers.[83] My own interviews with the builders of macroeconometric models elicited reminiscence of the same missionary spirit.

The first French large-scale macroeconometric models were built in the late 1960s, with a second important wave of innovation occuring during the second half of the 1970s. This is quite late compared with similar developments in countries like the United States, England, or the Nether-lands (Tinbergen's model for the Dutch economy was built in the mid-1930s).[84] The practice, indeed, was largely imported from these nations. Contacts with the "Anglo-Saxons" (notably Richard Stone at Cambridge, England) served to socialize a whole generation of practitioners trained at the ENSAE and at École Polytechnique into national accounting and modern economic analysis. Whereas model-building in other countries relied on a fairly broad institutional base, usually associating universities, research organizations, and public administrations, in France it remained chiefly an in-house, technocratic enterprise effected by the state (mostly at the INSEE and the Direction de la Prévision) and for the state. Further-more, it was legitimated politically by its formal incorporation into an in-stitutionalized framework of public policy decision-making: forecasts served for the establishment of the five-year plan, which gave them, and the institutions that produced them, considerable visibility.

A second important change was the development, after the late 1960s, of an economic research sector within the public administration itself. The IVth (1962–66) and Vth (1966–70) national plans singled out eco-nomics as the most advanced and scientific discipline of the social sci-ences and inaugurated a centralized policy of research contracts aimed at channeling social-scientific research toward specific uses. Purpose-oriented research organizations were created, many of them under the authority of the Planning Commissariat. In 1962, the then director of the agency, Pierre Massé, established the Centre de Recherches Mathé-matiques Appliquées à la Planification (or CERMAP), later renamed Centre pour la Recherche Économique et ses Applications (or CEPRE-MAP)[85] to serve as an advisory department for the public administra-tion. Similarly, the Centre d'Études des Revenus et des Coûts (CERC), another of Massé's creations, now past, was given the mission of analyz-ing the distribution of income at a time when France was trying to set up an income policy.[86]

Social-scientific research was also promoted through the development of contracts for various ministries. When state administrators set up the Comité de Coordination et d'Orientation des Recherches sur le Dével-oppement Économique et Social (CORDES) to contract out social-scientific research for state ministries, the arrangement, while ostensibly similar to U.S. government practices that helped feed the growth of uni-versities and consulting firms, ended up reinforcing the primacy of the state as a locus of professional research. In a process that exemplifies the self-reinforcing nature of state-centered technical expertise in France, CORDES further deepened the marginalization of universities.[87] (Pollak [1976, 114] has shown that already during the 1960s, the proportion of social science research funds going to universities was lagging further and further behind the state sector even as funds were growing overall; CORDES simply reinforced an ongoing trend.)

Finally, a particularly fateful development for postwar French economics took place as engineering-trained administrators grew increasingly close to the Anglo-American versions of scholarly economics. Members of the Corps des Ponts et Chaussées and the Corps des Administrateurs de l'INSEE were especially prominent in this evolution. In contrast to university academics, who looked mostly inward after 1945, the *grandes écoles* engineers and administrator-economists were well acquainted with foreign approaches and technical innovations, both in applied domains and in theoretical economics and econometrics through their participation in international meetings, such as those of the Econometric Society and the Cowles Commission (where, for instance, Malinvaud spent two years in the early 1950s).[88] These international linkages became more active during the 1970s, when a number of *corps* members and graduates of the *grandes écoles* went on to pursue graduate and postgraduate studies in economics in the United States. The first generations of these foreign-trained nationals came back with their PhDs at the beginning of the 1970s.

The engineers' training in social science, which had taken place largely outside the university or even outside the country, did not give them easy access to teaching and research positions, however. Without an *agrégation,* they were automatically barred from obtaining a university professorship. But as lifetime members of the Corps de l'Etat, many of them instead found employment in the specialized research organizations that had been set up to serve the public administration.

As their staff became increasingly socialized in international academic circles, a number of these organizations thus started to evolve toward "pure" research, sometimes against the intention of their institutional sponsors. The CEPREMAP offers the most striking example of such a transformation. Without letting go of its formal affiliation with the Planning Commissariat, the organization gradually moved away from its original function as a consulting bureau for the public administration to become one of the main academic centers in French economics. Some of the most important intellectual advances in postwar French economics originated there, either in applied studies, which evolved into theoretical endeavors, or in mathematical work by returning U.S.-trained engineers who were pursuing the American-inspired route to scientific professionalism: publications in Anglo-American economic reviews. This is the case, for instance, of the two main economic "schools" of the postwar period: the "regulation" approach (which followed the first path) and the "disequilibrium" approach (which followed the second).[89] In his conversation with me, one X-Ponts engineer described his dissatisfaction with the training he had received in France (he "did not understand what the French economists were up to") and his conversion to academic research in the United States in the following terms:

> I wanted to do economics, but I did not know under which form, so I went to the CERMAP. . . . I was doing applied studies there, but after two years I could not stand it anymore. . . . I met a colleague who gave me a book—*The Theory of Value*, by Gérard Debreu. It was in 1967, the book had been around for eight years, and it was one of the most important building blocks of economic theory at the time, but I did not know about it. And when I read that, after one–two months, I said: "*Now* I understand." And this is when I decided to leave for the United States.

He went on to describe his return to France:

> At the time, there were a few eminent personalities in French economic research, like Allais or Malinvaud. . . . Allais was very famous. But there was no school. Or there was just something that was the tradition of the French engineer-economists. Malinvaud had not created a school. What happened is that when I came back from the United States with my PhD, there was a small generation of people who, in spite of the French system, wanted to do research. It was located around the INSEE, and in a few other places. . . . All of a sudden four or five of us, some of whom had studied abroad, started to do research. Before that time, it was something people did not do. (research scholar, CEPREMAP, August 1995)

The intellectual path alluded to in this quotation was essentially the further development of mathematical economics, and in particular an attention to the microfoundations of macroeconomic functions and relations. Substantively the program in France (building on the work of American economists Barro, Grossman, Clower, and Leijonhufvud) involved reinterpreting Keynesian macroeconomics within a fixed-price general equilibrium analysis.[90] Almost forgotten today, the disequilibrium school occupied the energies of French mathematical economists for about a decade. Malinvaud synthesized the policy implications (in particular the distinction between "Keynesian" and "classical" unemployment) in an influential monograph in 1977.

In contrast with disequilibrium analysis, French engineers' innovative research on regulation was a more applied, more homegrown, and more heterodox affair. The school's leaders were Polytechniciens (mostly X-INSEE and X-Ponts) who worked on economic planning at the CGP, the Direction de la Prévision, INSEE, and CEPREMAP. Their international connections linked them more with the Cambridge neo-Keynesians and

Italian *operaismo* than with the neoclassical American-centered networks preferred by their more formally minded brethren. These connections were also less central to their intellectual approach, however: all the members of the regulation school were trained primarily in France. Lipietz (1994), in fact, described the "regulationists" (himself included) as the "rebel sons of Pierre Massé and Louis Althusser," emphasizing the pragmatic—but also conflictual—connection with the administrative apparatus, particularly Pierre Massé's Planning Commissariat, as well as with French structural Marxism, which was a dominant intellectual influence at the time.[91] Like their neoclassical counterparts, the regulationists offered a diagnosis of the emerging economic crisis. But their explanation emphasized structural factors, such as the exhaustion of the main social compromise upon which the Fordist "mode of regulation" had been based since the 1930s, whereby productivity gains were automatically transformed into salary increases.[92] Their scientific style also combined broad, somewhat literary ambitions with a resolute empiricism that set it apart from previous Marxist approaches. This orientation can be traced to the regulationists' positions within the public administration and their involvement with the empirical research programs of the Direction de la Prévision and INSEE: Michel Aglietta, Robert Boyer, Alain Lipietz, Jacques Mistral, and Jacques Mazier all started their careers there, working on macroeconometric modeling (Aglietta, Mistral, and Mazier went on to get a doctorate).

Both approaches had developed as pragmatic attempts to characterize and prognosticate about the then current economic crisis, in keeping with the consulting function of the CEPREMAP. Indeed, one of the regulation school's founding contributions was a 1977 report for the CORDES on inflation (CEPREMAP 1977), which led to several books by individual members of the original collective.[93] It is on the strength of their structural analyses predicting the future of French capitalism, for instance, that some regulationists enjoyed a short-lived stint as advisers to the socialist government after its election in the early 1980s.[94] Yet over time, many of these individuals drifted in different directions: some went into academia, joining a university, the EHESS or the CNRS; others into high administration, including ministerial cabinets, or business; many combined all three functions. Partly as a result of the weakening of the administrative institutions and philosophy that had produced it, the CEPREMAP progressively lost its applied dimension and redirected most of its activities toward scholarly research and student training. One after the other, the research centers affiliated with the Planning Commissariat closed and had most of their personnel transferred to the research consortium CNRS. The CEPREMAP itself was finally severed from the Commissariat Général au Plan in 2005 and incorporated into the Ministry of Research.

In other cases, however, administrative institutions fiercely resisted the push for research. For instance, while approving the involvement of administrators in academic economics (which contributed to the liveliness of the famous Roy-Malinvaud seminars), INSEE officials long opposed the emergence of a "pure" research pole within its walls on the grounds that it would divert energies from the real task at hand—serving administrative needs. The ambivalence of Edmond Malinvaud, one of France's most famous economists and the director of INSEE between 1974 and 1987, is well known among contemporary French economists. As one scholar put it: "The little story about Malinvaud—at least this is what he always said—is that he worked on research from five to seven in the morning and during weekends, and that research is not a profession.[95] My generation is a generation that establishes research as a real profession. . . . It's an important qualitative change" (research scholar, CEPREMAP, August 1995).

Despite this attitude, however, INSEE, with its enormous concentration of statisticians and econometricians, continued to be a central location for economic research. In the 1980s it was largely there that the next generation of neoclassicals (who finally succeeded in establishing an in-house research pole, the CREST) and also of heterodox economists (under the new label "school of conventions") would emerge (Dosse 1995, 283–84). Today, 9 percent of ENSAE graduates occupy teaching or research functions;[96] the CREST is over 140 members strong, nearly one-third of whom are INSEE administrators, a significant development given that those who designed the system never intended for it to house full-time scholars.[97]

The Internationalization of French Economics

All these developments magnified the influence of engineers (of various intellectual persuasions) within the academic field from the 1970s on. The *Revue Économique* started to attract nonuniversity authors.[98] Journals founded by the economic public administrations, INSEE and Direction de la Prévision, provided other (and perhaps more natural) publication venues.[99] Originally developed to publish analyses performed by these two administrations, these reviews held a virtual monopoly on applied economic research in France. During the 1980s, however, the review *Annales de l'INSEE* led the way toward a more assertive research orientation and edged closer to the theoretical world of the engineers. A 1982 bibliometric study thus found that these publications (*Économie et Statistique*, the *Annales de l'INSEE*, and *Statistique et Études Financières-Série Orange*) were routinely, even "zealously," cited by other French economic reviews, which deferred to their empirical and formal analyses. The *Annales de l'INSEE* today remains the most cited French economics publication worldwide.[100]

This centralization of economic research around public administrations and their associated *corps* may represent the most important change in French postwar economics. A simple measure of the magnitude of the transformation is the citation pattern in Blaug and Sturges's *Who's Who in Economics?* (1986), which shifts dramatically between the early part of the century, when the list of internationally well-known names in French economics includes a majority of university professors, and the 1970s and 1980s, when it is composed almost exclusively of engineers and INSEE administrators.[101] What separates the two periods is the gradual institutionalization through seminars, publication outlets, and graduate programs, of the (initially amateur) research orientation within the *grandes écoles* and the administrative world.

Economics training in the engineering schools themselves started to change in the late 1960s. Until then, it had remained, as one interviewee put it, "very elementary, in spite of the fact that it would have been very easy to teach mathematical economics at Polytechnique."[102] Except at ENSAE and, to a lesser extent, at École des Mines where Allais's influence was strong, the administrative authorities, who oversaw these institutions, continued to treat economics as a nonscientific subject. It took the students' rebellion of 1968 to force an expansion of economic research and teaching at Polytechnique into a more extensive and formal training program involving a younger generation of teachers and a resurrected version of Divisia's old econometrics laboratory. By the 1980s, economics had become a central part of the curriculum at many engineering schools, sometimes achieving the status of a "major" (e.g., the Economics section at École Centrale or the applied mathematics and economics section at Polytechnique).[103] Many schools had also added research centers and graduate programs. The École des Ponts created the CERAS, allegedly in order to provide expertise in the field of transport economics, but in fact granting relative intellectual freedom to its members. The École Normale Supérieure established the DELTA. These expansions are still unfolding. Perhaps the most interesting recent change is the regrouping of several leading economic research centers and their associated doctoral programs into large research consortiums: Paris-Sciences Économiques and Toulouse Sciences Economiques.

Not only have the *grandes écoles* become more economics-oriented, but they have also converged with the technical-administrative world of INSEE. In fact, the curriculum at ENSAE, where many are trained, inaugurated a stronger theoretical (i.e., microeconomic) component that complemented its traditional focus on statistical and econometric technique. Today, the training there resembles the standard graduate curriculum taught at top North American universities.[104]

The rise of the engineer-economists also had profound repercussions beyond the boundaries of the administrative world. As we have seen, some of the Polytechniciens who had been recruited into the economic administration via the CEPE and the Direction de la Prévision developed research interests of their own and undertook more academic careers either at the university (by completing a PhD and competing for the *agrégation*) or at the CNRS. At the same time, for younger generations of university economists, formalism represented a strategy for gaining access to international scientific networks and their symbolic and material rewards.[105] While some institutions, such as the CEPREMAP or the EHESS, were relatively open to the "mathematicians," others fiercely resisted the influx. The generalist orientation of the *agrégation* and the inevitably cliquish impulses of exam juries[106] often functioned as a gatekeeping device that put the most specialized and technically oriented economists at a disadvantage. Some failed, or placed poorly. The examination thus remained a site of struggle between different understandings of economic knowledge; that is, over the place and nature of erudition ("the myth of universal knowledge," as one recent critic put it) versus specialized research in the national diploma.[107] In that sense, the *agrégation* dramatized the contest over what Bourdieu would call different forms of capital: specialized, formalizing, and international on the one hand; intellectually broader, less technical, more politically (and therefore nationally) oriented on the other.

Still, from the mid-1970s on, the "mathematicians" progressed enough to launch their careers at the university, sometimes from peripheral locations in provincial towns. An especially interesting development, for instance, was the establishment of an "internationalized" and highly entrepreneurial organizational base at the University of Toulouse, led by two economists trained at the *grandes écoles* and U.S. universities, Jean-Jacques Laffont (ENSAE, Harvard PhD) and Jean Tirole (X-Ponts, MIT PhD). Although located outside the mainstream of power, the Industrial Economics Institute (IDEI) used its ties with the faculties to train PhDs for the academic market, including the *agrégation*. Through this strategy, "Toulouse" has had an important impact on the promotion of American-style professionalism at the very heart of the French university system. With Laffont and Tirole leading an intellectual revolution in industrial economics and drawing solid financial support from research contracts with the large public monopolies (mainly electricity and gas), the institution and its associated CNRS research center, the GREMAQ, were able to use the hierarchy of international standards dominated by American scientific reviews to establish their (now central) position within the French and, indeed, the European field.[108] To some extent, the microeconomic problems most IDEI economists dealt with belonged to the well-established tradition of the French economist-engineers going back to Dupuit, but they now pursued them from a different, more academically powerful, institutional base.

Since the 1970s, then, practitioners trained in the hard sciences have gradually increased their influence over doctoral programs and the *agrégation*, thus gaining access to chairs and contributing to the "scientization" of the university curriculum.[109] These developments, combined with international trends in the field as a whole, have reinforced the legitimacy of a "hard science model." The "econometrics major," for instance, has become the most selective and prestigious track almost everywhere. Paradoxically, owing to the strong formalizing orientation of many new professors, as well as the traditional disconnection between theory and applied studies, some French undergraduate economics curricula may today be yet more exclusively mathematical than their American counterparts, which are typically quite empirical and full of descriptive material. Indeed, this may have partly motivated the French students' revolt of 2000 with which this chapter opened. Mathematical techniques are increasingly integrated as routine elements of an academic profession that appears more "normalized" and less eclectic than in previous decades.[110]

The "Administrative Economists"

In contrast to both the United States and the United Kingdom, policy-relevant economic knowledge in France has involved the universities and the private world only in a limited manner. As we have seen, the French state organizes the training of its own economic specialists through two main career lines: one for technical purposes centered on the ENSAE, and one for policy-making purposes centered on the ENA. Whereas the two trajectories are often lumped together, they are in fact quite distinct. ENSAE graduates dominate the production of economic statistics and the technical *directions* of the Ministry of Finance (e.g., the Direction de la Prévision, the Direction de l'INSEE), while ENA alumni govern the production of economic advice and staff the key policy-making institutions (i.e., ministerial cabinets and powerful administrative departments in the Ministry of Finance like the Treasury and the Budget). The Inspection des Finances, for instance, by and large continues to reign supreme over financial matters. Both the production of economic information and the provision of policy advice are thus, by and large, organized as administrative monopolies.

Administrative Monopolies

This separation between "numbers" and "ideas," represented by the divide between ENSAE and ENA, has deep roots in French history. As far back as the nineteenth century, the professional and intellectual projects of statisticians and economists were more disconnected from one another than they were across the English Channel. A few Ponts et Chaussées engineers advocated forcefully for the incorporation of statistical tools in the development of economic knowledge,[111] but their influence on the field of political economy was only marginal. Resistance toward the use of statistical methods in economics came not only from liberal circles and the law faculties, but also from pioneers in mathematical economics like Cournot and Walras, who were principally interested in pure mathematical abstraction (Ménard 1987). The career of someone like Edgeworth, for instance, who held both the Drummond chair in economics at Oxford and the presidency of the Royal Statistical Society, would have been more improbable in the French context.

Nevertheless, it is through the administrative channel and the "social engineers" that the present-day synthesis between statistical and economic knowledge started to diffuse in France. In contrast to England, where statistical activities initially developed outside of state control among learned societies and social reform movements, in France they were closely associated with the state from the outset, as Libby Schweber (2006) and Alain Desrosiéres (1999) have shown. In particular, late nineteenth-century officials from administrative bureaus played an important role in diffusing new knowledge in mathematical statistics. Still, the central statistical apparatus remained poorly developed and staffed well into the twentieth century. Looking back on the interwar period, Alfred Sauvy (1984), for instance, compared unfavorably the staff of 120 of the Statistique Générale de France at the end of the 1930s to the nearly 2,400 employees of Germany's equivalent agency. The general lack of interest in data among French governing officials, and their poor knowledge of empirical facts, Sauvy argues, resulted in major economic policy mistakes.[112]

Sauvy's general account about the interwar period is corroborated by the history of the Institut Scientifique de Recherches Economiques et Sociales (ISRES), a small private observatory of economic conditions, created in 1933 under the direction of Charles Rist at the École Libre des Sciences Politiques. Rist devoted his institute's efforts almost exclusively to the collection and centralization of economic archives. Characteristically, however, he was able to set up his enterprise only by enrolling the financial support of the Laura Spellman Rockefeller Memorial Fund in the context of its worldwide promotion of empirical economic research (whose effects we have already discussed in the United States and in England). In addition, the organization's position as a private institute outside the administration limited its influence on official economic policy, foiling Rist's ambition to turn it into a French equivalent of the U.S. NBER.[113]

As in many other areas, the development of a modern statistical information system owed a lot to the advocacy of modernizers within the administration and among its corps of engineers. The activities of the ISRES during the 1930s prompted some state officials to recognize the need for coordinating a disparate system of economic and statistical information, although they believed that the system ought to be revamped on the administration's own terms. The main framework of the postwar economic information system was finally laid out under the Vichy government, which created the National Statistical Service in 1941 as a new "administrative body" of its own. This agency would soon be staffed by a new elite trained in a specialized school and associated *corps* of administrators (ENSAE and INSEE, already mentioned).[114]

Interestingly, these institutions, especially after the creation of the Service des Études Économiques et Financières (SEEF) at the Ministry of Finance with which they were closely linked, came to embody the institutionalized symbiosis between the generation of economic statistics, on the one hand, and the utilization of these data for economic planning and management, on the other.[115] This organizational design created a nearly absolute monopoly of governmental organizations and their unique breed of "economist-statisticians" over the construction of economic diagnostics, forecasts, and the production of policy-relevant economic information.[116] The state's statistics-gathering apparatus expanded considerably in the 1960s and 1970s, both quantitatively and qualitatively. The INSEE, for instance, went from a staff of about 2,500 in 1960 to 5,600 in 1970 and 7,000 in 1976, in pace with the institutionalization of national accounting and economic studies.[117] The number of INSEE administrators produced every year by ENSAE grew from 9 in 1960 to a peak of 24 in 1975. In 1965, the SEEF received a bureaucratic promotion, becoming the Direction de la Prévision, which was to serve as a think tank for the cabinet of the Ministry of Finance. Finally, various ministries established their own statistical and economic bureaus (e.g., at the Ministry of Labor), which also undertook significant amounts of research.[118]

By the end of the 1970s, public administrations, which controlled the production, release, and interpretation of economic numbers and figures, could shape much of the public debate about the state of the French economy. Whatever applied work was done under the aegis of contracts issued by government agencies (in economics, sociology, and urban studies) during the 1960s and 1970s, it was either carried out by the staff of specialized administrative agencies such as the INSEE or, when administrative resources proved insufficient, it was done on the cheap, by teams of contractual workers without formal status (the *hors-statuts*) and often without formal degrees.[119] As elsewhere, one consequence of this state-sponsored expansion in teaching, research, and contractual work was the diversification of recruitment in the social sciences, and the intellectual world more generally. Thus the intellectual transformations accompanying the social movements of the 1960s also left traces in the social-scientific organizations associated with the state, where experts working on national accounts, planning, and economic studies either for the administration or under contract for the CORDES flirted as comfortably with Marxism as they did with Keynesianism.

As ideological polarization grew during the 1970s, right-wing circles seized on the opportunity to express their concern. The ideological climate was changing on the Right, too. Across the Atlantic the champions of Keynesianism were under serious attack following Friedman's (1968) claims about the existence of a natural unemployment rate that no monetary policy could succeed in curbing.[120] In France, reemerging liberal currents at the margins of the administrative field (mostly in the universities and business schools and at Sciences-Po) contested the prevailing "Keynesian" orthodoxy of the public economic management apparatus. Rallying under the banner of the "new economists," they launched a partially successful media campaign to influence the political debate. The revival of liberal thought had been brewing for some time in France, and this seemed to be their moment.

And indeed the political atmosphere was different. The new president in power after 1974, Valéry Giscard d'Estaing, and especially his prime minister after 1976, Raymond Barre, introduced a dose of monetarism and attention to the supply side of the economy in an otherwise traditional Keynesian policy framework. A university economist, Barre also set out to dismantle the existing institutional machinery for the production of economic knowledge in France and enlisted his adviser, another university economist of *libéral* persuasion, in this effort. The first organization to go was the CORDES. Perceived as politically suspect by the right-wing government, its funding was cut off in 1979, though the Left partially revived it when it returned to power in 1981 (table 4-1).[121]

The recently acquired legitimacy of the social sciences within the research consortium CNRS appeared little more secure. A report submitted to the prime minister in 1978 argued that these disciplines required no great financial resources and were better off confined to teaching institutions.[122] Although it remained a dead letter thanks to resistance and a change in political administration in 1981, the report illustrates the vulnerability of the social sciences to political whim, in France as elsewhere.

TABLE 4-1
Research Contracts with the CORDES and the Planning
Commissariat (in millions of current French Francs)

Years	Program Authorizations	Annual Spending
1972	7.15	6.94
1973	5.686	5.58
1974	6.454	6.07
1975	7.703	6.358
1976	6.393	7.155
1977	8.582	7.508
1978	3.585	6.7
1979	—	—
1980	—	—
1981	6.94	2.29
1982	5.95	5.26
1983	4.59	6.19
1984	7.56	6.04
1985	9.5	7.9

Source: CORDES.

But the most serious attack of all was directed at the Gaullist-era legacy of a hypercentralized economic information system. The de facto monopoly of public administrations on the production, release, and interpretation of economic statistics became a growing concern as the deepening economic crisis fomented frequent disputes between the INSEE and the government.[123] The reform commission formed to look into the subject stated in its final report that "no team (outside the administration) has been able to attain a critical mass in order to have weighed in on the economic debate,"[124] and recommended the creation of new economic research organizations in order to introduce "pluralism." These organizations would be able to mobilize the INSEE's resource but would be encouraged to provide alternative interpretations and forecasts. The solution, patterned after the German model of several research institutes of comparable weight but different corporate affiliations, was implemented at the onset of the 1980s.

The government first established the Observatoire Français des Conjonctures Économiques (OFCE), a rather large institution that was expressly instructed to "liven up" the public debate. Designed as a more scientific center, it was also responsible for producing "independent" economic forecasts intended to compete with those of INSEE. The rest of the system consisted of two smaller structures, each representing different corporate groups: IPECODE,[125] on the employers' side, and IRES, established in 1982 by the socialist government and supervised by the unions.

How much pluralism these institutional transformations really introduced in the economic information apparatus is an open question. The administrative sphere in France still retains its unique position as both producer *and* first user of primary data. This situation differs from that in most other countries, where such a profound integration between official statistics and applied economic studies does not exist, and skills are more dispersed among the universities, the government, and the private sector. In addition, the French system does not support alternative sources of financing. The organizations created at the turn of the 1980s, for instance, remained highly dependent on the state for resources, contracts, and skilled personnel. In contrast to the think tanks that mushroomed in the Anglo-American world around the same period, the French initiative was largely organized from above, and has remained so to this day. Except for IPECODE, which was entirely private, the other structures were financed almost exclusively by public sources, via the Planning Commissariat.

More crucially, possibilities for staffing the new organizations were limited. Technical economic skills and competence are vested almost exclusively in state administrators, particularly among graduates from the ENSAE. By intellectual tradition, and because of a lack of resources, the university does not serve as a training ground for applied economic expertise. This situation played out very obviously in the case of the Observatoire Français des Conjonctures Économiques, which became a refuge of economists-statisticians from the INSEE. Here is how two observers described the change:

> The "new economists," they tried to use Barre so that he would set up these new structures. That was the original plan for the OFCE: to give money to the Fondation Nationale des Sciences Politiques so that they would produce a non-Keynesian counterweight to the INSEE. This plan was all over in a few days. Why? Because, of course, the state is not going to trust the "new economists" to build macroeconometric models. Rather, the state is going to trust people trained at Polytechnique, people from the INSEE. And all of these people were Keynesian at the beginning of the 1980s. Because, you see, as soon as economics becomes technical, the new economists are powerless. They do not count the likes of Sargent [a well-known conservative mathematical

economist in the United States] among their ranks, that is, people who are also excellent mathematicians. (research scholar, CEPREMAP, August 1995)

It's only people from the public administration who have resources. Because of that, they have secured a monopoly on applied macroeconomic and policy studies. There is a real feeling of inferiority among university-based economists vis-à-vis this dominant world; implicitly, they always think "we aren't going to take a position contrary to that of the administration economists, since we cannot base our opinion on an empirically secure foothold, as they can." (professor, Sciences-Po and university, July 1995)

There is no doubt that the creation of quasi-public economic research institutes has eroded the monopoly of INSEE. But from a wider comparative perspective, INSEE's ascendancy is remarkable. Indeed, the new pluralism actively promoted by public officials still remained under the tight control of administrative and, ultimately, political powers. An inescapable contradiction persists between actual financial dependence on the administration and the proclaimed mission of intellectual independence. For instance, the OFCE, which was perceived as favorable to the socialist party, found its budget sharply reduced during the first right-wing *cohabitation* government of 1986 to 1988. And the institution's public activism prior to the 1993 legislative election caused a certain amount of political agitation.[126]

The Enarchie

Teachers and professors—especially members of the law faculties and Sciences-Po—have traditionally played an important role in French politics. During the Third (1871–1940) and Fourth (1946–58) Republics, it was not uncommon for French economics professors to have a political career in the chamber of deputies or the senate, or even to serve as government ministers.[127] When it came to high-level positions in the administrative bureaucracy, however, the channels of access were generally closed to economic experts from universities. There were a few exceptions to this pattern, most notably during World War I.[128] But since World War II and the creation of the ENA, these exceptions have become rarer. If anything, reliance on experts drawn from administrative *corps* dramatically increased under the Fifth Republic. This is partly because French administrative practice does not routinely authorize temporary appointments of outsiders, as does British and U.S. practice. But the making of economic policy has also largely excluded members of the technical economic and statistical *corps*—something one interviewee characterized as "such a waste-when one knows how expensive it is to produce an Administrateur de l'INSEE" (High-level civil servant July 2005).

AN ECONOMIC ARISTOCRACY

The technocrats who dominate the Ministry of Finance and the ministerial cabinets typically conceive of themselves as a particular breed of "economic specialists." The mission of the Inspection des Finances, Sciences-Po, and the postwar ENA was to manufacture public experts in financial, and then economic, matters. The Ecole Libre des Sciences Politiques, as we have seen, was originally a private endeavor aimed at diffusing a liberal ideology among the higher civil service. (It was practically nationalized in 1945.)[129] The ENA, on the other hand, was created partly as a counterweight to the liberal orthodoxy of the high administration, which was held responsible for the economic disasters of the 1930s. In the words of Charles de Gaulle, president of the Republic in the provisional postwar government, the new institution was to "assist the state in its duty of economic direction of the country" (speech before the Consultative Assembly, March 2, 1945).[130]

Consistent with its founders' wishes, the ENA initially played an important role in diffusing modernist orientations within the Ministry of Finance, which had been dominated by a traditional "financial" conception of the economy. The first teachers there were recruited among the group of technocrats who had become acquainted with Keynesianism and modern methods of public management during the war. They "stressed economics . . . , taught it through case study, and made it more mathematical" (Kuisel 1981, 215).[131] And indeed economics' place in the school's curriculum increased almost continuously throughout the postwar period.

As it had done with the *grands corps* examinations in the nineteenth century, Sciences-Po soon established for itself a quasimonopoly on the training of students for the competitive examination that gave access to ENA. The school was so successful in this role that it controlled about 68 percent of ENA external admissions in the 1940s and 1950s and over 80 percent in the 1960s and 1970s.[132] In spite of the bold claims formulated by ENA's original sponsors, the continuity with prewar administrative training was thus strong, and became stronger as time went by. Factual and institutional knowledge of government operations and rules still occupied a privileged position in the curriculum at both institutions. The teaching of new subjects (such as economics) was directed toward concrete public policy uses and increasingly anchored in the dominant world of the administrative *grands corps* as opposed to the technical world of the engineering and statistical *corps*. By the mid-1990s, one of my interviewees, a professor at Sciences-Po and the University of Paris I, could thus observe:

> Teaching at the university is analytical. It is always possible to write an equation on the blackboard. But courses at Sciences-Po are always turned toward specific objectives. They are less analytical and more literary than at the university. Theoretical reflection is systematically linked to concrete problems of economic policy. It's quite frustrating. Theoretical reasoning does not go very far. The main objective remains to enter the ENA. And there, it's the same thing: it's literary talent that gets rewarded. (July 1995)

In the French context, an "economist" in charge of public policy or in an economic advisory position (e.g., at the Treasury or in a ministerial cabinet) is thus primarily a high-ranking technocrat who has gone through Sciences-Po, ENA, and (in the most elite cases) the Inspection des Finances. Such an individual has usually received training in economic and social policy, international questions, and administrative law (which remains the most prestigious subject) and has written many policy memos but done no actual piece of economic research. People who are selected for high positions in international organizations typically come from the same background. (Michel Camdessus, an *énarque* who directed the International Monetary Fund from 1987 to 2000, is one such example.) By contrast, specialized economists (in the sense of members of a professionalized scientific discipline) possess only limited institutionalized access to higher administrative and advice positions on the grounds that they are involved primarily in intellectual speculation and have a poor knowledge of the real world. A conflict of positions thus persists between the "economic managers" and the "economists," whether from university or from the technical *corps*. This struggle pits the public policy orientation of ENA graduates, who have been trained by higher civil servants and school alumni to the jurisdictional claims of disciplinary economists, who accuse the former group of having "lost touch" with the evolution of "economic science." Who the "proper" economic experts are is fraught with jurisdictional tensions rooted in the divided structure of the French state itself.

THE TRANSFORMATIONS OF ECONOMIC ADVICE

The main institutions of economic advice within the French governmental machinery are the ministerial cabinets affiliated with the various ministries (and with the presidency), and the various heads of "directions" at the Ministry of Finance, especially the Direction of the Treasury. All these agencies, for the most part, remain largely the province of ENA graduates. For instance, the latter have held 60 to 75 percent of positions as directors of ministerial cabinets from the mid-1980s to the late 1990s.[133]

Apart from the ministerial cabinets, the French government until 1997 possessed two "centralized" formal structures of economic advice. The Conseil Economique National (forerunner of the current Conseil Economique et Social) was created in 1925 as a consultative organ for the study and assessment of the economic situation in France. It was a large organization composed mainly of representatives of various economic sectors and interest groups. It had no research staff of its own, and its reports were usually written by top civil servants, who closely supervised the process.[134] In contrast with the British Economic Advisory Council of 1930, it did not include any outside economic experts such as university professors. The current Conseil Economique et Social includes forty members, but its composition, again, is more the outcome of complex negotiations between political and interest groups than it is a selection of specialists.

In 1952 public officials established the Commission des Comptes et des Budgets Économiques de la Nation at the Ministry of Finance for the purpose of producing a yearly report on the country's economic situation known as the *Report on National Accounts* (*Rapport sur les Comptes de la Nation*). The commission was designed as a sizable body of economic experts from the public and private sectors including, representatives of corporate groups, and members of the French Parliament. However, its role remained limited, often being confined to producing a consensus on economic growth forecasts. It did not provide any advice to the executive (as does the Council of Economic Advisers in the United States), nor was it allowed to give a critical assessment of governmental policy (as does the German Sachverständigenrat). Being large and politically heterogeneous, these organizations essentially exist to settle political and social conflicts under the clear oversight of administrative authorities. Thus the conception of "expertise" as embodied in the Economic and Social Council or the Commission des Comptes de la Nation, which mixes the "technical" and "political" characters, differs from the more narrow understanding of professional capacity based on formal training in America. Finally, the temporary commissions which French governments regularly set up to investigate specific topics also function in a similar way: they tend to be headed by *inspecteurs des finances* and include a broad range of members from across the political spectrum.

Given this history, the apparent move away from the politico-corporatist model that occurred during the 1990s seems all the more striking. Two steps were then taken to dissociate the provision of economic expertise to the government from the process of political negotiation of economic policy. The first step was the establishment (in 1997) of the Council of Economic Analysis (Conseil d'Analyse Economique) reporting directly to the prime minister. The second step was to dismantle the Commission des Comptes de la Nation and replace it by an expert organization (the Commission Économique de la Nation) composed mainly of economic specialists advising the minister of finance. In many respects, these organizations represent an important symbolic and material rupture with past practice, although several elements (such as their large size and the attempt to represent a wide spectrum of political perspectives) mark their continuity with previous institutions. Both are composed almost entirely of formally trained "economists," institutionalizing a more narrow definition of competence in economic matters. Nearly all members are professors who publish regularly in professional outlets rather than generalist administrators, and a large proportion were trained in the engineering schools or at ENSAE: of the sixty-six past and current members of the Council of Economic Analysis, thirty-eight have an economics doctorate (including seven PhDs), twenty are former Polytechnique students, and sixteen are former ENSAE students. (These categories are not mutually exclusive.) Most remarkably, perhaps, only two *énarques* (but 13 Sciences-Po graduates) have been members of the council, which is a measure of the somewhat atypical character of this institution. However, the relative absence of public administrators from the organization, its ambiguous mission (neither advising nor providing outside critique), and its narrow responsibilities (authoring circumscribed reports on specific topics rather than vision statements) also indicate its relatively peripheral status and the persistent role of non-administrative expert bodies as, essentially, political clearance mechanisms.[135]

THE MISSING PRIVATE JURISDICTION

> There is always in the air the idea that the private sector is impure, that it is only driven by the search for profit. Certainly this is less true today, but traces remain of that idea. In sum, it is the prejudice of the Catholic against money, which the Protestant does not suffer from.
>
> (Paul Delouvrier 1994, 137)

The French business world has historically shown little interest in making use of organized economic expertise, whether at the level of the firm or at that of the corporate group, either for practical, instrumental reasons or for ideological ones. In part this is due to the fact that businessmen see economic expertise largely as a capacity of the state and its private jurisdiction. The administration's presence in the domain of economic forecasts and applied analyses drives out competition from other sectors (such as universities or private agencies), both because of the magnitude of its influence and because of its distinctive competence: able, technically trained economists in France have traditionally come from the state administration. The university, on the other hand, has long remained at arm's length from the corporate world. Until the 1960s, universities did practically no teaching of business subjects, though business training was available in independent business schools.

After World War II, the theme of a French "managerial gap" began to take shape both among experts from American foundations and among French businessmen and public officials. To remedy the perceived problem, France sent some 4,500 emissaries to the United States on productivity missions. Conversely, American envoys provided training in France under the auspices of the Marshall Plan. The Ford Foundation also helped establish the INSEAD in 1957, a European business school modeled after Harvard's.

From the 1960s on, however, the state (in the form of the Planning Commissariat) took over the modernization of French business education by establishing a foundation (the FNEGE) to support instructor training in business subjects. Initially presented as a "National School of Administration for business people" and placed under the tutelage of three ministries, the foundation was only cautiously endorsed by the business sector. In the absence of a viable local institutional basis, the national goal of training a new generation of managers required continued reliance on the United States. Between 1968 and 1975, seven hundred students were awarded grants to study management in North American universities. Upon their return, they constituted the bulk of new recruits in business schools[136] and universities and promoted the professionalization of *gestion* (management science) as a new disciplinary enterprise, notably with the creation of specialized associations and research publications. In 1976, a separate examination, the *agrégation de sciences de gestion* finally completed the process of autonomization at the university level and permitted a rapid expansion of programs and enrollments.

In spite of its success among students, however, the expansion of *gestion* was not welcome everywhere. Business studies were looked down upon, and numerous voices arose in the 1960s to denounce the sellout of university education to capitalism. Research authorities "treated *gestion* as a particular branch of economic sciences," but one with much lower prestige (Perez 1998, 595; Chessel and Pavis 2001). Even today, the perception that French universities remain aloof from the business world is widespread. One business economist complained: "There is a formidable cultural difference [between business and the universities]. These are two worlds which look at each other with great suspicion. Our business executives do not have much intellectual interest. And on the side of universities, there is an immense laziness about engaging with the corporate world" (SEDEIS, July 1996).

Perhaps a cultural defiance of the world of commerce, ingrained in practices and inscribed in institutions, does indeed explain the still considerable gap of French business education vis-à-vis that in the United States or even the United Kingdom. By 2002, there were 1,350 university professors of business in France (against 1,650 in economics). Surveys for the United States, by contrast, show that the annual number of business BAs granted annually outweighs the quantity of economics BAs by nearly seventeen times.[137]

Likewise, the profession of "business economist" never put down institutional roots in France as it did in the other two countries. After World War II, only a few private corporations (typically, large oil firms) possessed in-house economic research services, but those were small and rarely staffed by specialists. Importantly, though, sophisticated microeconomic work was done in public monopolies such as the railways (SNCF), the coal-mining monopoly (Charbonnages de France), or the electricity monopoly (EDF) where engineers developed economic tools to price public goods and to evaluate investment returns. The Direction of General Economic Studies at EDF, was a prestigious department and a stepping-stone for higher positions in the organization. However, these developments took place for the most part in complete isolation from the rest of the business sector and had almost no impact on it (for instance, EDF was not even part of the Confederation of French Employers).[138]

The founding of REXECO, a research organization financed by the private sector in 1957, expressed employers' desires to participate in an economic debate largely monopolized by the state.[139] Corporations were also starting to manifest a greater interest in economic expertise. The establishment of an association of business economists, the AFEDE, in 1969,[140] formally marked the emergence in France of a specific professional space for economists working in business. By the mid-1990s, however, it still had fewer than 150 members. Compared with the more than 4,000 members of the American equivalent organization, the NABE, AFEDE remains a "traditional" association in the sense that the bulk of its members work in the industrial sector, where trade associations and large public and private enterprises traditionally reserve a few formal appointments for industry "economists" with highly specific professional expertise (notably, on oil, chemistry, and steel).

In France as elsewhere, the long-term decline of industry and manufacturing and the comparative rise of financial services (particularly after the deregulation of financial markets in the mid-1980s) have profoundly altered the composition of the business economics profession. In contrast to British, U.S., or German financial institutions, however, French banks are able to sustain less activity in this area because of their more traditional mode of operation and because of France's postwar history of overall financial underdevelopment. Still, the French twist to this story is that the expansion of economic research in the financial industry has, once again, benefited first and foremost graduates of the *grandes écoles*. As one interviewee put it, "broadly speaking, it is the Ministry of Finance which supplied recruits" to the banking sector as it expanded into financial services.[141] High-profile INSEE administrators were hired to fill the new "chief economist" positions, while rank-and-file analysts were disproportionately recruited among young graduates of ENSAE and from those university PhDs with demonstrable mathematical abilities. And indeed the existence of a pool of mathematical talent has transformed the way certain financial institutions operate in France: witness the case of the Société Générale, known for its highly complex financial engineering.[142] Today 25 percent of ENSAE graduates work in the banking sector, more than in any other sector (including the public sector, which employs only 15 percent).[143] Unsurprisingly, the economics profession in the business sector, whether public or private, thus reproduces the same status divisions that exist everywhere else.

The Difficult Commercialization of Economic Knowledge

In comparative perspective, France's commercial economic studies sector is relatively small. In part, this is due to the difficulty of supporting such activities in the context of a public sector monopoly and the large historical weight of public sector corporations, with their tradition of in-house studies.[144] In fact, some of the most important institutions in this domain have been closely linked to the state. During the 1950s and 1960s, research contracts with the Planning Commissariat supported not only the development of public sector institutions but also a constellation of small private research organizations (e.g., CREDOC, CERFI), some of which disappeared after the evisceration of the system in the late 1970s. Another good example is the BIPE, a consulting firm specializing in industry studies, which was established in 1959 with the support of large public administrations in order to provide the business sector (both public and private) with technical expertise on specific markets. A public financial institution, the Caisse des Dépôts, remains its main shareholder. Public administrations are also connected to the organization through leadership personnel. The first director of the BIPE was Claude Gruson (X-Mines, *inspecteur des finances*), who founded the Statistical Service of the Ministry of Finance (1952–61) and later became the head of the

INSEE (1961–67). Since then, high-level public administrators have continued to occupy leading positions in the organization.

Corporate groups in France are not important consumers or producers of economic knowledge. This is in part due to the internal fragmentation of both business and labor, which has prevented the emergence of powerful institutional structures like the American think tanks or the German institutes. The largest trade unions, on the other hand, all retain small teams of economic experts.[145] In principle, a state-sponsored research institute (the IRES) common to all union organizations handles economic studies relevant to the labor movement. Similarly, the IPECODE (now REXECODE) theoretically represents the voice of organized capital. However, both are much smaller in size and visibility than the corresponding German organizations (the DIW and the IFO) on which they are modeled. If corporatism was the intention, in effect the implementation of both institutions reflects the characteristically subdued nature of French corporatism. The following account is only one of many disillusioned statements I collected on this subject:

> Officially the main reason why the private sector in France does not finance economic research is fiscal. Taxpayers are not encouraged to put their money in foundations. And there is a grain of truth to it. . . . But I think that the main reason is the extraordinary polarization of French society. Everything is centered on the administration. I would go as far as saying that corporations are completely paralyzed in their face-to-face interactions with the administration. And in the end they prefer to act directly on political structures and the bureaucracy, rather than to try to produce a different vision. They prefer to lobby. Until recently, economic research was not part of their arsenal. What has struck me enormously over the years, for instance, is the extent to which many corporate executives do not believe in the price mechanism. They do not believe that if you increase supply, prices are going to drop. And the language of economic analysis is completely foreign to their worldview. By contrast, they put a lot of trust in their agreement with a functionary on this or that point.
>
> People who live in an economy where administrative power is dominant do not believe in the pertinence of an analysis centered on the market. They simply do not see the usefulness of an economic discourse. (professor at university and Sciences-Po, July 1995)

What this interview describes, then, is the way French capitalism's relationship to state institutions (and the absence, in contrast to the U.S. case, of a close connection between capitalism and the law) limits the jurisdictional niche of economics in France. Certainly, the patterns described here are evolving, partly as a result of the liberalization of the state, the transformations undergone by the French economy, and the changing economic rules that are accompanying the Europeanization process, as well as, on occasion, the entrepreneurship of certain individuals (such as the university-business partnerships formed by industrial economists at the University of Toulouse). But this is still a far cry from the systematic consulting activities that many American economists engage in, or the sophisticated use of economic knowledge by U.S. business corporations, courts, and state governments.

Economists as Intellectuals, Intellectuals as Economists

The preceding pages have described the rise and partial decline of what we may call a "statist" pattern in the organization of economic knowledge. Until about 1946, French public authorities' commitment to economics was ambivalent. The discipline was poorly represented in university and *grandes écoles* training, in spite of a few high-status outposts such as the early chair at the Collège de France. Free-market liberalism had long been dominant throughout the discipline in France, although it seriously weakened in the face of the Great Depression and the challenges raised by new generations of administrative elites. Few economic professors informed policy, and the Inspection des Finances retained its monopoly on all financial matters. It is only with the profound reevaluation of the role of the state after the war that the production of economic knowledge not only became attached to a national project—the modernization of the French economy, using the tools of national accounting, indicative planning and industrial policy—but was institutionally renovated through an efflorescence of special training and consulting institutions that took place, roughly, between the mid-1940s and the late 1960s. And although the economic project is by and large gone today, and many of the structures that sustained it have been dismantled (most symbolic, perhaps, was the gradual fading of the research apparatus supported by the Planning Commissariat), the legacies of this period are profound. They include the transformation of *grandes écoles* graduates (primarily from Polytechnique, ENSAE, École Normale Supérieure) into bona fide economists and the state's quasi monopoly on applied studies through the INSEE.

We have yet to examine the implications of this "statist" institutional pattern at the cognitive level: How does the organization of knowledge interact with its substantive content? Do French economists have a particular "intellectual style" compared with their American and British counterparts?

The basic fact mentioned in the introduction—that French economists hold more favorable attitudes toward state intervention than practitioners in other advanced industrialized countries[146]—is important but insufficient: it might simply be explained by similar "ideological" differences running across the national populations of the same countries. The comparison becomes more interesting, however, when we address the major schools of thought in the French context and their respective institutional provenance. I have suggested that economics in France has followed essentially three relatively independent routes for much of its history: a dogmatic, political, laissez-faire tradition, dominant in the nineteenth century, which has faded as the professionalization of the field progressed but retains a certain influence in universities; a "sociological" tradition, which affirmed the need for economists to "look for the human act behind any economic phenomenon" (Nogaro 1950, 31), often by means of historical work, and was generally sympathetic to socialist ideals; and finally, a (politically more eclectic) marginalist tradition, that was transmitted by trained mathematicians often turned public engineers whose interests centered on the development of microeconomic and econometric tools, on the one hand, and mathematical economics, on the other, with some important bridges between the two. What made these traditions relatively coherent is the fact that they largely originated in different (and indeed separate) institutional systems (though some elements overlapped: many of the engineer-economists prior to World War II were very *libéral*, too, for instance). In short, the organizational segmentation of the field between educational institutions (universities/ *grandes écoles*) and the careers they facilitated sustained important substantive and methodological cleavages.[147] Not only the use of formal methods but also the relevance of institutional and sociological factors to analyze the economy continue to divide French economists to a degree unparalleled in the United States or the United Kingdom.

At the same time, we should be careful not to reify these divisions. The autonomization of economics from law and the development of an academic orientation within the state sector have made the relation between institution and intellectual style more complicated. Though they evidently play a role, differences in mathematical capital are not the only structuring principle: there are Polytechniciens on both the sociological and the mathematical side of the divide (viz., the regulationists and the neoclassical theorists). If the ideal of a unified social science has persisted much longer in France, it is perhaps precisely because a significant segment of the state elite came to identify with it, and was supported in doing so by its relative institutional autonomy within the field.

Indeed, the divided but also largely noncompetitive nature of the French institutional context has sustained numerous specialized intellectual niches, many of which share little with each other but their claims to radical novelty. The contrast with the American academic structure, which relies—by design—on diversity of substantive interests within departments and mobility across them, is remarkable. The comparison presents us with the paradoxical outcome that French statism in the postwar period has harbored a considerable pluralism of economic theories, many of which came to acquire, at least for a time, a certain legitimacy as alternatives to orthodox approaches, while the competitive structure of the American economics profession has consecrated the rise of the neoclassical paradigm and the relative marginalization of heterodoxy.[148]

The economic historians of the Annales school, the structuralist pole after the 1940s, the school of "monopolist state capitalism" during the 1960s (born within the French Communist Party), the regulation school during the 1970s and 1980s, the "economics of conventions" that emerged at INSEE during the 1980s, and countless other original approaches have all shared an ambition to overturn the intellectual foundations of mainstream economics and bring down disciplinary boundaries between the social sciences. Furthermore, economists, not sociologists or political scientists, have occupied the intellectual terrain American scholars often recognize as "economic sociology" or "political economy" (Steiner 2005). The economics of conventions' reflection on individual rationality, which focuses on the normative "possible worlds" (Salais and Storper 1997) within which individual actions take place and make sense, or the regulation school's more structural approach to institutions would perhaps not have been recognized as part of the legitimate domain of economic science as readily in the United States as they are in France.[149]

"Everybody's Business"

Hence, contrary to the United States, where the economist's identity is often closely associated with a narrowly defined methodology and epistemology, practitioners in France may more easily adopt a broader "intellectual" posture. We have already seen that nineteenth-century *libéraux* believed in the necessities of widespread economic pedagogy and concentrated much of their action on popularizing their message: Jean-Baptiste Say, among others, encouraged such an understanding when he wrote that "political economy has not been seen for what it truly is, even among people who are subject to an arbitrary power: everybody's business."[150] In economics as elsewhere in France, the public sphere is often a key arena where individuals and collectives can help secure social recognition in the absence of easy channels of access into the administrative world. Partly as a result of the public administration's quasi monopoly on economic information, specialized economic journalism has been traditionally weak in France (especially compared with the United Kingdom).[151] But generalist newspapers constitute an important space where economists can air their views, and key intellectual and policy debates are generally well covered in the press. Many economists also routinely publish best sellers dealing with timely societal issues. There is a long tradition of public writing among high-level civil servants and academic economists, particularly university-based ones.[152] Economics is also present in the public sphere through small pedagogical books. For instance, the regulation school, which made a deliberate effort at popularization, was particularly effective at eliciting strong public validation via intellectual reviews such as the *Temps Modernes* or works directed at the general public.[153] It is also telling that the press—rather than some well-established professional organ, as in the United States—played a key role in the establishment, in the 1990s, of annual prizes for France's "best economist" (the magazine *Le Nouvel Économiste*) and the "best young economist" (the newspaper *Le Monde*).

But if economists may play an intellectual role, intellectuals are also authorized to speak about economic issues. Thus a vast range of individuals (directors of large enterprises and banks, higher civil servants, politicians, professors in other disciplines) and organizations (political parties, clubs, associations, intellectual reviews) may claim legitimacy in talking about economic matters and play an important role in the production of public economic discourse. French political parties, for instance, established "economic commissions" of experts during the 1950s as part of a strategy to enroll intellectuals. (*Économie et Politique*, the first Marxist economic review published in France, was affiliated with the Communist Party.) More important, perhaps, were the *clubs de réflexion* that brought together senior civil servants, intellectuals, journalists, and business and union leaders and helped disseminate ideas among governing elites. In the later part of the twentieth century, the most active of these organizations was the very selective Fondation Saint Simon, a center-left think tank created in 1982 (and dissolved in 1999). Composed mainly of higher civil servants, intellectuals who had often broken away from the Communist Party of their youth (many taught at the EHESS), journalists, and business leaders with a background in high administration, it sought to marshal ideas toward governing elites and the larger public by presenting itself as a group of experts and reasonable men standing above the political fray.

We should note that these pattern are not exclusive to the economics profession and reflect the larger structure of the intellectual and political fields in France, which, as Michèle Lamont has shown, emphasizes qualities of eloquence, general competence, *sens critique*, and capacity for abstraction (in contrast with the American valorization of the "professional" values of factualism, efficiency, expertise, and pragmatism) (1992, 98). This broad understanding of intellectual competence and skills is rooted in an educational system that reveres bright and articulate "generalists." It draws its strength from a social context where the celebration of reason (e.g., from eighteenth century philosophers to the present day) has been historically tied to political subversion and remains one of the founding myths of the French Republic. Against this cultural background, economic issues enter the public sphere not simply as technical issues that must be left to experts but as issues of reason that all *têtes bien faites* are entitled to take up. Of course economic subjects are highly political in the U.S., too, but political contention takes a different form there—that of a real "market of ideas" where institutions and individuals with vastly different resources and legitimacy struggle for attention. One interviewee, a high level public servant turned business leader, thus deplored in a (somewhat self-serving) statement to me that "the economic debate in France is a political debate . . . an ideological debate. For instance, [reports from the Planning Commissariate] are never perceived as expert reports, they are always perceived as political reports (from written notes, June 1995)." What he did not perceive, however, was that this very political contention entertains a symbiotic relation to the autonomy of technocratic monopolies that have no real competition and answer to no one but themselves.

THE SEGMENTED WORLDS OF FRENCH ECONOMICS

Let us now return to the problem posed in this chapter's introduction: How should we understand the contested status of economics in the French context? Tocqueville ([1856] 1998) suggested long ago that a closed and hierarchical form of political sovereignty tends unintentionally to foment rebelliousness. Perhaps the statist opposition between (administrative) center and (nonadministrative) periphery in French economic information, science, and expertise is the institutional vehicle that sustains the persistence of a political approach to economics in this country on both sides of the dividing line. The general suspicion aroused by liberal thought, to which classical and neoclassical economics is closely linked, among both the general public and state actors themselves can be understood in those terms. To this we must add, in the more recent period, fears that an "Anglo-Saxon" Trojan horse filled with U.S.-trained or U.S.-influenced personalities is seeking to smuggle neoliberalism into France. If anything, the economic liberalization of the post-1978 (and even more the post-1983) years and the general convergence of policy positions between left- and right-wing governments have intensified the contestation of economics outside the political center.

A second explanation refers more directly to the institutional makeup that has historically sustained the production of economic knowledge in France. As pointed out in chapter 1, the French state early on created a financial technocracy in the form of the Inspection des Finances, as well as various specialized elite *corps* (Mines, Ponts) in the interests of orchestrating the development of key industries. It is in these technocratic institutions that the tradition of microeconomic calculus was first established. But the intellectual developments that emerged there were not integrated into any comprehensive vision about the contribution of economic knowledge to public management. It was only after World War II, once ideas about planning and industrial modernization had taken hold, that French public officials started consciously to design an economic management elite, once again resorting to the creation of a new generation of specialized higher education institutions to do so.

The association of economic competence with administrative functions has constituted one of the most critical organizing mechanisms for the construction of the identity of French economists in the postwar era. There is probably nothing further removed from the French organization of economic ideas, information, expertise, and research than the American ideal of a decentralized and competitive market carried out by proclaimed professionals trained in universities. In French public practice, economic expertise came to be "built into" the generalist administrative function or understood as an essentially instrumental, problem-solving technique, which differed quite remarkably from the more scholarly orientation of the university-based discipline.

The status ordering and relative compartmentalization of career lines—particularly between *grandes écoles* and universities, and among graduates of the various *grandes écoles* themselves—means that different institutions relevant to the production of economic knowledge have come to develop different interests and views about the nature and purpose of economics. University professors typically control mass education and the main academic institutions and often have a close linkage with politics, but they are excluded from positions of administrative power, both in policy and in the economy. Technical administrators such as engineer-economists and economist-statisticians oversee the production of economic information and applied work, as well as a large portion of formalized theoretical research. Finally, civil administrators (ENA graduates) have a near monopoly on economic advice and policy design but are often poorly linked to academic "science" as practiced either by the universities or by technical administrators. As a result, "being an economist" is more contentious than in the United States and the United Kingdom since it is tangled up in unsolved conflicts over the legitimate definition of what the practice of economics should be about: traditional theory, statistical and econometric technique, mathematics, or factual knowledge.

In part, these categories are kept in place by the social roles and functions in which the actors find themselves caught. For instance, the relative lack of access of engineers to economic advice and decision-making positions has contributed to their intellectual isolation, but also to their autonomy. As one of the few who succeeded in making this transition put it, "Mathematical economists have found themselves confined to their scientificity and their milieu."[154] Paradoxically, however, it was also this very situation that helped transform the system. Institutions may be created for particular purposes, but once these logics are in place, individuals' interests and wishes may impel them to evolve in different directions. Two examples discussed abundantly in this chapter made this point clear: the colonization of scholarly institutions by engineers, and the development of a strong research orientation within the state administration. Both have brought about a reorganization of the field around formalized methods, which challenged the aforementioned boundaries. It is somewhat ironic that the centralized system that allowed French public engineers to blossom as economists was dismantled, in part, by the very economic ideas and international connections it had helped nurture.

Economists and Societies

THE MOST inescapable narratives about the history of economics in the twentieth century have to do with the discipline's increasingly assertive scientific style and growing methodological consensus, on the one hand, and its jurisdictional expansion and internationalization, on the other. Economists have abstracted economic processes into ever more sophisticated mathematical models, by and large based on constrained behavioral assumptions, such as the postulate of calculative agents who are able to rank their preferences. Academic, political, and economic institutions have rewarded formal and econometric technique above all other forms of scientific practice in economics, helping make them the dominant methods in the three national fields studied in this book.

At the same time, economic technologies have been brought to bear on societies in increasingly meticulous ways, thereby manufacturing —to a degree—the social conditions that make economic calculation possible and opening up (by depicting an economy in constant need of remediation vis-à-vis the ideal presented in the model) possibilities for jurisdictional expansion into new forms of economic expertise as well as new places.[1] As I have suggested elsewhere, these processes continuously feed into one another through dynamics of professional and scientific struggle.[2]

These changes, in turn, are closely intertwined with profound transformations in economic organization around the world, from the domestic interventionism of the 1960s to the dismantling and liberalizing movements of the 1980s, to the governmentalized welfarism of the current era, and who knows what in the future. But how should we think about the relationships among these different processes and entities? In short, what is the relationship between economists and the economy? The opening paragraph of this conclusion implies a generally "performative" line of analysis, which emphasizes the constant labor of economists to bring economies in line with their economic models. But might not the reverse be true as well? After all, aren't economic discourses and practices just as much made by society as they make it? Certainly this argument has been raised before.[3] For instance, George Steinmetz has recently suggested that discourses on society (what we call the social sciences) are interwoven with broader "regulation" regimes that structure their epistemology and scientific imagination. Reflecting on the trajectory of the American social sciences in the postwar period, he remarks that "social scientists' sense of the plausibility of different ways of thinking about the social" has been remarkably *homologous*, over time, to corresponding "large-scale social structural processes and cultural discourses."[4]

The metaphor is thus that of an elective affinity between the social sciences and the social, political, and economic regime they are a part of. To some extent, this way of thinking challenges the customary emphasis on the necessity to specify the nature of the causal relationship between knowledge and macroprocesses, or "ideas" and "institutions," as the abundant literature in political science and political sociology frames it. A great deal of ink has been spilled on this question, with no obvious conclusion. Empirical studies have offered support for both sides of the causal equation, showing that sometimes shifting institutional practices have made possible a rethinking of disciplinary frameworks; or that, at other times, social-scientific arguments have offered a strong rationale for institutional change. In fact, both of these arguments have been made concurrently about the same events (see, for instance, competing analyses of the Great Depression).[5]

The causal debate, then, has not been settled. Nor should it be. Perhaps the causal question makes sense only to the extent that it helps illuminate the processes at work within the various complexes of ideas-cum-institutions, or discourses-cum-practices complexes—in other words, help reveal how the realms of what is sayable, thinkable, doable in and about the economy change from time to time and from place to place. Historians of ideas have identified significant historical breaks in the genealogy of discourse about the economy. For instance, Albert Hirschman (1977) singled out the discursive opposition between peaceful economic "interests" and dangerous political "passions" as integral to the conceptual divorce between economy and politics at the end of the eighteenth century.[6] Karl Polanyi ([1944] 1957) has described the effort, at the turn of the nineteenth century, to disentangle economy from society (or the market from its sustaining social institutions) by extolling the virtues of self-regulation and crafting relief policies that facilitated the operation of the free market. Timothy Mitchell (1998) has noted the discursive reconstruction, starting in the late 1920s, of the economy as a coherent systemic order—a thing—still separate from the state, but which the state may now legitimately act upon, manipulate, and generally "fix" through the application of specialized expertise and technologies.[7] In all these cases, of course, economics itself was part and parcel of the process whereby the "economy" was constructed and reconstructed—first, as a self-contained object that obeyed natural laws (as in the writings, for instance, of Malthus, Ricardo, Senior or Say) and, second, as one that humans may manipulate for their own good (as in Keynes's view).[8] The economy as an object is a constantly moving target that cannot be separated from the projects, designs, and practices of economists—nor, for that matter, from the projects of accountants, financiers, planners, statisticians, lawyers, consultants, and, increasingly, other social scientists (see, for instance, Putnam's (1994) highly successful claims about the relevance of civil society organization for economic governance). And it is only because of this incessant work of articulation, this constant dialogue between representation, technique, and agents that the affinities between economic knowledge and its contextual base come into sight in the first place.

This book has been particularly concerned with one special type of affinity, that which ties knowledge to its social setting. Instead of focusing—in Foucault's manner—on what makes particular sorts of knowledge possible at a given historical moment, I have thus tried to analyze interactions between forms of political organization and forms of knowledge making within specific social contexts. The point was not to treat the United States, Great Britain, and France as self-contained cultures that would determine everything that happens within them but rather to show the structured, dialectical relationship between institutions (political institutions in particular) and knowledge. In other words, my purpose has been to lay bare certain commonalities and differences in the way the field of economics is institutionally, intellectually, and jurisdictionally structured across countries.

There are two main roads to establishing such regularities. For the case at hand, a first strategy amounts to ascertaining the *objective* differences that structure the production of economic knowledge in these three nations. This includes investigating the training of economists; the social and professional positions economists occupy and the authority granted to them; and the resources expended on different types of economic research. These elements fall classically under the broad label of comparative institutional analysis. A second strategy brings to light the *subjective* differences in the kinds of individuals who inhabit these worlds. This approach involves an examination of how economists (and those who cooperate or compete with them) in the United States, Great Britain, or France understand and talk about themselves and others; how they perceive the social world, including the problems they identify and the solutions they call for; and how they practice their science or expertise. In comparative sociology, this strategy is traditionally that of people who see themselves as the bearers of a cultural explanation.

A truly comprehensive sociological analysis must obviously be able to account for both of these moments. The professional habits of the mind of economists make sense only when we can trace them back to the social structures that have produced them. After all, social structures do not exist outside of people's subjective perceptions of them, which both sustain and eventually transform these structures. Still, as Pierre Bourdieu was always quick to point out, the objective moment should always be the first step of sociological analysis, if only because people's perceptions are always formed within, and indeed *out of*, preexisting social environments: "No doubt agents have an active apprehension of the world. No doubt they do construct their vision of the world. But this construction is carried out under structural constraints" (1990, 130).

Now it is important to note that the notion of "structural constraints" for Bourdieu referred essentially to people's biographical trajectories. He shows very effectively, for instance, that graduates of different *grandes écoles* (in *The State Nobility* [1996c]) or practitioners of different academic disciplines (in *Homo Academicus* [1988]) come from very different social backgrounds.[9] By contrast, this book has sought to conceptualize the problem in somewhat different ways, privileging instead the "structural constraints" that come out of the historical makeup of each national field. I have aimed to reveal how institutional differences in the very structure of these fields have shaped the social and intellectual trajectory of the groups of actors that populate them.[10] Hence chapter 1 was concerned essentially with establishing broad objective differences across the American, British, and French political, academic, and economic institutions, while chapters 2 through 4 went on to carry out both an objective and a subjective analysis of the paths followed by economics in these three countries.

This book thus strove to achieve a dual goal: to depict the "national" worlds economists inhabit, in a *structural* sense, through a detailed historical study of the specific rules and institutions that organize the production of and struggles over economic knowledge in each national field; and in a more *phenomenological* one, through an analysis of the subjective experiences that these contexts have given rise to, but which also serve to reproduce or change them. From this second point of view, the interview material presented here, though inevitably partial, remains indispensable: it not only offers precious information about the shape of the economics field in each country (and about the trajectories of individual economists themselves), but also provides a concrete illustration of the profound *inscription* or *embodiment* of these national-institutional logics in people's being and perceptions about themselves and the worlds they are part of. Understanding the traces institutions leave upon the people who traverse and enact them is the key to seeing how the various parts of the social world cohere. In the lives of the economists I interviewed, it is possible to follow the links in each national context between the national polity, the rules governing the production of economic knowledge, the substance of economic ideas and tools, and their effect on the economy and society more broadly.[11]

THE SOCIAL STRUCTURES OF ECONOMICS IN COMPARATIVE PERSPECTIVE

Economic discourse was largely born out of the liberal conception of a society made of free individuals.[12] But liberal thought, and the political and intellectual challenges it faced in order to legitimate itself, were not the same everywhere. Liberal thinkers enjoyed great prominence in England, yet they evolved in a thoroughly class-based polity, whose reality they had to grapple with—sometimes in sharp contradiction to their own liberal inclinations. The French liberals struggled against the centralizing tendencies of the state and contended with the weak legitimacy of the liberal perspective in general. Economics, however, gained prominence in the French context once its relevance for administrative practice became better established—though the stigma attached to liberalism still lingers. And while the ideology of free-market liberalism was better accepted in the United States, its central dilemma was repeatedly replayed in the recurrent democratic fears that unchecked liberalism leads to unfair practices that threaten what Tocqueville called "the equality of conditions." Much economic activity has focused on how to measure and resolve this very dilemma in different domains, in a way that was also shaped by the legal organization of the American economy. In short, the discipline and profession of economics that emerged in each country incorporated different conceptions and practices of the political, particularly the different exercise and understanding of the nature and purpose of "government."

How did this come about? The mechanisms are quite simple. What individuals—and the organizations employing them—might perceive as an important and engaging intellectual problem, or as a relevant and legitimate practical question, depends on preexisting habits, institutional patterns, and above all an accumulation of social experiences. All of these, in turn, have a particular national flavor. The actors I interviewed were themselves often keenly aware of such differences in scientific style and professional practice, though they typically conveyed them to me in a casual manner. My conversations with them inevitably elicited spontaneous cross-national comparisons (admittedly, the known comparative focus of my study was always an implicit reference point for these remarks).

Unsurprisingly, the most cosmopolitan among my interviewees were generally best equipped to volunteer these judgments, which relied not only on their experience but also on widely available cultural stereotypes. For instance, at the end of a long discussion, one Cambridge professor suddenly paused and said with an amused smile: "You see, in England, people are more prepared to be wrong than to sound pretentious. You talk things down, you are very pragmatic. For instance, the stuff I worked on all my life, the general equilibrium, and so on ... that's totally un-English. That's a French enterprise. Walras rather than Marshall" (June 1997).

A short while later, another British professor, this time from Oxford, contrasted the centrality of game theory in the United States, which he described as being "modeled on a representation of society as a bunch of interacting individuals," with the French economists' concern with planning and optimization problems. "The French," he added, "always have to show why it is optimal *not* to regulate" (June 1997), implicitly acknowledging the broader cultural skepticism the discipline faces in France and its insecurity vis-à-vis a political culture in which administrative control is practically second nature.

Implicitly, these interviewees were entertaining the idea that economic theories and approaches find their roots in the lived experiences of societies. We could certainly illustrate the point with our own examples. Is it just by coincidence, for instance, that public choice analysis, with its image of government actors as self-interested rent seekers, emerged primarily in the United States, where distrust for government action runs high and sometimes takes a visceral, unquestioned form? Or that Ordoliberalism, which promotes the state's role as the guarantor of a proper liberal economic order in which economic management responsibilities are rationally apportioned across social groups and institutions, was developed in Germany, where these patterns of political organization had a long-standing history? Certainly no idea is ever a purely "national" product. It is also true that public choice theories furnished a rhetorical background to the antigovernment backlash of the late 1970s and 1980s, and that Ordoliberalism served as a justification for the postwar German social market economy. But should we see these intellectual frameworks only as causes, rather than as consequences of specific political patterns? Part of sociology's, and particularly political science's, mistake in dismissing explanations based on ideas lies in the analytical conceit that ideas are exogenous to the political system. Rather than assuming this, social scientists should analyze the coevolution of politics, policy, and ideas as they are shaped by social and institutional structures.

In order to grasp the codependence between ideas and institutions, the present book has been centrally concerned with describing how the people who produce such ideas are trained, work, and position themselves vis-à-vis relevant others in the national or international context. As I have mentioned earlier, my way to address these two questions simultaneously was to analyze the actors themselves, who embody both ideas (through their analytical or political positions) and institutions (through their social trajectories). Put another way, I explored the social conditions of the production of economists across different societies. Now reaching the end of this analytical process, I draw two main conclusions. The first one, developed at length in this book, is that the social structures within which economists live are largely national, with specific histories, regulatory institutions, and struggles—both material and symbolic. Individual actors, with their social roles, ideas, and practices, are the product of specific relational patterns within specific national spaces. In particular, we have found that different social-institutional spaces create different *categories of agents*; they have different ways of producing people who make claims over economic discourse. For instance, the status distinctions between the *grandes écoles* and the university in France are quite different from the kinds of hierarchical distinctions that exist between Ivy League and other schools in the United States, or even between the old, new, and "new new" British universities. My French interviewees—particularly if they came from the university, arguably the dominated segment not only within the economics profession but also within the intellectual world as a whole—had much greater difficulty than interviewees from other countries in providing a homogeneous explanation of what being an economist means. Other social categories always came to their minds first. As the quotation that opens chapter 4 or the relative heterogeneity of professional outlets (associations, reviews) reminds us, in the French social space, institutionally specific occupational distinctions have been, for a long time, much more important than disciplinary ones: you were first an INSEE administrator, or an *inspecteur des finances*, and only secondarily an economist.

The second answer, which has been touched upon repeatedly (though not developed systematically) throughout this book, is that the social structures of economics are also international: being an economist means inhabiting not only a country-specific field, populated by fellow nationals, but also an international field (of course, this relation with the international domain, too, is constructed simultaneously at the objective and subjective levels). In particular, what goes on within the U.S. field of economics acts as a powerful structuring force for the rest of the world. Relations in the international field of economics (and particularly vis-à-vis the United States) can thus be just as important as relations within national fields in driving institutional or intellectual reproduction and change. For the remainder of this chapter we will thus examine each of these fields of relationships—the national one and the international one—in turn.

Social Processes and Categories in National Space

Let us begin by summarizing our findings concerning the place of economic knowledge in the order of learning, the administrative order, and the market order in each of the three countries examined in this study. Table 5-1 synthesizes the information presented in the case studies. It is important to read the table as an analytical portrait, rather than as an enumeration of causal influences. In other words, we should not think that each line constitutes a separate *influence* on the social character of economics across nations, whose causal contribution can be drawn out in precise ways. Rather, we should imagine that all lines are interdependent and combine to jointly *constitute* what being an economist means in each country.

Let us take each of our cases with this point in mind. When describing the shape of American economics, we cannot think of the respective structures of public administrations, universities, and markets as completely independent forces. In the United States, a relatively nontechnocratic form of administrative organization and the market-enhancing strategies of governments at all levels (including those serving their own internal knowledge needs) are precisely among the factors that have turned American universities into one of the main vehicles of professionalism. It is thus only in relation to the dynamics among all of these institutions that the distinctive pattern of scientific and merchant professionalism in American economics emerges and makes sense.[13]

In Britain the same pattern of interdependent institutions holds true, but in a different manner. Britain has historically been governed by public-minded social and cultural elites, where service to the state traditionally bore both an amateur and a highly prestigious character. Universities, particularly elite ones, long remained tied to a conception of learning that was less professional and more geared toward general cultivation than in the United States. These historical patterns also help us understand the breakdown of this system during the late twentieth century and its evolution toward the American model. The broadening of higher education and Margaret Thatcher's populist attacks on traditional elite rule combined to compel modifications to the organization of the field.

Finally, in France, the long prevalence of an *administrative* approach to political and economic governance (while it has often been used in the pursuit of liberal economic principles)[14] explains, perhaps, the country's institutionally and culturally ambivalent stance toward a discipline that has traditionally asserted the relative illegitimacy of the state in *directing* the economic process. It also explains the unsettled character of French understandings of what an "economist" is. The immense social and educational prestige of state managers, in particular, entitles them to define

TABLE 5-1
Summary of the Case Studies

	United States	Britain	France
Academia			
Institutionalization in the higher education system	Contemporaneous with the rise of the modern university, extensive	Late (relative to academic institutions), yet extensive	Piecemeal and segmented
Formalization of the training process	High: PhD	Low, but increasingly formalized	High, but divided between universities and *grandes écoles*
Organization of research	Diversified basis (public and private). Foundations and government agencies prominent.	Mostly state; initially at arm's length, but increasingly state-controlled	State-dominated, separation between research and teaching (though weakening)
Intellectual patterns	Applied quantification Price theory dominant	Macroeconomic orientation prominent; broad concept of welfare	Segmented, with strong mathematical tradition and operational microeconomics
Policy/politics			
Civil service	Economic specialists trained in universities	Experienced "amateurs," but expansion of specialists through the Government Economic Service	Generalists from administrative *corps* and specialists from technical *corps*
Economic advice	Formal channels of executive advice since 1946; congressional hearings	Permanent secretaries, informal networks and expert commissions	*Cabinets ministériels*: dominated by members of the *corps de l'Etat* (Fifth Republic especially)

(continued)

TABLE 5-1 (Continued)

	United States	Britain	France
Think tanks	Numerous, powerful, and well institutionalized	Important, but weaker and less institutionalized	Weak, mostly linked to the state
Public sphere	Economists incorporated as experts mainly, though a few generalist columnists Strong business press	Important role of both economic columnists and economists Strong economic and financial press	More generalist public sphere, though growing specialization
Business			
Private jurisdiction	Very well developed: strong ties to the legal profession and the financial markets; private consulting for government agencies	Historically small but growing after economic reforms of the 1980s	Limited

economic expertise in a way that captures their own role in managing the French economy. Yet here, too, the growing strength of an international scholarly community organized around academic professionalism has been one of the main vehicles of an evolution toward American-style disciplinarization of French economics. I shall come back to this point shortly.

POLITICAL ORDERS AND THE MAKING OF CATEGORIES

More than anything, this book has focused on the importance of the organization and exercise of "government" in shaping the economists' professional and intellectual enterprises. It has shown that the relationship between economic knowledge and state power defines in large part the field's social purposes and the distinctive identity of its practitioners. In postwar France, economics grew markedly within the institutional framework of the state as it expanded its economic management capabilities. As French public officials saw it, the organization of France's economic "modernization" required the creation of new administrative elites—and universities could not be trusted with this task. Economics was thus incorporated into the government profession itself, as an element in the training of generalist administrators (the *énarques* and members of the *grands corps*), and as a basis for the development of a new, specialized *corps* of technical administrators (the INSEE administrators). This system was set up alongside—and to some extent in competition with—universities, the traditional home of economic expertise. In Britain and America, on the other hand, economic knowledge production possessed more autonomy, its center and legitimacy continuing to be located mainly outside of political institutions. Therefore, the incorporation of economists in government relied on the technical relevance of their skills to practical policy tasks. The United States, with its administrative structure articulated around specialist functions and the use of external experts in senior positions, best exemplifies this model. Britain represents a much more mixed case due to the presence of a generalist class of career civil servants (a group that bears some resemblance to its French counterparts). Yet in contrast to France, the civil service is less homogeneous and sufficiently permeable to allow specialists some access to decision-making roles.

Whatever its forms, the institutionalization of economic knowledge into the state apparatus was the single greatest impetus propelling the transformation of economics into a highly technical, mathematically oriented discipline. In fact, public or quasi-public agencies often harbored the most mathematical types of economic research before they became well accepted within academia. Kenneth Arrow and Thomas Schelling, for instance, produced much of their early work while employed by the

RAND Corporation; many of the French engineer-economists did something similar from their official positions in public agencies and national enterprises. More generally, the birth of macroeconomics and its redefinition of policy making as the application of objective expertise to the pursuit of well-specified national goals encouraged a more technical orientation among economists in all three countries, especially between World War II and the late 1960s, when the so-called Keynesian paradigm was in full swing. Whether it gave rise to the use of automatic stabilizers (in the United States), stop-go policies (in England), or indicative planning (in France), confidence in the predictive power and fine-tuning capabilities of economic knowledge was at its highest during this period. Yet within this common technocratic framework, idiosyncratic factors at the national level still reinforced certain intellectual styles over others. Each economics profession became embedded in different political projects, different ideas about the legitimate economic goals of the nation, and different understandings about the best ways to achieve these goals, as Dobbin (1994) points out.

One important difference in the relationship between the political sphere and economic knowledge stems from national differences in the exercise and legitimacy of state power as a whole. Thus, economics' penetration of political institutions in France could be characterized as both pervasive (every *énarque* receives a significant training in economics) and yet superficial. In the country where state officials are most autonomous, the need for economic evaluations of state action has also been somewhat irrelevant. Hence France has produced comparatively little post hoc analysis of the effectiveness of its public policies, and the state proprietors of economic data have seen little need to share it with potential users outside the state's jurisdiction.[15] In the United States, by contrast, government action has needed more justification—indeed, the very political contentiousness of the policy process means that detailed expert reports show up in congressional hearings, lobbying institutions, think tanks, and government agencies, pulling economists into the orbit of the state in a desperate quest for scientific impartiality.

Differences in each country's substantive political preoccupations in the wake of World War II also help explain the distinctive intellectual and technological emphases of their economists. Thus economic growthmanship was coupled with different *political* projects across countries, the most salient of which were the buildup of industrial power in France, redistribution in England, and military and economic supremacy in the United States. These projects provided the background against which the development of national research infrastructures for social scientists and the imagination and practices of economists grew. They supported certain particular skills with which economists came to be identified and oriented their theoretical or empirical work. The French microeconomic tradition, the British approach to welfare economics, and the remarkable development of growth theory and game theory in the United States, for example, are each deeply intertwined with these profoundly different implementations of public power.

Finally, the manner in which each state has drawn upon economic expertise has made an important symbolic statement about the character of the discipline in each country, helping define the way economics is seen in society at large and thus powerfully shaping the way economists see themselves. Thus, as Bourdieu (1994, 1996c) and Starr (1993) have suggested, the state is not simply a material institution oriented to the monopolization of certain resources; it is also, importantly, a *symbolic* institution with a power of *certification, consecration, legitimate classification, and categorization.* Sometimes this power is very explicit, as when the state does, or does not, *recognize* racial categories. At other time, it is much more subtle. In this perspective, the formalization of the role of economists within the structure of U.S. government, though much less direct than the making of special classes of economic experts within French administration (the *énarques*, the *INSEE administrators*), has probably no less *symbolic* importance. The existence of professionally exclusive agencies, such as the Council of Economic Advisers and the National Economic Council, and the manner in which they function send powerful messages about what it means to be an economist, and who is granted authority to claim expertise on economic issues. The involvement of economists in the constant back-and-forth between state and nonstate actors on matters of public policy also define their identity. Whether they serve as CEA appointees on loan from a university, prepare econometric analyses for special interest lobbying bodies, or testify as experts before congressional hearings, American economists officially enter the realm of the state as people who possess a specific form of expertise generally validated through research training in universities. The recent rise of think tanks and the political fortunes of pseudoacademics paradoxically confirm, in fact, the symbolic and cultural force of this institutional pattern.

As I have argued, the British state created a quite different identity for economic experts. In the United Kingdom, an official body created in 1964 (the Government Economic Service) organizes the long-term careers of economists as a distinct expert group in government, with access to so-called "technical" positions. Although the requirements for such positions have become increasingly specialized over time, economists in Britain do not, unlike their peers in America, possess a de jure claim on any one government agency. High-level administrators trained in the arts have historically dominated the provision of economic advice at the highest levels of government. The tradition of having businesspeople govern important economically oriented agencies has also been enduring. Yet Britain has also experienced a subtle movement of professionalization, particularly marked under the Blair government (1997–2007), which appointed academic economists in prominent positions at the Bank of England, the Competition Commission, and the Office of Fair Trading. Economic professors may also play significant roles in British public life through their involvement in Royal commissions of inquiry, as well as through their more informal ties to politicians and civil servants in political parties and clubs, and finally, as authors of accessible commentary in the British public sphere.

The French state accords even less deference to the independent technical expertise of university economists, denying them any monopoly on the production of legitimate economic knowledge. Public administration in France relies on a highly stratified labor market, with sharply divided training and career lines for decision making, technical expertise, and academic production. Generalist technocrats trained in the art of public policy are the main purveyors of advice to governments, a pattern that was only reinforced with the advent of the Fifth Republic. By contrast, academic credentials (a PhD) have traditionally held little currency in a world dominated by other forms of legitimation. In Bourdieu's terms, the academic capital of university professors has been dominated by the administrative capital of technocrats in the field of power. Steps to mitigate the influence of high administration, by delocalizing the ENA to Strasbourg, for instance, or by creating a Council of Economic Analysis staffed with economics professors, have not yet managed to significantly erode the system.

ORDERS OF LEARNING AND THE MAKING OF DISCIPLINES

The French case, more than any other, points out the complexity of what I have called the "order of learning" as a strategic site for understanding patterns of professional development. Strangely enough, education has often been overlooked in studies of professions. Furthermore, particular academic professions, such as the one investigated here, have rarely attracted interest in their own right.[16] Yet my examination of economics in France, with its separate tracks for expertise and in England, with its powerful academic and social hierarchies, hopefully makes a convincing case for the need to fill this void with more work that denaturalizes the American system of academic professions (while recognizing the mechanisms of its influence today). First, we have seen that the shape of the educational system is extraordinarily important to understand how people make jurisdictional claims to theorize about and act on the economy—whether this requires a PhD (in the United States), passage through an elite university (in Britain), or a *grande école*, or a central examination like the *agrégation de sciences économiques* (in France). Hence this book ought to make sociologists rethink some of the categories (such as "academia") that we often take for granted as being exclusive of other categories (such as "the state"). In the United States, the scholar's legitimacy as expert is such that some government and independent agencies (such as the Federal Reserve) have been thoroughly staffed by PhDs and a significant amount of scholarly research takes place within them. To some extent, the International Monetary Fund in Washington follows a similar model. France exemplifies a reverse pattern where public engineers and administrators who were destined for other careers developed scientific interests and then moved into traditional academic institutions such as the CNRS or the university. The Corps de l'Etat were certainly not geared toward academic production, and still aren't. Rather, they were essentially intended to provide the nation with well-trained, versatile leaders in public administration and business—and, for the most part, this is what they accomplished. Yet as we have shown, these institutions (and those they fed into within the state administration) came, sometimes reluctantly, to house some of the most influential scholarly activity to come out of France in the last century. In fact, it is this sector that has remained over time the most closely integrated with the world of American and British economics. What initially allowed such connections to take place was not that Polytechniciens and Normaliens were trained in economic theory and economic methods (indeed, as we saw, such training was very limited, particularly in the earlier periods) but the fact that they were all mathematicians, and approached economics from a logical point of view, as a form of applied mathematics.

Perhaps the most interesting consequence of the structure of training has to do with national and historical variations in the relative integration of the discipline of economics. In the United Kingdom, once economics succeeded in securing a niche, the overwhelming social authority of the oldest and most powerful institutions (mainly Oxford and Cambridge) at first ensured a high degree of intellectual homogeneity. The main reason is that these universities could see themselves (and be seen) as the apex of a continuum in a way the French *grandes écoles* would never be able to. (As pointed out earlier, the difference between the *grandes écoles* and French universities was perceived to be one of nature rather than simply of degree.) At the same time, the transformations undergone by British higher education over the course of the twentieth century had powerful intellectual effects: once international leadership in the field of economics shifted toward the United States, the original academic power structure weakened (though it has not disappeared). By the 1970s the country's academic stars (Sen, Miralees) had decamped to the United States, foreigners had acquired a dominant presence within "British" economics. Two Hungarians, Balogh and Kaldor, dominated the discipline's public face, the *Economic Journal* published mostly foreign, and especially U.S. authors, and the LSE was probably one of the most cosmopolitan universities in the world. Part of the traditional center (Cambridge) had become absorbed in the bitter struggle over the legacy of Keynesianism: "They were stuck there, a historic pocket, like the church of Saint Paul in Jerusalem," one interviewee told me. In the meantime, newer institutions eagerly tried to raise their profile by aligning themselves on the transatlantic mainstream.

The American path bears some similarities to the British situation, most notably in the continuous (though more fluid) nature of hierarchies in higher education. Certainly the geographical size and diversity of the United States are such that plenty of niches exist for multiple approaches. The American Social Science Association, let us again point out, is an umbrella organization that, *in principle*, tolerates more diversity than its British counterpart, the Royal Economic Society. American economics also harbors fierce political debates over theory, methodology, and policy. In practice and in comparative perspective, however, the main trend over the course of the twentieth century has been the standardization of training as well as a homogenization of evaluation criteria that has marginalized nonorthodox approaches.[17] After institutionalism was dethroned by the rise of mathematical economics and more politically challenging forms of intellectual heresy (such as Marxism) were relegated to peripheral institutions and sometimes to other disciplines, American economists installed themselves confidently within the neoclassical paradigm. It is within this paradigm that the major intellectual debates in the discipline have taken place. Many of the trials of strength and internal conflicts concern the compatibility of models (and, often, empirical results) with the standard framework. In other words, the dominant conversations within the discipline have centered around which hypotheses in the neoclassical framework may be modified or tweaked to account for observed empirical patterns. But American economists implicitly agree to keep disturbances to a minimum; as a result, the framework is almost never questioned as a whole.

The French situation has been quite different. Out of an initially quite tightly bound disciplinary project—remember the overwhelmingly *libéral* orientation of French economics in the nineteenth century—two factors have combined to produce both weak disciplinary institutions and significant intellectual segmentation after World War II. The first of these is the sharp cultural and institutional boundary between the state and the rest of society, which has led to sharp divisions in the training of economists and the definitions of economic expertise. The second factor is the relative isolation and fragmentation of the intellectual sector itself. This fragmentation of the intellectual sphere is sustained by an institutional separation between teaching (university) and research (CNRS), the persistence of mandarin traditions at the university, which is a common pattern across all of continental Europe, and an early tenure system, all of which favor a high degree of intellectual entrenchment.[18] It is important to note, however, that intellectual divisions today do not map perfectly on institutional ones, though they often *originated* there. Rather, intellectual styles cut across institutional boundaries as each side seeks to enroll allies in the other sector. For instance, public engineers' connections to universities give them access to students and positions, while university-trained academics strive for better linkages to the public administration such as research contracts and appointments on special commissions.

It is interesting to note that Japan appears to harbor patterns similar to France, for similar institutional reasons. Studies of postwar Japanese economic policy describe a strong disconnection between the universities, which have historically been dominated by "literary" approaches, and a technocratic state administration that, as in France, recruits from elite higher learning institutions such as Tokyo University. And, as in France, it is within the latter that Keynesian economics became institutionalized and later morphed into a powerful indigenous school (*kanchu ekonomikusu*)[19] (Gao 1997; Hein 2003, 2004). Likewise, the dominant paradigms in French economics during the postwar period, whether neoclassical or not, have arguably come from the research sector which is most closely connected to the public administration. Even the recent rise of a school of industrial economics in Toulouse is in great part attributable to the patronage of the public sector: contracts with large public corporations were of paramount importance to its emergence and survival.

ECONOMIC ORDERS AND THE MAKING OF MONEY

Sociologists have generally recognized the fundamental importance of material factors in shaping the rise of professions. All professional enterprises, including disciplinary ones, essentially strive to establish an economic monopoly over certain activities.[20] Nevertheless, the influence of *specific* dimensions of economic organization over the process and content of professionalization has received less attention. If professions are essentially about securing rents, then *how* the particular profession of economics allows (or does not allow) its members to make money in different countries is of paramount importance to its structure as well as its ideational dimensions.

The United States occupies a unique place in this narrative. With weaker status distinctions in the educational system and the society at large, American academic groups and the institutions that sustained them (universities and foundations), have relied extensively on professionalization and disciplinarization to achieve legitimacy and secure jurisdictional monopolies. Hence the remarkable place of the PhD in establishing occupational identities, the tight control exerted by top institutions over resources and rewards, and the relative uniformity of training and work expectations. Still, American economists earn significantly higher salaries than other social scientists, in both the academic and the nonacademic sector. In 2003, for instance, the median annual salaries of doctoral economists were, on average, about 40 percent higher than those of sociologists and 33 percent higher than those of political scientists. Salary differences were greatest in the private sector and lowest in government, which suggests that economists' salaries are high because of high demand from the private sector, particularly finance and consulting.[21]

As we have seen, the fact that social and economic regulation in the United States occurs mainly through legal means implies that economists' work options in the private sector are much more abundant than in other nations. The ambiguous and contestable character of legal rules propel organizations, firms, courts, and government offices to resort to economists to provide quantifiable standards of decision making. This applied work has in turn expanded economic knowledge into new terrains, yielding considerable material profit. Hence the intellectual imperialism of American economics *as a discipline* may not be purely a consequence of its universalistic method and scientific rigor, as some optimistic practitioners (e.g., Lazear 2000) would have it. Instead, it might be tied to the particular professional ecology in which the American economics profession finds itself and, beyond it, to the prevailing mode of economic regulation in America. The United States is, after all, an economist's economy, which proclaims more than any other its conformity to the laissez-faire ideals that anchor the dominant streams of modern economic theory. It is also the country where the techniques of economists have flourished most broadly and have most systematically been turned into commercial ventures; where the social function of economists is best institutionalized and sustained by a comparatively cohesive (both materially and symbolically) scientific base; and perhaps where the language of economics carries greatest social authority, both in the wider public sphere and in specific institutional settings such as corporations, courts, public policy.

These considerations warrant a more general argument about the implications of this book for the study of professions and disciplines, in relation to Andrew Abbott's *System of Professions* in particular. On the one hand, Abbott's central assumption that professions and disciplines exist and evolve through their competition with other professions and disciplines is indeed illuminating when applied to U.S. economics. It helps us understand the imperialistic tendencies of the discipline, its drive to conquer new jurisdictions, and the jurisdictional and intellectual challenges it faces from other knowledge-based enterprises. Two points are worth mentioning, however. First, the dynamic processes at work are more complex than a simple competition over turf. The U.S. case also exemplifies a *jurisdictional nesting* of economics within other professions and disciplines, a nesting that is supported by a particular mode of exercise of public power in which the law is essential. Second, relations among professions are always defined and governed by *specific social, economic, and political circumstances*. In the United States, the jurisdictional interpenetration between economics and the law depends, for instance, on forms of economic regulation that emphasize legal instruments, and on the adversarial nature of the judicial process (and the concomitant role of experts, including economic experts, in litigation). Likewise, the development of finance and the commercialization of economic technologies in the financial world, both of which are very extensive in the United States, have depended on the size and particular organization of American financial markets. By contrast, the limited development of financial economics in France may be related to the underdevelopment of the French financial markets (at least prior to the 1986 reform). The general point here is that the social organization of other relevant professions and professional markets (law, finance, public administration, etc.) is of paramount importance in shaping the jurisdictional and intellectual opportunities available to the profession of economics. From this point of view, a "system of professions" is first and foremost a set of social, economic, and political conditions that govern the (external) relations among various social projects and thereby define these projects' (internal) character and identity. As these conditions change, for instance, as countries increasingly turn toward neoliberal forms of economic governance that give legal instruments the upper hand over administrative ones, so does the bundle of professional relations upon which economics depends, and, consequently, the discipline's jurisdictional and intellectual scope.

Social Processes and Categories in International Space

One of the paradoxes of this comparative project is that many economists, in fact, see national disciplinary differences as incidental and like to think of themselves as participating in an international scientific field where national boundaries are largely irrelevant. The sentiment that economics is an integrated, global science is widely shared, particularly among those economists who identify with the neoclassical mainstream. A professor from the University of Paris I thus stated bluntly: "As a first approximation there is no difference between France and other countries. This does not exclude differences of belief or ideology, but economic research takes place within a common field. People know and recognize each other" (June 1995). Interestingly, however, he immediately qualified his statement: "Many institutional and heterodox economists, who are very well represented in French universities, would probably not recognize themselves as part of this field" and proceeded to explain, in great detail, the idiosyncratic organization of French economics.

There is no paradox here. Both moments of the story obviously capture an essential part of the processes at work. We can, however, make two points about the self-evident character of the international space for economists. First, we should not forget that this global field is just as much a historical achievement as the national fields described earlier. Like them, it has been sustained over the years by many institutions and practices: by the international circulation of individuals, credentials, prizes, and honors—of which the most important may be U.S. PhDs returning home and emulating the training they have received; by the global political economy of publications and consulting work; and by the rise of international departmental and individual rankings, which economists seem to be particularly obsessed about.[22] Second, we should nonetheless be puzzled by the fact that while the importance of this space is well acknowledged, its specific organization is so often overlooked by those who see themselves as taking part in it. The primary empirical fact about the international field of economics has been, since World War II at least, the overwhelming domination of U.S.-based scholars, scholarship, and institutions and their commensurate power over the rules of the game that prevail in it.[23] Thus the belief in an international disciplinary field oriented toward the progress of knowledge, where "people know and recognize each other," also serves to obscure the structure of domination that produced this belief in the first place. Here the analogy with Bourdieu's description of social space (in *Distinction* [1984] for instance), or of any other specific field, is useful. Just in the same way that the dominants in social space tend to ignore the sociological principles of their own domination, which, in essence, are their superior endowments in the relevant forms of capital, the dominants in the international field of economics also fail to see the importance of national divisions and so overlook the benefits that accrue to them from being physically situated in or connected to this particular segment of the field. This is all the more surprising since they are better acquainted with its control mechanisms and its most influential members. Similarly, at the receiving end of American imperialism in the field of economics, the negation of national boundaries helps scholars overcome the necessarily more peripheral position to which their national location condemns them while raising their profile vis-à-vis less (or differently) internationally minded segments of the local profession. As Dezalay and Garth (2002) have brilliantly shown in their analysis of the transformation of Latin American states, connections to the United States are a form of capital in and of themselves.[24]

Clearly the field of economics is much more "international" when seen from Europe than it is seen from the United States, in the sense that the relation to the U.S. field is always much more defining of people's identities in Europe than is American scholars' relations to Europe. American economists worry little about the rest of the world. As Bourdieu observed, the dominants' privilege is automatically transformed into a natural attitude toward their own domination that rationalizes it as a consequence of talent or meritocratic achievement. The rest of the world, by contrast, is more anxious about its international position (i.e., in essence, its position relative to the United States). This is because the social positions of European economists, economic departments, and research centers are—at least in part—made and unmade in the United States: in U.S.-based credentials, conferences, reviews, and invitations. Parallel European distinctions, by contrast, are much less relevant to the position of American economists. Ironically, this does not preclude ideas and techniques coming out of Europe, such as Keynesianism or general equilibrium analysis, from being mobilized in scientific and political battles within the U.S. field and then being exported back to their place of origin. There is a fundamental asymmetry here that representations centered on the notion of an international scientific community largely miss.

To say this, however, amounts neither to denouncing the idea of a global intellectual enterprise as a pure mystification nor to assuming that the imperialistic structure of the international field is simply coercively imposed. Rather, my purpose is to suggest that international scientific power hierarchies, by anchoring certain national positions in a global (and naturalized) disciplinary common ground, become part and parcel of the processes that structure the distribution of power and resources within the national fields themselves. How they do so, of course, is contingent and may vary a lot across time and space. For instance, as leadership in economics moved away from Europe to the United States, some institutions and groups within Europe increasingly used their connections to the United States, whether material or intellectual or both, to advance their own position at home. In England, this was the case for the London School of Economics vis-à-vis Oxford and especially

Cambridge; later some of the newer universities (Warwick, Essex) and polytechnics adopted similar strategies of differentiation vis-à-vis both older and peer institutions. In France, the first major conduit of internationalization was the milieu of engineer-economists and the main statistical agency, INSEE; today, however, many universities also eagerly seek and claim international integration. So the international field has, in effect, become the world to which economists worldwide "naturally" orient themselves.

Finally, this international field itself is highly differentiated between mainstream and heterodox networks, and between academic and more overtly political ones.[25] Across all networks, however, international social structures and relations retain a pervasive influence on local struggles because they affect people's and institutions' positions in local fields and consequently shape the classificatory judgments that apply to them and the strategies of action that derive from these judgments. In the course of several years of research, I heard economists in the United Kingdom, France, and also Germany (where I completed nineteen interviews of economists in the summer of 1997) bemoan or celebrate the "Americanization" of their local profession, which generally meant the same thing: an emphasis on formalization, the standardization of evaluative criteria, and the diffusion of the neoclassical approach. Contemptuous statements about the spread of "Anglo-Saxon economics" or, as one interviewee put it, "French-style axiomatization,"[26] like accusations of "backwardness" or calls for "scientific rigor" or "pluralism," are always, implicitly or explicitly, also relational statements about proximity and distance vis-à-vis other segments of the national or international field. As Bourdieu's theoretical apparatus predicts, the subjective positions people take on these issues should map nicely onto people's objective position vis-à-vis the dominant social structures (i.e., the U.S. economic mainstream). We would expect, for instance, the strongest "boundary work" (Lamont 1992; Lamont and Thévenot 2000) against the United States to come from people holding those forms of capital and intellectual affinities that are most marginal or threatened in the current configuration of power (e.g., people with local as opposed to international reputations or heterodox as opposed to mainstream inclinations). In England, I thus met a "traditional Cambridge economist" (in his own words) who condemned the mainstream for being "very much subservient to America" (research scholar, Cambridge University, June 1997). Another economist, also self-identified as a Cambridge heterodox, said:

> For Cambridge, and perhaps for Britain too, the problem is that they are copying the Americans, but they are twenty years late. That's the

worst situation. Not only are we going in the wrong path, but we are following blindly, with the dedication of religious pilgrims, way way way behind. Don't think about it and just do it. A lot of these people have studied in America. And they want to turn our place into North America. (professor, University of Cambridge, June 1997)

Other good examples of the homology between (objective) field position and (subjective) position taking would be the "post-autistic" movement's plea for pluralism in economics and a moratorium on the abuse of mathematical language, or the role of noneconomists (including Pierre Bourdieu himself) in the "resistance" against the "tyranny of the market" (e.g., see Bourdieu 1999a). Conversely, we would expect that calls for the modernization of the practice of economics and economic management should come from those holding dominant or rising forms of capital (such as international connections, mathematical capital). An illustration of this type of connection would be the mounting calls to rationalize performance measures for individual scholars and institutions in England and France by ranking them according to publication or citation record, a practice that clearly favors actors with international connections and reputation.[27] As some research on the British experience suggests, the institutionalization of such forms of professional regulation has tended to completely exclude nonmainstream economists from the top end of the academic job market.[28]

It is through such local struggles, largely fought within national economics fields by actors pushing those institutional strategies that will allow them to best reap the rewards of their different forms of capital (e.g., local vs. imported capital), that an international "field" of economics gets produced and stabilizes itself. And what brings this international field into existence for French and British economists, so that an "international mainstream" can be identified and argued about (or against), is the scientific and institutional influence of this field's dominant international player, the United States. However, as Bourdieu (1999b) points out, to understand *how* American influence gets locally mobilized, rejected, translated, and used by actors, and to explain the ultimate outcome of their struggles, we need a meticulous analysis of all the stakes involved, both local and nonlocal.

Like their national counterparts, the international social structures of economics legitimize certain definitions of how to practice economics and who is qualified to produce economic discourse and to govern economic policy. Perhaps the best illustration of this process is the displacement of the generalist economic policy maker, who can be trained in the arts, engineering, law, or public administration, by the professional scholar trained in economic *science* (as certified by a PhD). The shift has been particularly marked in the United States and Latin America, but it is quite noticeable elsewhere too.[29]

Interviews I conducted at the French and German central banks illustrate the kind of transition I am evoking here and underscore the importance of international relationships to that transformation. They also suggest the fragility of the process, and the fact that these changes never occur without a great deal of ambivalence. Three officials I spoke to (two at the Banque de France in Paris and one at the Bundesbank in Frankfurt) praised the efficacy of their practically oriented central banks, in which economic research has traditionally been relatively unimportant. One French official went as far as to say that "there is a feeling at the Bank that it is often the less credible central banks that have the best economic research departments. Look at the Bundesbank, there is almost no research, but it is the best central bank; contrast this with the Bank of Italy or the Bank of Spain, which have large research units [but are less effective]."[30] At the same time, all three officials fervently embraced the conception, best exemplified by the U.S. Federal Reserve system, that a modern central bank should have a top-notch economic research department that is on par with the best academic institutions. As the following quotation from the Bundesbank official suggests, the primary reason was not that such a strategy would help his institution better perform its function. Like his French counterparts, he was rather doubtful of that. Rather, his explanation was phrased in entirely symbolic terms: conforming to this institutional model, he said, would allow the Bundesbank to be a more legitimate player in international circles: "It is very important to compete with the IMF or the OECD. Often when we meet, they present sophisticated papers. If we do not do the same we will lose power in international discussion, and, especially, in the EMU context. Our position really has to be supported by academic work, or it does not look as credible." (economist, research department, Bundesbank, July 1997).

For these institutions, hiring trained economists, creating economic advisory councils in which economists play an important role, disbursing money for economic research, or relying on economic consultants clearly has a profound ceremonial dimension and cannot be separated from broader dynamics within the international field of central banking in which displays of scientific firepower are increasingly equated with technocratic authority. Hence the international social structures of economics neither erase the national structures nor stand separately from those structures. Rather, they play into the struggles that continuously reshape the national fields themselves, by shifting the way people and institutions are categorized and evaluated, by influencing the distribution of resources, and by sustaining the diffusion of policy fashions.

Contribution of a Sociology of Economic Knowledge to Economic Sociology

Economic questions are sites where societies articulate their conceptions of themselves and their relations to others in the international arena. As an intellectual and disciplinary corpus, economics serves as a vehicle for cultural representations about the proper shape of the economy—what it is supposed to look like. As a professional practice, economics formulates ideas about the proper way to achieve this ideal, suggesting *how* the economy is supposed to be acted upon and *who* has authority to speak about economic issues.

Studying the social, institutional, and intellectual foundations of this authority across societies thus serves as a point of entry into an analysis of the institutional mechanisms whereby cultural representations or national paradigms about economic order are routinely formed. As such, a sociology of economic knowledge should be a precondition to any form of economic sociology: first, because analyzing the particular social conditions that lie behind what we know about the economy provides a natural foundation for potentially reconstructing that very knowledge; second, and more important, because economics is part and parcel of the economy as it exists today. More precisely, *specific*, context-dependent forms of economic knowledge are part and parcel of *particular* economies as they exist today.

One way to read the present study is as a critique of economics' universalizing discourse and practical claims. In the first instance, this book should thus serve as a reminder that the search for universalism gets constructed in quite different ways across social contexts. Economic knowledge gets entrenched with different force across countries, in different places and institutions, and for different purposes, and its very substance can also differ in subtle ways—in the problems posed, methods used, tools developed, and identities forged. I have sought to locate these differences in what I call the "exercise of public power." The French technocracy's legitimation by reason and mathematics produced (at its core) an economics that was highly formal, and mainly concerned with the efficiency and productivity of the large (sometimes public) enterprises. From the technocracy's point of view, all else was just politics or worse, corporate solidarities, which one should keep at bay. The British clerisy ideal produced an economics that struggled to reconcile ethics with economic freedom and efficiency. Politics was therefore at the center of British economics, but the fact that it was all a conversation between gentlemen of goodwill took some of the political edge off. Finally the American emphasis on professionalism produced an economics that was practically oriented and much more utilitarian (in the sense of rational choice) in its theoretical imagination. Here was a discipline whose results could be marshaled much more aggressively to arbiter political and legal conflicts and grow businesses.

This book thus aims to offer a more complex and, I hope, more sociological critique of economics than the oft-heard complaint about the lack of fit between economic theory and reality. First, it shows that economists remain intensely concerned with, and constantly struggle over, their representations of an underlying economic "reality," even in their most abstract endeavors.[31] Second, much of economics' intellectual development across the last century has been driven by economic *practice*—whether this involved an operational problem to be solved, an effort to reform or modernize society and advise power, or the desire to make inert data speak through technology. The widely shared skepticism of economics among less formalizing disciplines, whether it is legitimate or not, provides no grounds for avoiding a serious reflection on the social conditions under which economists produce *their visions* of economic reality. And this sort of reflection, incidentally, should also send us back to ourselves. The work of sociologists is, after all, evidently subject to the same logics as those I have tried to expose in our powerful neighbor in the social-scientific field.

Appendix

TABLE 6-1
Chronology of the Rise of Economics

	Academicization (1870s–1920s)	Public Management (1930s–1960s)	Marketization (1960s–1990s)
Economics	• Founding of scientific associations, academic reviews, specialized training programs and advanced degrees	• Macroeconomic and econometric revolutions • Governmental and semi-governmental economic advice / research units • New economic administrations (emphasis on planning and budgeting) • State funding for economic research • Specialized schools and corps (France)	• Microeconomic and financial revolutions • Economic departments in banks/corporations • Commercialization of economic tools toward both the private and public sectors • Rise of business schools • Business economics associations
Illustrative examples (list is non-exhaustive)	• U.S.: American Economic Association (1885); *American Economic Review* (1911); First economics PhDs (1880s) • U.K.: Royal Economic Society (1890); *Economic Journal* (1891); Cambridge Tripos (1903) and London School of Economics and Political Science (1895) • France: Société d'économie politique (1842); Incorporation in the law curriculum (1877); *Revue d'économie politique* (1887).	• U.S.: NBER (1920); Brookings (1927); Council of Economic Advisers (1946) • U.K.: *General Theory* (1936); Economic Section of the war cabinet (1941); Government Economic Service/Department of Economic Affairs (1964); Economic Quangos. • France: École Nationale d'Administration (1945); INSEE (1946); Economic laboratories of the Planning Commissariat (1960s)	• U.S.: Carnegie and Ford foundation reports on business education (1959); National Economic Research Associates (1961), Charles River Associates (1965); Long Term Capital Management (1994) • U.K.: Bank reviews (1960s); • France: professionalization of *gestion* (management science)

DATA

Data for this research consist mainly of interviews, statistics obtained from various institutions regarding the education and labor market for economists (both current and past), and a large a variety of primary material ranging from published personal memoirs, government reports, newspaper and magazine articles, information obtained from professional associations, individual corporations and state agencies. Finally, I used a large amount of historical studies as secondary sources, which are all listed in the bibliography.

The following is the list of 95 interviews I conducted in France, the United Kingdom, Germany, and the United States between June 1995 and March 2005 (this book, however, does not report on the German case). Interviewees were selected on the basis of their professional qualifications and age, and sometimes their specific knowledge about the broader field of economics and its history. My principal concern was to meet economists who had diverse professional experiences (in academia, government, business, or the think tanks), and would also represent a variety of generations. I proceeded by constructing a series of networks. I directly contacted a first group of people, basing my selections from various directories of professional associations and from my own assessment of who would be a good "point of entry" into a particular segment of the profession given their personal trajectory. Most of the following interviews, in turn, were the result of individual recommendations from these first contacts. The larger number of interviews in France corresponds to the necessity to make up, to a greater extent than in the other two countries, for the smaller secondary literature on the history of French economics as well as for the smaller number of publicly available interviews.

Interviews lasted between one-half hour and five hours, with a majority around one hour and one half. Most were taped, but always under condition of anonymity. I met some people twice. The interview data contain a clear bias in favor of academics, as one of my chief concerns was to understand disciplinary differences across countries, in addition to institutional ones. Among academics, I also interviewed a larger number of people who are active in "macroeconomics" (broadly conceived), because the latter is often the most conflictual domain within economics, as well as its most visible.

Except where indicated, interviews were conducted at the site of the main professional function and are listed according to this function. Hence OFCE means "Economist working at OFCE." Except where indicated, the title "professor" means "professor of economics." One should remember that many people often combine several functions (this is particularly true in France). Finally, a certain number of economists located

TABLE 6-2
List of Interviewees/Informants

	Main Professional Function (at Time of Interview)
France	
June 1, 1995	Economic Studies, Indosuez Bank
June 3, 1995	PhD Student, University of Paris X
June 5, 1995	IFRI
June 6, 1995	Professor, École Normale Supérieure and university
June 8, 1995	INSEE administrator, CSERC
June 9, 1995	OFCE
June 12, 1995	Direction de la Prévision
June 14, 1995	OFCE
June 15, 1995	Research scholar, CREST
June 16, 1995	Direction de la Prévision
June 19, 1995	Economic Studies, INSEE
June 20, 1995	Economic Studies, Bank of France
June 22, 1995 and July 10, 1995	Professor, Sciences-Po and University of Paris I
June 26, 1995	Professor, University of Paris I
June 29, 1995	High-level civil servant, Inspection des Finances
July 3, 1995	OFCE
July 3, 1995	Bank of France
July 4, 1995	BIPE
July 5, 1995	Economic Studies, National Bank of Paris (BNP)
July 7, 1995	Cour des Comptes
July 19, 1995	Research scholar, CEPREMAP
July 20, 1995	Euro 92 (think tank)
July 25, 1995	Professor, Sciences-Po
July 26, 1995	French Confederation of Insurance Companies
July 27, 1995	REXECODE
August 2, 1995	IRES
August 3, 1995	Professor, University of Aix-Marseille
August 4, 1995	Research scholar, CEPREMAP
August 4, 1995 and August 22, 1995	Research scholar, CEPREMAP (2 interviews)
August 9, 1995	Economic Studies, INSEE
August 13, 1995	Professor, INSEAD
August 21, 1995	Research scholar, CEPII
August 22, 1995	Research scholar, CEPREMAP

(continued)

TABLE 6-2 (*Continued*)

	Main Professional Function (at Time of Interview)
June 21, 1996	French Association of Business Economists
June 26, 1996	SEDEIS
May 26, 2005 and July 4, 2005	High-level civil servant and Professor at Paris-Dauphine
United Kingdom	
June 2, 1997	Professor, University of Oxford
June 3, 1997	3 business economists, on the board of the Society of Business Economists (interviewed together in London)
June 4, 1997	Professor, London Business School
June 5, 1997	Professor, London School of Economics
June 6, 1997	Professor, University of Sussex Journalist, *Financial Times*
June 9, 1997	Professor, University of Oxford
June 9, 1997	Professor, University of Oxford
June 10, 1997	Reader, University of Bristol
June 11, 1997	Professor, University of Cambridge
June 11, 1997	Senior Research Fellow, University of Cambridge
June 12, 1997	Reader, University of Birmingham
June 16, 1997	Two senior economists, Department of Trade and Industry (interviewed together)
June 17, 1997	Professor, University of Cambridge
June 19, 1997	Reader, University of Cambridge
June 20, 1997	Senior Lecturer, De Monfort University
United States	
December 11, 1996	Assistant professor, Harvard University
January 4, 1997	Professor, University of Wisconsin (interview conducted at the AEA meeting, New Orleans)
January 4, 1997	Official, National Association of Business Economists (interview conducted at the AEA meeting, New Orleans)
January 5, 1997 and April 9, 1997	Professor, MIT (first interview conducted at the AEA meeting, New Orleans; second interview conducted at MIT)
April 8, 1997	Professor, MIT
April 10, 1997	Professor, Harvard University (*)

(continued)

Table 6-2 *(Continued)*

	Main Professional Function (at Time of Interview)
April 11, 1997	Professor emeritus, Harvard University
January 3, 1998	Professor, University of Iowa (conducted at the AEA meeting, Chicago; also e-mail correspondence)
May 14, 1999	Economic journalist/essayist
May 19, 1999	Professor, Harvard University
July 31, 1999	Professor, Princeton University (*)
August 11, 1999	Economic consultant, Washington
August 11, 1999	Economist, US government (Small Business Administration)
August 12, 1999	Senior Fellow, Brookings Institution
August 12, 1999	Economist, Congressional Budget Office
August 13, 1999	Senior Fellow, American Enterprise Institute
August 13, 1999	Economist, Congressional Budget Office
October 20, 1999	Professor, New York University (*)
November 8, 1999	Professor, Princeton University
November 26, 2003	Professor, University of California, Berkeley (*)
March 11, 2005	Professor, University of California, Berkeley (*)
Germany	
June 26, 1997	Research staff member, IFO, Münich
June 29, 1997	Assistant Professor, University of Münich
June 30, 1997	Professor, University of Stuttgart-Höhenheim
July 1, 1997	Professor, University of Mannheim and ZEW
July 2, 1997	Professor, University of Mannheim (business administration)
July 3, 1997	Professor, University of Mannheim
July 7, 1997	Economist, Ministry of Finance, Bonn
July 8, 1997	Staff member, Economic Studies, Westlandes Bank, Düsseldorf
July 9, 1997	Professor, University of Hamburg
July 11, 1997	Librarian, Kiel Institute of World Economics
	Researcher, Kiel Institute of World Economics

(continued)

TABLE 6-2 (*Continued*)

	Main Professional Function (at Time of Interview)
July 12, 1997	Professor, Humboldt University, Berlin
July 14, 1997	Professor, Free University, Berlin
	Interviewed together:
	Staff member, Economics Department at Bank Gesellschaft Berlin and Assistant Professor, Free University, Berlin
July 15, 1997	DIW, Berlin
July 16, 1997	Professor, University of Frankfurt
July 17, 1997	Economic Research Department, Bundesbank, Frankfurt
	Economic Research Department, Bundesbank, Frankfurt
July 18, 1997	Professor, University of Tübingen

in the United States had taught for long periods of time in England, or been educated there, hence I also recorded substantial information on that aspect of their experience. These people are marked with a (*) in the table below. Also tremendously helpful on Britain are the interview volume by Keith Tribe (1997) and the autobiographical essays in Backhouse and Middleton (2000).

Other useful interview volumes, mostly of American economists or at least economists teaching in the United States, include: Hargrove and Morley (1984), Swedberg (1990), Breit and Spencer (1997, 3rd edition), Colander and Klamer (1990), Colander and Landreth (1997), Snowdon and Vane (1999), Colander, Holt and Rosser (2004), Colander (2007). Several professional journals, such as the *Journal of Economic Perspectives*, *Macroeconomic Dynamics* and *The Region* (publication of the Federal Reserve Bank of Minneapolis) also publish very detailed interviews of American economists. Also see the Nobel prize internet archive at http://nobelprize.org/nobel_prizes/economics/laureates/ for detailed autobiographies by Nobel prize winners.

Notes

INTRODUCTION
ECONOMICS AND SOCIETY

1. The literature on these historical transformations is extremely vast and is partially covered throughout this book. For excellent overviews of the institutional development of economics, see especially Schumpeter [1954] 1994; Morgan 2003; and Backhouse 2005. For introductions to the three themes just mentioned, however, see in particular Wagner, Wittrock and Whitley, 1991; Coats 1993a, 1993b; Fourcade-Gourinchas 2001 on the process of academicization across nations; and more specifically Dorfman 1949; 1959; Furner 1975; Ross 1979; Barber 1993; and Morgan and Rutherford 1998 on the United States; Maloney 1985; and Tribe and Kadish 1993 on Britain; and Le Van–Lemesle 2004 on France. On state-led transformations in economics and related social sciences, see Furner and Supple 1990a; Wagner, Wittrock, and Whitley 1991; Porter 1995; Rueschemeyer and Skocpol 1996; and Steinmetz 2005a; more specifically Klein and Morgan 2000; Bernstein 2001; and Mirowski 2002b on the United States; Winch 1969; Coats 1981 on Britain; Fourquet 1980 on France. On the commercialization of economic science, see in particular Whitley 1987a; Faulhaber and Baumol 1988; MacKenzie 2006. On international processes in economics, see notably Coats 1997; Bockman and Eyal 2002; Charle, Shriewer and Wagner 2004; Fourcade 2006. See appendix for a schematic presentation of these trends.

2. See Krüger, Daston, and Heidelberger 1987; Mirowski 1989b; Backhouse and Biddle 2000; Klein and Morgan 2001; Morgan 2003.

3. This theme has been particularly well developed by Ellul 1967; Habermas 1971; Abbott 1988; Meyer 1994; Schofer 1999.

4. See Whitley 1984, 1987b; Cole 1983; Han 2003. The image of consensus is also being engineered by academic economists' remarkable love affair with ranking systems (based mainly on citations or publication output).

5. On cross-national economic policy variations, see especially Weir and Skocpol 1985; Hall 1989; Dezalay and Garth 2002; Fourcade-Gourinchas and Babb 2002; Prasad 2006.

6. Views on each of the propositions reported in table 0-2, however, are likely to have changed quite substantially since the surveys were administered. For instance, with central banking institutions across Europe evolving in the sense of a greater independence from political control, it should be expected that French economists' views on the subject are now more closely aligned with the views of their American and German colleagues. (The Bundesbank has been independent since it was created in 1948. The Banque de France became independent from government control in 1993, the Bank of England in 1997. The European Central Bank was created in 1999.)

7. See Frey and Eichenberger 1993. There is little reason to think, however, that such appointments have generally rewarded economists per se (in a manner that would be analogous to the recent "rise of economists" in Latin America and Central and Eastern Europe [Markoff and Montecinos 1993]). Rather, these patterns seem to correspond to the higher prestige of the civil service in those societies, as well as the traditional public role played by professors (Krause 1996), *including* economics professors.

8. All translations are mine unless otherwise noted.

9. See Mayhew 1998; Dobbin and Dowd 2000 for such an argument.

10. Szreter 1993; Perkin 1989; Krause 1996.

11. I disagree somewhat with Ragin's characterization of Mill's method (particularly as it is used by Skocpol and other institutionalist scholars) as "case-oriented." I consider it to be qualitative, yet essentially variable-oriented: the logic of exposition in the method is driven by the imperative of demonstrating causal relationships between variables, not to reconstruct the coherence of a case in its historical and anthropological thickness. Therefore, my own understanding of the "case-oriented" method is closer to what Skocpol and Somers (1980) call "contrast-oriented comparative history" and Tilly (1984) labels "individualizing comparisons": that is, a style of exposition driven by the assumption of the relative uniqueness of each case. Also see Skocpol 1984 on these debates.

12. On the term "free trade," see Trentmann 1998, 226; on "labor," see Biernacki 1995; on "civil society," see Koselleck 2002. Also see the superb analysis of the use of the term "public" in France and the United States in Moody and Thévenot (2000, 317–18). In the United States, the term is used to refer to procedures by which individual opinions are collected and expressed to others in a deliberative process (as in *public* hearing). In the French case, "public" designates mainly an activitity that is carried out by the state in the name of the common good (as in "enquête d'utilité *publique*").

13. I am deeply indebted to Libby Schweber for sharpening my awareness of this point.

14. This practice is especially frequent among members of the generalist-trained higher administration (ENA and grands corps), who can present themselves as historians, economists, essay writers, etc.

15. E.g., see Bonnell and Hunt 1999; Sewell 2005 on the cultural turn in the social sciences.

16. My own view of agency here is similar to William Sewell's: "Agency is formed by a specific range of cultural schemas and resources available in a person's particular social milieu. The specific forms that agency will take vary enormously and are culturally and historically determined" (1992, 20).

17. See Bourdieu 1977b, 1988, 1992.

18. For a beautiful theoretical exposition of this view, see Meyer, Boli, and Thomas 1987; DiMaggio 1994; Dobbin 1994.

19. Meyer, Boli, and Thomas 1987; Sewell 1992; Dobbin 1994, 2001; Swidler 2001.

20. These are: verticality/horizontality, individualism/collectivism, polarization/integration.

21. Also see Johnson (1973) identifies "national styles of economic research" and Abend (2006) does the same for sociology. Boltanski and Thévenot 1991 on this important theoretical point.

22. See, e.g., Dumont 1977; Hirschman 1977; Rosanvallon 1989b on the connections between political theory and economic economics.

23. Source: *Dictionnaire historique de la langue francaise* (ed. Le Robert, 1992), etymological definition for *économiste*.

24. Trentmann 1998, 228; Rohrlich 1987; Bowden and Seabrooke 2006.

25. Tribe 1988; Lindenfeld 1997. See Mitchell 1999 on the emergence of the macroeconomy as a "thing" to be acted upon.

26. See Berger and Luckmann 1966; Bourdieu 1992; Meyer, Boli, and Thomas 1987.

27. Also see Wuthnow 1987.

28. See in particular Wagner, Wittrock, and Whitley 1991; Rueschemeyer and Skocpol 1996; Heilbron, Magnusson, and Wittrock 1998; Sarfatti-Larson 1977; Abbott 1988, 2005; Heidenheimer 1989; Krause 1996.

29. This paragraph draws on a very helpful comment by Frank Dobbin.

30. Sewell distinguishes between high-power/low-depth political structures (which tend to be not very persistent) and high-power/high-depth ones, which are especially durable. Among the latter, Sewell cites the American constitutional system, the French public bureaucracy, and English community legal structures (1992, 24).

31. See notably Schweber (2006) on the interconnection between discipline assertion and inferential style of statistical reasoning. Also see Heilbron 1991.

32. Jarausch 1983; Lepenies 1988; Collins 1998; Fourcade-Gourinchas 2001; Schweber 2006; Bourdieu 1975, 1988; Ringer 1992; Heilbron 1995.

33. See, e.g., Chenu 2002 on French sociology (the case of economics will be treated at length in the following chapters).

34. These documents, however, also exemplify the diversity of national understandings concerning the proper and legitimate economic goals for the nation, and the role of government in achieving them. For instance, the "basic law" in Germany insists mainly on the need for the state to maintain the "requirements of economic equilibrium" but barely mentions economic growth.

35. Dawson 1953.

36. Etner 1987; Porter 1995; Ekelund and Hébert 1999.

37. See Jasanoff 1995.

38. See, for instance, auctioneers (Quemin 1997), notaries (Suleiman 1987).

39. For excellent literature reviews on the social analysis of science and ideas, see Swidler and Arditi 1994; Shapin 1995; Gieryn 1995; Camic and Gross 2001.

40. See, again, the important body of institutionalist scholarship dealing with the influence of economic ideas on policy (Weir and Skocpol 1985; Hall 1989; Rueschemeyer and Skocpol 1996; Campbell 1998; Stryker 1989; Campbell and Petersen 2001) or with the massive "economicization" of public bureaucracies and political elites that has accompanied the turn toward neoliberal policies (Markoff and Montecinos 1993, forthcoming; Centeno 1994; Loureiro 1996; Centeno and Silva 1998; Montecinos 1998; Eyal 2000; Babb 2001; Dezalay and Garth 2002).

CHAPTER ONE
INSTITUTIONAL LOGICS IN COMPARATIVE PERSPECTIVE

1. See Dobbin 1994, 31; Kaufman forthcoming; Bensel 1990 on the buildup of central state capacities after the Civil War.

2. See, e.g., the classic treatment of American individualism in Bellah et al. 1985.

3. See Birnbaum and Badie 1983, 128–29. In this perspective, it is not surprising that the main theoretical frameworks for analyzing American political institutions (pluralism and Marxism) both lay considerable stress on the influence of social interests.

4. Silberman 1993, 227. I rely heavily on Silberman's account in this entire section.

5. Silberman 1993, 281.

6. Heclo 1984, 14.

7. Birnbaum and Badie 1983, 128; Cohen-Tanugi 1992, 95–126; Kingdon 1995; Heclo 1988.

8. As in Britain, the expansion of the American public service was also contemporaneous with the expansion of universities, which means that the state, unlike its counterparts in continental Europe, did not need to rely on specialized institutions.

9. Silberman 1993, 263; also see Heclo 1984, 11.

10. Kaufman 2008.

11. Tocqueville [1835–40] 2000; Cohen-Tanugi 1992, 132.

12. Hollingsworth 1996, 180–81. Also see G. Wilson 1990, 39–66.

13. See Voss 1994 on this point.

14. The Federal Reserve Board is technically one of those agencies, in charge of the supervision of the banking system in addition to the management of monetary policy.

15. See Dobbin 1994, 1995; Roy 1997; Fligstein 1990; Djelic 2002. The Interstate Commerce Commission emerged as a state response to the concentration of power in the railroad sector. By the end of the New Deal, the model of the regulatory agency had been extended to the stock market, radio, trade, electricity, finance, communications, and labor relations.

16. See, for instance, the breakup of the Standard Oil Company in 1911 or the breakup of AT&T in 1982. See Campbell and Lindberg 1990 and Prasad 2006 for further developments on this point.

17. The agency in charge was the Office of Price Administration (1941–47). Price controls were reinstated during the Korean War and again in 1971 under Nixon (Goodwin 1975).

18. Vogel 1996b; Schultze 1984. See, for instance, Sidney Blumenthal, "Drafting a Democratic Industrial Plan" *New York Times*, August 28, 1983.

19. See Vogel, 1996a.

20. But see Schneiberg 2005 on the significant presence of municipal and cooperative utilities, particularly in the Midwest.

21. Blinder 1999.

22. See Clark and Youn 1976. On the *Trustees of Dartmouth College vs. Woodward* case, see Menand 2001, 240–43.

23. Burke 1983, 111. Also see Hofstadter 1963a; Veysey 1965; Shils 1979; Charle and Verger 1994.

24. On the influence on the German model on American higher education, see Herbst 1965 and Ben-David 1960. A significant number of American students were trained in Germany during the second half of the nineteenth century.

25. Bledstein 1976; Trow 1993, 286; Clark and Youn 1976.

26. Professional schools were initially created as independent institutions. By the 1930s, however, the vast majority of professional schools had been incorporated into universities (Goldin and Katz 1999).

27. Oleson and Voss 1979.

28. Gumport 1993a, 232.

29. Geiger 1986; Mirowski and Mirjam-Sent 2007.

30. Birnbaum and Badie 1983; Nettl 1968.

31. See, for instance, Lipset 1963b on the respect for and social acceptance of the aristocracy in British society.

32. See Charle 1997. Also see Silberman 1993 on the structure of the civil service.

33. See the critiques raised by the Plowden (HMSO 1961) and Fulton (HMSO 1968) reports; also Committee on the Reorganization of Central Government (HMSO 1970).

34. See, for instance, the establishment of the Civil Service College for the in-house training of public officials in 1970.

35. Theakston 1996, 37. Permanent secretaries are the most senior civil servants, who head government departments and serve as personal advisers to ministers. Only one permanent secretary of the Treasury since World War I—Terence Burns, who occupied the position from 1991 to 1998—was a professional economist. Source: Author's survey derived from Browning 1986; Barberis 1996; Middleton 1998.

36. The recent deterioration of the civil service status (in relative terms) has led to higher levels of turnover. A Treasury experience, for instance, has become a valuable background for entry into the City. Source: Interviews.

37. Birnbaum and Badie 1983; Bulmer 1987; Christoph 1975; Rose 1984; Harris 1990a.

38. See Jepperson 1992, 115; Steinmo 1989.

39. See, e.g., Himmelfarb's (2004) comparative analysis of the Enlightenment in Britain, France, and the United States, where she describes the British Enlightenment as the "Age of Benevolence."

40. As Thompson puts it, "The considerably autonomy of the commercially oriented, Morrisonian public corporations, by means of which the commanding heights of the economy were nationalized, militated against their use by a central planning authority. . . . There was, in effect, a definite reluctance to go down the road traversed by the French in the postwar period and establish something comparable to the Commissariat Général au Plan" (2006, 140–41). Also, the British nationalizations were much more political, made in the name of the

reduction of wealth inequalities, while in the French nationalizations the desire to increase the productivity and efficiency of the economy seemed more prominent. See, again, Thompson's discussion of the redistributive arguments in favor of public ownership (2006, 166–67).

41. See, for instance, Weir 1989, 75.

42. The National Economic Development Council was "a committee of government, employers and union representatives, which (met) monthly to discuss economic and industrial problems" (Keegan and Pennant-Rea 1979, 109).

43. The British practice of planning acknowledges a greater role for interest groups (especially trade unions) than its French model, which Shonfield characterizes as a "voluntary collusion between senior civil servants and big business" (1965, 128). Also see Zysman 1983; Hall 1986; Prasad 2006 on the differences between France and Britain.

44. See Tomlinson 2005.

45. Longstreth 1979; Fourcade-Gourinchas and Babb 2002.

46. Green 1992, 212. Also see Longstreth 1979; Ingham 1984; Kynaston and Roberts 2001; Cassis 1999. Brittan 1964, chap. 11, offers a firsthand account of the "priority to the pound policy" of the Treasury, and Booth 2001, details the Treasury's attempt to impose the "Robot" approach to monetary policy in the 1950s, according to which the "main aim of economic policy should be to support the sterling" (289).

47. See Thelen 2004.

48. Trow 1993, 282.

49. In the institutional fashion already encountered elsewhere, the University Grants Committee was an arm's-length organization that preserved the universities' governance autonomy and established block grants on the basis of regular consultations. Oxford and Cambridge, whose wealth was derived from ancient endowments, were excluded from the scheme at first.

50. Fisher 1977, 79.

51. See Ringer 1979, 229–30; Charle and Verger 1994, 121–22.

52. A recent survey thus found that among university social science staff in post during the academic year 1989–90, 33.5 percent had a doctorate, 27.8 percent a master's degree, and 38.7 percent a bachelor's degree (the same figures for economics were, respectively 30.7, 36.4, and 32.9 percent) (Pearson et al., 1991).

53. See Anderson 1992; Wittrock 1985. The traditional view among the British business elite was that the art of "affairs" (like that of law, or medicine) was learned after long years of work experience, rather than through education. Indeed, available surveys of the educational background of business leaders show that British entrepreneurs and managers have been fewer to attend a college or a university than their American, German, and French counterparts, and that such a pattern has remained consistent since the nineteenth century (although the proportion of those receiving university training over the period still increased markedly over time, as it did elsewhere) (Kaelble 1980, 417).

54. Clark 1983. State grants' share of total university income rose from about 34 percent in 1920 to 73 percent in 1967 (Halsey and Trow 1971, 63). Similarly, the status of the Ministry of Education was progressively enhanced, and a sepa-

rate Department for Education and Science (DES) with responsibilities for higher education was created in 1964 (Premfors 1980).

55. Rothblatt 1990, 73.

56. This represents only a slight decline from 1900, where the corresponding numbers were, respectively, 68 percent for the Royal Society and 82 percent for the British Academy (Halsey 1992, 77).

57. The percentage of self-recruitment of teachers at Oxbridge in 1992 was 31 percent (Halsey 1992, 140), which is still important, but significantly down from its level a few decades earlier (78.1 percent in 1961–62, 59 percent in 1976) (Halsey and Trow 1971, 85).

58. See Soares 1999 for a history of Oxford.

59. The Franks Report (1966) led to the establishment and funding (half government, half business) of the London Business School and Manchester Business School.

60. However, management studies has been taught at Oxford since 1965.

61. See Alter 1987.

62. It has since then been renamed the Higher Education Funding Council. The UGC provides a block grant to universities that covers salaries, research assistants, and libraries.

63. Edgerton 1997, 770.

64. Birnbaum and Badie 1993, 109; Tocqueville [1856] 1998.

65. Rosanvallon 1990.

66. Under the Third (1871–1939) and Fourth Republics (1946–58), the Parliament and its committees used to have more authority in the determination of economic policy orientations. Kuisel places the shift in influence toward the executive and the central bureaucracy in the early 1950s, when a string of "strong-willed premiers or finance ministers like Antoine Pinay, René Mayer, Joseph Laniel, Edgar Faure, and Mendès-France took charge of economic affairs" (1981, 254–55).

67. Hall 1986, 177–78; Kuisel 1981, 254.

68. See Rosanvallon 1989a, 178.

69. E.g., Charles Spinasse, at the Ministry of National Economy, and Alfred Sauvy at the ministry's Statistical Agency (Kuisel 1981, 121). Also see Margairaz 1991 on this period.

70. 1936–37. See Kuisel 1981; Bloch-Laîné and Bouvier 1986, 94.

71. Paxton (1982), in particular, pointed out the "modernist" dimension of the Vichy regime, which he sees as a precursor of the postwar *économie dirigée*.

72. A statutory reform in 1936 had already increased the role of public authority in supervising the bank's activity.

73. The Inspectorate of Finances is, with the Conseil d'État, the most prestigious of the *grands corps*. Created by Napoleon in 1801, it now recruits principally the top graduates of the École Nationale d'Administration. Its members have a quasi monopoly on the top positions in the Ministry of Finance.

74. Kuisel 1981, 253. See Mamou 1988 on the Treasury.

75. Stevens 1980, 95; Shonfield 1965, 166–71. Also see Zysman 1983; Hayward 1986, 22–23. The Caisse des Dépôts et Consignations is a formidably powerful financial institution that "commands all the money accumulated in

small savings in the post office and savings banks; it holds the vast pension funds of the nationalized industries and local authorities, and any tax revenues which the Government has not yet spent" (Shonfield 1965, 167).

76. See Bauchet 1964, 62; Shonfield 1965, 129–31; Hall 1986 on the French Planning Commissariat.

77. Schmidt 1996; Gordon and Meunier 2001.

78. During the period following World War I, partnerships between private and public capital were promoted on a large scale, as a means to further industrial expansion. Examples of this policy included mixed capital companies (e.g., the Compagnie Française des Pétroles) and a specialized banking institution, the Crédit National, designed to handle credits to private industry (Shonfield 1965, 82).

79. The quotation is from Landes 1949, 50. Kuisel argues that the stereotype of the cautious, "Malthusian" French businessman emerged around 1900 (1981, 29).

80. Général De Gaulle, Letter to Alain Peyrefitte, December 12, 1962. Cited in Jeanneney 2007, 26.

81. Also see Fourcade-Gourinchas and Babb 2002.

82. Caron mentions that the movement of state administrators into industry started around 1860 (1981, 77–81). Also see Charle 1987 and Bourdieu 1996c, chap. IV-2, "Establishment Schools and Power over the Economy."

83. As opposed to 41 percent in 1985 (Bauer and Bertin-Moutrot 1997).

84. See Kramarz and Thesmar 2006.

85. Suleiman (1978, 210) points out that this diversification can be understood as a strategy of survival for certain corps and schools faced with changing economic conditions. Thus the Corps des Mines' move into private industry was, to some extent, geared at offsetting the consequences of decline in the mining sector. In 1970, for instance, about one-third of the members of the Corps des Mines occupied functions in the private sector (while another third was employed in public or semipublic enterprises).

86. Roughly one-fifth of École Nationale d'Administration alumni currently work in the business sector (of these, three-quarters are in private enterprises and one-quarter in public enterprises). But about one-third of all graduates of the École Nationale d'Administration have been employed in business at one point in their careers. Source: www.ena.fr, 1999.

See Lebaron 2000 on the (contested) evolution of Polytechnique toward the business school model.

87. The expression is from Wittrock 1985, 19. Also see Silberman 1993, 114–16, on Napoleon's higher education policy.

88. Prior to 1830 they were under the control of the Ministry of Interior (Fox and Weisz 1980, 8). Today the École des Ponts et Chaussées is under the control of the Ministry of Equipment (Public Works), and the École des Mines is administered by the Ministry of Industry.

89. Fox and Weisz 1980, 8.

90. The Superior School of Commerce of Paris (École Supérieure de Commerce de Paris [ESCP]), 1820; the School of High Commercial Studies (École des Hautes Etudes Commerciales [HEC]), 1881.

91. Silberman 1993, 116. Also see Suleiman 1978.

92. The students ranked at the top of their class at the end of their studies at École Polytechnique (roughly the top third) are typically recruited into technical *corps* of the state (of which the Corps des Mines and Corps des Ponts et Chaussées are the most prestigious). Similarly, students ranked at the top of their class at the end of their studies at ENA are typically recruited into *grands corps* of the state (of which the Inspection des Finances and the Conseil d'État are the most prestigious).

93. Prost 1968; Clark 1973; Karady 1986; Musselin 2004.

94. Suleiman 1980, 49–50; Suleiman 1978; Birnbaum 1982; Charle 1991. The proportion of graduates of the École Nationale d'Administration among ministers has been oscillating between 24 and 45 percent between the mid-1980s and the mid-1990s. "Les énarques omniprésents," *Le Monde*, June 27, 1997.

95. Literally, National School of Statistics and Economic Administration.

96. As Bourdieu has demonstrated, the field of the *grandes écoles* is far from homogeneous. In *State Nobility*, he examines in detail the "palace wars," which have led to the domination of the generalist *énarques* over administrative functions, and the relegation of the graduates of top engineering schools into high-level technical positions (1996c, 197–214).

97. Bourdieu, 1996c, 192. A survey by Jean-Michel Eymeri of ENA admits between 1987 and 1996 confirms the persistence, if not reinforcement, of this pattern (2001, 25).

98. Premfors 1980. Data from the World Bank indicate that public expenditures per student in tertiary education as a percentage of the GNP per capita were 29.3 percent for France in 1980, against 79.9 percent in the United Kingdom and 48.2 percent in the United States. In 2000, however, the three countries were closer together, with approximately 30 percent, 23 percent, and 32 percent, respectively, of the GNP per capita (France's more enviable position in the recent period is due essentially to the fact that British public funding for tertiary education has not kept pace with the massive expansion in student numbers during the 1980s and 1990s). As an alternative comparison, figures for Germany, the Netherlands, or Sweden in 2000 are all above 40 percent. Source: World Bank, World Development Indicators.

99. See Bienaymé 1978, 5.

100. See Bourdieu 1996c, 193–95.

101. See Clark 1973; Fox 1980; Weisz 1983, 77; Fox and Weisz 1980.

102. See Papon 1998.

103. Perhaps the most famous example is France's civil nuclear engineering program. See Hecht 1998.

104. Gilpin 1968.

105. Since the 1982 reform, the coordination between the CNRS and institutions of higher education (both universities and *grandes écoles*) has been much more pronounced. For instance, the latter now house a large number of CNRS laboratories. Yet the subject continues to be a matter of strong controversy in France. In 1998, a proposition by the minister of education to shift research resources toward the universities (following the American model) provoked a major outcry within French research circles.

CHAPTER TWO
THE UNITED STATES: MERCHANT PROFESSIONALS

1. For details, see Nobel internet archive at http://nobelprize.org/nobel_prizes/economics/

2. On control processes and consensus in American economics, see especially Baron and Hannan 1994 for an overview. Also Cole 1983; Whitley 1984, 1987b; Zhao 2004; and Lamont forthcoming on relative consensus; Han 2003 on labor market processes; Klamer and Colander 1990 and Colander 2007 on graduate training; Siegfried 1994 and Ellison 2002 on publishing. Healy 2006 on philosophy.

3. Hansen 1991; Klamer and Colander 1990; Krueger 1991.

4. Alston, Kearl, and Vaughan 1992; Caplan 2001.

5. See Cohen's (1999) beautiful study of the cultural appeal of numbers in the United States.

6. E.g., Reverend John McVickar, *Outlines of Political Economy* (1825) and Reverend Francis Wayland, *Elements of Political Economy*, (1837), the principal economics textbooks used in the Northeast from 1837 to the 1860s (O'Connor 1944, 214).

7. See Finkelstein 1984; Dorfman 1946, 512; Coats 1993b, 349; O'Connor 1944, 100, 106; Barber 1993.

8. Haskell 1977, 91–122.

9. Haskell 1977, 107.

10. With a few notable exceptions, such as Henry C. Carey, who led a protectionist school tied to Pennsylvania industrial interests.

11. Barber 1993, 9. See also Camic 1995 on localism in American sociology.

12. Coats 1993b, 436.

13. See Hofstadter 1963b on "anti-intellectualism in American life."

14. Reuben 1996, 157–76; also see Smith 1994, chap. 1, "American Social Science: Moralism and Scientific Method."

15. Richard T. Ely and E.R.A. Seligman were among the founders of the AAUP (Metzger 1987, 167–68).

16. With the Institute of Economics (established in 1922 and directed by Harold Moulton, a Chicago professor) and the Brookings Institute. All three institutions were promoted by the steel magnate Robert Brookings, a businessman who had served in economic agencies during World War I, and were financially supported by various foundations (Carnegie, especially). The Brookings Institution per se emerged in 1928. See Saunders 1966.

17. The Laura Spelman Rockefeller Memorial was absorbed into the Rockefeller Foundation in 1929. Its main characteristic was its involvement in the field of the social sciences (with, in particular, the support of the Social Science Research Council from 1924), which built up under the direction of Beardsley Ruml from 1922 to 1929 (see in particular Fischer 1993 on the SSRC and Condliffe Lagemann 1992 on the Carnegie Corporation).

18. Lyons 1969; Leonard 1991; Larsen 1992; Bernstein 2001.

19. Robinson's data (1983) show that both philanthropic foundations and federal agencies (including the National Science Foundation) have historically

lent stronger support to economic research than to other types of social-scientific work. The general decline (in real terms) in federal resources after 1980 appears much less pronounced in economics than, for instance, in sociology (whose share of all federal social-scientific research expenses drops from about 33 percent during the first half of the 1970s to less than 4 percent in 1997).

20. William Barber suggests that the "recession" of economics degrees during the 1970s is explained by the outbreak of college radicalism and antiwar activism, which drew students' interests away from a discipline regarded as "an apologia of *status quo* capitalism" and third world oppression (1998, 109).

21. See Silk 1960; and figure 2-2, second axis.

22. Partly as a strategy to ensure its own financial survival, the American Economic Association continued to run membership drives aimed at laypeople through the 1920s (Coats 1964a; Bernstein 2001, 17–18). Figure 2-2, which shows the relative stagnation of AEA membership figures from World War I to the late 1930s, is evocative of this struggle.

23. See Stigler 1965, 45; Bernstein 2001, 28–29.

24. See Khurana 2007, 159–67.

25. Gordon and Howell 1959, 244; Pierson 1959, 721; Jacoby et al. 1956.

26. Gordon and Howell 1959, 343n8.

27. Pierson 1959, 253.

28. See Fourcade and Khurana forthcoming.

29. On the rise (and fall) of management as a profession, see, e.g., Khurana 2007.

30. Columbia Business School, for instance, admitted its last class of undergraduates in 1952.

31. Reuben 1996, 209.

32. These numbers contrast with national percentages of less than 2 percent. (Source: National Science Foundation.) There seems to have been an especially rapid expansion of the percentage of economics majors at Harvard and Princeton during the second part of the 1990s, fueled by the performance of the stock market and the attraction exerted by Wall Street. At Harvard, for instance, the percentage of economics concentrators has oscillated between 9.5 and 12.5 percent of each year's class since 1982 (data could not be obtained for prior dates). At Princeton, the number of undergraduates obtaining a degree in economics went from 7 percent in 1991 (a proportion that had remained relatively stable since the late 1960s) to more than 11 percent in 1995. Sources: Harvard University and Princeton University, Office of the Registrar, 2000.

33. About 15 percent of business school faculty had an economics PhD in the early 1970s. See White, Billings and Brown 1981. This proportion, however, is much higher in elite business schools, often reaching above 50% of the faculty.

34. American Economic Association, *Report on Committee on the Status of Women in the Economics Profession*, 2004, http://www.vanderbilt.edu/AEA/CSWEP/annual_reports/2004_CSWEP_Annual_Report.pdf (accessed March 29, 2006).

Of the Nobel Prize winners affiliated with business schools, George Stigler (1982), Merton Miller (1990), Ronald Coase (1991), Gary Becker (1992), Robert Fogel (1993), and James Heckman (2000) all have an affiliation with the graduate school of business at the University of Chicago. The list also includes Robert Merton (1997) at Harvard Business School; William Sharpe (1990) and Myron Scholes (1997) at Stanford Business School; John Harsanyi at the Haas School of Business (Berkeley) (1994); and Robert Engle (2003) at NYU's Stern School.

35. Heilbroner reports that George was considered by the University of California for its first chair in political economy but lost all chances to the position after stating loud and clear that "for the study of political economy you need no special knowledge, no extensive library, no costly laboratory. You do not even need textbooks nor teachers, if you will but think for yourselves" (Heilbroner [1953] 1992,186). Henry George (1839–97) is best known for the best seller *Progress and Poverty* (1879), which expounded his positions for a single massive tax on land to absorb all rent and abolish poverty.

36. The first economist to be granted a PhD in the United States was Stuart Wood at Harvard in 1875 (but his degree was in political science, with "economics" as the subject). Doctorates in political economy were generalized in the 1890s (Mason and Lamont 1982, 390). Also Silva and Slaughter 1984.

37. Max Weber, for instance, who had a doctorate in law, could successively hold a chair in economics and in political science, while at the same time playing a prominent role in the development of an institutional basis for professional sociology in his country.

38. Coats 1985, 1709.

39. Out of 372 business members of the AEA in 1938, only 165 provided information on the highest degree attained. The figures for 1969 are based on a sample survey of the 1969 AEA directory.

40. This stands in sharp contrast to the limited role played by the master's degree as a marker of professional abilities in economics. The master's, by contrast, constitutes the "professional trademark" of political scientists. Source: National Science Foundation. Also Bowen and Rudenstine 1992.

41. Data from Spellman and Gabriel 1978, 183.

42. Spellman and Gabriel 1978; Whitley 1987b; Coats 1992; Gumport 1993b, 273.

43. By contrast, seventy-four percent of sociology doctorates and seventy percent of political science doctorates are still found in education. Source: National Science Foundation.

44. See Collins 1990, 159; also Bernstein 2001, 113–14; Bronfenbrenner 1948, 378. Keyserling was a student of Rexford Tugwell, the prominent institutionalist economist and New Deal adviser, at Columbia. Only twenty-five in 1933, he was hired as a member of Senator Wagner's staff and helped draft the National Labor Relations Act and the United States Housing Act of 1937. Keyserling remained throughout his life suspicious of orthodox economic theory. He was also not shy about testifying publicly on policy matters and writing pamphlets to state his views, which were often perceived as utterly hostile to the business community. Academic critiques presented his political activism (and his lack of formal credentials) as inconsistent with the expert role.

45. Campbell 1998; Bernstein 2001.

46. See, for instance, Krugman 1994, 1998, 2003. Among the most interesting debates, see the article "Economic Culture Wars" (Krugman, October 24, 1996)

and following articles (with James Kenneth Galbraith) on the electronic magazine *Slate* (www.slate.com); or the debate with Robert Kuttner after the article "Peddling Krugman" (Kuttner, *American Prospect*, no. 28, September–October 1996). Paul Krugman (MIT PhD, 2008 Nobel prize in economic sciences) taught at many of the top U.S. universities (Yale, MIT, Berkeley, Stanford, Princeton) and became a columnist for the *New York Times* in 2000.

47. A left-wing think tank, created in 1986 (see figures 2-7a and 2-7b).

48. Reay (2004) suggests that this combination of abstract, formalized knowledge and practical success is a major paradox of economics and a clear anomaly when looked at from the perspective of the sociology of professions (Abbott 1988).

49. Bowen 1953, 136–37. The AEA report, like the SSRC report on the Mathematical Training of Social Scientists a few years later (Social Science Research Council 1955), also recommends that economics departments actively seek to recruit mathematically trained undergraduates. These efforts received the support of philanthropic foundations, most notably Rockefeller and Ford.

50. See Bateman and Kapstein 1999; Yonay 1998.

51. In fact, a plan for the creation of a more radical Society for the Study of National Economy, explicitly modeled on the German Verein für Sozialpolitik, had failed a few months earlier due to advocacy of a clearly statist agenda and the competition of Ely's own organization. See Rodgers 1998, 97–11 for a brilliant analysis of the impact of the German model in America. Also Haskell (1977, esp. 181).

52. Cited in Seligman 1925, 148–49. Interestingly, one of the major differences is the reference to the role of the church, which was absent from the Verein's platform.

53. Coats 1993b.

54. Mason and Lamont 1982, 392. This allows Haskell (1977) to argue that the AEA's commitment to reform was always quite superficial and in any case ought to be attributed more to the activism of the organization's principal architects (e.g., Richart T. Ely) than to a general consensus among the members.

55. Commons 1963, 56–58.

56. Hofstadter and Metzger 1955; Furner 1975; Bledstein 1976, 328; Silva and Slaughter 1984, 147.

57. See Sass 1993.

58. In addition to Furner's (1975) groundbreaking study, see also Bledstein 1976; Haskell 1977; Ross 1979; Sass 1982; Manicas 1991; Bender 1993.

59. This argument is nicely developed in Church 1975.

60. Bateman 1998, 2001; Bulmer 1987; Fisher 1993; Richardson and Fisher 1999; Ross 1979, 400–401; Skocpol 1987.

61. "When the executive committee of the Laura Spellman Rockefeller fund established the official funding policy in 1924, . . . [it] refused to fund organizations concerned with legislation, to become involved in any social or economic reform, to try to influence findings or ever deal directly with researchers, or to fund non-empirical studies. The fund retained this approach throughout its history and in its final report identified its commitment to value neutrality as its greatest legacy" (Smith 1994, 26–27).

Mitchell's involvement with the Committee on Recent Economic Changes (discussed later), for instance, was sharply criticized by officials at the Carnegie Corporation (Biddle 1998b, 64).

62. See Herbst 1965 on the connection to Germany. This, however, does not mean that there was not a large amount of intellectual overlap between all these departments. Each of them exhibited a degree of internal diversity and included members of the other "camp." See Reder 1982 on the presence of an important institutionalist contingent at the University of Chicago during the interwar period.

63. Ross (1979, 186–95) develops this argument.

64. Yonay 1998, 73–75.

65. On institutionalism, see especially Witte 1957; Ross 1979; Yonay 1994 and 1998; Biddle 1998.

66. Rutherford 2000; Smith 1994. Indeed, of eight "institutionalist" presidents of the American Economic Association, several are famous for their contribution to issues of measurement (e.g., Mitchell, Copeland, and Burns).

67. See Mirowski 1989b, 221–22.

68. This work, known as the IS-LM model, reinterpreted Keynes's framework within the standard neoclassical tradition but introduced imperfections (such as wage rigidities) to account for the Keynesian result of unemployment equilibrium.

69. William Nordhaus has joined Samuelson as a coauthor since the thirteenth edition of *Economics*.

70. Interview in Breit and Spencer 1997.

71. Backhouse 1998. The journals are *American Economic Review*, *Quarterly Journal of Economics*, and *Journal of Political Economy*. This is, of course, without counting *Econometrica*, an international journal, which was throughout the period the most representative publication for the mathematical approach. Another trend noted by Backhouse is the rise in the proportion of theory articles themselves.

72. Breslau (2003) remarks that "searches of economic literature and reference sources have not turned up a single use of that sense of the word "economy" [to describe the aggregate of a nation's productive activities] before the development of Keynesian macroeconomics in the 1940s, although econometricians at the Cowles commission did refer to the economic system as a thing" (380).

73. Morgan 1990, 248; Krüger, Daston, and Heidelberger 1987. Originally, the term "econometric" had a much broader acceptance than its current narrow meaning of statistical testing of a model against data. "Econometrics" referred to any type of economic analysis involving numbers and/or mathematical figures. After all, Mitchell was elected president of the Econometric Society (see, for instance, Fisher 1941).

74. See Morgan 1990, 55–56; Koopmans 1947.

75. Quotation from Williamson in Smelser and Swedberg 1994, 78. See Rutherford 2005 for an analysis of the persistence of institutionalist work at the NBER after World War II.

76. Alfred Cowles had also a distant family connection to the mathematical economist Irving Fisher at Yale.

77. These figures come from Divisia 1953.

78. Mirowski 2002b is the most extensive study of the Cowles Commission.

79. The Cowles Commission was initially located in Colorado Springs, where Alfred Cowles was trying to recover from tuberculosis. It was renamed the Cowles Foundation after its move to Yale in 1955.

80. On Cowles, read notably Christ 1996; Hildreth 1986; Arrow 1991; Mirowski 2002b.

81 The names are Ragnar Frisch (1969), Kenneth Arrow (1972), Tjalling Koopmans (1975), Herbert Simon (1978), Lawrence Klein (1980), James Tobin (1981), Gérard Debreu (1983), Franco Modigliani (1985), Robert Solow (1987), Trygve Haavelmo (1980), and Harry Markowitz (1990). Source: Christ 1996.

82. On the wartime involvement of economists, see in particular Bernstein 1995; Guglielmo 2008.

83. Bernstein 1994, 369; Bernstein 2001; Mirowski 2002b.

84. Mirowski summarizes this point by saying that economics was partially "drafted into the ranks of the cyborg sciences as a consequence of the overall wartime reorganization of science in America" (2002b, 157).

85. Mirowski 2005; Amadae 2003.

86. See, e.g., Mirowski 1999, 707–8; 2002b.

87 See, in particular, McCloskey 1994; Blaug 2003.

88. Hence Mirowski (2002b) argues that the development of the Walrasian research program at Cowles ultimately signaled the abandonment of the cyborg route in American economics.

89. Not only had several Cowles members (Oskar Lange, of course, but also Marschak) made major contributions to the "socialist calculation debate" in the 1920s and 1930s, but the later generation of general equilibrium theorists was also fairly left-wing. The Arrow-Debreu theorem had mathematically proved that for a competitive equilibrium to exist, a number of very unlikely conditions had to be met, which implicitly vindicated the role of government as a substitute.

90. Lyons 1969, 278–79.

91. See Jacoby 1987, 175–77. Howard and King argue that Paul Baran was then the only *avowedly* Marxist professor of economics in the entire United States (1989, 114).

92. Mirowski 2002b, 242–49; Mirowski 2002a; Solberg and Tomlinson 1997.

93. Samuelson in Colander and Landreth 1996, 170. It is important to note that one did not have to wait for the McCarthy era for such political understandings of Keynesianism to take hold. The Tufts-Harvard Keynesian pamphlet *An Economic Program for American Democracy* (1937), which I discuss later, had received the same critique from alumni that it was a "Red" tract (Colander and Landreth 1996, 64–65). Also see Samuelson's recollection of the political attacks which his textbook and other Keynesian texts (Loris Tarshis's most prominently) weathered (Samuelson 1997, 157–59).

94. Weir 1989 develops this point. Also see below.

95. American Economic Association 1955.

96. Established in 1968. See Lee 2004 and Mata 2006 for a history of radical economics.

97. Riecken 1983, 40–41.

98. From the review of NSF funding patterns presented in Newlon 1989.

99. The term is from Samuelson (1955, vi).

100. See, for instance, Arrow 1967, 735. Also Warsh 2006 for a history of neoclassical growth theory.

101. Goodwin (1998), citing Leonard (1991) makes this point about the Ford Foundation. See also Amadae 2003.

102. Samuelson, however, certainly had credentials to undertake such a project, having written extensively (albeit quite critically) on the subject.

103. See, e.g., Warsh 2006 for an emphasis on the role of mathematical technique in the evolution of economic theory.

104. Attewell 1984, 26.

105. In fact, I found in my own interviews that even officially "dissenting" economists still agree widely on the virtues of the standard neoclassical micro economics/macroeconomics sequence as a pedagogical tool. This contrasts quite markedly with France, where Marxists generally rejected the neoclassical framework *en bloc*.

106. Kreps (1998), citing Romer, calls this an "hourglass" model of intellectual development.

107. Another striking example is the revival of economic history along cliometrics lines, that is, by scholars using essentially economic theory and statistical techniques.

108. This argument is not without parallel with the rhetoric of pragmatist philosophy. See, for instance, Dewey in *Experience and Nature*: "Thus there is here supplied, I think, a first rate test of the value of any philosophy which is offered to us: Does it end in conclusions which, when they are referred back to ordinary life experiences and their predicaments, render them more significant, more luminous to us, and make our dealings with them more fruitful?" (1958, 7).

109. Here is a classic presentation of the "as if" by Friedman (1953, 40):

It is frequently convenient to present such a hypothesis by stating that the phenomena it is desired to predict behave in the world of observation *as if* they occurred in a hypothetical and highly simplified world containing only the forces that the hypothesis asserts to be important. In general, there is more than one way to formulate such a description—more than one set of "assumptions" in terms of which the theory can be presented. The choice among such alternative assumptions is made on the grounds of the resulting economy, clarity, and precision in presenting the hypothesis; their capacity to bring indirect evidence to bear on the validity of the hypothesis by suggesting some of its implications that can be readily checked with observation or by bringing out its connection with other hypotheses dealing with related phenomena; and similar considerations.

See Hands 2003 for a summary of interpretations of the "as if".

110. On the relationships between Chicago and institutionalism, see in particular Rutherford 2008. Also see Friedman and Friedman (1998) for further information on Friedman's biography.

111. E.g., see Van Horn and Mirowski 2005; Nik-Khah 2007 on conservative foundations' support for the Chicago school.

112. See Robert Solow's review for the *Public Interest*, cited in Parker 2005, 442–43.

113. That is, it was never subjected to econometric tests (where the competitive market model is *not* the null hypothesis). On this point, see especially Leeson 2000.

114. The paper by Lawrence Summers states that "in order to have a 50% chance of rejecting the null hypothesis [of efficient securities markets] it would be necessary to have data for just over 5,000 years" (1986, 596).

115. Later vindicated by the famous "Lucas critique" (Lucas 1976). As critics have pointed out, Chicago economists have often effectively ignored theoretical approaches and empirical studies that contradicted this description of the workings of the economy. As Robert Lucas wrote quite openly in a personal memoir: "The construction of theoretical models is our way to bring order to the way we think about the world, but the process necessarily involves ignoring some evidence or alternative theories—setting them aside. That can be hard to do—facts are facts—and sometimes my unconscious mind carries out the abstraction for me: I simply fail to see some of the data or some alternative theory. This failing can be costly and embarrassing to me, but I don't think it has any effect on the advance of knowledge" (Lucas n.d., 5).

116. For an example of the calibration method, see, e.g., Kydland and Prescott 1982.

117. The "rational expectations" generation of the Chicago school was indeed much more sophisticated mathematically than its predecessors, bringing the general equilibrium modelizing techniques that the earlier generation had looked down upon to bear, for instance, on Friedman's (nonformalized) critique of the Philips curve (Friedman 1968).

118. Chamberlin 1933; Robinson 1933.

119. See how the work of Stigler and others expounded the absent or harmful effects of all sorts of regulations—from electricity to finance and real estate, from aeronautics to trucking.

120. See Emmett 2007 on the history of the workshop system. Also Overtveldt 2007 for an interesting but uncritical account of the rise of the "Chicago school." The term "intelligent conservatives" comes from Hackney 2007a.

121. Source: Federal Reserve Board. As a result of this, the Fed has largely turned into an appendage of academia. After the top ten departments, Federal Reserve jobs are some of the most sought-after positions for PhDs. In fact, one interviewee described the Federal Reserve as basically an academic institution.

122. Commons's autobiography was written during the early years of the New Deal and first published in 1934.

123. "In 1908, at the high point of the Progressive era collaboration between university-based experts and Progressive state administration, forty-one University of Wisconsin faculty members occupied seats on at least one official state commission. Within a year after a change of administration in 1914, the professors had been cleaned out to the last appointee" (Rodgers 1998, 110).

124. On Commons also see Dorfman 1959, 288; Henderson 1993. Wisconsin economists played an important role in the design and implementation of social welfare policies throughout the 1920s (Schweber 1996; McNutty 1980), a form of activity that prefigured their (and other institutionalists') involvement in the early New Deal (Brinkley, 1995).

125. The first president of the American Economic Association, Francis Amasa Walker (1840–96), for instance, had been associated with government service for much of his career, as superintendent of the U.S. census.

126. Coats 1964a, 274; Bernstein 2001, 34–37.

127. Silva and Slaughter 1984, 289.

128. On the Federal Reserve, see Caporale 2003. On the Bureau of Agricultural Economics, see Lyons 1969; Alchon 1985; Hawley 1990; Barber 1981. The BAE in 1930 was "employing more social scientists than all other agencies combined" (Hawley 1990, 299).

129. Grossman 1982; Alchon 1985; Barber 1985; Hawley 1990.

130. Again, with the notable exception of the Bureau of Agricultural Economics.

131. See Alchon 1985; Barber 1985; Cook 1982.

132. See, for instance, the case of Wharton professor Joseph Willits, who sat on Hoover's Emergency Committee for Employment and advocated for national unemployment insurance.

133. Kindleberger 1991, 43; Stein 1986; interviews.

134. This is how several prominent figures have explained their switch from physics to economics in the 1930s. See, for instance, the interview with Paul Samuelson in Breit and Spencer (1997) and the quotation by Koopmans in Mirowski (2002b, 251).

135. Among others: the Agriculture Adjustment Administration, National Recovery Administration, Tennessee Valley Authority, National Labor Relations Board, Social Security Administration, Committee on Economic Security, Securities and Exchange Commission.

136. See, for instance, Zelizer 2000.

137. Barber 1996; Davis 1971; Weir and Skocpol 1985; Hall 1989; Tugwell 1957. Leon Keyserling, who was at the National Planning Board during the 1930s, commented: "With all due respect to Keynes, I have been unable to discover much reasonable evidence that the New Deal would have been greatly different if he had never lived, and if a so-called school of economics had not taken on his name" (1972, 135).

138. Yonay 1998, 63; Biddle 1998.

139. Tugwell was nominated undersecretary of agriculture in June 1934.

140. See Barber 1996, 68; Clawson 1981; Dobbin 1993; Merriam 1944; Stryker 1989, 1990; Sweezy 1972.

141. Roosevelt's 1934 budget was unbalanced.

142. J. Viner, F. Knight, P. Douglas, H. Simons. See Davis 1971, Laidler 1993, Tavlas 1998, and Skidelsky 1994 for a discussion of the "pre-Keynesian" Chicago economists' ideas.

143. These personalities include, among many others: Laughlin Currie, adviser to the governor of the Federal Reserve Board (and later at the White House);

Richard Gilbert at the Industrial Economics Division at the Department of Commerce (and director of research at the Office of Price Administration during the war); Robert Nathan, at the National Income Division (and chairman of the Planning Committee of the War Production Board after 1942). See Stein 1996; Weir and Skocpol 1985.

144. In spite of Galbraith's often quoted claim that "Harvard was the main avenue by which Keynes' ideas passed to the United States" (1971, 48), the "new" policy approach institutionalized in Washington before it did so in academia. As Barber recalls, "None of the junior economists who [together with their colleagues at Tufts University] participated in drafting one of the pioneering American statements of Keynesian doctrine—*An Economic Programme for Recovery*, published in 1938—achieved tenured status at Harvard" (1997, 14).

145. Stigler 1965, 45. These journals were the *Quarterly Journal of Economics*, the *American Economic Review*, the *Review of Economics and Statistics*, and *Econometrica*.

146. Bernstein 1990; 2001 83.

147. Interview, professor emeritus, Harvard University, April 1997. The slide rule is a manual computing instrument based on a logarithmic scale. The earliest version was created in 1624. From that time until the invention of the electronic calculator (in the 1960s), the slide rule was the most widely used tool for finding powers and roots, performing multiplication, division, and trigonometric calculations.

148. See Ikenberry 1992 on the role of experts in forging the postwar international economic institutions.

149. See, e.g., Carson 1975 on the development of national accounts.

150. This is as of 2006. Leon Keyserling (1950–53), and Alan Greenspan (1974–77) are the two exceptions; in addition, Beryl Sprinkel (1985–89) and Martin Bailey (1999–2001) came from business, though both have an economics PhD (and Bailey was an economics professor).

151. Schultze 1996; Porter 1983, 405.

152. Tobin and Weidenbaum 1988, ix.

153. Silk (1964) reports that a survey of more than five hundred university economists conducted in 1963 found that 84 percent favored an immediate tax cut, despite imbalance in the federal budget (595). Also see Tobin 1966; Okun 1970; Schultze 1996; and in particular Bernstein 2001 on this period.

154. Weir 1989; Weir and Skocpol 1985.

155. See Weir 1988; Bernstein 2001.

156. Martin 1991, 111–12.

157. The lowering of taxes automatically weakens the operation of automatic stabilizers. This is explained by Robert Solow:

My own particular view is that we have done something foolish regarding fiscal policy. We used to depend a lot—more than people other than economists knew—on what were called automatic stabilizers. Just as an example, if the economy began to boom, the first part of income to gain would be profits. Profits were very heavily taxed. So when the economy boomed, the federal budget moved in the direction of surplus.

On the other hand, if the economy began to turn down, transfer expenditures would rise rapidly, profits would turn into losses, and corporate tax revenues would fall. So you'd get the kind of shift in federal budgets that any good Keynesian type would have wanted, but you got it without legislation.

Over the years we have weakened those stabilizers. We've weakened them by, for good or evil, diminishing welfare and other transfer expenditures. It might have been right or wrong to do that, but it was not done in order to weaken automatic stabilization. That was a side effect. We also tax corporate profits relatively much less. We depend much more on personal income taxes now than we used to.

The beauty of these automatic stabilizers was that they didn't depend on the stupid Congress getting its act together. It just happened. It wasn't exactly a policy rule but it operated almost as if it were. And so one of the things I think we could do right now is to go back and try to find ways of strengthening those automatic stabilizers again. (Solow 2002)

158. Rhoads 1985; Schultze 1996; De Long 1996.

159. This figure is from White 1937.

160. It is interesting to note that the first Reagan term was associated with a sharp *decrease* in the number of economists in government.

161. See "Report of the Committee on Economists in Public Service," *American Economic Review,* March 1946, supplement, cited in Bowen 1953, 16.

162. See Position Classification Standard for Economist Series, GS-0110, http://www.opm.gov/fedclass/gs0110.pdf. Economists are now one among more than three hundred specialist groups listed by the federal government's Office of Personnel Management, and are further classified into narrower subfields according to their specific area of competence. Under the 1964 status, these classifications are economist, financial economist, labor economist, regional economist, industry economist, international economist, and agricultural economist. Source: Office of Personnel Management, U.S. government.

163. See this example from an economic analyst at the Congressional Budget Office:

The CBO is in two halves. There's the Budget Analysis Division, which are the folks who are responsible for the cost estimates on legislation. And they typically are master's level. The new folks now have a master's in either economics or public policy, more often. . . . Then the other half of CBO is the program divisions, like Natural Resources and Commerce (where I am). There's a Macro Division, National Security, Health, that sort of thing. Tax Analysis. In those divisions, we do research that supports, and we help the folks in the Budget Analysis Division, but we also do these longer-term things. And it's the Program Division folks that I'm referring to when I say that you have to have a PhD. And I would guess there's probably—in the Program Divisions, there's probably . . . I don't know . . . 80 analysts? And most of them have a PhD, and any of them would have to, to be starting. (August 13, 1999)

164. The Rand Corporation, a private organization working almost exclusively from contracts with the Department of Defense, also played a pioneering

role in the formulation and diffusion of PPBS. See Smith 1966; Smith 1991, chap. 5.

165. The model for the CBO came largely from the Brookings Institution and its influential book series Setting National Priorities (started in 1971). Brookings provided the first two directors of the Congressional Budget Office (Alice Rivlin and Robert Reischauer, both authors in the Setting National Priorities series).

166. See, for instance, the arguments developed by Milton Friedman in his best seller *Capitalism and Freedom* (1967).

167. See Schultze 1977 and Rhoads 1985 on the role of economists in advocating for efficiency in public policy, and Derthick and Quirk 1985; Noll 1985; Sunstein 2002 on deregulation. Derthick and Quirk (1985, 36) report, for instance, that the Ford Foundation gave a total of $1.8 million to the Brookings Institution between 1967 and 1975 to support economic studies of regulation, which resulted in Brookings becoming one of the most vocal and relentless advocates of microeconomic efficiency and deregulation in Washington. Also see Crichtlow 1993, 287–89, on the evolution of the Brookings Institution.

168. Greenberg, Schroder, and Onstott 1999. In many cases, however, the outcome of this research was a mixed bag for social reformers—the negative income tax experiment being perhaps the most dramatic one. In this case, the experiments demonstrated some work disincentive effects and some increase in family breakup among recipients. These were widely reported in the press and got their principal proponent, Senator Daniel Patrick Monhiyan, to recant his support for the measure (Steensland 2007).

169. See, e.g., O'Connor's (2001) wonderful historical analysis of the transformations of "poverty knowledge" and Steensland's (2007) fascinating and nuanced analysis of the failure of guaranteed income policies. Note that economists could be found on both sides of the issue of guaranteed income.

170. See Heckman's Nobel Prize lecture (2000) for a useful presentation of "microeconometrics" and Heckman and Smith 1995 for a presentation of the differences between this approach and social experiments.

171. See Pierson 1994 on the movement of defederalization of policy. Greenberg, Schroder, and Onstott discuss the importance of federalism in the following terms:

> Reformers often find themselves in a situation where they don't have the power or the votes to enact nationwide changes, but they can enact funding for demonstrations. Moreover, federal funds for particular programs may be used with considerable discretion by states, encouraging the view that the states should literally be the laboratories of democracy. Social experimentation in the United States is sometimes also encouraged by private foundations. No other country has a nonprofit, nongovernmental, nonreligious sector with comparable resources and social policy interests. (1999, 170)

172. In the scientific jargon, this is referred to as the "treatment effect."

173. Heclo (1980), for instance, has shown that the expansion of government bureaucracy after the war proceeded at a much slower pace than that of government spending.

174. Greenberg, Schroder, and Onstott 1999, 166. For instance, the twelve-year research effort on the negative income tax was led by Mathematica Policy Research, a company set up in the late 1950s by a group of Princeton University economists specialized in the development of mathematical models for military decision-making. (With the dwindling of government funds for public policy research under the Reagan administration, however, the company developed into a software business. See Karen W. Anderson, "Mathematica's Shift into the Software Field," *New York Times*, February 22, 1983.)

175. See Mirowski and Nik-Khah 2007 for a similar account.

176. See National Science Foundation 1985, *Science and Engineering Personnel: A National Overview* for figures on self-identification. (According to this document, roughly 50 percent of self-identified economists are in business.)

177. Source: National Science Foundation. This is against 59 percent for educational institutions and 11 percent for government. These figures stand in sharp contrast with comparable figures for sociologists, which are, respectively, 11 percent (business), 74 percent (education) and 7 percent (government) in 2001.

178. Source: Interview with NABE official. This figure includes the members of the local chapters of the NABE. Also see www.nabe.com.

179. *Business Week* thus reports that economics is the second most popular college subject (after engineering) among America's "corporate elite" ("The Corporate Elite," October 11, 1993, 64).

180. The "ABC curves": A curve: "speculation"; B curve: "business"; C curve: "money."

181. Samuelson 1987; Dominguez, Fair, and Shapiro 1988.

182. The notable exception to this is the Federal Reserve, which has been historically quite active in macroeconometric model-building. The Federal Reserve of Saint Louis built one of the first "monetarist" models in the 1970s, and the Federal Reserve Board developed FRBUS, a large computer model, for forecasting and policy simulation.

183. Economic consultant, Washington, August 1999.

184. Not only was macroeconometric modeling not at the scientific frontier anymore, but its scientific credibility had been seriously damaged by the Lucas critique (1976), which showed that under the rational expectations hypothesis, econometric models could not serve to formulate forecasts on the future behavior of the economy:

> The progressive intellectual agenda was doing the heavy lifting for the development of ever better macroeconometric models. Academia stopped contributing to that effort around the time of Lucas critique. But in the practical world they needed these models, and so there was essentially no academic input to that endeavor for a very long time. . . . It just stopped after the Lucas critique and migrated into the for-profit sector. Models became ad hoc and opportunistic except for the Fed's, which, having academics, continued that agenda. (professor, Ivy League university, November 1999)

185. Bodkin, Klein, and Marwah 1991.

186. See Faulhaber and Baumol 1988. On Otto Eckstein, see Wilson 1984. On Wharton, see Sass 1982, chap. 9.

187. See the symposium on this question in the *Journal of Economic Perspectives* 13(2)–(Spring 1999): 91–99. Also Posner 1987.

188. Stigler 1982; Mayhew 1998.

189. This discussion refers to a more general argument about how the "weak" nature of the American state (and in particular the forms of legal governance) encourages the development of professionalism (see, for instance, Jepperson and Meyer 1991; Dobbin and Sutton 1998).

190. Eisner 1991 argues that due to the general influence of the Chicago school in the field of economics (and especially law and economics) during this period, the policy and enforcement processes came to reflect "Chicago school" concerns. Also see Hackney 2007b.

191. Eisner 1991, 115.

192. See Hurdle 1992; Mandel 1999.

193. Richard Schmalensee for Microsoft, and Franklin Fisher for the federal government. Fisher previously had been one of the main experts involved in the IBM case (on the defense side).

194. Mirowski and Nik-Khah 2007.

195. The rise of finance as a separate profession is a subject in itself, which goes well beyond the scope of this book. But see Whitley 1987a; MacKenzie 2006.

196. For instance, Herbert Stein, a Chicago economics PhD who worked as an economist at the CED between 1945 and 1967 (and was later appointed chairman of Nixon's Council of Economic Advisers), is often seen as the architect of the CED's growing receptivity to discretionary fiscal policy in the 1960s (Collins 1981; also see Stein's obituary in the *New York Times*, September 9, 1999).

197. Smith (1991) identifies more than 1,000 private think tanks in the United States, with a little more than 100 in Washington alone. Of the 112 Washington-based "think tanks" existing in 1986, two-thirds (74) had been created since 1970 (McGann 1995).

198. Blyth 2001, 152–201.

199. Vogel 1989, 226. Also see Vogel 1983, and figure 2-7b, which details the budgets of a number of public policy organizations.

200. The literature on think tanks, especially regarding the rise of a strongly ideological public policy research sector during the 1970s and 1980s, is quite large. See, notably, Blumenthal 1988; Smith 1991; Weiss 1992; Crichtlow 1993; Ricci 1993; McGann 1995; Medvetz 2007.

201. With the notable exception of Robert Mundell, who since then earned the 1999 Nobel Prize in economics. See Krugman 1994, 87–89.

202. For a sense of the European migration into U.S. economics before the mid-1960, see Grubel and Scott 1967.

203. For instance, Ashenfelter and Oaxaca argue that Gary Becker's 1957 "*The Economics of Discrimination* (which provides an 'economic' definition of discrimination), coupled with simple, modern econometric methods, has become the standard from which the litigation of disputes over allegations of race and sex discrimination proceeds" (1987, 325).

CHAPTER THREE
BRITAIN: PUBLIC-MINDED ELITES

1. The theory of imperfect or monopolistic competition was developed separately by Joan Robinson in Cambridge, England (1933) and Edward Chamberlin at Harvard (1933).

2. Blaug and Towse 1988; Machin and Oswald 1999, 2000; Commission on the Social Sciences 2003. See the June 2000 issue of the *Economic Journal* for a summary (Propper and Dasgupta 2000).

3. "Economists. Doctored," *Economist*, May 9, 1998.

4. On the clerisy ideal, see Rothblatt 1983; Collini 2006; Schweber 1996, 2006.

5. Prussia, for instance, established its first "chairs" in "Oekonomie, Policei und Kammersachen" in 1727 (Hennings 1988, 43).

6. The very first chair was occupied by Malthus, at the Training Institution of the East India Company (1805). Oxford got its first chair in 1825; University College, London, in 1828; and Dublin in 1832.

7. Tribe and Kadish, 1993.

8. Also see Sanderson 1972, 191; Howson and Winch 1977, 5; Silberman 1993, 394.

9. Middleton 1996, 71. Walter Bagehot lived from 1826 to 1877. The front page of The *Economist* still displays its original motto, a wonderful example of its claim to "enlighten" the wider public: "First published in September 1843 to take part in a severe contest between intelligence, which presses forward, and an unworthy, timid ignorance obstructing our progress."

10. Founded in 1821 (and still well alive today), and dominated by businessmen and bankers (Coats 1993b, chap. 18).

11. Sidney Webb (along with his wife, Beatrice) was the main "thinker" of the Fabian Society (est. 1884), a circle of intellectuals interested in social reform who sought to "educate" society toward the goal of social justice, as well as to promote the use of rational expertise in government and politics. The organization subsequently played, and still does, an important role in the Labour Party. See Thompson 2006.

12. As Winch remarks, the results of the original plan were mixed:

> The École Libre and the British Association report of 1894 were twin inspirations to Beatrice and Sidney Webb when they resolved to make an attempt to start a centre of economic teaching and research in London on the lines of that of Paris. Ironically, however, the institution that emerged was more like a business school than a training ground for budding public administrators destined to play a part in furthering the cause of bureaucratic collectivism. (1990, 52; see also Sanderson 1972, 192–93; Rutherford 2007)

13. See Sanderson 1972; Tribe and Kadish 1993; Tribe (2003, 692–702) on Manchester.

14. On the role of Marshall in the professionalization of British economics, see Maloney 1985; Groenewegen 1995. Marshall had proposed in *The Economics of Industry* (1879) to replace the words "political economy" with "economic

science" or "economics." The term caught on with the publication of his *Principles of Economics* (1890) and his obsession to assert the scientific character of the disciplinary enterprise to which he had given his life. Heilbroner reports that Stanley Jevons was first to have planned the writing of a book titled *Principles of Economics*, but "did not live to do so" ([1953] 1992, 177).

15. Chester 1986, 169–73; Guillebaud 1954, 104–5.

16. About 20 percent of recruits came from PPE. See Waterfield 1958, 7.

17. Economics also became a popular field in the "O" and "A" levels (preuniversity diploma) in the 1960s (Lumsden, Attiyeh, and Scott 1980).

18. Middleton 1998, 71.

19. Source: Commission on the Social Sciences, 2003.

20. Pearson et al. 1991, 123. Also see Lisle 1984.

21. Unfortunately, this survey contains information only on single-honors economics degrees; we could not isolate data on joint degrees, such as economics and history, or combination degrees such as PPE, which continue to play an important role in British undergraduate education. Similarly, no separate information was available on the specific employment patterns of PhD/D.Phil. graduates.

22. Bulmer 1982; Desrosières 1993, 203–17; Schweber 2006.

23. Middleton 1998, 122; Edwards 1993, 614. In the postwar period, the latter evolved into a major research consultancy.

24. The main influences on the creation of the LCES were Beveridge, Bowley, Keynes, and Robertson. The LCES used the Harvard method for the study of the business cycle. See Middleton 1998, 159; Robinson 1978.

25. See Young and Lee 1993, 128–36.

26. See Fisher (1977, 1980) for detailed studies of the role of American foundations in British social-scientific (and especially economic) research between the wars.

27. Dahrendorf 1995, 317–18. The two institutions ended up "divorcing" from each other later on, however.

28. See Jones 1988 on the foundation of the NIESR; Tribe 2003 on the Economic Research Section.

29. Report of the HMSO, 1946, 12. Also see mention in King 1998, 432; Donovan 2001, 67–68.

30. Source: HMSO, Education Statistics for the United Kingdom. The MRC received a much larger amount of funding overall, though it came from other sources.

31. This happened at the cost of a 30 percent budget cut, however, and of the SSRC losing the term "science" from its title, which from then on became Economic and Social Research Council. Between 1979 and 1988, the ESRC budget decreased in real terms. It is only in 1993 that the real-term level of the 1979 budget was reached again. Source: ESRC. See Johnson 1973, 71; Smith and Larsen 1989; King 1997, 1998; Donovan 2001 on the question of "relevance" and the history of the SSRC/ESRC more generally. About one-third of the SSRC's budget in the 1980s was going to forecasting agencies, such as the NIESR, the DAE in Cambridge, the (now defunct) Macroeconomic Bureau in Warwick, and forecasting units at the University of Liverpool and the London Business School.

32. By contrast, only eleven economists from the London School of Eco nomics signed the letter (Wood 2006). See Wickham-Jones 1992 about the manifesto.

33. Cited in Soffer 1978, 69. Middleton 1998, 108. Also see Coats 1964b and Whitley 1987b about the concentration of intellectual authority.

34. "British" by birth or residency in the United Kingdom.

35. This is based on my own coding of all economists who are British citizens and British residents in Blaug 1999.

36. See Backhouse 1997, 1999.

37. At Oxford, Firsts in Greats thus provided a number of fellows for the PPE School at the time of its creation (see Chester 1986, 48). Also see Collard 1990 on endogamous practices in pre–World War II Cambridge.

38. See, for instance, Young and Lee 1993, 89–118 on the "cross-fertilization" of ideas between these core institutions.

39. The two main figures of the British historical school, Thomas Cliffe Leslie and John Kells Ingram, were Irish. See Koot 1987.

40. Public schools are old, fee-paying independent boys schools (though several have gone coed since World War II). In contrast to France, and even more so than in the United States, these independent schools, as well as the free but selective grammar schools, have traditionally played an essential role in maintaining an upper-class control of the education system. The grammar schools were dismantled in 1976, though some of them reconverted to fee-paying independent schools.

41. See, for instance, Brown's biography of Harrod, which notes that Harrod's "mother lying on the playing field [at Saint Paul's] heard cockney accents among the boys, and was determined that her son should go to Westminster" (1980, 3).

42. Johnson and Johnson 1978, 91, 132.

43. Coats and Coats's (1970, 1973) detailed studies of the social and educational background of the members of the Royal Economic Society also show that this was true until the 1960s at least.

44. See Robinson 1990.

45. The AUTE was created in 1924 as part of a movement of unionization in higher education but was revived as a more active professional forum in the 1960s.

46. Through the 1960s the *Economic Journal* remained in the hands of Carter and E.A.G. Robinson. However, starting about 1971, editorial teams for the journal became larger and more diverse, though editors continued to have long tenures. Finally, council members of the Royal Economic Society are now elected, which they were not earlier.

47. See Mirowski 1989a.

48. See Peter Manicas's analysis of methodological writings in English nineteenth-century economics (1987, 49–52).

49. Rosanvallon 1989b, 137. Also see Somers 2001.

50. Soffer 1970, 1943; also see Richards's (1991) discussion of the "exemplary" use of mathematics in British liberal education in the early nineteenth century, which she contrasts with the French "separatist" view.

51. As a matter of fact, the first tripos in Cambridge (in the eighteenth century) were primarily mathematical. It was only in the nineteenth century that a classical tripos, then a moral sciences and a natural sciences tripos were added. See Rothblatt 1997; Weintraub 2002.

52. Frank Ramsey (1903–30) was a brilliant mathematician and philosopher (he was a fellow of King's College at age twenty-one), who made fundamental contributions to economic theory in two papers in the *Economic Journal* (in 1927 and 1928). Ramsey notably developed the notion known as "Ramsey pricing" concerning the pricing rule a monopolist should set in order to maximize social welfare (also developed by Marcel Boîteux in France).

53. Sanderson 1972, 46–47.

54. The British Association for the Advancement of Science was closely connected to both the throne and the Parliament to which it provided expert advice. See Haskell 1977.

55. Soffer 1978. Economic history, however, developed on a separate and distinguished path in England (Koot 1987). The other reason for the failure to institutionalize historical methods as the core of British economics is that the intellectual program of the discipline, as it was synthesized by Marshall, called not only for rigorous theory but also for a strong applied component, which made historical economics less relevant as a separate approach. See Groenewegen 1995.

56. Schabas 1990, 116; also see Schweber 2006.

57. Schabas 1990, 112. Also see Schabas 1991.

58. For instance, in Section F (economics and statistics) of the British Association for the Advancement of Science. At Oxford, the department of economics still bears the title "economics and statistics."

59. Young and Lee 1993, 23–24.

60. See Backhouse, Middleton, and Tribe 1997.

61. By contrast, Stigler's survey of economic articles in five prominent American professional journals shows that by 1942, 65 percent still used "no special technique" (Stigler 1965, 48). The reviews are *American Economic Review*, *Quarterly Journal of Economics*, *Review of Economics and Statistics*, *Journal of Political Economy*, and *Econometrica*. By 1960, however, the percentages for both countries were similar (with about 33 percent of purely literary articles). We should, however, be careful with these numbers, especially the most recent figures, since all the journals are partly "internationalized" in their authorship. This is especially true of the *Economic Journal* (as well as, for that matter, the other important U.K. publication, *Economica*), both of which had only about 50 percent British authors by 1960, and 30 percent "American" authors (the latter also had an even stronger presence in the pages of the *Review of Economic Studies* almost from its creation) (Backhouse 1997).

62. See Shackle 1967, 291–92.

63. See Skidelsky 1994, 414. Also see Keynes 1939; Patinkin 1976.

64. See Gaspard 2001.

65. Mirowski, using a different metric (the percentage of *pages* containing mathematical formulas, as opposed to the number of *articles* using mathematics) than Backhouse, Middleton, and Tribe (1997) found that the U.S.-based *Journal of Political Economy* and *Quarterly Journal of Economics* were more

mathematical than the *Economic Journal* by the late 1920s, which supports the interpretation given here (Mirowski 1991, 150). Perhaps we should interpret the difference as showing that even though more authors were accustomed to using mathematics in the British than in the American journals through the 1950s, each "British" article using mathematics was less thoroughly mathematical than its U.S. counterpart.

66. Robbins himself does not seem to have been very at ease with sophisticated mathematics. Source: Interviews.

67. See Tintner 1954 (in UNESCO report). Notable exceptions include Roy G. Allen, who was a professor of statistics at the London School of Economics and published a textbook: *Mathematical Economics* (London: MacMillan, 1956).

68. In the *American Economic Review*, the same percentage went up from 50 to 54 percent (Morgan 1988).

69. Though historians still debate the relative importance of this cause, there is substantial evidence that the enclosure movements (by which control over a large proportion of rural land was transferred from communal to wealthy hands) dramatically worsened the situation of the rural population, prompting the "poor laws" movement (see Polanyi [1944] 1957; Block and Somers 2003).

70. Economists argued that poor rates interfered with the wage mechanism and discouraged demographic and moral restraint among the poor. They also pointed out that tying the poor to their parish of origin where they could receive relief only worsened the problem of poverty by preventing the emergence of a mobile labor force—in truth, what we would come to call a labor market (see, for instance, Block and Somers 2003).

71. Cited in Himmelfarb's wonderful chapter on Marshall (1992, 287). See the rest of the book, particularly chapter 1, for a superb analysis of compassion in Victorian England.

72. For a brilliant exposé of this dilemma, see Robinson 1962, 51–57.

73. Keynes's *theoretical* departure from classical theory was firmly grounded in his understanding of human psychology (see Laidler 1999 on this point). The irrational and erratic "psychology of the public"—translated into investment decisions, spending patterns, monetary policy, and nominal illusion with respect to wages—means that prices do not adjust, and output and employment are liable to fluctuations. Consequently, he saw the future as fundamentally uncertain— nothing guarantees that the economic system will evolve in an orderly and predictable manner:

> All these pretty, polite techniques, made for a well-paneled board room and a nicely regulated market, are liable to collapse. At all times the vague panic fears and equally vague and unreasoned hopes are not really lulled and lie but a little way below the surface. . . . I accuse the classical economic theory of being one of these pretty, polite techniques, which tries to deal with the present by abstracting from the fact that we know very little about the future. (1937, 215)

74. See Harris 1977, 407, 424.

75. As Milton Friedman clearly saw when commenting upon this passage of Keynes's letter to Hayek, Keynes's penchant for government action was, in es-

sence, informed by his own social trajectory and intimate experience of government. Friedman's analysis is worth quoting at length here:

> Keynes believed that economists (and others) could best contribute to the improvement of society by investigating how to manipulate the levers actually or potentially under control of the political authorities so as to achieve desirable ends, and then persuading benevolent civil servants and elected officials to follow their advice. The role of voters is to elect persons with the right moral values to office and then let them run the country. . . . The persuasiveness of Keynes' view was greatly enhanced in Britain by historical experience, as well as by the example Keynes himself set. Britain retains an aristocratic structure—one in which noblesse oblige was more than a meaningless catchword. . . . The situation was very different in the United States. The United States is a democratic not an aristocratic society, as Tocqueville pointed long ago. It has no tradition of an incorruptible or able civil service. Quite the contrary. The spoils system formed public attitudes far more than a supposedly non-political civil service. As a result, Keynes' political bequest has been less effective in the United States than in Britain, which partly explains, I believe, why the "public choice" revolution in the analysis of politics occurred in the United States. Economists, myself included, have sought to discover how to manipulate the levers of power more effectively, and to persuade—or educate— governmental officials to serve the public interest (Friedman 1997, 21–22).

76. Friedrich Hayek had arrived at the LSE; Karl Popper would follow in 1946.

77. See Robbins 1938; Hicks 1939. I am very indebted to Roger Backhouse for his extensive comments on this particular section.

The new approach to welfare caught on for essentially three reasons. First, it fit in better with the neoclassicals' redefinition of economics as the science of allocation and exchange, as opposed to the classical economists' focus on production and distribution. Second and more important, "the mathematics [that was implied] proved to be capable of enormous development," and it far outstripped the competition in terms of scientific presentation (Hicks 1975, 323; Cooter and Rappoport 1984). Third, consistent with the theory, the models "proved" that society was best off under laissez-faire: in the 1950s, Arrow and Debreu in the United States demonstrated mathematically the "two fundamental theorems of welfare"—where they equated Pareto optimality with market equilibrium under perfect competition.

78. See, for instance, Harrod 1938, 397.

79. See Skidelsky 1995, 98–99 on Keynes.

80. The original formulation of the second-best theorem by Lipsey and Lancaster states that "in a situation where there exist many constraints preventing the fulfillment of the Paretian optimum conditions, the removal of any one constraint may affect welfare efficiency either by raising it, by lowering it, or by leaving it unchanged" (1956, 12). Also see Baumol 1965.

81. Mirrlees 1982, 63.

82. See, for instance, the British contributions to the measurement of inequalities, going from Pigou, Hugh Dalton, and Meade to Atkinson, Sen, Cowell, and

Champernowne. One of my U.S. interviewees lamented: "Here we never even got to that point. Growth was always supposed to take care of everything" (professor, West Coast university, November 2003).

83. See, for instance, Broome 1999, but also the flourish of books on ethics (particularly utilitarian ethics) by economists themselves.

84. In this cogent little piece, Deaton contrasts the (British) *Stern Review on the Economics of Climate Change*'s strictly egalitarian position giving equal weight to the welfare of all generations with the modal attitude among American economists that market returns rates are high enough that global warming might be better left to future generations to deal with: "If zero discounting (with perhaps a touch of paternalism) is the British vice, the refusal to consider ethical questions explicitly but to leave them to the market is surely the American vice" (2007, 4).

85. It is worth noting that the French were much closer to the Americans than to the British on the subject. The rationale for the French welfare state (*la sécurité sociale*) was essentially political.

86. This section's title is obviously in reference to Meade's book.

87. The broadness with which Keynes famously defined the economist's role, which certainly reflects the confidence of high, gentlemanly culture, contrasts quite remarkably with the more narrow and specialized understanding of American definitions. See the quotation from Keynes in chapter 1.

88. Inaugural lecture at the London School of Economics, February 1948, quoted in Howson 1988a, 139. Also see Meade's entry in Blaug 1986.

89. Hicks 1975, 325. Catallactics: The science of exchanges.

90. See, e.g., Galbraith 1971 and Hirschman 1989 on this point.

91. See Marjorie Turner's *Joan Robinson and the Americans* (1989). Also Millmow 2003.

92. Cambridge retaliated with the creation of the *Cambridge Journal of Economics* in 1977, federating various forms of heterodoxy.

93. Backhouse 1999.

94. Halsey 1982, 219.

95. Lipsey is also the author of the first economics textbook in the modern, positive format, widely diffused in England during the 1960s and 1970s, *Introduction to Positive Economics* (1963).

96. See Backhouse 1997, and interviews of Richard Lipsey and Sir Albert Sloman (vice-chancellor of Essex from its founding in 1962 to 1987) in Tribe 1997. As Sloman recalls, this strategy did not go too well with the University Grants Committee, which struck down Essex's founding in 1972–73. Also see the article by Sargent (who founded the department of economics at Warwick) titled: "Are American Economists Better?" (1963).

97. Source: Interviews, Backhouse 1997.

98. Economists who served in the Treasury repeatedly brought up the tension between specialists and generalists. See, for instance, the revealing titles *Don and Mandarin: Memoirs of an Economist* (MacDougall 1987) and *An Economist among Mandarins: A Biography of Robert Hall* (1901–1998) (Jones 1994).

99. Cairncross and Watts 1989, 7.

100. Middleton 1998, 80–81.

101. MacLeod and Andrews 1969.

102. A post of chief economic adviser to the government had been created in 1919, but scholars agree that it was mostly honorary and served primarily for quasi-diplomatic functions until World War II (Coats 1981; Harris 1990b, 100).

103. On the EAC, see Howson and Winch 1977; Bennett 1978; Middleton 1982; Weir and Skocpol 1985. Howson and Winch argue that the works of the Council and the Committee on Economic Information contributed to alter Treasury views in a Keynesian direction, though others are generally more cautious about this claim.

104. On the wartime employment of economists, see in particular Cairncross 1996, 33; Booth 1986; Coats 1993b, 557; Howson 1988a.

105. On staffing problems in the postwar Economic Section, also see Cairncross and Watts, 1989, 135.

106. On the key period of the immediate after-war, and the policy choice between planning and demand management, see Weir 1989. She shows that the "conversion" of the Treasury to Keynesian demand management was partly a "negative" choice, motivated by the desire to avoid the stronger alternative of planning promoted by members of the Labour Party.

107. The CEPS (1947–54) was a small advice structure (twenty-five people), which served as a de facto cabinet for successive chancellors before being absorbed into the regular Treasury machinery. It consisted of a mix of regular civil servants and outsiders, both generalists and specialists (including trained economists) (Hennessy 1989, 153–154).

108. Booth 2001; Cairncross and Watts, 1989, 132–61.

109. On NEDC, see Denton, Forsyth, and MacLennan 1968; Wood 2000.

110. Middleton 1998, 378.

111. See Balogh 1959.

112. On the DEA, see MacDougall 1987; Hennessy 1989, especially 182–88; Blick 2006. Within government, the devaluation of the sterling was opposed by the Chancellor of the Exchequer (James Callahan), the minister of economic Affairs (George Brown), and the prime minister himself, Harold Wilson (Targetti 1992, 20–21).

113. The NEDC was first downgraded under the premiership of Margaret Thatcher, then finally abolished under the Major government.

114. On the rise of specialists within the civil service, see notably Booth and Coats 1978; Coats 1981; Middleton 1998; Edgerton 2006 (on military specialists).

115. See Baker 1999.

116. To some extent, these policies were by then also a way to attract good candidates in an administrative labor market depressed by budget cuts.

117. Emblematic of this latter change was the 1991 appointment of Sir Terence Burns, a former economics professor at London Business School and chief economic adviser to HM Treasury under Margaret Thatcher, to the post of permanent secretary of the Treasury (the top administrative job). Also see Dowding 1995, 27, 122, on the growing visibility of specialists in higher grades.

118. See Harris 1990a. For instance, Alfred Marshall served on the Royal Commission on Labour and was heard at the Gold and Silver Commission, the

Royal Commission on the Aged and Poor, the Indian Currency Committee, and the Royal Commission on Local Taxation (Soffer 1978, 88).

119. See Blick 2004 on special advisers. Because of the absence of a system of political appointments at the top of the administrative hierarchy (as in the United States), and the stability of the civil service, the latter may appear committed to the particular economic strategies of the party in place. When Harold Wilson came to power in 1964, the Treasury had been under conservative rule for eighteen years. Similarly, Margaret Thatcher was wary of the regular civil service's willingness to implement her economic program, which was antagonistic to the prevailing "Keynesian" economic policy consensus. Finally, Tony Blair's reliance on special advisers has been even more extensive.

120. That was true of several of my interviewees. The Treasury, in particular, is often considered an invaluable training ground, both by academics and by City bankers. One of my interviewees, a macroeconomics professor at the London School of Economics, told me:

> I went to the university in Cambridge, then worked for the Treasury for four years. In Cambridge I started my first year in mathematics, then I switched to economics (I had done economics before in high school). I guess I did not miss much by not doing the first year in economics. Economics was hopeless at Cambridge at the time. It was dominated by the post-Keynesians. . . . All the macro I learnt I got it from the Treasury. (professor, London School of Economics, June 1997)

121. This trend has been particularly obvious in the 1990s. See, for instance, the careers of John Flemming, who returned to Oxford in 1992 after eleven years at the Bank of England (including six as chief economist), and one year at the European Bank for Reconstruction and Development, or Charles Goodhart, back to the London School of Economics in 1985 after seventeen years as monetary adviser to the Bank of England. Other, more recent, examples include Mervyn King, a LSE professor who has been (in successive order since 1991) the bank's executive director, chief economist, and now the first academic governor, or John Vickers, an Oxford professor who was chief economist of the Bank in the late 1990s before heading the Office of Fair Trading.

122. Hence as late as 1972, Donald MacDougall, a Treasury mandarin whose career at Oxford was long past, could become president of the Royal Economic Society.

123. Source: Royal Economic Society, *Directory of Members*, 1994. In 1994, academic members represented 64 percent of the RES membership, and business members 10 percent.

124. See Portes 2001.

125. Coats 1993b, 402.

126. Middleton 1998, 128–29. Middleton also analyzes in depth the episode of the tariff reform campaign in 1903, which witnessed the first public action of a collective of economists in the publication of a free-trade manifesto by fourteen professors, among them Marshall, Edgeworth, and Bastable. According to Middleton, the campaign marked a decisive step in the constitution of the British economics profession as a separate and self-conscious entity (1998, 132–41).

127. E. Johnson 1978, 22; Brown 1980.

128. Rueschemeyer and Van Rossem 1996.

129. E.g., the New Fabian Research Bureau, the XYZ Club.

130. Thompson 2006, 87–88; also see Howson 1988b.

131. "The strength of the LSE is that it is close to the political process: the present director Sir Howard Davies moved there from running the Bank of England, and his place was taken by former LSE professor Mervyn King. The chairman of the Commons education committee, Barry Sheerman, sits on its board of governors, along with Labour peer Lord (Frank) Judd. Also on the board are Tory MPs Virginia Bottomley and Richard Shepherd, not to mention Lord Saatchi and Lady Howe." (MacLeod 2005).

132. Middleton 1998; interviews; *Economist* 1985.

133. On the role of think tanks in Thatcherism, see notably Hall 1992; Cockett 1995; Blyth 2002; Tribe forthcoming.

134. "I Think, Therefore I Tank," *The Economist*, November 25, 1989. Budget figures for 2004 are from American Enterprise Institute, Annual Report 2004, from U.K. Charity Commission, Register of Charities, and from IEA Report and Financial Statement 2004.

135. For instance, some German interviewees stated that their own research organizations were facing strong competition from "the British institutes," even at home. The CEPR's near monopoly of the market of EC contracts is also notorious.

136. Kynaston 1988. This role was in large part linked to the international institutionalization of the gold standard after 1870.

137. Examples: *Midland Bank Review*, 1920–87; *Lloyd's Bank Review*, 1930–87; *Westminster Bank Review*, 1936–68, continued by *National Westminster Bank Quarterly Review*, 1968–93; *Three Banks Review*, 1949–85, continued by *Royal Bank of Scotland Review*, 1985–92. See Roberts 1995.

138. See Parsons 1989, 189; also Middleton 1998, 290; Hall 1986, 1992.

139. On the role of journalists in the supply-side revolution, see especially Blumenthal 1988; Bartley 1995.

140. Still, the question remains how the recent internationalization of the British economic press has transformed the field of economic journalism in that country. The international editions of the *Economist* and the *Financial Times* represent an increasingly large percentage of these publications' overall market. Indeed, by the 1990s, The *Economist* was, from the point of view of its readership, more an American than a British magazine. In 1993, The *Economist* had a weekly worldwide circulation of 530,000, nearly 40 percent of it going to North America, 20 percent to the United Kingdom, and 20 percent to the rest of Europe (Edwards 1993, 951).

In 1986 the *Financial Times* had a daily circulation of over 254,000, with nearly 75 percent going to the British market (Kynaston 1988). Since the 1990s the *FT* has launched a series of foreign editions (including a U.S. edition in 1997). In 2007 the *FT*'s total circulation was 426,830, with about one-third going to the U.K. market and one-third to the U.S. market. As a comparison, the *Wall Street Journal* European edition sells about 88,000 copies. Source: Audit Bureau of Circulations, consultation online at http://www.abc.org.uk (accessed September 12, 2007).

141. Cassis 1995, 224.

142. See chapter 1. On business education, see Sanderson 1972; Napier 1996. Also Arena (2008) and Besomi (1998) on industrial economics at Oxford.

143. Established as the Business Economists Group in 1953. The association adopted its present name (Society of Business Economists) in 1969. Source: Society of Business Economists.)

144. *Economist*, July 20, 1993.

145. See, for instance, Leyland 1992; Naisbitt 1995.

146. It is, for instance, quite revealing that the New Labour in power has been relying on businesspeople to manage a large number of important social programs.

147. *Economist*, May 9, 1998.

148. E.g., Baumol 1995; Backhouse 1999.

CHAPTER FOUR
FRANCE: STATIST DIVISIONS

1. "Lettre ouverte des étudiants en économie aux professeurs responsables de l'enseignement de cette discipline," *Le Monde*. June 21, 2000 (open letter of economics students to economics teachers).

2. Today known as "post-autistic economics."

3. "Appel des économistes pour sortir de la pensée unique" (1996), which crystallized after the December 1995 strikes wave. See Lebaron 2000, 79–80.

4. See Viviane Forrester, *L'Horreur Économique*, which sold 350,000 copies in France alone and of which The *Guardian* said it was set to be "the greatest economic bestseller since *Das Kapital*" ("L'horreur, L'horreur," October 26, 1999). Characteristically, the book also did very well in Germany, Spain, and South America but failed to attract an audience in the United States and the United Kingdom. Among the more "intellectual" pamphlets, one may consult some of the "militant/scientific" books of the *Liber/Raisons d'agir* collection, such as P. Bourdieu, *Contre-feux: Propos pour servir à la résistance contre l'invasion néo-libérale.*

5. ATTAC is the Association pour la Taxation des Transactions pour l'Aide aux Citoyens (which in English presents itself as the "international movement for democratic control of financial markets and their institutions"). Founded in 1998, its main goal is to regain the "space lost by democracy to the sphere of finance," and its main motto is that "the world is not for sale."

6. Source: Membership directory, conversation with treasurer of AFSE. The French Association of Economics Doctors (ANDESE, created in 1953) has a similar number of members: around 750. (1995 figures)

7. Source: Royal Economic Society in *Economic Journal* 113 (2003); Verein für Sozialpolitik, *Register of Members*, 2005. Many of the members of the Verein für Sozialpolitik are nonacademic.

8. These differences may also reflect the lesser propensity of the French to organize altogether; see, for instance, Schofer and Fourcade-Gourinchas 2001.

9. Source: Tableau de classement des personnels enseignants titulaires et sta-giaires. Section 05 (droit, sciences économiques et gestion); groupe 02 (sciences économiques). Ministère de l'Education Nationale, Paris, France.

10. See Tribe 2007 on the German case.

11. See, for instance, the case of Michel Chevalier during the Second Empire, or the Socialists (e.g., Blanc and Proudhon) during the Second Republic.

12. As shown by Whatmore (1998, 464), this is especially clear in the work of Jean-Baptiste Say.

13. See Alcouffe 1989. Also Schumpeter [1954] 1994.

14. Le Van–Lemesle 1991.

15. It was fashioned after the British magazine the *Economist*.

16. National Conservatory for the Industrial Arts, an engineering school.

17. See Etner 1986. Regarding the two business schools, the Superior School of Commerce of Paris (École Supérieure de Commerce de Paris [ESCP]) and the School of High Commercial Studies (École des Hautes Etudes Commerciales [HEC]), see Le Van-Lemesle 1993, 2004. A move toward commercial teaching, initiated by industrialists and chambers of commerce, had led to the emergence of a dozen "superior commercial schools" around the country during the 1870s and 1880s. However, most of these provincial schools were aimed at providing vocational training for young apprentices. These two Parisian institutions were the only ones to address a public of post-*baccalauréat* graduates.

18. However, a strange mix of Saint-Simonian industrialism and free trade found its way to political power in the person of Michel Chevalier during the Second Empire.

19. Ingrao and Israel 1990, 89.

20. Vinokur 1986, 190. Also see Walras, who, in his autobiography, relates his inability to obtain an authorization from the Interior Ministry to create a new political economy journal: "my authorization was refused, for the good reason that it had been decided that nobody was going to get one" (Walras, 1965, 3–4).

21. Rosanvallon 1990, 217.

22. See, e.g., Armatte 1994.

22. Le Van–Lemesle 2004.

23. Alcouffe 1989, 329.

24. Silberman 1993, 52.

25. Favre 1981, 459–60.

26. Koen (1986) reports that the proportion of professors among French con-tributors to political economy writings shot from 16 percent in 1800–1849 to 54 percent in 1850–1910, while the proportion of nobles and clergy members de-creased from 16 percent to 7 percent.

27. Said Charles Gide: "The literary production of the Institute has not been at all prolific during the last few years. This is not owing to the enfeebled activity of its members, least of all its veterans, but because it spent itself in action rather than in meditation, partly along the lines of social work, partly in journalism or politics" (Gide 1907, 194). Of course, Gide himself was a leader in a political movement, too, called *solidarisme*—which advocated the creation of worker co-operatives as an alternative to market capitalism.

28. The *agrégation du supérieur* is the recruitment device for full professorship in the law faculties. In the original format of 1896, it is a competitive examination which has both a written and an oral component (during which candidates have to prepare four lectures on a randomly assigned subject within four broad areas [on general political economy; the history of economic doctrines; finance; and an optional subject], disposing of twenty-four hours of preparation for each). Only people holding a doctorate in the required fields can take the examination. There exists also (since 1980) a lower-rank "social science" *agrégation* for recruitment into the secondary education system.

29. See Gide 1907.

30. James 1954.

31. Zylberberg 1990, 28; Armatte 1994; Etner 1987.

32. See UNESCO 1953, particularly the chapter by Emile James.

33. Mossé 1957.

34. Jeannin 1996; Steiner 2000.

35. Source: Econometric Society 1957. I did not count foreigners in post in Paris (mostly at the OEEC), nor Frenchmen who resided outside of France (in the United States notably).

36. See Pouch (2001), who documents the exclusion of Marxist economists from French universities in the early postwar period. Ironically, it is in a Rockefeller-funded institution, the VIth section of the EPHE, that many of them will find refuge. See, for instance, the case of Charles Bettelheim studied by Denord and Zunigo 2005.

37. UER: Unité d'Enseignement et de Recherche.

38. Like elsewhere, the most dynamic growth came from the "business" (*gestion*) and "law and economics" (*droit et économie*) sections, which are the ones more directly oriented toward practice—in the private sector for the former and in the civil service for the latter. The AES sections (*administration économique et sociale* or "social and economic administration") are specialized programs combining law and economics, which constitute a major channel of recruitment into the lower civil service. Today, about the same number of students (among the two- and three-year diploma courses) graduates in "AES" as in regular "economics." Also see Fitoussi 2001.

39. See Pouch on how Marxism came to establish a strong place within French universities after 1968: for instance, the percentage of Marxist theses in the two largest universities (Paris I and Nanterre) was substantial in the 1970s: 17 percent in 1972–74 (Paris I only); 8.6 percent in 1975–77; 10.6 percent in 1978–80). (2001, 119).

40. Association for the Critique of Economic and Social Sciences. See especially De Brunhoff, Beaud, and Servolin 1973a, 1973b; Attali 1973. See Lesourne 1975 for a reply.

41. In French: "une pure chimère, une vraie duperie" (Leroy-Beaulieu 1900, 88).

42. Pirou, 1937.

43. Ekelund and Hébert 1999, 36.

44. See Etner 1989; Breton 1986, 42. The liberal school can certainly not be characterized as methodologically backward, however. For instance, it embraced Mengerian marginalism with great enthusiasm.

45. See, for instance, the cases of two disciples of Walras (Aupetit and Antonelli) during the 1900s, who repeatedly failed the *agrégation* and were reproached their utilization of mathematical methods in their doctoral theses (Antonelli finally passed the examination in 1919) (Breton 1992, 35–36).

46. The *agrégation*, however, has been reformed in 2000, in order to give more room to the research already accomplished by candidates.

47. See also the critique by Bousquet cited by Le Van–Lemesle (2004, 400–403).

48. Cited in Mazon 1988, 85.

49. One exception was the Institut de Recherches Économiques et Sociales, a private observatory created in 1933 with Rockefeller support, with the mission to produce empirical work (quantitative studies and surveys). The IRES was directed by one of the most eminent university professors at the time, Charles Rist. After the war the institute was integrated into Sciences-Po (see Mazon 1988, 43–45).

50. Flouzat 1962–63.

51. Steiner (2005), for instance, shows that economists represented the main contributors to the "economic sociology" section of the Durkheimian review *Année Sociologique* until the 1960s.

52. See Simiand 1912.

53. See Camic 1992, 1995 on the relationship between economics and sociology in the United States.

54. *Revue Économique*, May 1950, 4; cited in Steiner 2005.

55. This VIth section, founded in part thanks to a grant from the Rockefeller Foundation, later gave birth to the Maison des Sciences de l'Homme and finally to the École des Hautes Études en Sciences Sociales in 1975 (Mazon 1988).

56. See, for instance, Favereau 2000.

57. Cournot was a mathematician by training (who had spent time at the École Normale Supérieure before it was closed down).

58. See Breton 1986; Ekelund and Hébert 1978, 1999; Dumez 1985; Etner 1987; Zylberberg 1990; Porter 1995, 68–71.

59. Colson's tenure at École Polytechnique lasted from 1914 to 1928, and from 1892 to 1926 at the École Nationale des Ponts et Chaussées. Divisia's tenure at École Polytechnique lasted from 1929 to 1939, from 1926 to 1950 at the École Nationale des Ponts et Chaussées and École Supérieure des Mines de Paris (Le Van–Lemesle 2004, 435). Colson also taught at the École des Hautes Études Commerciales (HEC) and the École Libre des Sciences Politiques; Divisia, at the National Conservatory of Arts (CNAM).

60. See Gide 1907, 203.

61 See, for instance, the little book by Divisia titled *Exposés d'économique: L'Apport des ingénieurs français aux sciences économiques* (Economic exposés: The contribution of French engineers to economic science) (Divisia 1951).

62. Graduates of École Polytechnique are commonly referred to as "X." X-Mines refers to the career path leading from a top exit ranking from École Polytechnique to the technical corps of the mining administration, the Corps des Mines; likewise, X-Ponts refers to an École Polytechnique / Corps des Ponts et Chaussées (bridges and roads administration) career; X-INSEE to an École Polytechnique / Corps des Administrateurs de l'INSEE (economic and statistical administration) career.

63. See, e.g., Divisia 1951; Drèze 1964, 1989, on the economic contributions of engineers in the twentieth century.

64. Le Van–Lemesle 2004, 640.

65. Gérard Debreu is a French mathematician trained at the École Normale Supérieure, who spent most of his career at the University of California, Berkeley. He won the Nobel Prize in economics in 1983. He played an important role in training a generation of younger French emigrants to the United States, many of whom returned to France to develop general equilibrium theory.

66. See, for instance, the work of Wittrock and Wagner, esp. Wagner, Weiss et al. 1991; Wagner 1989; Wittrock 1989. Also, on a similar theme for earlier periods, see Rueschemeyer and Skocpol 1996; Furner and Supple 1990; and Furner and Lacy 1993; Wagner, Wittrock, and Whitley 1991.

67. Margairaz 1991, 31; Le Van–Lemesle 1993; Terray 2002, 44.

68. Alumni of the École Polytechnique (or "X") made up 49 percent of the members of X-Crise at its founding (Sauvy 1984, 381; Le Van–Lemesle [2004, 505] cites the figure of 54 percent of Polytechniciens in 1939). X-Crise published a monthly bulletin, which analyzed the current French economic situation. It is important to note that X-Crise was far from an ideologically homogeneous group. There was, for instance, a small minority favorable to economic liberalism around Jacques Rueff, François Divisia, and Clément Colson. The majority of the group, however, leaned toward a certain *dirigisme* within the framework of a liberal capitalist economy and consorted with "planist" milieus (in unions and the political Left), though they did not generally share their socialist orientations. Margairaz (1991, 316–17).

69. Boltanski (1990, 1987) has shown how the diffusion and implementation of this technocratic ideology from the mid-1930s to the mid-1950s came to be identified with a new social group ("les cadres"). Also see Djelic 1998.

70. Rueff 1947. See Denord 2001 on the origins and development of French neoliberalism and the history of the Mont-Pèlerin Society in France.

71. Fourquet 1980, 114. "We were all more or less leaning towards the left, since you have to be Marxist to grant economic management techniques the weight we gave them. . . . But our analysis was mainly technical" (Gruson 1976, 75).

72. Rosanvallon 1989a, 181. Also see Boyer 1985, 81–82; Sauvy 1984, 394. See, for instance, the trajectory of Robert Marjolin, who would become one of the architects of French planning in the postwar period. Marjolin had spent time in the United States during the mid-1930s, studying labor unions on a Rockefeller fellowship.

73. Andrieu, Le Van, and Prost 1987. See, for instance, a little textbook by two high functionaries, P. Mendès-France (later president of the council) and G. Ardant, *Economics and Action* (New York: Columbia University Press, 1955), which exposes the detailed policy implications of the Keynesian framework.

74. See Kessler 1986, 211–12. Le Van–Lemesle 1987, 2004.

75. Institute of Applied Economic Science.

76. Fourquet 1980; Abraham-Frois and Labre 1998. For instance, the first issues of the ISEA review *Économie Appliquée* are composed of (translated) articles by eminent foreign scholars on various developments in Keynesian economics. The ISEA cultivated its image of a bridge with foreign (essentially Anglo-Saxon)

economic science very self-consciously and largely used its pages to provide pedagogical exposés of various advances in economic analysis. The personality of François Perroux (the director of the ISEA) was of course crucial to this orientation. A university professor who published essentially in the "literary" mode, Perroux was nonetheless a firm supporter of the development of mathematical economic theory. (He had studied under Etienne Antonelli, a disciple of Walras.) Through the ISEA seminars, but also his courses at the university and at Sciences-Po (and later at the Collège de France), Perroux influenced a whole generation of postwar economists.

77. Out of the fusion of the National Statistical Service and the Institute for the Study of the Business Cycle (see Terray 2002). The Institut de Conjoncture (Institute for the Study of the Business Cycle) was created in 1938 within the Ministry of National Economy, and integrated into the Service National de la Statistique (the French central statistical office) in 1941. It was finally replaced by an administrative direction in 1946 (Sauvy 1954, 23).

78. The Service des Études Économiques et Financières was founded in 1947. The Commissariat Général au Plan was established in 1946.

79. Literally, Forecasting Direction.

80. See Fourquet 1980; Gruson 1968; Perroux, Uri, and Marczewski 1947.

81. Center for the Study of Economic Programs.

82. See Rosanvallon 1989a, 185–86. There are, of course, a few exceptions, for instance, Perroux or Prou, who were also economics professors.

83. See notably Fourquet 1980.

84. Courbis 1991, 231. The first of these models were ZOGOL (short term), built in 1966, and FIFI (medium term), built in 1966–68, and used from 1968 to 1978, for preparation of the Sixth and Seventh Plans.

85. CERMAP: Research Center in Mathematics Applied to Planning. CEPREMAP: Center for Applied Economic Research.

86. Center for the Study of Revenues and Costs.

87. Committee for the Coordination and Orientation of Research on Economic and Social Development. This complex research apparatus extended to many domains of the social sciences: similar organizations were thus affiliated to the Ministry of Education (e.g., CEREQ.), the Ministry of Labor (e.g., CEE, or Center for the Study of Employment), the Ministry of Transportation (e.g., IRT), and so on. For an exhaustive list, see Aliénor 1980.

88. The Rockefeller Foundation sponsored research and study trips to the United States and recruited many of its grantees among engineers. For instance, both Debreu (Nobel Prize, 1983) and Malinvaud spent a year at the Cowles Commission (Bungener and Joël 1989).

89. The disequilibrium approach originates largely in the work of Jean-Pascal Bénassy (École Normale Supérieure, Berkeley PhD, 1973) and was further developed by research scholars at the CEPREMAP, INSEE (Malinvaud), and the university. The *régulation* school started with the work of Michel Aglietta and was also developed mainly within the state apparatus (INSEE and CEPREMAP).

90. Interestingly, however, the reference to Marxism was also present—for instance, one important exponent of the disequilibrium approach insisted explicitly

on the intellectual proximity of his formalization to Marx's arguments about the causes of economic crises in *Capital* (Bénassy 1976, 797–800).

91. See Massé 1965. Another important influence was the debate around the theory of state monopolistic capitalism. Its manifesto (Boccara 1973) sold more than fifty thousand copies (Pouch 2001).

92. For an introduction, see Boyer 1990; Boyer and Saillard 2002. For a history, see Vidal 2001.

93. A former member narrated the formative years of the regulation school:

Aglietta comes back from the United States in 1974 with his dissertation [a French doctorate on the subject of the American economy titled *A Theory of Capitalist Regulation: The U.S. Experience.* New York: Verso (1979) originally published in French in 1976. Aglietta's adviser was Raymond Barre]. Well, it is arcane and impossible to understand. Because nobody gets it, he wants to discuss it and he proposes to the finest representatives of French neo-Marxism at the time to organize a seminar at INSEE. So they meet every month. He's there, of course, and so are Guibert, Cartelier, Benedetti, Suzanne de Brunhoff. And we decide that we should do something similar with the CORDES, a contract, but on France [Bénassy et al. 1977]. And that is how we developed the classical form of the theory of regulation. (Research scholar, CEPREMAP, August 1995)

Also see Lipietz 1979; Boyer 1986; Delorme 2000.

94. Pouch 2001, 85.

95. See the interview Malinvaud gave to the *Journal of Economic Perspectives* in 2003, which confirms this orientation: "You must realize that when I returned to *INSEE* [in the 1950s] I wasn't assigned to research. I had the intention of devoting most of my spare time to research and teaching in economics. So I wasn't hesitating on my vocation, from that point of view. I had one hesitation—that's whether I would be able to do fruitful research. That I didn't know, and I had an ethic of serving." (Malinvaud in Krueger 2003, 188).

96. See Dosse 1995: 283–84. Source: ENSAE alumni association (Association des Anciens de l'ENSAE).

97. This is according to the latest (2004) activity report. The CREST stands for Centre de Recherche en Economie et Statistique.

98. Jeannin 1996 finds that between 1980 and 1994, more than 40 percent of the articles published in the *Revue Économique* came from nonuniversity institutions.

99. The first two reviews are published by the INSEE. *Annales de l'INSEE* (called *Annales d'Économie et de Statistique* after 1986) and *Économie et Statistique* were started in 1969. The former is a fairly theoretical review, while the latter is more applied. *Statistique et Études Financières* (renamed *Économie et Prévision* after 1982) is published by the Direction de la Prévision (formerly SEEF).

100. Koen, 1986; Malouin and Outreville 1987.

101. Also see Combes and Linnemer 2001.

102. High-level civil servant (interviewed on July 9, 2005).

103. Schmidt 1999, 132.

104. See Lebaron's detailed study of the ENSAE in Lebaron 1995; 2000, chap. 3, "Les transformations de l'ENSAE." From this point of view, the ENSAE was ahead of the engineering schools, where economics training remained fairly elementary until the early 1980s.

> If you go to ENSAE, you have no incentive to read Smith, or Marshall or Walras. What you learn is taken from current research. The history of ideas is not present. In the early 1970s the professor in the history of ideas was Gérard Maarek, who is now at the Crédit Agricole (a French bank). You just have to read his book to see how he approaches the subject. You learn the economics of Marx as an economist of today understands and modelizes it. You are being explained what Marx said in a Debreu-like framework. It's clear, it helps you have a model, but you really get no clue about class struggle.
>
>   At Polytechnique, economics was not so technical. It was much less hard science than at ENSAE. There was an urbane side to it, very economic policy, very "énarque" if you will. It was not very serious. But that has changed. It has become much more hard science. (INSEE administrator, French Bank, August 1995)

105. A university economist, who received his doctorate in 1970, thus recollected that he was among the first people in his generation to do so. "What was very revealing," he said, "is that when I went to the United States and met Ken Arrow, he asked me: 'are you X [Polytechnicien] or Normalien?' He could not understand that in France, it was possible to do modern economics without being X or Normalien" (professor, University Paris I and CEPREMAP).

106. See the results of Linnemer and Perrot (2004) and Legendre and L'Horty (2004), who show that *agrégation* candidates connected to the selection jury have between two and four times more chances of succeeding than nonconnected candidates.

107. Jean-Jacques Laffont, an ENSAE-Harvard graduate, denounced the *agrégation* as one of the principal obstacles to the successful integration of French universities into the international scientific field—curiously echoing Gide's and Perroux's remarks earlier in the century:

> The existence of the *agrégation* has unfortunate consequences, not because of its national character, not because it is an examination, not because of the possible political manipulations of examination boards, but because it provides the wrong incentives to future Ph.Ds in the most crucial period of their intellectual life. . . . Anticipating a generalist examination, a clever student will not choose a highly specialized dissertation subject and thus will not engage in the most advanced type of research. . . . After the doctorate, s/he will prepare for the *agrégation*. For several years s/he will thus pursue the myth of universal knowledge, while neglecting research. (Laffont 1995, 354)

Also see Martin 2004, who makes a similar point.

108. Combes and Linnemer 2001, 2003b.

109. See Lebaron 2000 for an analysis of the mathematization of university curricula.

110. See Steiner 2000 on the *Revue Économique*.

111. Schweber, for instance, points to the role of Cheysson and Levasseur, two state engineers, in establishing a connection between statistics and political economy in France (2006).

112. On this point, see, e.g., Ménard 1987. Sauvy 1984, 376–89. Sauvy speaks of "the atrocities of the deflation of 1935, and the blind outburst of 1936." In particular, he argues that the Blum government's decision to reduce the workweek to forty hours contributed to destroying the coming recovery of the economy in 1936.

113. See Tournès 2006.

114. These are the names they came to assume later.

115. Desrosières, Mairesse, and Volle 1977, 517.

116. See Jobert 1979; Desrosières 1994.

117. Source: INSEE 1996 and Lenoir and Prot 1979, 16. In 1961, the INSEE, which until then had been confined essentially to statistical tasks, inherited part of the responsibilities of the Statistical Service at the Ministry of Finance. See Jobert 1979 on the statistical monopoly and Jobert and Théret 1994 on the dismantling of the system.

118. INSEE 1996, 124.

119. See Machin 1984; Lisle 2002. These *hors-status* (or nonstatutory, contractual researchers) were ultimately "integrated" into the CNRS in the late 1970s, amid considerable resentment due to their lesser formal training.

120. The NAIRU: non-accelerating inflation rate of unemployment.

121. Also see Spenlehauer 2004 on the relative weakness of a "public policy evaluation" culture in French administration. Machin 1984, 226.

122. Michel Massenet, *Rapport sur l'Emploi Scientifique*, cited in Lisle 2002.

123. We should also not underestimate the personal rivalry between two of the most prominent economists at the time: Barre (then prime minister) and Malinvaud (then director of the INSEE).

124. Lenoir and Prot 1979, 139.

125. Now merged with REXECO into a new structure (REXECODE).

126. Source: Interviews. During the 1993 legislative campaign, the OFCE released a study supporting the position of the socialist party. Comparing the economic programs of the three main candidates, the study concluded that only a reduction in the workweek (the socialist proposition, later implemented by the Jospin government) would significantly decrease the level of unemployment. Reflecting on the episode, an officer of the organization told me: "We have the monopoly of independence. And it is sometimes difficult to manage" (research scholar, OFCE, August 1995). An older, also left-leaning institution, the CERC, also experienced a similar quandary, and was brutally dismantled by Parliament on January 1, 1994. See for instance *Le Monde*, January 11, 1994, "La Controverse sur la Disparition du *Centre d'Étude des Revenus et des Coûts*." See, for instance, "La Controverse sur la Disparition du *Centre d'Étude des Revenus et des Coûts*," Le Monde, January 11, 1994.

127. For the 1900–39 period, Le Van–Lemesle shows that out of a total of eighty-eight people teaching economics, 12.5 percent were deputies and 7 percent were ministers (1993, 728–29). Also see Charle 1994, 286; Margairaz 1990;

Bourdieu 1988, particularly the section titled "The Conflict of Faculties" (on the more recent period). Among the most well-known names, let us mention, for instance, Louis-Germain Martin (minister of finance, 1934–35), Jean-Marcel Jeanneney (minister of industry, 1959–62), Raymond Barre (prime minister, 1976–81), Edmond Alphandéry (minister of finance, 1993–95), Dominique Strauss-Kahn (minister of finance, 1997–99).

128. For instance, a handfull of university economics professors (Rist, Nogaro, Antonelli, Germain-Martin, Gignoux) consulted in the Armament Ministry of Albert Thomas during World War I (Le Van–Lemesle 2004, 495; Kuisel, 1981). Charles Rist, the university expert par excellence (including a consultant to many foreign governments), was also appointed vice-governor of the Bank of France during the 1920s.

129. Technically, this was not a "nationalization." The new Sciences-Po (renamed Institut d'Etudes Politiques de Paris) was made dependent on a "national foundation of political sciences," financed by the state but with a nonprofit status, fairly unusual in France.

130. Cited in Kesler 1985, 369.

131. Kesler 1997, 32.

132. Also see Boyer 1985, 81; Kesler 1985.

133. "Les énarques omnipresents," *Le Monde*, June 27, 1997.

134. Hayward 1966; Margairaz 1991, 338.

135. These figures are as of November 2005.

136. See, for instance, the tight links between HEC and Harvard Business School.

137. See chapter 2. For French figures, see Pavis 2005 and Marco 2006, 174. Also see Boltanski 1990, Fridenson 2001, and Chessel and Pavis 2001 on the history of French business education.

138. See Boiteux 1997; Hecht 1998.

139. Another organization, the SEDEIS, created in 1948, was already an attempt to "diversify" this debate (see Merlin 1997).

140. Association Française des Économistes d'Entreprise. However, an earlier association had been created in 1953 to promote economics doctorates and encourage their employment in the corporate sector (the ANDESE; see note 2).

141. Economist, Indosuez Bank, June 1, 1995.

142. Source: Interviews at REXECODE, BNP (National Bank of Paris), Indosuez Bank.

143. Source: ENSAE alumni association, 2005.

144. See, for instance, the comment: "You can do serious applied work only if your base activities are highly profitable. Since the public administration has a monopoly on these base activities, it becomes too expensive for us to do anything too specialized" (economist, AFEDE/GIM, June 1996).

145. E.g., The ISERES (for the communist union CGT) has a team of fewer than five people. The CFDT (socialist union) also recruits economic experts, often directly from the public administration, most noticeably the Commissariat Général au Plan.

146. At the beginning of the 1980s.

147. In a survey carried out in 1981, Bobe and Etchegoyen also noted a clustering of economists' opinions around three poles: public administration, the university, and the private sector.

148. See Weiller and Carrier 1994 for a survey of French heterodox currents in this century.

149. For an introduction, see the special issue of the *Revue Économique* 40(2) (1989) titled "L'Économie des conventions"; Batifoulier 2001; Favereau 2002. For a critique, see Amable and Palombarini 2005.

150. Say, *Traité d'Économie Politique* (1803, 1:xxviii), cited in Whatmore 1998, 463. And of course Say himself was the author of the widely read *Catéchisme d'économie politique* (catechism of political economy, first published in 1821). Many liberals after him, Bastiat first among them, defended the same position.

151. See Lenoir and Prot 1979. However, see the beautiful study by Duval (2004) of the French field of economic journalism, showing its subordination to the broader economic field.

152. See, for instance, Jacques Attali, Michel Albert, François Bloc-Laîné, or Simon Nora among the high functionaries; Daniel Cohen or Jean-Paul Fitoussi among the more academic economists.

153. La Découverte publishing house played a key role in this process.

154. High-level civil servant and university professor, July 9, 2005.

CONCLUSION
ECONOMISTS AND SOCIETIES

1. See Callon 1998b for a brilliant analysis of cases of market failure, where society "overflows" the designed market frame. Economists consider such cases to be deviant and bring them together under the concept of "externalities," whereas sociologists would generally regard them as the norm.

2. Fourcade 2006.

3. See, especially, Wagner, Wittrock, and Whitley, 1991.

4. Steinmetz 2000a, 278; also see Wagner 1989 for a similar argument.

5. Weir and Skocpol (1985), for instance, interpret the activism of the early New Deal as a form of pragmatically inspired proto-Keynesianism, which anticipated by a long shot the full deployment of Keynesian ideas in the postwar period. Conversely, Mark Blyth (2002) makes a strong case for the causal relevance of economic ideas to the great transformations in economic governance that have marked the twentieth century—including the Great Depression. On the relationship between ideas and institutions, also see Campbell 1998; Hall 1989.

6. Also see Rothschild 1992.

7. Note, however, that the construction of the concept of the "national economy," which Mitchell sees as contemporaneous with the emergence of macroeconomics, can certainly be traced to earlier scholarship—for instance, the work of Friedrich List and even before: the circuit of François Quesnay.

8. Arguably, the modern separation between finance and the economy (and the correlative emergence of finance as a discipline separate from economics) could be read as another chapter of this process of discursive transformation.

9. For instance, Sciences-Po, ENA, and HEC are the most "bourgeois" of the French *grandes écoles* from the point of view of their social recruitment.

10. A more focused analysis would, for instance, trace the complex battles over discursive and scientific style and relate them to the social and intellectual trajectories of *particular* actors and groups of actors within their own (national) field. Outstanding examples of this research strategy include Pierre Bourdieu's analysis of Heidegger's philosophy (1996a) and Flaubert's novel writing (1996b), Lebaron's study of the field of French economics in the 1990s (2000), as well as—in a less Bourdieuian fashion—Babb's description of the transformation of Mexican economics (2001) and Schweber's close historical examination of the creation of the discipline of statistics in nineteenth-century France and Britain (2006). Bourdieu describes the necessity of this detailed exercise beautifully in *The Political Ontology of Martin Heidegger*:

> Any adequate analysis [of Heidegger's thought] must accommodate a dual refusal, rejecting not only the claim of the philosophical text to absolute autonomy, with its concomitant rejection of all external references, but also any direct reduction of the text to the most general conditions of its production. We may recognize its independence, but on condition that we openly admit that this is only another name for dependence on the specific rules governing the internal functioning of the philosophical field. (Bourdieu 1996a, 2).

11. See Callon 1998a, 2007.

12. Foucault 1991; Wolin 2004, 270–71.

13. See Abbott 2005 on the mutual constitution of universities, states, and professions.

14. See, for instance, Caron 1981; Kuisel 1981; Prasad 2006; Landier and Thesmar 2007.

15. This is one of the conclusions of the Bourdin report to the French Senate about the French system of economic information (Sénat 2001).

16. But see Clark, 1987; Bender and Schorske 1998; Lamont forthcoming.

17. See Klamer and Colander 1990; Colander 2007.

18. The limited research I conducted on the German case also suggests fragmentation for reasons similar to the second factor mentioned here. Aside from a small number of PhD programs, graduate education and careers in Germany have been traditionally organized around a personalized system of apprenticeship, a situation that—almost by design—favors intellectual reproduction. Germany's higher learning system is much more egalitarian than any of the systems discussed in this book, so no institution or person really dominates *in principle*—though each individual professor has a legitimate claim to his or her own sphere of influence (this is partly because social differentiation in German education traditionally occurs much earlier, in secondary school, between the vocational and generalist tracks) (Maurice, Sellier, and Sylvestre 1986; Mayer, Müller, and Pollak 2003).

19. On Japanese postwar economics, see, e.g., Gao 1997; Hein 2003, 2004.

20. See, notably, Sarfatti-Larson 1977.

21. National Science Foundation 2006. Without doubt, U.S. academics (and economists in particular) are also used to "work the market" to their advantage

in ways that would be unthinkable in countries like Britain and especially France, where salaries are fixed centrally (or nearly so), with limited variations across individuals and disciplines.

22. See Coupé 2003. A recent article in the French newspaper *Le Monde* bemoans the fact that 40 percent of the French economists who rank in the top 1,000 economists worldwide (as measured by the "impact factor" of their publications) work in the United States (Kahn 2007).

23. See, e.g., Coats 1997; Fourcade 2006.

24. Also see Bourdieu and Wacquant 1997.

25. See the neoliberal networks described in Mirowski and Plehwe, forthcoming.

26. One U.S. interviewee thus revealed her strong contempt for what she called "French-style axiomatization," completely at odds, she thought, with the "American" way of doing science. In her interpretation, "Axiomatization in economics was imported from France by Arrow. There is a French quality to any kind of rationalism. But Arrow-style economics cannot survive in the U.S. Rationalism is an episode that has infected the field but will go away. American economics will go back to pragmatism" (professor, University of Iowa, January 1998).

27. See Combes and Linnemer (2003a), who show that a fictitious research center composed of the top twenty-eight French economists working outside of France would have a citation impact far greater than any currently existing French economics research center.

28. E.g., see Harley and Lee 1997 and Lee and Harley 1998 on the consequences of the British Research Assessment Exercises for academic economics in the United Kingdom.

29. On Latin America, see Babb 2001; Dezalay and Garth 2002; Markoff and Montecinos 1993, forthcoming.

30. Economist, Research Department, Banque de France, June 1995. These interviews took place before EMU, when the national central banks still had an important role in monetary policy. The "modern" Italian school in economics was in large part produced by the Bank of Italy, which sponsored U.S. PhDs through a close connection with a famous Italian émigré scholar, Franco Modigliani at the Massachusetts Institute of Technology. A similar pattern is found in many Latin American countries.

31. See Yonay and Breslau's (2006) wonderful exposé of the ways in which mathematical models seek to account for economic reality. Also see the discussion of Chicago in chapter 2.

References

Abbott, Andrew. 1988. *The System of Professions: An Essay in the Division of Expert Labor*. Chicago: University of Chicago Press.

———. 2000. *Chaos of Disciplines*. Chicago: University of Chicago Press.

———. 2005. "Linked Ecologies: States and Universities as Environments for Professions." *Sociological Theory* 23(3):245–74.

Abend, Gabriel. 2006. "Styles of Sociological Thought: Sociologies, Epistemologies, and the Mexican and U.S. Quests for Truth." *Sociological Theory* 24(1): 1–41.

Abraham-Frois, Gilbert, and Françoise Labre. 1998. "La diffusion de la Théorie Générale dans le milieu universitaire français: Retard ou spécificité?" *Revue d'Économie Politique* 108(1):109–30.

Adler, Emanuel, and Peter Haas. 1992. "Epistemic Communities, World Order, and the Creation of a Reflective Research Program." *International Organization* 46(1):367–90.

Aglietta, Michel. 1976. *Régulation et crise du capitalisme: l'expérience des États-Unis*. Paris: Calman-Levy.

Ahlstrom, Göran. 1982. *Engineers and Industrial Growth: Higher Technical Education and the Engineering Profession during the Nineteenth and Early Twentieth Century: France, Germany, Sweden and England*. London: Croom Helm.

Alchon, Guy. 1985. *The Invisible Hand of Planning: Capitalism, Social Science and the State in the 1920s*. Princeton, N.J.: Princeton University Press.

Alcouffe, Alain. 1989. "The Institutionalization of Political Economy in French Universities, 1819–1896." *History of Political Economy* 21(2):313–44.

Alexander, Kenneth, John Wilson, Alexander G. Kemp, and T. M. Rybczynski. 1967. *The Economist in Business*. Oxford: Basil Blackwell.

Aliénor. 1980. "Les enjeux politiques et Idéologiques de la crise actuelle en sciences sociales." *Critique de l'économie Politique*, April–June,:11.

Allais, Maurice. 1954. "Puissance et dangers de l'utilisation de l'outil mathématique en économique." *Econometrica* 22(1):58–71.

———. 1989. "My Life Philosophy." *American Economist* 33(2):3–17.

Allen, William R. 1977. "Economics, Economists and Economic Policy: Modern American Experiences." *History of Political Economy* 9(1):48–88.

Alston, Richard M., J. R. Kearl, and Michael B. Vaughan. 1992. "Is There a Consensus among Economists in the 1990s?" *American Economic Review* 82(2):203–9.

Alter, Peter. 1987. *The Reluctant Patron: Science and the State in Britain, 1850–1920*. Oxford: Berg.

Amable, Bruno, and Bob Hancke. 2001. "Innovation and Industrial Renewal in France in Comparative Perspective." *Industry and Innovation* 8(2):113–33.

Amable, Bruno, and Stefano Palombarini. 2005. *L'économie n'est pas une science morale*. Paris: Raisons d'Agir.

Amadae, Sonja M. 2003. *Rationalizing Capitalist Democracy: The Cold War Origins of Rational Choice Liberalism*. Chicago: University of Chicago Press.

American Economic Association. 1938. "Directory of Members." *American Economic Review* 28(3, suppl.):1–103.

———. 1955. "Report of the Exploratory Committee on the Status of the Profession." *American Economic Review* 45(2):677–84.

———. 1989. "Biographical Listing of Members." *American Economic Review* 79(6):23–640.

Anders, George. 2007. "An Economist's Courtroom Bonanza." *Wall Street Journal*, March 19, A1.

Anderson, R. D. 1992. *Universities and Elites in Britain since 1800*. London: Macmillan.

Andrieu, Claire, Lucette Le Van, and Antoine Prost, eds. 1987. *Les nationalisations de la Libération: De l'utopie au compromis*. Paris: Presses de la Fondation nationale des sciences politiques.

Appleby, Joyce. 1978. *Economic Thought and Ideology in Seventeenth-Century England*. Princeton, N.J.: Princeton University Press.

Arena, Lisa. 2008. "The Marshallian Tradition of Industrial Economics in Oxford, 1940s–1970s." Presented at the workshop "History of Economics as History of Science." École Normale Supérieure de Cachan, June 20.

Armatte, Michel. 1994. "L'économie à l'École Polytechnique." Pp. 375–96 in *La Formation Polytechnicienne 1794–1994*, edited by Bruno Belhoste, Amy Dahan Dalmedico, and Antoine Picon. Paris: Dunod.

Arrow, Kenneth J. 1967. "Samuelson Collected." *Journal of Political Economy* 75(5):730–737.

———. 1991. "Cowles in the History of Economic Thought." Pp. 1–24 in *Cowles Fiftieth Anniversary*, edited by Kenneth J. Arrow, Gerard Debreu, Edmond Malinvaud, and Robert M. Solow. New Haven, Conn.: Cowles Foundation for Research in Economics.

Ashenfelter, Orley, and Ronald Oaxaca. 1987. "The Economics of Discrimination: Economists Enter the Courtroom." *American Economic Review* 77(2):321–25.

Ashmore, Malcolm, Michael Mulkay, and Trevor Pinch. 1989. *Health and Efficiency: A Sociology of Health Economics*. Philadelphia: Open University Press.

Attewell, Paul A. 1984. *Radical Political Economy since the 1960s: A Sociology of Knowledge Analysis*. New Brunswick, N.J.: Rutgers University Press.

Audit Bureau of Circulations. 2006. "ABC." http://www.abc.org.uk.

Babb, Sarah. 1998. "The Evolution of Economic Expertise in a Developing Country: Mexican Economics, 1929–1998." PhD diss., Northwestern University.

———. 2001. *Managing Mexico: Mexican Economists from Nationalism to Neoliberalism*. Princeton, N.J.: Princeton University Press.

Backhouse, Roger. 1997. "The Changing Character of British Economics." Pp. 33–60 in *The Post-1945 Internationalization of Economics*, edited by A. W. Bob Coats. Durham, N.C.: Duke University Press.

———. 1998. "The Transformation of U.S. Economics, 1920–1960, Viewed through a Survey of Journal Articles." Pp. 85–107 in *From Interwar Pluralism to Postwar Neoclassicism*, edited by Mary S. Morgan and Malcolm Rutherford. Durham, N.C.: Duke University Press.

———. 1999. "Economics in Mid-Atlantic: British Economics, 1945–1995." Pp. 20–41 in *The Development of Economics in Western Europe since 1945*, edited by A. W. Bob Coats. London: Routledge.

———. 2005. "The Rise of Free Market Economics: Economists and the Role of the State since the 1970s." *History of Political Economy* 37(1): 355–92.

———. 2007. "Robbins and Welfare Economics: A Reappraisal." Mimeo, University of Birmingham.

Backhouse, Roger, and Jeff Biddle, eds. 2000. *Toward a History of Applied Economics*. Annual supplement to *History of Political Economy* 32. Durham, N.C.: Duke University Press.

Backhouse, Roger E., and Roger Middleton. 2000. *Exemplary Economists*. Vol 1, *North America*. Vol. 2, *Europe, Asia and Australasia*. Aldershot, U.K.: Edward Elgar.

Backhouse, Roger E., Roger Middleton, and Keith Tribe. 1997. "Economics Is What Economists Do: But What Do the Numbers Tell Us?" Paper presented at the Annual History of Economic Thought Conference, University of Bristol, September 3–5.

Baker, Andrew. 1999. "Nébuleuse and the 'Internationalization of the State' in the UK? The Case of HM Treasury and the Bank of England." *Review of International Political Economy* 6(1):79–100.

Ball, James, and Sean Holly. 1991. "Macroeconometric Model-Building in the United Kingdom." Pp. 195–230 in *A History of Macroeconometric Model-Building*, edited by Ronald G. Bodkin, Lawrence Klein, and Kanta Marwah. Aldershot, U.K.: Edward Elgar.

Balogh, Thomas. 1959. "The Apotheosis of the Dilettante: The Establishment of the Mandarins." Pp. 11–53 in *The Establishment*, edited by H. S. Thomas. London: Blond.

Barber, William J. 1981. "The United States: Economists in a Pluralistic Polity." Pp. 175–209 in *Economists in Government: An International Comparative Study*, edited by A. W. Bob Coats. Durham, N.C.: Duke University Press.

———. 1985. *From New Era to New Deal: Herbert Hoover, the Economists, and American Economic Policy, 1921–1933*. Cambridge: Cambridge University Press.

———. 1993. "Political Economy and the Academic Setting before 1900: An Introduction." Pp. 3–14 in *Breaking the Academic Mold: Economists and American Higher Learning in the Nineteenth Century*, edited by William J. Barber. New York: Transaction.

———. 1996. *Designs within Disorder: Franklin D. Roosevelt, the Economists, and the Shaping of American Economic Policy, 1933–1945*. Cambridge: Cambridge University Press.

———. 1997. "Postwar Changes in American Graduate Education in Economics." Pp. 12–30 in *The Post-1945 Internationalization of Economics*, edited by A. W. Bob Coats. Durham, N.C.: Duke University Press.

———. 1998. "Reconfigurations in American Academic Economics: A General Practitioner's Perspective." Pp. 105–121 in *American Academic Culture in Transformation: Fifty Years, Four Disciplines*, edited by Thomas Bender and Carl E. Schorske. Princeton, N.J.: Princeton University Press.

Barberis, Peter. 1996. *The Elite of the Elite: Permanent Secretaries in the British Higher Civil Service*. Brookfield, Vt.: Dartmouth University Press.

Baron, James N., and Michael T. Hannan. 1994. "The Impact of Economics on Contemporary Sociology." *Journal of Economic Literature* 32(3):1111–46.

Barre, Raymond. 1959. *Économie politique*. Paris: Presses Universitaires de France.

Bartley, Robert. 1995. *The Seven Fat Years*. New York: Free Press.

Bateman, Bradley W. 1998. "Clearing the Ground: The Demise of the Social Gospel Movement and the Rise of Neoclassicism in American Economics." Pp. 29–52 in *From Interwar Pluralism to Postwar Neoclassicism*, edited by Mary S. Morgan and Malcolm Rutherford. Durham, N.C.: Duke University Press.

———. 2001. "Make a Righteous Number: Social Surveys, the Men and Religion Forward Movement, and Quantification in American Economics." *History of Political Economy* 33(5):57–85.

Bateman, Bradley W., and Ethan B. Kapstein. 1999. "Between God and Market: The Religious Roots of the American Economic Association." *Journal of Economic Perspectives* 13(4):249–58.

Batifoulier, Philippe, ed. 2001. *Théorie des conventions*. Paris: Economica.

Bauchet, Pierre. 1964. *Economic Planning: The French Experience*. Ann Arbor: The University of Michigan Press.

Bauer, Michel, and Bénédicte Bertin-Moutrot. 1997. *Radiographie des grands patrons français: Les conditions d'accès au pouvoir, 1985–1994*. Paris: L'Harmattan.

Baumol, William. 1965. "Informed Judgment, Rigorous Theory and Public Policy." *Southern Economic Journal* 32(2):137–45.

———. 1995. "What's Different about European Economics?" *Kyklos* 48(2): 187–92.

Béchaux, Auguste. 1902. *L'École économique française*. Paris: Rousseau et Guillaumin.

Becker, Gary S. 1976. *The Economic Approach to Human Behavior*. Chicago: University of Chicago Press.

Bellah, Robert N., Richard Madsen, William M. Sullivan, Ann Swidler, and Steven M. Tipton. 1985. *Habits of the Heart: Individualism and Commitment in American Life*. New York: Harper and Row.

Ben-David, Joseph. 1960. "Scientific Productivity and Academic Organization in Nineteenth-Century Medicine." *American Sociological Review* 25(6): 828–43.

Bénard, Jean. 1976. "Crise de la science économique ou des économistes?" *Revue Economique* 2:297–300.

Bénassy, Jean-Pascal. 1976. "The Disequilibrium Approach to Monopolistic Price Setting and General Monopolistic Equilibrium." *Review of Economic Studies* 43(1):69–81.

Bénassy, Jean-Pascal, Robert Boyer, R. M. Gelpi, Alain Lipietz, Jacques Mistral, J. Munoz, and C. Ominami 1977. *Approches de l'inflation: L'exemple francais, un rapport au CORDES*. Paris: CEPREMAP.

Bender, Thomas. 1993. *Intellect and Public Life: Essays on the Social History of Academic Intellectuals in the United States*. Baltimore: Johns Hopkins University Press.

———. 1998. "Politics, Intellect, and the American University." Pp. 17–54 in *American Academic Culture in Transformation: Fifty Years, Four Disciplines*, edited by Thomas Bender and Carl E. Schorske. Princeton, N.J., Princeton University Press.

Bender, Thomas, and Carl E. Schorske, eds. 1998. *American Academic Culture in Transformation: Fifty Years, Four Disciplines*. Princeton, N.J.: Princeton University Press.

Bennett, Anthea. 1978. "Advising the Cabinet—the Committee of Civil Research and the Economic Advisory Council: A Brief Comparison." *Public Administration* 56(1):51–71.

Bensel, Richard F. 1990. *Yankee Leviathan: The Origins of Central Authority in America, 1859–1877*. Cambridge: Cambridge University Press.

Berger, Peter, and Thomas Luckmann. 1966. *The Social Construction of Reality*. New York: Anchor Books.

Bernstein, Michael A. 1990. "American Economic Expertise from the Great War to the Cold War: Some Initial Observations." *Journal of Economic History* 50(2):407–16.

———. 1994. "American Economics and the American Economy in the American Century: Doctrinal Legacy and Contemporary Policy Problems." Pp. 361–94 in *Understanding American Economic Decline*, edited by Michael A. Bernstein and David E. Adler. Cambridge: Cambridge University Press.

———. 1995. "American Economics and the National Security State, 1941–1953." *Radical History Review* 63: 8–26.

———. 2001. *A Perilous Progress: Economists and the Public Purpose in America*. Princeton, N.J.: Princeton University Press.

Besomi, Danièle. 1998. "Roy Harrod and the Oxford Economists' Research Group's Inquiry on Prices and Interest, 1936–39." *Oxford Economic Papers* 50(4):534–62.

Beveridge, William. 1944. *Free Employment in a Free Society*. London: Allen and Unwin.

Biddle, Jeffrey. 1998a. "Institutional Economics: A Case of Reproductive Failure?" Pp. 108–133 in *From Interwar Pluralism to Postwar Neoclassicism*, edited by Mary S. Morgan and Malcolm Rutherford. Durham, N.C.: Duke University Press.

———. 1998b. "Social Science and the Making of Social Policy: Wesley Clair Mitchell's Vision." Pp. 43–79 in *From Interwar Pluralism to Postwar Neoclassicism*, edited by Mary S. Morgan and Malcolm Rutherford. Durham, N.C.: Duke University Press.

Bienaymé, Alain. 1978. *Systems of Higher Education: France*. New York: International Council for Educational Development.

Biernacki, Richard. 1995. *The Fabrication of Labor*. Berkeley: University of California Press.

Birnbaum, Pierre. 1982. *The Heights of Power: An Essay on the Power Elite in France*. Chicago: University of Chicago Press.

Birnbaum, Pierre, and Bertrand Badie. 1983. *The Sociology of the State*. Chicago: University of Chicago Press.

Blackstone, Tessa, and William Plowden. 1988. *Inside the Think Tank: Advising the Cabinet, 1971–1983*. London: Mandarin.

Blaug, Mark. 1992. *The Methodology of Economics: How Economists Explain*. 2nd ed. Cambridge: Cambridge University Press.

———. 1999. *Who's Who in Economics*. 3rd ed. Cheltenham, U.K.: Edward: Elgar.

———. 2003. "The Formalist Revolution of the 1950s." Pp. 395–410 in *A Companion to the History of Economic Thought*, edited by Warren J. Samuels, Jeff E. Biddle, and John B. Davis. Malden, Mass.: Blackwell.

Blaug, Mark, and Paul Sturges. 1986. *Who's Who in Economics? A Biographical Dictionary of Major Economists, 1700–1986*. 2nd ed. Cambridge, Mass.: MIT Press.

Blaug, Mark, and Ruth Towse. 1988. *The Current State of the British Economics Profession*. London: Royal Economic Society.

Bledstein, Burton. 1976. *The Culture of Professionalism: The Middle Class and the Development of Higher Education in America*. New York: Norton.

Blick, Andrew. 2004. *People Who Live in the Dark: The History of the Special Adviser in British Politics*. London: Politico's.

———. 2006. "Harold Wilson, Labour and the Machinery of Government." *Contemporary British History* 20(3):343–62.

Blinder, Alan. 1999. "Life Imitates Art: How the Economy Came to Resemble the Model." Adam Smith Award Address at the National Association of Business Economists, San Francisco, September 27.

Bloch-Laîné, François. 1976. *Profession, Fonctionnaire: Entretiens avec Françoise Carrière*. Paris: Seuil.

Bloch-Laîné, François, and Jean Bouvier. 1986. *La France restaurée: Dialogue sur les choix d'une modernisation, 1944–1954*. Paris: Fayard.

Block, Fred, and Margaret Somers. 2003. "In the Shadow of Speenhamland: Social Policy and the Old Poor Law." *Politics and Society* 31(2):283–323.

Block, Walter and Michael Walker. 1988. "Entropy in the Canadian Economic Profession: Sampling Consensus on Major Issues." *Canadian Public Policy* 14(2):137–150.

Blumenthal, Sidney. 1983. "Drafting a Democratic Industrial Plan." *New York Times*, August 28.

———. 1988. *The Rise of the Counter-Establishment: From Conservative Ideology to Political Power*. New York: Perennial Library.

Blyth, Mark. 2002. *Great Transformations: Economic Ideas and Institutional Change in the Twentieth Century*. Cambridge: Cambridge University Press.

Bobe, Bernard, and Alain Etchegoyen. 1981. *Économistes en désordre: Consensus et dissensions*. Paris: Économica.

Boccara, Paul. 1973. *Études sur le capitalisme monopoliste d'État, sa crise et son issue*. Paris: Éditions Sociales.

Bockman, Johanna. 2007. "The Origins of Neoliberalism between Soviet Socialism and Western Capitalism: 'A Galaxy without Borders.'" *Theory and Society* 36(4):343–71.

Bockman, Johanna, and Gil Eyal. 2002. "Eastern Europe as a Laboratory for Economic Knowledge: The Transnational Roots of Neo-Liberalism." *American Journal of Sociology* 108(2):310–52.

Bodkin, Ronald G., Lawrence Klein, and Kanta Marwah. 1991. *A History of Macroeconometric Model-Building*. Aldershot, U.K.: Edward Elgar.

Boiteux, Marcel. 1997. "La pédagogie, art du grand patron: Entretien avec Marcel Boiteux." *Annales des Mines: Gérer et Comprendre* 49 (September): 4–16.

Boland, Lawrence A. 1979. "A Critique of Friedman's Critics." *Journal of Economic Literature* 17(2):503–22.

Boltanski, Luc. 1990. "Visions of American Management in Postwar France." Pp. 343–72 in *Structures of Capital*, edited by Sharon Zukin and Paul DiMaggio. Cambridge: Cambridge University Press.

Boltanski, Luc, and Laurent Thévenot. 1991. *De la justification: Les économies de la grandeur*. Paris: Gallimard.

Bonnell, Victoria, and Lynn Hunt, eds. 1999. *Beyond the Cultural Turn*. Berkeley: University of California Press.

Booth, Alan E. 1986. "Economic Advice at the Centre of British Government, 1939–1941." *Historical Journal* 29(3):655–75.

———. 2001. "Britain in the 1950s: A 'Keynesian' Managed Economy?" *History of Political Economy* 33(2):283–14.

Booth, Alan E., and A. W. Bob Coats. 1978. "The Market for Economists in Britain. 1945–1975: A Preliminary Survey." *Economic Journal* 88 (351):474–95.

Booth, Philip. 2006. "A List of the 364 Economists Who Objected to Thatcher's Macro Policy." *Econ Journal Watch* 3(2):380–92.

Bourdieu, Pierre. 1975. "The Specificity of the Scientific Field and the Social Conditions of the Progress of Reason." *Social Science Information* 14(6):19–47.

———. 1977a. *Outline of a Theory of Practice*. Cambridge: Cambridge University Press.

———. 1977b. "La production de la croyance: Contribution à une économie des biens symboliques." *Actes de la Recherche en Sciences Sociales* 13:3–43.

———. 1984. "Quelques propriétés des champs." Pp. 113–120 in *Choses Dites*. Paris: Minuit.

———. 1988. *Homo Academicus*. Stanford, Calif.: Stanford University Press.

———. 1990. *In Other Words: Essays toward a Reflexive Sociology*. Stanford, Calif: Stanford University Press.

———. 1992. *The Logic of Practice*. Stanford, Calif.: Stanford University Press.

———. 1994. "Rethinking the State: Genesis and Structure of the Bureaucratic Field." *Sociological Theory* 12(1):1–18.

———. 1996a. *The Political Ontology of Martin Heidegger*. Stanford, Calif.: Stanford University Press.

———. 1996b. *The Rules of Art: Genesis and Structure of the Literary Field*. Stanford, Calif.: Stanford University Press.

———. 1996c. *The State Nobility: Elite Schools in the Field of Power*. Cambridge: Polity Press.

———. 1999a. *Acts of Resistance: Against the Tyranny of the Market*. New York: Free Press.

———. 1999b. "The Social Conditions of the International Circulation of Ideas." Pp. 220–28 in *Bourdieu: A Critical Reader*, edited by R. Shusterman. Oxford: Blackwell.

———. 2004. *Science of Science and Reflexivity*. Chicago: University of Chicago Press.

Bourdieu, Pierre, and Loïc Wacquant. 1997. "On the Cunning of Imperialist Reason." *Theory, Culture and Society* 16(1):41–58.

Bowden, Brett, and Leonard Seabrooke. 2006. *Global Standards of Market Civilization*. London: Routledge.

Bowen, William, and Neil Rudenstine. 1992. *In Pursuit of the Ph.D*. Princeton, N.J.: Princeton University Press.

Bowles, Samuel. 1974. "Economists as Servants of Power." *American Economic Review* 64(2):129–32.

Bowen, Howard R. 1953. "Graduate Education in Economics." *American Economic Review* 43(4):ii–xv, 1–223.

Boyer, Robert. 1976. "La croissance française de l'après-guerre et les modèles macroéconomiques." *Revue Économique* 27(5):882–939.

———. 1985. "The Influence of Keynes on French Economic Policy: Past and Present." Pp. 77–115 in *The Policy Consequences of John Maynard Keynes*, edited by Harold Wattel. Armonk, N. Y.: M. E. Sharpe.

———. 1990. *The Regulation School: A Critical Introduction*. New York: Columbia University Press. Originally published as *L'École de la régulation: Une analyse critique*. Paris: La Découverte, 1986.

———. 1999. "Le paradoxe des sciences sociales: Les vues d'un économiste 'dissident.'" *Current Sociology* 47(4):19–45.

Boyer, Robert, and Yves Saillard, eds. 2002. *Regulation Theory: The State of the Art*. London: Routledge. Originally published as *Théorie de la régulation: l'état des savoirs*. Paris: La Découverte, 1995.

Breit, William, and Roger Spencer, eds. 1997. *Lives of the Laureates: Seven Nobel Economists*. 3rd ed. Cambridge, Mass.: MIT Press.

Breslau, Daniel. 2003. "Economics Invents the Economy: Mathematics, Statistics, and Models in the Work of Irving Fisher and Wesley Mitchell." *Theory and Society* 32(3): 379–411.

Breton, Yves. 1986. "Les économistes libéraux français et l'emploi des mathématiques, 1800–1914." *Économies et Sociétés* 20(3):25–63.

———. 1992. "L'économie politique et l'emploi des mathématiques en France, 1800–1940." *Histoire et Mesure* 7(1/2):25–52.

Brinkley, Alan. 1995. *The End of Reform: New Deal Liberalism in Recession and War*. New York: Knopf.

Brint, Steven G. 1994. *In an Age of Experts: The Changing Role of Professionals in Politics and Public Life*. Princeton, N.J.: Princeton University Press.

Brittan, Samuel. 1964. *The Treasury under the Tories, 1951–1964*. London: Penguin.

Bronfenbrenner, Martin. 1948. "Postwar Political Economy: The President's Reports." *Journal of Political Economy* 56(5):373–91.

Broome, John. 1999. *Ethics Out of Economics*. Cambridge: Cambridge University Press.

Brown, Henry Phelps. 1980. "Sir Roy Harrod: A Biographical Memoir." *Economic Journal* 90(357):1–33.

Browning, Peter. 1986. *The Treasury and Economic Policy, 1964–1985*. London: Longman.

Bulmer, Martin. 1982. *The Uses of Social Research*. London: Unwin Hyman.

———. 1987. "The Governmental Context: Interaction between Structure and Influence." Pp. 27–39 in *Social Science Research and Government: Comparative Essays on Britain and the United States*, edited by Martin Bulmer. Cambridge: Cambridge University Press.

Bungener, Martine, and Marie-Eve Joël. 1989. "L'essor de l'économétrie au CNRS." *Cahiers pour l'Histoire du CNRS* 4:45–78.

Burke, Colin. 1983. "The Expansion of American Higher Education." Pp. 108–30 in *The Transformation of Higher Learning, 1860–1930: Expansion, Diversification, Social Opening, and Professionalization in England, Germany, Russia, and the United States*, edited by Konrad Jarausch. Chicago: University of Chicago Press.

Cain, P. J. 1997. "British Capitalism and the State: An Historical Perspective." *Political Quarterly* 68(1):95–98.

Cairncross, Sir Alec. 1971. "Economic Forecasting: Further Reflections." Pp. 139–58 in *Essays in Economic Management*. London: Allen and Unwin.

———. 1996. *Economic Ideas and Government Policy: Contributions to Contemporary Economic History*. London: Routledge.

Cairncross, Sir Alec, and Nita Watts. 1989. *The Economic Section, 1939–1961: A Study in Economic Advising*. London: Routledge.

Cairnes, John Elliott. 1875. *The Character and Logical Method of Political Economy*. London: Macmillan.

Caldwell, Bruce J. 1980. "Positivist Philosophy of Science and the Methodology of Economics." *Journal of Economic Issues* 14(1):53–76.

———. 1982. *Beyond Positivism: Economic Methodology in the Twentieth Century*. London: Allen and Unwin.

Callon, Michel. 1998a. "The Embeddedness of Economic Markets in Economics." Pp. 1–57 in *The Laws of the Markets*, edited by Michel Callon. Oxford: Blackwell.

———. 1998b. "An Essay on Framing and Overflowing: Economic Externalities Revisited by Sociology." Pp. 244–69 in *The Laws of the Markets*, edited by Michel Callon. Oxford: Blackwell.

———. 2007. "What Does It Mean to Say That Economics Is Performative?" Pp. 311–57 in *Do Economists Make Markets? On the Performativity of Economics*, edited by Donald MacKenzie, Fabian Muniesa, and Lucia Siu. Princeton, N.J.: Princeton University Press.

Camic, Charles. 1992. "Reputation and Predecessor Selection: Parsons and the Institutionalists." *American Sociological Review* 57(4):421–55.

———. 1995. "Three Departments in Search of a Discipline: Localism and Interdisciplinary Interaction in American Sociology 1890–1940." *Social Research* 62(4):1003–23.

Camic, Charles, and Neil Gross. 2001. "The New Sociology of Ideas." Pp. 236–50 in *The Blackwell Companion to Sociology*, edited by Judith R. Blau. Malden, Mass.: Blackwell.

Camic, Charles, and Yu Xie. 1994. "The Statistical Turn in American Social Science: Columbia University, 1890 to 1915." *American Sociological Review* 59(5):773–805.

Campbell, John L. 1998. "Institutional Analysis and the Role of Ideas in Political Economy." *Theory and Society* 27:377–409.

Campbell, John L., and Leon Lindberg. 1990. "Property Rights and the Organization of Economic Activity by the State." *American Sociological Review* 55(5):634–47.

Campbell, John L., and Ove K. Petersen, eds. 2001. *The Rise of Neoliberalism and Institutional Analysis*. Princeton, N.J.: Princeton University Press.

Campion, Henry. 1958. "Recent Development in Economic Statistics." *Journal of the Royal Statistical Society, Series A (General)* 121(1):1–17.

Canterbery, E. Ray, and Robert J. Burckardt. 1983. "What Do We Mean by Asking Whether Economics Is a Science?" Pp. 15–40 in *Why Economics Is Not Yet a Science*, edited by Alfred S. Eichner. London: Macmillan.

Caplan, Bryan. 2001. "What Makes People Think Like Economists? Evidence on Economic Cognition from the 'Survey of Americans and Economists on the Economy.'" *Journal of Law and Economics* 44(2):395–426.

Caporale, Barbara. 2003. "The Influence of Economists on the Federal Reserve Act." *Scottish Journal of Political Economy* 50(3):311–25.

Caron, François. 1981. *Histoire économique de la France: XIXème–XXème siècle*. Paris: Armand Colin.

Carruthers, Bruce. 1996. *City of Capital: Politics and Markets in the English Financial Revolution*. Princeton, N.J.: Princeton University Press.

Carson, Carol S. 1975. "The History of the United States National Income and Product Accounts: The Development of an Analytical Tool." *Review of Income and Wealth* 21(2):153–81.

Cassidy, John. 1996. "The Decline of Economics." *New Yorker*, December 2, 50–60.

Cassis, Youssef. 1995. "Big Business in Britain and France." Pp. 214–26 in *Management and Business in Britain and France: The Age of the Corporate Economy*, edited by Youssef Cassis, François Crouzet, and T. R. Gourvish. Oxford: Clarendon Press.

———. 1999. *Big Business: The European Experience in the Twentieth Century*. Oxford: Oxford University Press.

Centeno, Miguel Angel. 1994. *Democracy within Reason: Technocratic Revolution in Mexico*. College Station: Pennsylvania State University Press.

Centeno, Miguel Angel, and Patricio Silva, eds. 1998. *The Politics of Expertise in Latin America*. New York: St. Martin's Press.

Chamberlin, Edward H. 1933. *The Theory of Monopolistic Competition*. Cambridge, Mass.: Harvard University Press.

Chandler, J. A. 2000. "The United States." Pp. 200–223 in *Comparative Public Administration*, edited by J. A. Chandler. New York: Routledge.

Charle, Christophe. 1987. "Le Pantouflage en France, 1880–1980." *Annales-Histoire Sciences Sociales* 42(5):1115–37.

Charle, Christophe, Jürgen Schriewer, Peter Wagner (eds.). 2004. *Transnational Intellectual Networks, Forms of Academic Knowledge and the Search for Cultural Identities*. Frankfurt and New York: Campus Verlag.

———. 1991. "Savoir durer: La nationalisation de l'Ecole libre des sciences politiques, 1936–1945." *Actes de la Recherche en Sciences Sociales* 86–87:99–105.

———. 1994. *La République des universitaires, 1870–1940*. Paris: Seuil.

———. 1997. "Legitimités en péril: Eléments pour une histoire comparée des élites de l'État en France et en Europe occidentale (XIXème–XXème siècles)." *Actes de la Recherche en Sciences Sociales* 116–117:39–53.

Charle, Christophe, and Jacques Verger. 1994. *Histoire des universités*. Paris: Presses Universitaires de France.

Chenu, Alain. 2002. "Une Institution sans intention : La sociologie en France depuis l'après-guerre." *Actes de la recherche en sciences sociales* 1/2 (141–142):46–61

Chessel, Marie-Emmanuelle, and Fabienne Pavis. 2001. *Le Technocrate, le patron et le professeur: Une histoire de l'enseignement supérieur de gestion*. Paris: Belin.

Chester, Norman. 1986. *Economics, Politics, and Social Studies in Oxford, 1900–85*. London: Macmillan.

Christ, Carl F. 1996. "History of the Cowles Commission, 1932–1952." Pp. 3–65 in *Econometrics, Macroeconomics and Economic Policy: Selected Papers of Carl F. Christ*. Cheltenham, U.K.: Edward Elgar. Originally published in *Economic Theory and Measurement: A Twenty Year Research Report*. Chicago: Cowles Commission for Research in Economics, 1952.

Christoph, James B. 1975. "High Civil Servants and the Politics of Consensualism in Great Britain." Pp. 25–62 in *The Mandarins of Western Europe: The Political Role of Top Civil Servants*, edited by Mattei Dogan. New York: Sage.

Church, Robert. 1975. "Economists as Experts: The Rise of an Academic Profession in the United States, 1870–1920." Pp. 571–609 in *The University in Society*, vol. 2, edited by Lawrence Stone. Princeton, N.J.: Princeton University Press.

Clark, Burton R. 1983. *The Higher Education System: Academic Organization in Cross-National Perspective*. Berkeley: University of California Press.

———, ed. 1987. *The Academic Profession: National, Disciplinary, and Institutional Settings*. Berkeley: University of California Press.

Clark, Burton R., and Ted I. K. Youn. 1976. *Academic Power in the United States: Comparative Historic and Structural Perspectives*. Washington, D.C.: American Association for Higher Education.

Clark, Colin. 1977. "The 'Golden Age' of the Great Economists: Keynes, Robbins, et al. in 1930." *Encounter* 48:80–90.

Clark, Terry. 1973. *Prophets and Patrons: The French University and the Emergence of the Social Sciences*. Cambridge, Mass.: Harvard University Press.

Clawson, Marion. 1981. *New Deal Planning*. Baltimore: Johns Hopkins University Press.

Coats, A. W. Bob. 1961. "The Political Economy Club: A Neglected Episode in American Economic Thought." *American Economic Review* 51(4):624–37.

———. 1964a. "The American Economic Association, 1904–29." *American Economic Review* 54(4):261–85.

———. 1964b. "The Role of Authority in the Development of British Economics." *Journal of Law and Economics* 7:85–106.

———. 1981. "Britain: The Rise of Specialists." Pp. 27–66 in *Economists in Government: An International Comparative Study*, edited by A. W. Bob Coats. Durham, N.C.: Duke University Press.

———. 1985. "The American Economic Association and the Economics Profession." *Journal of Economic Literature* 23(4):1697–1727.

———. 1992. "Economics in the United States, 1920–1970." Pp. 407–58 in *On the History of Economic Thought*. Vol. 1 of *British and American Economic Essays*. London: Routledge.

———. 1993a. "The Educational Revolution and the Professionalization of American Economics." Pp. 340–75 in *Breaking the Academic Mold: Economics and American Higher Learning in the 19th century*, edited by William Barber. New York: Transaction.

———. 1993b. *The Sociology and Professionalization of Economics*. Vol. 2 of *British and American Economic Essays*. London: Routledge.

———, ed. 1997. *The Post-1945 Internationalization of Economics*. Annual supplement to *History of Political Economy* 28. Durham, N.C.: Duke University Press.

Coats, A. W. Bob, and Sonia Coats. 1970. "The Social Composition of the Royal Economic Society and the Beginnings of the British Economic 'Profession,' 1890–1915." *British Journal of Sociology* 21(1):75–85.

———. 1973. "The Changing Social Composition of the *Royal Economic Society* 1890–1960 and the Professionalization of British Economics." *British Journal of Sociology* 24(2):165–87.

Cockett, Richard. 1995. *Thinking the Unthinkable: Think Tanks and the Economic Counter-Revolution*. New York: HarperCollins.

Cohen, Arthur M. 1998. *The Shaping of American Higher Education: Emergence and Growth of the Contemporary System*. San Francisco: Jossey-Bass.

Cohen, Patricia Cline. 1999. *A Calculating People: The Spread of Numeracy in Early America*. New York: Routledge.

Cohen-Tanugi, Laurent. 1992. *Le droit sans l'État*. Paris: Presses Universitaires de France.

Colander, David and Arjo Klamer. 2007. *The Making of an Economist, Redux*. Princeton, N.J.: Princeton University Press.

Colander, David, and Harry Landreth. 1996. *The Coming of Keynesianism to America: Conversations with the Founders of Keynesian Economics*. Cheltenham, U.K.: Edward Elgar.

Colander, David C., Richard P. F. Holt, and J. Barkley Rosser Jr. 2004. *The Changing Face of Economics: Conversations with Cutting-Edge Economists*. Ann Arbor: University of Michigan Press.

Cole, Stephen. 1983. "The Hierarchy of the Sciences?" *American Journal of Sociology* 89(1):111–39.

————. 1992. *Making Science: Between Nature and Society.* Cambridge, Mass.: Harvard University Press.

Collard, David A. 1990. "Cambridge after Marshall." Pp. 164–92 in *Centenary Essays on Alfred Marshall,* edited by John K. Whitaker. Cambridge: Cambridge University Press.

Collini, Stefan. 2006. *Absent Minds: Intellectuals in Britain.* New York: Oxford University Press.

Collins, Randall. 1998. *The Sociology of Philosophies: A Global Theory of Intellectual Change.* Cambridge, Mass.: Harvard University Press.

Collins, Robert M. 1978. "Positive Business Responses to the New Deal: The Roots of the Committee for Economic Development, 1933–1942." *Business History Review* 52(3):369–91.

————. 1981. *The Business Response to Keynes, 1933–1964.* New York: Columbia University Press.

————. 1990. "The Emergence of Economic Growthmanship in the United States: Federal Policy and Economic Knowledge in the Truman Years." Pp. 138–69 in *The State and Economic Knowledge,* edited by Mary Furner and Barry Supple. Cambridge: Cambridge University Press.

Colson, Clément. 1901–07. *Cours d'économie politique professé à l'École des Ponts et Chaussées.* 6 vols. Paris: Gauthier-Villars.

Colvin, Phyllis. 1985. *The Economic Ideal in British Government: Cal culating Costs and Benefits in the 1970s.* Manchester: Manchester University Press.

Combes, Pierre Philippe, and Laurent Linnemer. 2001. "La publication d'articles de recherche en économie en France." *Annales d'Economie et de Statistique* 62:5–50.

————. 2003a. "L'impact international des articles de recherche français en économie." *Revue Économique* 54(1) :181–217.

————. 2003b. "Where Are the Economists Who Publish? Publication Concentration and Rankings in Europe Based on Cumulative Publications." *Journal of the European Economic Association* 1(6):1250–1308.

Commission on the Social Sciences. 2003. *Great Expectations: Social Sciences in Britain.* Report. Reading, U.K.: Academy of Learned Societies for the Social Sciences. http://www.the-academy.org.uk/GtExpectations.pdf.

Commons, John R. 1963. *Myself.* Madison: University of Wisconsin Press.

Condliffe Lagemann, Ellen. 1992. *The Politics of Knowledge: The Carnegie Corporation, Philanthropy and Public Policy.* Chicago: University of Chicago Press.

Cook, Paul B. 1982. *Academicians in Government from Roosevelt to Roosevelt.* New York: Garland.

Cooter, Robert, and Peter Rappoport. 1984. "Were the Ordinalists Wrong about Welfare Economics?" *Journal of Economic Literature* 22(2):507–30.

Copeland, Morris A. 1941. "Economic Research in the Federal Government." *American Economic Review* 31(3):526–36.

Coupé, Tom. 2003. "Revealed Performances: Worldwide Rankings of Economists and Economics Departments, 1990–2000." *Journal of the European Economic Association* 1(6):1309–45.

Courbis, Raymond. 1991. "Macroeconomic Modeling in France." Pp. 231–66 in *A History of Macroeconometric Model-Building*, edited by Ronald G. Bodkin, Lawrence Klein, and Kanta Marwah. Aldershot, U.K.: Edward Elgar.

Crichtlow, Donald T. 1993. "Think Tanks, Antistatism, and Democracy: The Nonpartisan Ideal and Policy Research in the United States." Pp. 279–322 in *The State and Social Investigation in Britain and the United States*, edited by Mary Furner and Michael Lacey. Washington, D.C.: Woodrow Wilson Center Press; Cambridge: Cambridge University Press.

Dahrendorf, Ralf. 1995. *LSE: A History of the London School of Economics and Political Science, 1895–1995*. Oxford: Oxford University Press.

Davis, J. Ronnie. 1971. *The New Economics and the Old Economists*. Ames: Iowa State University Press.

Davis, John B., ed. 1998. *New Economics and Its History*. Annual supplement to *History of Political Economy* 29. Durham, N.C.: Duke University Press.

Dawson, A. A. P. 1953. "The United Nations and Full Employment." *International Labor Review* 67(5).

Day, Alan J. 1993. *Think Tanks: An International Directory*. Essex: Longman Current Affairs; Detroit: Gale Research.

Deaton, Angus. 2007. "On Transatlantic Vices, or Stern in America." *Royal Economic Society Newsletter* 139:3–4. http://www.res.org.uk/society/pdfs/newsletter/oct07.pdf (accessed May 21, 2008).

Debreu, Gérard. 1983. "Economics in the Mathematical Mode." Nobel Prize lecture. http://nobelprize.org/nobel_prizes/economics/laureates/1983/debreu lecture.pdf. (accessed February 9, 2007).

De Brunhoff, Suzanne, Michel Beaud, and Claude Servolin. 1973a. "La crise de la science économique." *Le Monde*, May 22.

———. 1973b. "La crise de l'économie politique: Un choix ineluctable." *Le Monde*, October 9.

De Long, J. Bradford. 1996. "Keynesianism, Pennsylvania Avenue Style: Some Economic Consequences of the Employment Act of 1946." NBER Working Paper No. W5611.

Delorme, Robert. 2000. "Introduction." Pp. 1–12 in *Institutional Economics in France and Germany: Ordnungstheorie versus the Regulation School*, edited by Agnès Labrousse and Jean-Daniel Weisz. Berlin: Springer Verlag.

Delouvrier, Paul. 1994. *Paul Delouvrier ou la passion d'agir*. Paris: Seuil.

De Marchi, Neil. 1991. "The League of Nations Economists and the Ideal of Peaceful Change in the Decade of the Thirties." Pp. 143–78 in *Economics and National Security: A History of Their Interaction*, edited by Craufurd D. Goodwin. Durham, N.C.: Duke University Press.

Denord, François. 2001. "Aux origines du néoliberalisme: Louis Rougier et le colloque Walter Lippman." *Le Mouvement Social* 195:9–34.

Denord, François, and Xavier Zunigo. 2005. "'Révolutionnairement vôtre': Economie marxiste, militantisme intellectual et expertise politique chez Charles Bettelheim." *Actes de la Recherche en Sciences Sociales* 158 (June):8–29.

Denton, Geoffrey, Murray Forsyth, and Malcolm MacLennan. 1968. *Economic Planning and Policies in Britain, France, and Germany*. London: Allen and Unwin.

Derthick, Martha, and Paul J. Quirk. 1985. *The Politics of Deregulation.* Washington, D.C.: Brookings Institution Press.

Desrosières, Alain. 1985. "Histoires de formes: Statistiques et sciences sociales avant 1940." *Revue Française de Sociologie* 26(2):277–310.

———. 1993. *La politique des grands nombres: Histoire de la raison statistique.* Paris: La Découverte.

———. 1994. "Une particularité française: L'économiste-statisticien." *Courrier des Statistiques* 70:49–54.

———. 1995. "De l'École de l'INSEE à l'ENSAE et l'ENSAI, 1942–1994: Éléments d'histoire d'une école de statistique et d'économie." *Courrier des Statistiques* 75–76 (December).

———. 1999. *The Politics of Large Numbers: A History of Statistical Reasoning.* Cambridge, Mass.: Harvard University Press.

Desrosières, Alain, Jacques Mairesse, and Michel Volle. 1977. "Les temps forts de la statistique française depuis un siècle." Pp. 509–17 in *Pour une histoire de la statistique,* edited by F. Bédarida et al. Paris: Institut National de la Statistique et des Études Économiques.

Dewey, John. 1958. *Experience and Nature.* New York: Dover.

Dezalay, Yves, and Bryant Garth. 2002. *The Internationalization of Palace Wars: Lawyers, Economists and the Transformation of Latin-American States.* Chicago: University of Chicago Press.

DiMaggio, Paul. 1994. "Culture and Economy." Pp. 27–57 in *Handbook of Economic Sociology,* edited by Neil Smelser and Richard Swedberg. Princeton, N.J.: Princeton University Press.

DiMaggio, Paul, and Walter Powell. 1983. "The Iron Cage Revisited: Institutional Isomorphism and Collective Rationality in Organizational Fields." *American Sociological Review* 48(2):147–160.

Divisia, François. 1928. *Économique rationnelle.* Paris: Gaston Douin.

———. 1951. *Exposés d'économique: L'apport des ingénieurs français aux sciences économiques.* Paris: Dunod.

———. 1953. "La Société d'Économétrie a atteint sa majorité." *Econometrica* 21(1):1–30.

Djelic, Marie-Laure. 1998. *Exporting the American Model.* Oxford: Oxford University Press.

———. 2002. "Does Europe Mean Americanization? The Case of Competition." Paper presented at the Thirteenth Biennial Conference of Europeanists, Chicago, March.

Dobbin, Frank. 1992. "Metaphors of Industrial Rationality: The Social Construction of Electronics Policy in the United States and France." Pp. 185–206 in *Vocabularies of Public Life: Empirical Essays in Symbolic Structure,* edited by Robert Wuthnow. London: Routledge.

———. 1993. "The Social Construction of the Great Depression: Industrial Policy during the 1930s in the United States, France and Britain." *Theory and Society* 22:1–56.

———. 1994. *Forging Industrial Policy.* Princeton, N.J.: Princeton University Press.

———. 1995. "The Origins of Economic Principles: Railway Entrepreneurs and Public Policy in 19th-Century America." Pp. 277–301 in *The Institutional Construction of Organizations: International and Longitudinal Studies*, edited by Richard W. Scott and Soren Christensen. Thousand Oaks, Calif.: Sage.

———. 2001. "Why the Economy Reflects the Polity." Pp. 401–24 in *The Sociology of Economic Life*, 2nd ed., edited by Mark Granovetter and Richard Swedberg. Boulder, Colo.: Westview Press.

———. 2004. "The Sociological View of the Economy." Pp. 1–46 in *The New Economic Sociology: An Anthology*, edited by Frank Dobbin. Princeton, N.J.: Princeton University Press.

Dobbin, Frank, and Timothy Dowd. 2000. "Antitrust and the Market for Corporate Control: Railroading, 1825–1922." *American Sociological Review* 65:635–57.

Dobbin, Frank, and John R. Sutton. 1998. "The Strength of a Weak State: The Rights Revolution and the Rise of Human Resources Management Divisions." *American Journal of Sociology* 104(2):441–76.

Dominguez, Kathryn M., Ray C. Fair, and Matthew Shapiro. 1988. "Forecasting the Depression: Harvard versus Yale." *American Economic Review* 78(4):595–612.

Donovan, Claire Angela. 2001. *Government Policy and the Direction of Social Science Research*. DPhil thesis, Social and Political Thought, University of Sussex.

Dorfman, Joseph. 1946. *The Economic Mind in American Civilization 1606–1865*. New York: The Viking Press.

———. 1949. *The Economic Mind in American Civilization*. Vol. 3, *1865–1918*. New York: Viking Press.

———. 1959. *The Economic Mind in American Civilization, 1918–1933*. Vols 4 and 5. New York: Viking Press.

Dosse, François. 1995. *L'empire du sens: L'humanisation des sciences humaines*. Paris: La Découverte.

———. 1997. *History of Structuralism*. Vol. 2, *The Sign Sets, 1967–Present*. Minneapolis: University of Minnesota Press.

Dowding, Keith M. 1995. *The Civil Service*. London: Routledge.

Drèze, Jacques. 1964. "Some Postwar Contributions of French Economists to Theory and Public Policy, with Special Emphasis on Problems of Resource Allocation." *American Economic Review* 54(4):1–64.

———. 1989. "Maurice Allais and the French Marginalist School." *Scandinavian Journal of Economics* 91(1):5–16.

———. 2001. "Economics and Universities in Europe." Unpublished manuscript. CORE. http://www.core.ucl.ac.be/services/psfiles/dp01/EconUnivEur.pdf (accessed June 7, 2007).

———. 2007. "Research and Higher Education in Economics: Can We Deliver the Lisbon Objectives?" *Journal of the European Economic Association* 5(2–3):271–304.

Dumez, Hervé. 1985. *L'économiste, la science et le pouvoir: le cas Walras*. Paris: Presses Universitaires de France.

Dumont, Louis. 1977. *From Mandeville to Marx: The Genesis and Triumph of Economic Ideology*. Chicago: University of Chicago Press.

———. 1986. *Essays on Individualism: Modern Ideology in Anthropological Perspective*. Chicago: University of Chicago Press.

Durkheim, Émile. [1915] 1965. *The Elementary Forms of Religious Life*. New York: Free Press.

———. 1985. *The Rules of Sociological Method*. New York: Free Press.

Duval, Julien. 2004. *Critique de la raison journalistique. Les Transformations de la presse économique en France*. Paris: Seuil (Liber).

Dyson, Kenneth. 1980. *The State Tradition in Western Europe: Study of an Idea and Institution*. Oxford: Martin Robertson.

Eatwell, John. 1985. "Keynes, Keynesians and British Policy." Pp. 61–75 in *The Policy Consequences of John Maynard Keynes*, edited by Harold Wattel. Armonk, N.Y.: M. E. Sharpe.

Econometric Society. 1957. "Directory of Members." *Econometrica* 25(5):1–208.

Economist. 1985. "Economising on Economists." September 7, 35.

———. 1992. "Cambridge versus Cambridge." January 3.

———. 1998. "Economists. Doctored." May 9.

———. 1989. "I Think, Therefore I Tank." November 25.

Edgerton, David. 1997. "Science in the United Kingdom: A Study in the Nationalization of Science." Pp. 759–76 in *Science in the Twentieth Century*, edited by John Krige and Dominique Pestre. Amsterdam: Harwood Academic Publishers.

Edgerton, David. 2006. *Warfare State. Britain, 1929–1970*. Cambridge: Cambridge University Press.

Edwards, Ruth Dudley. 1993. *The Pursuit of Reason: The Economist 1843–1993*. London: Penguin.

Eisner, Marc Allen. 1991. *Antitrust and the Triumph of Economics: Institutions, Expertise and Policy Change*. Chapel Hill: University of North Carolina Press.

Eisner, Marc Allen, and Kenneth J. Meier. 1990. "Presidential Control versus Bureaucratic Power: Explaining the Reagan Revolution in Anti-Trust." *American Journal of Political Science* 34(1):269–87.

Ekelund, Robert B., and Robert F. Hébert. 1978. "French Engineers, Welfare Economics, and Public Finance in the Nineteenth Century." *History of Political Economy* 10(4):636–68.

———. 1999. *Secret Origins of Modern Microeconomics: Dupuit and the Engineers*. Chicago: University of Chicago Press.

Ellison, Glenn. 2002. "The Slowdown of the Economics Publishing Process." *Journal of Political Economy* 110(5):947–93.

Ellul, Jacques. 1967. *The Technological Society*. New York: Vintage.

Emmett, Ross. 2007. "Sharpening Tools in the Workshop: The Workshop System and the Chicago School's Success." Paper presented at the Conference on the Chicago School. University of Notre Dame, September 14–15.

Esping-Andersen, Gosta. 1990. *The Three Worlds of Welfare Capitalism*. Princeton, N.J.: Princeton University Press.

Etner, François. 1986a. "L'enseignement économique dans les grandes écoles au XIXe siècle en France." *Economie et Sociétés* 20(6):159–73.

———. 1987. *Histoire du calcul économique en France*. Paris: Economica.

———. 1989. "Partisans et adversaires de l'économie mathématique en France." *Revue Economique* 40(3):541–48.

Evans, Eric J. 1978. *Social Policy 1830–1914: Individualism, Collectivism and the Origins of the Welfare State*. London: Routledge and Kegan Paul.

Evans, Peter, Dietrich Rueschemeyer, and Theda Skocpol, eds. 1985. *Bringing the State Back In*. Cambridge: Cambridge University Press.

Eyal, Gil. 2000. "Anti-politics and the Spirit of Capitalism." *Theory and Society* 29(1):49–92.

Eymeri, Jean-Michel. 2001. *La fabrique des énarques*. Paris: Economica.

Fabricant, Solomon. N.d. *Toward a Firmer Basis of Economic Policy: The Founding of the National Bureau of Economic Research*. Cambridge, Mass.: National Bureau of Economic Research.

Faulhaber, Gerald, and William J. Baumol. 1988. "Economists as Innovators: Practical Products of Theoretical Research." *Journal of Economic Literature* 26(2):577–600.

Favereau, Olivier. 2002. "Conventions et regulation." Pp. 511–20 in *Regulation Theory: The State of the Art*, edited by Robert Boyer and Yves Saillard. London: Routledge.

Favre, Pierre. 1981. "Les sciences de l'État entre déterminisme et libéralisme: Emile Boutmy (1835–1906) et la création de l'École Libre des Sciences Politiques." *Revue Française de Sociologie* 22:429–65.

Feldstein, Martin. 1986. "Supply Side Economics: Old Truth and New Claims." *American Economic Review* 76(2):26–42.

———. 1992. "The Council of Economic Advisers and Economic Advising in the United States." *Economic Journal* 102:1223–34.

Fetter, Frank. 1925. "The Economists and the Public." *American Economic Review* 15:13–26.

Finkelstein, Martin J. 1984. *The American Academic Profession: A Synthesis of Social Scientific Inquiry since World War II*. Columbus: Ohio State University Press.

Fisher, Donald. 1977. "The Impact of American Foundations on the Development of British University Education. 1900–1939." PhD diss., University of California, Berkeley.

———. 1980. "The Impact of American Philanthropy on the Development of the Social Sciences in Britain." Pp. 234–68 in *Philanthropy and Cultural Imperialism: The Foundations at Home and Abroad*, edited by Robert F. Arnove. Boston: G. K. Hall.

———. 1993. *Fundamental Development of the Social Sciences: Rockefeller Philanthropy and the United States Social Science Research Council*. Ann Arbor: University of Michigan Press.

Fisher, Irving. 1941. "Mathematical Methods in the Social Sciences." *Econometrica* 9(3/4):185–97.

Fitoussi, Jean-Paul. 2001. *L'enseignement supérieur de l'économie en question*. Rapport au Ministre de l'Education Nationale. Paris: Fayard.

Fligstein, Neil. 1990. *The Transformation of Corporate Control*. Cambridge, Mass.: Harvard University Press.

Flouzat, Denise. 1962–63. *L'étudiant économiste*. Paris: Cujas.

Fontaine, Philippe. 1996. "The French Economists and Politics, 1750–1850: The Science and Art of Political Economy." *Canadian Journal of Economics* 29(2):379–93.

Foucault, Michel. 1972. *The Archaeology of Knowledge*. New York: Pantheon Books.

———. [1978] 1991. "Governmentality." Pp. 87–104 in *The Foucault Effect: Studies in Governmentality*, edited by Graham Burchell, Colin Gordon, and Peter Miller. Hemel Hampstead: Harvester Wheatsheaf.

Fourcade, Marion. 2006. "The Construction of a Global Profession: The Transnationalization of Economics." *American Journal of Sociology*. 112(1):145–94.

Fourcade, Marion, and Kieran Healy. 2007. "Moral Views of Market Society." *Annual Review of Sociology* 33: 285–311.

Fourcade, Marion, and Rakesh Khurana. Forthcoming. "From Social Control to Financial Economics: The Linked Ecologies of Economics and Business in Twentieth-Century America." In *Making, Evaluating, and Using Social Science Knowledge: The Underground of Practice*, edited by Charles Camic, Neil Gross, and Michèle Lamont. New York: Russell Sage Foundation.

Fourcade, Marion, and Evan Schofer. 2006. "The Multifaceted Nature of Civic Engagement: Forms of Political Activity across Nations." Working Paper, University of California, UC Berkeley, and University of California, Irvine.

Fourcade-Gourinchas, Marion. 2001. "Politics, Institutional Structures and the Rise of Economics: A Comparative Study." *Theory and Society* 30(3): 397–447.

Fourcade-Gourinchas, Marion, and Sarah L. Babb. 2002. "The Rebirth of the Liberal Creed: Paths to Neoliberalism in Four Countries." *American Journal of Sociology*. 108(3):533–79.

Fourquet, François. 1980. *Les comptes de la puissance: Histoire de la comptabilité nationale et du plan*. Paris: Encres.

Fox, Robert. 1980. "The Savant Confronts His Peers: Scientific Societies in France, 1815–1914." Pp. 240–82 in *The Organization of Science and Technology in France, 1808–1914*, edited by Robert Fox and George Weisz. Cambridge: Cambridge University Press.

Fox, Robert, and George Weisz. 1980. "The Institutional Basis of French Science in the Nineteenth Century." Pp. 1–28 in *The Organization of Science and Technology in France, 1808–1914*, edited by Robert Fox and George Weisz. Cambridge: Cambridge University Press.

Frank, David, and Jay Gabler. 2000. "The Social Sciences in the University: Change and Variation over the Twentieth Century." Unpublished manuscript. Harvard University.

Frank, David, John Meyer, and David Miyahara. 1995. "The Individualist Polity and the Prevalence of Professionalized Psychology: A Cross-National Study." *American Sociological Review* 60(3):360–77.

Franks Report. 1966. *Report of Commission of Inquiry*. 2 vols. University of Oxford.

Frey, Bruno S., and Reiner Eichenberger. 1993. "American and European Economics and Economists." *Journal of Economic Perspectives* 7(4):185–93.

Frey, Bruno S., Werner Pommerehne, Friedrich Schneider, and Guy Gilbert. 1984. "Consensus and Dissension among Economists: An Empirical Inquiry." *American Economic Review* 74(5):986–93.

Fridenson, Patrick. 2001. Preface to *Le Technocrate, le patron et le professeur: Une Histoire de l'enseignement supérieur de gestion,* by Marie-Emmanuelle Chessel and Fabienne Pavis. Paris: Belin.

Friedman, Milton. 1953. "The Methodology of Positive Economics." In *Essays in Positive Economics.* Chicago: University of Chicago Press.

———. 1967. *Capitalism and Freedom.* Chicago: University of Chicago Press.

———. 1968. "The Role of Monetary Policy." *American Economic Review.* 58(1):1–17.

———. [1988] 1997. "John Maynard Keynes." *Federal Reserve Bank of Richmond Economic Quarterly* 83(2):1–23.

Friedman, Milton, and Rose D. Friedman. 1998. *Two Lucky People: Memoirs.* Chicago: University of Chicago Press.

Froman, Lewis A. 1930. "Graduate Students in Economics 1904 to 1928." *American Economic Review* 20(2):235–47.

———. 1952. "Graduate Students in Economics 1904 to 1928." *American Economic Review* 42(4):602–08.

Fry, Geoffrey K. 1990. "The Fulton Committee and the 'Preference for Relevance' Issue." *Public Administration* 68:175–90.

Furner, Mary. 1975. *Advocacy and Objectivity: A Crisis in the Professionalization of American Social Science, 1865–1905.* Lexington: University Press of Kentucky.

Furner, Mary, and Michael Lacy. 1993. *The State and Social Investigation in Britain and the United States.* Cambridge: Cambridge University Press.

Furner, Mary O., and Barry Supple. 1990a. "Ideas, Institutions and State in the United States and Britain: An Introduction. Pp. 3–39" in *The State and Economic Knowledge: American and British Essays,* edited by Mary O. Furner and Barry Supple. Cambridge: Cambridge University Press.

———. 1990b. *The State and Economic Knowledge: American and British Essays.* Cambridge: Cambridge University Press.

Galbraith, John Kenneth. 1971. "How Keynes Came to America." Pp. 3–59 in *A Contemporary Guide to Economics, Peace and Laughter,* edited by Andrea D. Williams. Boston: Houghton Mifflin.

Galtung, Johan. 1981. "Structure, Culture and Intellectual Style: An Essay in Comparing Saxonic, Teutonic, Gallic, and Nipponic Approaches." *Social Science Information* 6:817–56.

Gao, Bai. 1997. *Economic Ideology and Japanese Industrial Policy: Developmentalism from 1931 to 1965.* Cambridge: Cambridge University Press.

Gaspard, Marion. 2001. "Les démonstrations de la règle de Ramsey: Les mathématiques comme 'self-control.'" *Revue Économique* 52(3):595–604.

Geiger, Roger. 1986. *To Advance Knowledge: The Growth of American Research Universities 1900–1945.* New York: Oxford University Press.

———. 1992. "The Dynamics of University Research in the United States, 1945–1990." Pp. 3–17 in *Research and Higher Education: The United*

Kingdom and the United States, edited by Thomas G. Whiston and Roger L. Geiger. Buckingham, U.K.: Open University Press.

Gide, Charles. 1907. "Economic Literature in France at the Beginning of the Twentieth Century." *Economic Journal* 17(66):192–212.

Gieryn, Thomas F. 1995. "Boundaries of Science." Pp. 393–443 in *Handbook of Science and Technology Studies*, edited by S. Jasanoff et al. Thousand Oaks, Calif.: Sage.

———. 1999. "The U.S. Congress Demarcates Natural Science and Social Science (Twice)." Pp. 65–114 in *Cultural Boundaries of Sciences: Credibility on the Line*. Chicago: University of Chicago Press.

Gilpin, Robert. 1968. *France in the Age of the Scientific State*. Princeton, N.J.: Princeton University Press.

Goldin, Claudia, and Lawrence F. Katz. 1999. "The Shaping of Higher Education: The Formative Years in the United States, 1890 to 1940." *Journal of Economic Perspectives* 13(1):37–62.

Goodwin, Craufurd D. W. 1972. "Marginalism Moves to the New World." *History of Political Economy* 4(2):551–70.

———. 1975. *Exhortation and Controls: The Search for a Wage-Price Policy, 1945–1971*. Washington, D.C.: Brookings Institution.

———. ed. 1991. *Economics and National Security: A History of Their Interaction*. Annual supplement to *History of Political Economy* 23. Durham, N.C.: Duke University Press.

———. 1998. "The Patrons of Economics in a Time of Transformation." Pp. 53–81 in *From Interwar Pluralism to Postwar Neoclassicism*, edited by Mary S. Morgan and Malcolm Rutherford. Durham, N.C.: Duke University Press.

Gordon, Philip, and Sophie Meunier. 2001. *The French Challenge: Adapting to Globalization*. Washington, D.C.: Brookings Institution.

Gordon, Robert A., and James E. Howell. 1959. *Higher Education for Business*. Ford Foundation Report. New York: Columbia University Press.

Gordon, Scott. 1955. "The London *Economist* and the High Tide of Laissez-Faire." *Journal of Political Economy* 63(6):461–88.

Granovetter, Mark. 1985. "Economic Action and Social Structure: The Problem of Embeddedness." *American Journal of Sociology* 91(3):481–510.

Green, E.H.H. 1992. "The Influence of the City over British Economic Policy c1880–1960." Pp. 193–218 in *Finance and Financiers in European History, 1880–1960*, edited by Youssef Cassis. Cambridge: Cambridge University Press.

Greenaway, David. 1990. "On the Efficient Use of Mathematics in Economics: Results of an Attitude Survey of British Economists." *European Economic Review* 34:1339–51.

Greenberg, David, Mark Schroder, and Matthew Onstott. 1999. "The Social Experiment Market." *Journal of Economic Perspectives* 13(3):157–72.

Groenewegen, Peter D. 1995. *A Soaring Eagle: Alfred Marshall 1842–1924*. Aldershot, U.K.: Edward Elgar.

Grossman, David M. 1982. "American Foundations and the Support of Economic Research, 1913–1929." *Minerva* 20(1/2):59–82.

Grubel, Herbert G., and Anthony D. Scott. 1967. "The Characteristics of Foreigners in the U.S. Economics Profession." *American Economic Review* 57(1):131–45.

Gruson, Claude. 1968. *Origine et espoirs de la planification française*. Paris: Dunod.

———. 1976. *Programmer l'espérance: Conversations avec Philippe Dominique*. Paris: Stock.

Guillebaud, C.W. 1954. "Le Royaume-Uni." Pp. 103-115 in *Les sciences sociales dans l'enseignement supérieur: Sciences économiques*. Paris: UNESCO.

Guillén, Mauro F. 1989. *La Profesión de Economista: El Auge de Economistas, Ejecutivos y Impresarios en España*. Barcelona : Ariel.

———. 1994. *Models of Management: Work, Authority, and Organization in a Comparative Perspective*. Chicago: University of Chicago Press.

———. 2001. *The Limits of Convergence*. Princeton, N.J.: Princeton University Press.

Gumport, Patricia J. 1993a. "Graduate Education and Organized Research in the United States." Pp. 225–60 in *The Research Foundations of Graduate Education: Germany, Britain, France, the United States, Japan*, edited by Burton R. Clark. Berkeley, CA: The University of California Press.

———. 1993b. "Graduate Education and Research Imperatives: A View from American Campuses." Pp. 261–90 in *The Research Foundations of Graduate Education*, edited by Burton R. Clark. Berkeley, CA: University of California Press.

Habermas, Jürgen. 1971. *Knowledge and Human Interests*. Boston: Beacon Press.

———. 1984. *The Theory of Communicative Action*. 2 vols. Boston: Beacon Press.

Hacking, Ian. 1987. "Prussian Numbers, 1860-1882." In *The Probabilistic Revolution, Vol. 1*, edited by L. Krüger, L. Daston and M. Heidelberger. Cambridge, Mass.: MIT Press.

———. 2004. *Historical Ontology*. Cambridge, Mass.: Harvard University Press.

Hackney, James. 2007a. Interview with Richard Posner, September 25, 2007. Transcript obtained from J. Hackney.

———. 2007b. *Under Cover of Science: American Legal-Economic Theory and the Quest for Objectivity*. Durham, N.C.: Duke University Press.

Hall, Peter A. 1986. *Governing the Economy: The Politics of State Intervention in Britain and France*. Oxford: Oxford University Press.

———, ed. 1989. *The Political Power of Economic Ideas: Keynesianism across Nations*. Cambridge, Mass.: Harvard University Press.

———. 1990. "Policy Paradigms, Experts, and the State: The Case of Macroeconomic Policy-Making in Britain." Pp. 53–78 in *Social Scientists, Policy and the State*, edited by Stephen Brooks and Alain Gagnon. New York: Praeger.

———. 1992. "The Movement from Keynesianism to Monetarism: Institutional Analysis and British Economic Policy in the 1970s." Pp. 90–113 in *Structuring Politics: Historical Institutionalism in Comparative Analysis*, edited by Sven Steinmo, Kathleen Thelen, and Frank Longstreth. Cambridge: Cambridge University Press.

———. 1993. "Policy Paradigms, Social Learning and the State: The Case of Economic Policymaking in Britain." *Comparative Politics* 25(3):275–96.

Halsey, A. H. 1982. "The Decline of the Donnish Dominion?" *Oxford Review of Education* 8(3):215–29.

———. 1992. *The Decline of the Donnish Dominion: The British Academic Professions in the Twentieth Century*. Oxford: Clarendon Press.

Halsey, A. H., and M. A. Trow. 1971. *The British Academics*. Cambridge, Mass.: Harvard University Press.

Han, Shin-Kap. 2003. "Tribal Regimes in Academia: A Comparative Analysis of Market Structure across Disciplines." *Social Networks* 25(3): 251–80.

Hands, D. Wade. 2003. "Did Milton Friedman's Methodology License the Formalist Revolution?" *Journal of Economic Methodology* 10(4):507–20.

Hansen, W. Lee. 1991. "The Education and Training of Economics Doctorates: Major Findings of the Executive Secretary of the American Economic Association's Commission on Graduate Education in Economics." *Journal of Economic Literature* 29(3):1054–87.

Hargrove, Edwin C., and Samuel A. Morley. 1984. *The President and the Council of Economic Advisers: Interviews with CEA Chairmen*. Boulder, Colo.: Westview Press.

Harley, Sandra, and Frederic Lee. 1997. "Research Selectivity, Managerialism, and the Academic Labour Process: The Future of Nonmainstream Economics in U.K. Universities." *Human Relations* 50(11):1427–60.

Harris, José. 1977. *William Beveridge: A Biography*. Oxford: Clarendon Press.

———. 1988. "William Beveridge in Whitehall: Maverick or Mandarin?" Pp. 224–41 in *Government and Expertise: Specialists, Administrators, and Professionals, 1860–1919*, edited by Roy McLeod. Cambridge: Cambridge University Press.

———. 1990a. "Economic Knowledge and British Social Policy." Pp. 379–400 in *The State and Economic Knowledge: The American and British Experiences*, edited by Mary Furner and Barry Supple. Cambridge: Cambridge University Press.

———. 1990b. "Society and the State in Twentieth Century Britain." Pp. 63–117 in *The Cambridge Social History of Britain, 1750-1950*. Vol. 3, *Social Agencies and Institutions*, edited by F.M.L. Thompson. Cambridge: Cambridge University Press.

———. 1994. "The Arts and Social Sciences, 1939–1970." Pp. 217–50 in *The History of the University of Oxford. Vol. 8, The Twentieth Century*, edited by Brian Harrison. Oxford: Clarendon Press.

Harris, Seymour E., Robert D. Calkins, Thomas H. Carroll, Philip H. Coombs, Solomon Fabricant, Lloyd G. Reynolds, and Tjalling C. Koopmans. 1959. "Round Table on the Organization and Financing of Economic Research." *American Economic Review* 49(2):559–80.

Harrod, Roy F. 1938. "Scope and Method of Economics." *Economic Journal* 48(191):383–412.

Hartz, Louis. 1955. *The Liberal Tradition in America*. New York: Harcourt, Brace.

Haskell, Thomas. 1977. *The Emergence of Professional Social Science*. Urbana: University of Illinois Press.

Hausman, Daniel M., ed. 1994. *The Philosophy of Economics: An Anthology*. Cambridge: Cambridge University Press.

Hawley, Ellis W. 1990. "Economic Inquiry and the State in New Era America: Antistatist Corporatism and Positive Statism in Uneasy Coexistence." Pp. 287–324 in *The State and Economic Knowledge: American and British Essays*, edited by Mary O. Furner and Barry Supple. Cambridge: Cambridge University Press.

Hayek, Friedrich August von. 1967. *Studies in Philosophy, Politics and Economics*. Chicago: University of Chicago Press.

Hayward, Jack. 1966. *Private Interests and Public Policy: The Experience of the French Economic and Social Council*. New York: Barnes and Noble.

———. 1986. *The State and the Market Economy: Industrial Patriotism and Economic Intervention in France*. New York: New York University Press.

Healy, Kieran. 2006. "Specialization and Status in Philosophy." Working paper. University of Arizona.

Hecht, Gabrielle. 1998. *The Radiance of France: Nuclear Power and National Identity after World War II*. Cambridge, Mass.: MIT Press.

Heckman, James. 2000. "Microdata, Heterogeneity, and the Evaluation of Public Policy." Pp. 255–322 in *Nobel Lectures: Economics, 1996–2000*, edited by Torsten Persson. Singapore: World Scientific Publishing Company. http://nobelprize.org/economics/laureates/2000/heckman-lecture.pdf.

Heckman, James J., and Jeffrey A. Smith. 1995. "Assessing the Case for Social Experiments." *Journal of Economic Perspectives* 9(2):85–110.

Heclo, Hugh. 1977. *A Government of Strangers*. Washington, D.C.: Brookings Institution.

———. 1980. "Issue Networks and the Executive Establishment." Pp. 87–124 in *The New American Political System*, edited by Anthony King. Washington, D.C.: American Enterprise Institute for Public Policy Research.

———. 1984. "In Search of a Role: America's Higher Civil Service." Pp. 8–34 in *Bureaucrats and Policy-Making: A Comparative Overview*, edited by Ezra Suleiman. New York: Holmes and Meier.

———. 1988. "The In-and-Outer System: A Critical Assessment." *Political Science Quarterly* 103(1):37–56.

Heclo, Hugh, and Aaron Wildavsky. 1974. *The Private Government of Public Money: Community and Policy inside British Politics*. Berkeley: University of California Press.

Heidenheimer, Arnold J. 1989. "Professional Knowledge and State Policy in Comparative Historical Perspective: Law and Medicine in Britain, Germany and the United States." *International Social Science Journal* 41:529–53.

Heilbron, Johan. 1991. "The Tripartite Division of the French Social Sciences." Pp. 73–92 in *Discourses on Society: The Shaping of the Social Sciences Disciplines*, edited by Peter Wagner, Björn Wittrock, and Richard Whitley. Dordrecht: Kluwer Academic Publishers.

———. 1995. *The Rise of Social Theory*. Minneapolis: University of Minnesota Press.

Heilbron, Johan, Lars Magnusson, and Björn Wittrock, eds. 1998. *The Rise of the Social Sciences and the Formation of Modernity: Conceptual Change in Context, 1750–1850.* Boston: Kluwer Academic Publishers.

Heilbroner, Robert. [1953] 1992. *The Worldly Philosophers: The Lives, Times and Ideas of the Great Economic Thinkers.* New York: Simon and Schuster.

Heilman, Ralph E., E. L. Bogart, William H. Kiekhofer, C. O. Ruggles, and George W. Dowrie. 1928. "The Relationship between Departments of Economics and Collegiate Schools of Business." *American Economic Review* 18(1):73–84.

Hein, Laura E. 2003. "Statistics for Democracy: Economics as Politics in Occupied Japan." *Positions* 11(3):765–74.

———. 2004. *Reasonable Men, Powerful Words: Political Culture and Expertise in Twentieth-Century Japan.* Berkeley: University of California Press.

Henderson, John P. 1993. "Political Economy and the Service of the State: The University of Wisconsin." Pp. 318–39 in *Breaking the Academic Mold: Economists and American Higher Learning in the Nineteenth Century*, edited by William J. Barber. New York: Transaction.

Hennessy, Peter. 1989. *Whitehall.* London: Secker and Warburg.

Hennings, Klaus. 1988. "Die Institutionalisierung der Nationalökonomie an Deutschen Universitäten." Pp. 43–54 in *Die Institutionalisierung der Nationalökonomie an Deutschen Universitäten: Zur Erinnerung an Klaus Hennings (1937–1986)*, edited by Norbert Waszek. St. Katherinen: Scripta Mercura Verlag.

Herbst, Jürgen. 1965. *The German Historical School in American Scholarship: A Study in the Transfer of Culture.* Ithaca, N.Y.: Cornell University Press.

———. 1983. "Diversification in American Higher Education." Pp. 196–206 in *The Transformation of Higher Learning, 1860–1930: Expansion, Diversification, Social Opening, and Professionalization in England, Germany, Russia, and the United States*, edited by Konrad H. Jarausch. Chicago: University of Chicago Press.

Hey, John D., and Donald Winch, eds. 1990. *A Century of Economics: 100 Years of the Royal Economic Society and the Economic Journal.* Oxford: Basil Blackwell.

Hicks, John R. 1939. "The Foundations of Welfare Economics." *Economic Journal* 49(196):696–712.

———. 1975. "The Scope and Status of Welfare Economics." *Oxford Economic Papers* 27(3):307–26.

Hildreth, Clifford. 1986. The *Cowles Commission in Chicago, 1939–1955.* Berlin: Springer Verlag.

Himmelfarb, Gertrude. 1985. *The Idea of Poverty: England in the Early Industrial Age.* New York: Vintage.

———. 1992. *Poverty and Compassion: The Moral Imagination of the Late Victorians.* New York: Vintage.

———. 2004. *The Roads to Modernity: The British, French and American Enlightenments.* New York: Vintage.

Hirschman, Albert O. 1977. *The Passions and the Interests: Political Arguments for Capitalism before Its Triumph.* Princeton, N.J.: Princeton University Press.

———. 1989. "How the Keynesian Revolution Was Exported from the United States." Pp. 347–59 in *The Political Power of Economic Ideas*, edited by Peter A. Hall. Princeton, N.J.: Princeton University Press.

HMSO. 1942. *Social Insurance and Allied Services*. Cmnd. 6404. London: HMSO. [Beveridge report]

———. 1946. *Report of the Committee for the Provision for Social and Economic Research*. Cmnd. 6868. London: HMSO. [Clapman report]

———. 1961. *Control of Public Expenditures*. Cmnd. 1432. [Plowden report]

———. 1963. *Report of the Committee on Higher Education*. Cmnd. 2154. London: HMSO. [Robbins report]

———. 1965. *Report of the Committee on Social Studies*. Cmnd. 2660. London: Hmso. [Heyworth report]

———. 1968. *Report of the Committee 1966–1968 on the Civil Service*. London: HMSO. [Fulton report]

———. 1970. *White Paper on the Reorganization of Central Government*. Cmnd. 4506. London: HMSO.

Hobsbawm, Eric. 1987. *The Age of Empire, 1875–1914*. New York: Pantheon.

———. 1990. *Industry and Empire: An Economic History of Britain since 1750*. Harmondsworth, U.K.: Penguin.

Hodgson, Geoffrey M. 1997. "The Fate of the Cambridge Capital Controversy." Pp.95–110 in *Capital Controversy, Post-Keynesian Economics and the History of Economics: Essays in Honour of Geoff Harcourt*, vol. 1, edited by Philip Arestis, Gabriel Palma, and Malcolm Sawyer. London: Routledge.

Hofstadter, Richard. 1963a. *Anti-intellectualism in American Life*. New York: Knopf.

———. 1963b. "The Revolution in Higher Education." Pp. 269–290 in *The Paths of American Thought*, edited by Morton White and Arthur Schlesinger Jr. Boston: Houghton Mifflin.

Hofstadter, Richard, and Walter P. Metzger. 1955. *The Development of Academic Freedom in the United States*. New York: Columbia University Press.

Hollingsworth, Rogers. 1996. "L'imbrication du capitalisme américain dans les institutions." Pp. 179–99 in *Les Capitalismes en Europe*, edited by Colin Crouch and Wolfgang Streeck. Paris: La Découverte.

Howard, M. C., and J. E. King. 1989. *A History of Marxian Economics*. Vol. 2, *1919–1990*. Princeton, N.J.: Princeton University Press.

Howson, Susan K. 1988a. "Economists as Policy-Makers: Editing the Papers of James Meade, Lionel Robbins, and the Economic Advisory Council." Pp. 129–52 in *Editing Modern Economists*, edited by D. E. Moggridge. New York: AMS Press.

———. 1988b. "'Socialist' Monetary Policy: Monetary Thought in the Labour Party in the 1940s." *History of Political Economy* 20(4):543–64.

Howson, Susan K., and Donald Winch. 1977. *The Economic Advisory Council, 1930–1939: A Study in Economic Advice during Depression and Recovery*. Cambridge: Cambridge University Press.

Huntington, Samuel P. 1968. "Political Modernization: America vs. Europe." Pp. 93–139 in *Political Order in Changing Societies*. New Haven, Conn.: Yale University Press.

Hurdle, James A. 1992. "Economists Inside and Outside the Law: Providing Economic Advice to Attorneys." *Business Economics,* October, 57–61.

Hutchison, Terence W. 1976. "Economists and Social Justice in the History of Economic Thought." Pp. 47–65 in *Economics and Equality*, edited by Aubrey Jones. London: Philip Allan.

———. 1978. *On Revolutions and Progress in Economic Knowledge*. Cambridge: Cambridge University Press.

Hutton, William. 1986. *The Revolution That Never Was: An Assessment of Keynesian Economics*. London: Longman.

Ikenberry, John. 1992. "A World Economy Resorted: Expert Consensus and the Anglo-American Post-war Settlememt." *International Organization* 46(1): 289–321.

Ingham, Geoffrey K. 1984. *Capitalism Divided? The City and Industry in British Social Development*. New York: Schocken Books.

Ingrao, Bruno, and Giorgio Israel. 1990. *The Invisible Hand: Economic Equilibrium in the History of Science*. Cambridge, Mass.: MIT Press.

INSEE. 1996. *Cinquante ans d'INSEE ou la conquête du chiffre*. Paris: INSEE.

Jacoby, Neil, George L. Bach, Melvin G. de Chazeau, Donald W. O'Connell, Arthur M. Weimer, and Ewald T. Grethe. 1956. "Economics in the Curricula of Schools of Business." *American Economic Review* 46(2):551–77.

Jacoby, Russell. 1987. *The Last Intellectuals: American Culture in the Age of the Academe*. New York: Basic Books.

James, E. 1954. "France." Pp. 71–81 in *Les Sciences sociales dans l'enseignement supérieur: Sciences économiques*. Paris: UNESCO.

Jarausch, Konrad H., ed. 1983. *The Transformation of Higher Learning, 1860–1930: Expansion, Diversification, Social Opening, and Professionalization in England, Germany, Russia, and the United States*. Chicago: University of Chicago Press.

Jasanoff, Sheila. 1995. *Science at the Bar*. Cambridge, Mass.: Harvard University Press.

———. 2005. *Designs on Nature: Science and Democracy in Europe and the United States*. Princeton, N.J.: Princeton University Press.

Jeanneney, Jean-Noel. 2007. *Google and the Myth of Universal Knowledge. A View from Europe*. Chicago: University of Chicago Press.

Jeannin, Philippe. 1996. "La *Revue Économique* ou la modernité des économistes français (1980–1994)." Pp. 197–229 in *Les Revue d'économie en France, 1751–1994*, edited by Luc Marco. Paris: L'Harmattan.

Jepperson, Ronald. 1991. "Institutions, Institutional Effects and Institutionalism." Pp. 143–63 in *The New Institutionalism in Organizational Analysis*, edited by Walter W. Powell and Paul J. DiMaggio. Chicago: University of Chicago Press.

———. 1992. "National Scripts: The Varying Construction of Individualism and Opinion across the Modern Nation-States." PhD diss., Yale University.

———. 2002. "Political Modernities: Disentangling Two Underlying Dimensions of Institutional Differentiation." *Sociological Theory* 20(1):61–85.

Jepperson, Ronald, and John W. Meyer. 1991. "The Public Order and the Construction of Formal Organizations." Pp. 204–31 in *The New Institutionalism in Organizational Analysis*, edited by Walter W. Powell and Paul J. DiMaggio. Chicago: University of Chicago Press.

Jobert, Bruno. 1979. "Un monopole d'État: La prévision économique et sociale en France." *Revue Française d'Administration Publique* 9:11–42.

Jobert, Bruno, and Bruno Théret. 1994. "France: La consécration républicaine du néo-libéralisme." Pp. 21–86 in *Le Tournant néo-libéral en Europe: Idées et recettes dans les pratiques gouvernementales*, edited by Bruno Jobert. Paris: L'Harmattan.

Johnson, Elizabeth S. 1978. "Scientist or Politician?" Pp. 17–30 in *The Shadow of Keynes: Understanding Keynes, Cambridge and Keynesian Economics*, edited by Harry Johnson and Elizabeth S. Johnson. Oxford: Basil Blackwell.

Johnson, Harry G. 1971. "The Keynesian Revolution and the Monetarist Counter-Revolution." *American Economic Review* 61(2):1–14.

———. 1973. "National Styles in Economic Research: The United States, the United Kingdom, Canada, and Various European Countries." *Daedalus* 102:65–74.

———. 1977. "The American Tradition in Economics." *Nebraska Journal of Economics and Business* 16(3):17–26.

Johnson, Harry, and Elizabeth S. Johnson. 1978. *The Shadow of Keynes: Understanding Keynes, Cambridge and Keynesian Economics*. Oxford: Basil Blackwell.

Jones, Byrd L. 1972. "The Role of Keynesians in Wartime Policy and Post-War Planning, 1940–1946." *American Economic Review* 62(1/2):125–33.

Jones, Kit. 1988. "Fifty Years of Economic Research: A Brief History of the National Institute of Economic and Social Research 1938-1988." *National Institute Economic Review* 124:36–59.

———. 1994. *An Economist among Mandarins: A Biography of Robert Hall (1901–1988)*. Cambridge: Cambridge University Press.

Kadish, Alon. 1982. *The Oxford Economists in the Late Nineteenth Century*. Oxford: Clarendon Press.

———. 1989. *Historians, Economists, and Economic History*. London: Routledge.

Kadish, Alon, and Keith Tribe, eds. 1993. *The Market for Political Economy: The Advent of Economics in British University Culture, 1850–1905*. London: Routledge.

Kaelble, Hartmut. 1980. "Long-Term Changes in the Recruitment of the Business Elite: Germany Compared to the U.S., Great Britain and France since the Industrial Revolution." *Journal of Social History* 13(3):404–23.

Kahn, Annie. 2007. "Relativiser la fuite des cerveaux." *Le Monde*, June 26.

Karabel, Jerome. 1996. "Towards a Theory of Intellectuals and Politics." *Theory and Society* 25(2):205–33.

Karady, Victor. 1986. "De Napoléon à Duruy: Les origines et la naissance de l'université contemporaine." Pp. 261–322 in *Histoire des universités en France*, edited by Jacques Verger. Toulouse: Privat.

Kaufman, Jason. 2008. "Corporate Law and the Sovereignty of States." *American Sociological Review* 73:402–425.

Kearle J. R., Clayne L. Pope, Gordon C. Whiting, and Larry T. Wimmer. 1979. "A Confusion of Economists?" *American Economic Review* 69(2):28–37.

Keegan, William, and Rupert Pennant-Rea. 1979. *Who Runs the Economy? Control and Influence in British Economic Policy*. London: Maurice Temple Smith.

Kesler, Jean-François. 1985. *L'E.N.A., la société, l'État*. Paris: Berger-Levrault.

———. 1997. "L'énarchie n'existe pas." *Pouvoirs* 80:23–41.

Kessler, Marie-Christine. 1978. "Recruitment and Training of Higher Civil Servants in France: the École Nationale d'Administration." *European Journal of Political Research* 6:31–52.

———. 1986. *Les Grands Corps de l'État*. Paris: Presses de la Fondation Nationale des Sciences Politiques.

Keynes, John Maynard. 1924. "Alfred Marshall, 1842–1924." *Economic Journal* 34(135):311–72.

———. 1937. "The General Theory of Employment." *Quarterly Journal of Economics* 51(2):209–23.

———. 1939. "Professor Tinbergen's Method." *Economic Journal* 49(195): 558–77.

Keynes, John Neville. 1891. *The Scope and Method of Political Economy*. London: Macmillan.

Keyserling, Leon. 1972. "The Keynesian Revolution and Its Pioneers: Discussion." *American Economic Review* 62(1/2):134–38.

Khurana, Rakesh. 2007. *From Higher Aims to Hired Hands: The Social Transformation of American Business Schools and the Unfulfilled Promise of Management as a Profession*. Princeton, N.J.: Princeton University Press.

Kindleberger, Charles P. 1991. *The Life of an Economist: An Autobiography*. Cambridge: Basil Blackwell.

King, Desmond. 1997. "Creating a Funding Regime for Social Research in Britain: The Heyworth Committee on Social Studies and the Founding of the Social Science Research Council." *Minerva* 35:1–16.

———. 1998. "The Politics of Social Research: Institutionalizing Public Funding Regimes in the United States and Britain." *British Journal of Political Science* 28(3):415–44.

Kingdon, John. 1995. *Agendas, Alternatives and Public Policies*. New York: Harper Collins.

Kirman, Alan, and Moegens Dahl. 1996. *Economic Research in Europe*. Florence: European University Institute Monographs.

Klamer, Arjo, and David Colander. 1990. *The Making of an Economist*. Boulder, Colo.: Westview Press.

Klein, Judy L., and Mary S. Morgan, eds. 2000. *The Age of Economic Measurement*. Annual supplement to *History of Political Economy* 33. Durham, N.C.: Duke University Press.

Knorr-Cetina, Karin. 1999. *Epistemic Cultures: How the Sciences Make Knowledge*. Cambridge, Mass.: Harvard University Press.

Koen, Vincent. 1986. "La production française de connaissances économiques: Analyse bibliométrique." *Revue Économique* 37(1):117–36.

Koopmans, Tjalling C. 1947. "Measurement without Theory." *Review of Economics and Statistics* 29(3):161–72.

Koot, Gerard M. 1987. *English Historical Economics, 1870–1926: The Rise of Economic History and Mercantilism.* Cambridge: Cambridge University Press.

Koselleck, Reinhart. 2002. *The Practice of Conceptual History: Timing History, Spacing Concepts.* Stanford, Calif.: Stanford University Press.

Kramarz, Francis, and David Thesmar. 2006. "Beyond Independence: Social Networks in the Boardroom." CEPR discussion paper 5496.

Krause, Elliott. 1996. *Death of the Guilds.* New Haven, Conn.: Yale University Press.

Kreps, David M. 1998. "Economics: The Current Position." Pp. 77–103 in *American Academic Culture in Transformation: Fifty Years, Four Disciplines,* edited by Thomas Bender and Carl E. Schorske. Princeton, N.J.: Princeton University Press.

Krueger, Alan B. 2003. "An Interview with Edmond Malinvaud." *Journal of Economic Perspectives* 17(1):181–98.

Krueger, Anne O. 1991. "Report of the Commission on Graduate Education in Economics." *Journal of Economic Literature* 29(3):1035–53.

Krüger, Lorenz, Lorraine J. Daston, and Michael Heidelberger, eds. 1987. *The Probabilistic Revolution.* 2 vols. Cambridge, Mass.: MIT Press.

Krugman, Paul. 1994. *Peddling Prosperity: Economic Sense and Nonsense in the Age of Diminished Expectations.* New York: Norton.

———. 1996a. "Economic Culture Wars." *Slate,* October 24. http://www.slate.com/id/1911/.

———. 1996b. "Of Economists and Liberals: Paul Krugman Debates Robert Kuttner." *American Prospect* 7(29):13-16.

———. 1998. *Pop Internationalism.* Cambridge, Mass.: MIT Press.

———. 2003. *The Great Unraveling: Losing Our Way in the New Century.* New York: Norton.

Kuhn, Thomas S. 1962. *The Structure of Scientific Revolutions.* Chicago: University of Chicago Press.

Kuisel, Richard. 1981. *Capitalism and the State in Modern France.* Cambridge: Cambridge University Press.

Kuttner, Robert. 1985. "The Poverty of Economics." *Atlantic Monthly,* February, 74–84.

Kydland, Finn E., and Edward C. Prescott. 1982. "Time to Build and Aggregate Fluctuations." *Econometrica* 50:1345–71.

Kynaston, David. 1988. *The Financial Times: A Centenary History.* London: Viking Press.

Kynaston, David, and Richard Roberts. 2001. *City State: A Contemporary History of the City of London: How the Markets Came to Rule Our World.* London: Profile.

Laffont, Jean-Jacques. 1995. "Réflexions sur l'agrégation d'économie." *Revue d'Économie Politique* 105(2):353–56.

Laidler, David. 1993. "Hawtrey, Harvard, and the Origins of the Chicago Tradition." *Journal of Political Economy* 101(6):1068–1103.

Lamont, Michèle. 1987. "How to Become a Dominant French Philosopher: The Case of Jacques Derrida." *American Journal of Sociology* 93(3):584–622.

———. 1992. *Money, Morals and Manners: The Culture of the French and the American Upper-Middle Class.* Chicago: University of Chicago Press.

———. Forthcoming. *Cream Rising: Finding and Defining Excellence in the Social Sciences and the Humanities.* Cambridge, Mass.: Harvard University Press.

Lamont, Michèle, and Laurent Thévenot, eds. 2000. *Rethinking Comparative Cultural Sociology.* Cambridge: Cambridge University Press.

Lamontagne, Michael. 1947. "Some French Contributions to Economic Theory." *Canadian Journal of Economics and Political Science* 13(4):514–32.

Landes, David S. 1949. "French Entrepreneurship and Industrial Growth in the Nineteenth Century." *Journal of Economic History* 9(1):45–61.

Landier, Augustin, and David Thesmar. 2007. *Le Grand Méchant Marché: Décryptage d'un fantasme français.* Paris: Flammarion.

Larsen, Otto N. 1992. *Milestones and Millstones: Social Science and the National Science Foundation, 1945–1991.* New Brunswick, N.J.: Transaction.

Latour, Bruno. 1987. *Science in Action.* Cambridge, Mass.: Harvard University Press.

Laufenberger, Henry. 1937. "Enquête sur quelques instituts européens de recherche économique." Pp. 194–259 in *L'Enseignement économique en France et à l'étranger,* edited by Charles Rist. 50th anniversary issue of *Revue Économique.* Paris: Sirey.

Lazear, Eddie. 2000. "Economic Imperialism." *Quarterly Journal of Economics* 115(1):99–147.

Lebaron, Frédéric. 1995. "La culture économique à l'ENSAE: Quelques éléments et hypothèses." *Bulletin du C.R.E.D.H.E.S.S.,* February 7.

———. 1997. "La dénégation du pouvoir: Le champ des économistes français au milieu des années 1990." *Actes de la Recherche en Sciences Sociales* 119:3–26.

———. 2000. *La croyance économique: Les économistes entre science et politique.* Paris: Seuil.

Lee, Frederic S. 2004. "History and Identity: The Case of Radical Economics and Radical Economists, 1945–1970." *Review of Radical Political Economy* 36(2):177–95.

Lee, Frederic S., and Sandra Harley. 1998. "Peer Review, the Research Assessment Exercise and the Demise of Non-mainstream Economics." *Capital and Class* 66:23–51.

Leeson, Robert. 2000. *The Eclipse of Keynesianism: The Political Economy of the Chicago Counter-Revolution.* New York: Palgrave.

Legendre, François et Yannick L'Horty. 2004. "Agrégation d'économie 2004: Une Affaire Politique." *Alternatives Economiques: L'Économie Politique* 23:8–14.

Lekachman, Robert. 1966. *The Age of Keynes.* New York: McGraw-Hill.

Lenoir, René, and Baudouin Prot. 1979. *L'information économique et sociale.* Report to the President of the Republic. Paris: La Documentation Française.

Leonard, Robert. 1991. "Essays in the History of Economic Thought: Theory and Institutions in the Mid–Twentieth Century." PhD diss., Duke University.

Leontief, Wassily. 1982. "Academic Economics." *Science* 217(4555):104–7.

Lepenies, Wolf. 1988. *Between Literature and Science: The Rise of Sociology.* Cambridge: Cambridge University Press.

Leroy-Beaulieu, Paul. 1900. *Traité théorique et pratique d'économie politique*. Paris: Guillaumin.

Lesourne, Jacques. 1973. "Un programme pour les économistes." *Le Monde*, May 26.

Letwin, William. 1965. *Law and Economic Policy in America: The Evolution of the Sherman Antitrust Act*. New York: Random House.

Le Van–Lemesle, Lucette. 1987. "Les économistes officiels experts ou politiques?" In *Les nationalisations de la libération: De l'utopie au compromis*, edited by Claire Andrieu, Lucette Le Van, and Antoine Prost. Paris: Presses de la Fondation Nationale des Sciences Politiques.

———. 1991. "L'institutionalisation de l'économie politique en France." In *L'économie politique au XIXeme siècle*, edited by Yves Breton and Michel Luftalla. Paris: Economica.

———. 1993. "L'enseignement de l'économie politique en France, 1860–1939." Doctoral thesis. Université de Paris I.

———. *Le juste ou le riche: L'enseignement de l'économie politique 1815–1950*. Paris: Comité pour l'histoire économique et financière de la France.

Leyland, Jill. 1992. "Where Do Economists Work and What Do They Do?" *Business Economist* 23(suppl.):6–13.

Lindenfeld, David F. 1997. *The Practical Imagination: The German Sciences of the State in the Nineteenth Century*. Chicago: University of Chicago Press.

Lipietz, Alain. 1979. *Crise et inflation, pourquoi?* Paris: François Maspero.

———. "De l'approche de la régulation à l'écologie: Une mise en perspective historique." Interview with Giuseppe Cocco, Fadela Sebaï, and Carlo Vercellone. *Futur Antérieur*, September, 71–100.

Lipset, Seymour Martin. 1963a. *The First New Nation: The United States in Historical and Comparative Perspective*. New York: Basic Books.

———. 1963b. "The Value Patterns of Democracy: A Case Study in Comparative Analysis." *American Sociological Review* 28(4):515–31.

Lipsey, Richard G., and Kelvin Lancaster. 1956. "The General Theory of the Second Best." *Review of Economic Studies* 24(1):11–32.

Lisle, Edmond. 1984. "Social Science Research in the United Kingdom: From Clapham to Rothschild." Pp. 11–141 in *Traversing the Crisis: The Social Sciences in Britain and France*, edited by Edmond Lisle, Howard Machin, and Sy Yasin. London: ESRC.

———. 2002. "Les sciences sociales en France: Developpement et turbulences dans les années 1970. Entretien entre Edmond Lisle et Olivier Martin, 27 juin 2001." *Revue Pour l'Histoire du CNRS* 7(November).

Locke, Robert L. 1984. *The End of Practical Man: Entrepreneurship and Higher Education in Germany, France, and Great Britain, 1880–1940*. Greenwich, Conn.: JAI Press.

Longstreth, Frank. 1979. "The City, Industry and the State." Pp. 157–90 in *The State and Economy in Contemporary Capitalism*, edited by Colin Crouch. New York: St. Martin's Press.

Lowi, Theodore J. 1969. *The End of Liberalism: Ideology, Policy, and the Crisis of Public Authority*. New York: Norton.

Lubin, Isador. 1937. "Government Employment as a Professional Career in Economics." *American Economic Review* 27(1):216–24.

Lucas, Robert. 1976. "Econometric Policy Evaluation: A Critique." *Journal of Monetary Economics,* supplementary series 1(2):19–46.

———. N.d. "Professional Memoir." Lecture presented at the Nobel Economists Lecture Series, Trinity College, San Antonia, Texas. (accessed June 6, 2007).

Lumsden, Keith, Richard Attiyeh, and Alex Scott. 1980. *Economics Education in the United Kingdom.* London: Heinemann Educational Books.

Lyons, Gene. 1969. *The Uneasy Partnership: Social Science and the Federal Government in the Twentieth Century.* New York: Russell Sage Foundation.

MacDougall, Donald. 1987. *Don and Mandarin: Memoirs of an Economist.* London: John Murray.

Machin, Howard. 1984. "The CNRS and Social Science Research in France." In *Traversing the Crisis: The Social Sciences in Britain and France*, edited by Edmond Lisle, Howard Machin, and Sy Yasin. London: Economic and Social Research Council.

Machin, Stephen, and Andrew Oswald. 1999. *Signs of Disintegration: A Report on UK Economics PhDs and ESRC Studentship Demand.* London: Economic and Social Research Council.

———. 2000. "UK Economics and the Future Supply of Academic Economists." *Economic Journal* 110(464):334–49.

MacKenzie, Donald A. 1981. *Statistics in Britain, 1865–1930: The Social Construction of Knowledge.* New York: Columbia University Press.

———. 2006. *An Engine, Not a Camera.* Princeton: Princeton, N.J.: University Press.

MacLeod, Donald. 2005. "A Time-Honoured Tradition." *Guardian*, June 27.

MacLeod, Roy M., and E. Kay Andrews. 1969. "The Committee of Civil Research: Scientific Advice for Economic Development 1925–1930." *Minerva* 7(4):680–705.

Maier, Charles S. 1978. "The Politics of Productivity: Foundations of American International Economic Policy after World War II." Pp. 23–49 in *Between Power and Plenty: Foreign Economic Policies of Advanced Industrial States*, edited by Peter J. Katzenstein. Madison: University of Wisconsin Press.

Malinvaud, Edmond. 1977. *Theory of Unemployment Reconsidered.* Oxford: Blackwell.

Maloney, John. 1985. *Marshall, Orthodoxy and the Professionalisation of Economics.* Cambridge: Cambridge University Press.

Malouin, Jean-Louis, and Jean-François Outreville. 1987. "The Relative Impact of Economic Journals: A Cross-Country Comparison." *Journal of Economics and Business* 39(3):267–77.

Mamou, Yves. 1988. *Une machine de pouvoir: La direction du Trésor.* Paris: La Découverte.

Mandel, Michael J. 1999. "Going for the Gold: Economists as Expert Witnesses." *Journal of Economic Perspectives* 13(2):113–20.

Manicas, Peter. 1987. *A History and Philosophy of the Social Sciences.* Oxford: Basil Blackwell.

———. 1991. "The Social Science Disciplines: The American Model." Pp. 45–71 in *Discourses on Society: The Shaping of the Social Sciences Disciplines*, edited by Peter Wagner, Björn Wittrock, and Richard Whitley. Dordrecht: Kluwer Academic Publishers.

Mannheim, Karl. [1936] 1985. *Ideology and Utopia*. New York: Harcourt Brace.

Marchal, André. 1953. *La pensée économique en France depuis 1945*. Paris: Presses Universitaires de France.

Marco, Luc. 2006. "L'agrégation de sciences de gestion (1976–2005)." *Revue d'Histoire des Sciences Humaines* 14(1):173–98.

Margairaz, Michel. 1990. "Les Ministres des Finances: Personnalités, structures, conjonctures." *Pouvoirs* 53:101–8.

———. 1991. *L'Etat, les finances et l'économie: histoire d'une conversion, 1932–1952*. Comité pour l'Histoire Économique et Financière de la France. Paris: Ministère de l'Économie, des Finances et de l'Industrie.

Markoff, John, and Verónica Montecinos. 1993. "The Ubiquitous Rise of Economists." *Journal of Public Policy* 13(1):37–68.

———. Forthcoming. *Economists in the Americas*. Aldershot: Edward Elgar.

Marshall, Alfred. 1879. *The Economics of Industry*. London: Macmillan.

———. 1890. *Principles of Economics*. London: Macmillan.

———. 1907. "The Social Possibilities of Economic Chivalry." *Economic Journal* 17(65):7–29.

Martin, Cathie Joe. 1991. *Shifting the Burden*. Chicago: University of Chicago Press.

Martin, Philippe. 2004. "L'agreg d'éco échoue au concours." *Libération*, March 8.

Mason, Edward S., and Thomas S. Lamont. 1982. "The Harvard Department of Economics from the Beginning to World War II." *Quarterly Journal of Economics* 97(3):383–433.

Massé, Pierre. 1965. *Le plan ou l'anti-hasard*. Paris: Gallimard.

Mata, Tiago. 2004. "Constructing Identity: The Post-Keynesians and the Capital Controversies." *Journal of the History of Economic Thought* 26(2): 241–59.

———. 2006. "Dissent in Economics: Making Radical Political Economics and Post-Keynesian Economics, 1960–1980." Ph.D. diss., London School of Economics and Political Science.

Maurice, Marc, François Sellier, and Jean-Jacques Sylvestre. 1986. *The Social Foundations of Industrial Power: A Comparison of France and Germany*. Cambridge, Mass.: MIT Press.

Mayer, Karl-Ulrich, Walter Müller, and Reinhard Pollak. 2003. "Institutional Change and Inequalities of Access in German Higher Education." Working paper. http://www.mpibberlin.mpg.de/en/institut/dok/full/Mayer/institut/institutional_change.pdf (accessed January 27, 2007).

Mayhew, Anne. 1998. "How American Economists Came to Love the Sherman Antitrust Act." Pp. 179–201 in *From Interwar Pluralism to Postwar Neoclassicism*, edited by Mary S. Morgan and Malcolm Rutherford. Durham, N.C.: Duke University Press.

Mazon, Brigitte. 1988. *Aux origines de l'École des Hautes Études en sciences sociales: Le rôle du mécénat américain*. Paris: Editions du Cerf.

McCloskey, Deirdre. 1994. *Knowledge and Persuasion in Economics*. Cambridge: Cambridge University Press.

McCloskey, Donald N. 1985. *The Rhetoric of Economics*. Madison: University of Wisconsin Press.

McGann, James. 1995. *The Competition for Dollars, Scholars and Influence in the Public Policy Research Industry*. Lanham, Md.: University Press of America.

McKee, C. W., and H. G. Moulton. 1951. *A Survey of Economic Education*. Washington, D.C.: Brookings Institution.

McNutty, Paul J. 1980. *The Origins and Development of Labor Economics*. Cambridge, Mass.: Harvard University Press.

Meade, James. 1975. *The Intelligent Radical's Guide to Economic Policy*. London: Allen and Unwin.

Medema, Steven G. 1998. "Wandering the Road of Pluralism to Posner: The Transformation of Law and Economics in the Twentieth Century." Pp. 202–24 in *From Interwar Pluralism to Postwar Neoclassicism*, edited by Mary S. Morgan and Malcolm Rutherford. Durham, N.C.: Duke University Press.

Medvetz, Thomas. 2007. "Think Tanks in America: Anti-Intellectualism and the Production of Policy Knowledge." Unpublished Dissertation. Department of Sociology: University of California, Berkeley.

Meiksins, Peter, and Smith, Chris. 1996. *Engineering Labour: Technical Workers in Comparative Perspective*. London: Verso.

Menand, Louis. 2001. *The Metaphysical Club: A Story of Ideas in America*. New York: Farrar, Straus and Giroux.

Ménard, Claude. 1987. "Trois formes de résistance à la statistique: Say, Cournot, Walras." Pp. 417–29 in *Pour une histoire de la statistique*, by INSEE. Paris: Economica.

Mendès-France, Pierre, and Gabriel Ardant. 1955. *Economics and Action*. New York: Columbia University Press.

Merlin, Albert. 1997. "Albert Merlin et la culture économique dans l'industrie: Entretien avec Albert Merlin." *Annales des Mines: Gérer et Comprendre* 48:4–15.

Merriam, Charles. 1944. "The National Resources Planning Board: A Chapter in American Planning Experience." *American Political Science Review* 38(6):1075–88.

Merton, Robert. K. 1973. *The Sociology of Science: Theoretical and Empirical Investigations*. Chicago: University of Chicago Press.

Metzger, Walter. 1987. "The Academic Profession in the United States." Pp. 123–208 in *The Academic Profession*, edited by Burton Clark. Berkeley: University of California Press.

Meyer, John W. 1994. "Rationalized Environments." Pp. 28–54 in *Institutional Environments and Organizations: Structural Complexity and Individualism*, edited by W. Richard Scott and John W. Meyer. Thousand Oaks, Calif.: Sage.

Meyer, John W., John Boli, and George Thomas. 1987. "Ontology and Rationalization in the Western Cultural Account." Pp. 12–37 in *Institutional Structure: Constituting State, Society, and the Individual*, edited by George M. Thomas, John W. Meyer, Francisco Ramirez, and John Boli. London: Sage.

Meyer, John W., John Boli, George Thomas, and Francisco O. Ramirez. 1987. "World Society and the Nation-State." *American Journal of Sociology* 103(1): 144–81.

Meyer, John W., and Brian Rowan. 1977. "Institutional Organizations: Formal Structure as Myth and Ceremony." *American Journal of Sociology* 83(2):340–363.

Middleton, Roger. 1982. "The Treasury in the 1930s: Political and Administrative Constraints to Acceptance of the "New" Economics." *Oxford Economic Papers* 34(1):48–77.

———. 1996. *Government versus the Market: The Growth of the Public Sector, Economic Management and British Economic Performance, c. 1890–1979.* Cheltenham, U.K.: Edward Elgar.

———. 1998. *Charlatans or Saviours? Economists and the British Economy from Marshall to Meade.* Cheltenham, U.K.: Edward Elgar.

Mill, John Stuart. 1987. *System of Logic.* Book 6, *The Logic of the Moral Sciences.* London: Duckworth.

Millmow, Alex. 2003. "Joan Robinson's Disillusion with Economics." *Review of Political Economy.* 15(4):561–74.

Mirowski, Philip. 1989a. *More Heat Than Light: Economics as Social Physics, Physics as Nature's Economics.* Cambridge: Cambridge University Press.

———. 1989b. "The Probabilistic Counter-revolution, or How Stochastic Concepts Came to Neoclassical Economic Theory." *Oxford Economic Papers* 41(1):217–35.

———. 1991. "The When, the How and the Why of Mathematical Expression in the History of Economic Analysis." *Journal of Economic Perspectives* 5(1):145–57.

———. ed. 1994. *Natural Images in Economic Thought: "Markets Read in Tooth and Claw."* Cambridge: Cambridge University Press.

———. 1999. "Cyborg Agonistes: Economics Meets Operations Research in Mid-Century." *Social Studies of Science* 29(5):685–718.

———. 2002a. "Cowles Changes Allegiance: From Econometric Empiricism to Cognition as Intuitive Statistics." *Journal of the History of Economic Thought* 24:165–94.

———. 2002b. *Machine Dreams: Economics Becomes a Cyborg Science.* Cambridge: Cambridge University Press.

———. 2005. "How Positivism Made a Pact with the Postwar Social Sciences in the United States." Pp. 142–72 in *The Politics of Method in the Human Sciences: Positivism and Its Epistemological Others,* edited by George Steinmetz. Durham, N.C.: Duke University Press.

Mirowski, Philip, and D. Wade Hands. 1998. "A Paradox of Budgets: The Postwar Stabilization of American Neoclassical Demand Theory." Pp. 260–92 in *From Interwar Pluralism to Postwar Neoclassicism,* edited by Mary Morgan and Malcolm Rutherford. Durham, N.C.: Duke University Press.

Mirowski, Philip, and Esther Mirjam-Sent. 2007 "The Commercialization of Science and the Response of STS." Pp. 635–690 in *Handbook of Science, Technology and Society Studies,* edited by Ed Hackett, Olga Amsterdamska, and Michael Lynch. Cambridge, Mass.: MIT Press.

Mirowski, Philip, and Edward Nik-Khah. 2007. "Markets Made Flesh: Callon, Performativity, and the Crisis in Science Studies, Augmented with Consideration of the FCC Auctions." Pp. 190–224 in *Do Economists Make Markets? On the Performativity of Economics*. edited by Donald MacKenzie, Fabian Muniesa, and Lucia Siu. Princeton, N.J.: Princeton University Press.

Mirowski, Philip, and Dieter Plehwe. Forthcoming. *The Making of the Neoliberal Thought Collective*. Princeton, N.J.: Princeton University Press.

Mirrlees, James. 1982. "The Economic Uses of Utilitarianism." Pp. 63–84 in *Utilitarianism and Beyond*, edited by Amartya Sen and Bernard Williams. Cambridge: Cambridge University Press.

Mitchell, Timothy. 1998. "Fixing the Economy." *Cultural Studies*. 12(1):82–101.

———. 1999. "State, Economy and the State Effect." Pp. 76–97 in *State/Culture: State Formation after the Cultural Turn*. Ithaca, N.Y.: Cornell University Press.

Mitchell, Wesley C. 1925. "Quantitative Analysis in Economic Theory." *American Economic Review* 15(1):1–12.

Montecinos, Veronica. 1998. "Economists in Party Politics: Chilean Democracy in the Era of the Markets." Pp. 126–41 in *The Politics of Expertise in Latin America*, edited by Miguel Angel Centeno and Patricio Silva. New York: St. Martin's Press.

Moody, Michael, and Laurent Thévenot. 2000. "Comparing Models of Strategy, Interests and the Public Good in French and American Environmental Disputes." Pp. 273–306 in *Rethinking Comparative Cultural Sociology*, edited by Michèle Lamont and Laurent Thévenot. Cambridge: Cambridge University Press.

Morgan, Mary S. 1990. *A History of Econometric Ideas*. Cambridge: Cambridge University Press.

———. 2003. "Economics." Pp. 275–305 in *The Cambridge History of Science*. Vol. 7, *The Modern Social Sciences*, edited by Theodore Porter and Dorothy Ross. Cambridge: Cambridge University Press.

Morgan, Mary S., and Malcolm Rutherford. 1998a. "American Economics: The Character of the Transformation." Pp. 1–26 in *From Interwar Pluralism to Postwar Neoclassicism*, edited by Mary S. Morgan and Malcolm Rutherford. Durham, N.C.: Duke University Press.

———, eds. 1998b. *From Interwar Pluralism to Postwar Neoclassicism*. Annual supplement to *History of Political Economy* 30. Durham, N.C.: Duke University Press.

Morgan, Theodore. 1988. "Theory versus Empiricism in Economics: Update and Comparisons." *Journal of Economic Perspectives* 2(4):159–64.

Mossé, Robert. 1957. "The New Economics Curriculum in the French Facultés de Droit." *Economic Journal* 67(265):145–48.

Mougeot, Michel. 1989. "La pensée économique française après 1945: A propos d'un ouvrage d'André Marchal." *Revue Économique* 40(3):567–74.

Musselin, Christine. 2004. *The Long March of French Universities*. London: Routledge.

Mustar, Philippe, and Philippe Larédo. 2002. "Innovation and Research Policy in France (1980–2000) or the Disappearance of the Colbertist State." *Research Policy* 31:55–72.

Naisbitt, Barry. 1995. "The Changing World of the Business Economist." *Business Economist* 26(2):26–37.

Napier, Christopher J. 1996. "Accounting and the Absence of a Business Economics Tradition in the United Kingdom." *European Accounting Review* 5(3):449–81.

National Science Board. Various years. *Science and Engineering Indicators.* Arlington, VA: National Science Foundation.

National Science Foundation, Division of Science Resources Statistics. *Characteristics of Science and Engineering Doctorate Recipients: Selected Trend Tables 1993, 1995, and 1997.* http://www.nsf.gov/statistics/srs00412/ (accessed June 22, 2007).

National Science Foundation. Division of Science Resources Statistics. 1985. *Science and Engineering Personnel: A National Overview.* Arlington, Va.: National Science Foundation.

———. 2004. *Federal Obligations for Research by Agency and Detailed Field of Science and Engineering: Fiscal Years 1970–2002.* NSF 04-313. Project Officer, Ronald L. Meeks. Arlington, Va.: National Science Foundation.

———. 2006. *Academic Research and Development Expenditures: Fiscal Year 2004.* NSF 06-323. Project Officer, Ronda Britt. Arlington, Va.: National Science Foundation.

———. Various years. *Characteristics of Doctoral Scientists and Engineers in the United States.* Arlington, Va.: National Science Foundation.

Nelson, Robert H. 1987. "The Economics Profession and the Making of Public Policy." *Journal of Economic Literature* 27:49–91.

———. 2002. *Economics as Religion: From Samuelson to Chicago and Beyond.* University Park: Pennsylvania State University Press.

Nettl, J. P. 1968. "The State as a Conceptual Variable." *World Politics* 20(4):559–92.

Newlon, Daniel H. 1989. "The Role of the NSF in the Spread of Economic Ideas." Pp. 195–233 in *The Spread of Economic Ideas,* edited by David Colander and A. W. Bob Coats. Cambridge: Cambridge University Press.

Nik-Khah, Edward. 2007. "George Stigler, the GSB and the Pillars of the Chicago School." Presented at the conference "Revisiting the Chicago School" University of Notre Dame, September.

Nogaro, Bertrand. 1950. *La méthode de l'économie politique.* Paris: Librairie générale de droit et de jurisprudence.

Noll, Roger G., ed. 1985. *Regulatory Policy and the Social Sciences.* Berkeley: University of California Press.

Norton, Hugh S. 1977. *The Employment Act and the Council of Economic Advisers, 1946–1976.* Columbia: University of South Carolina Press.

Novick, David, and Daniel J. Alesch. 1970. "Program Budgeting: Its Underlying Concepts and International Dissemination." Unpublished manuscript, Rand Corporation.

Noyelle, Henri. 1951. "A propos de l'enseignement économique en France: Le rapport sur le concours d'agrégation 1950." *Revue Économique* 2(2): 189–208.

O'Connor, Alice. 2001. *Poverty Knowledge: Social Science, Social Policy, and the Poor in Twentieth-Century U.S. History*. Princeton, N.J.: Princeton University Press.

O'Connor, Michael J. L. 1944. *Origins of Academic Economics in the United States*. New York: Columbia University Press.

Okun, Arthur. 1970. *The Political Economy of Prosperity*. Washington, D.C.: Brookings Institution.

Oleson, Alexandra, and John Voss. 1979. "Introduction." Pp. vii–xxi in *The Organization of Knowledge in Modern America 1860–1920*, edited by Alexandra Oleson and John Voss. Baltimore: Johns Hopkins University Press.

Orloff, Ann Shola, and Theda Skocpol. 1984. "Why Not Equal Protection? Explaining the Politics of Public Social Spending in Britain, 1900–1911, and the United States, 1880s–1920." *American Sociological Review* 49:726–50.

Ormerod, Paul. 1999. *The Death of Economics*. New York: St. Martin's Press.

Orr, Larry L. 1999. *Social Experiments: Evaluating Public Programs with Experimental Methods*. Thousand Oaks, CA: Sage.

Overveldt, Johan van. 2007. *The Chicago School: How the University of Chicago Assembled the Thinkers Who Revolutionized Economics and Business*. Chicago: Agate B2 Books.

Papon, Pierre. 1998. "Research Institutions in France: Between the Republic of Science and the Nation-State in Crisis." *Research Policy* 27(8):771–80.

Parker, Richard. 2005. *John Kenneth Galbraith: His Life, His Politics, His Economics*. New York: Farrar, Straus and Giroux.

Parsons, D. W. 1989. *The Power of the Financial Press: Journalism and Economic Opinion in Britain and America*. Aldershot, U.K.: Edward Elgar.

Patinkin, Don. 1976. "Keynes and Econometrics: On the Interaction between the Macroeconomic Revolutions of the Interwar Period." *Econometrica* 44(6):1091–1123.

Patterson, Orlando. 1991. *Freedom in the Making of Western Culture*. New York: Basic Books.

Pavis, Fabienne. 2005. "La division du travail entre disciplines de sciences sociales en France: Gestion, économie, sociologie (1960–2000)." Paper presented at the conference "National Traditions in the Social Sciences," Amsterdam, May 6–7.

Paxton, Robert O. 1982. *Vichy France: Old Guard and New Order, 1940–1944*. New York: Columbia University Press. Original edition, New York: Knopf, 1972.

Pearson, Richard, et al. 1991. *Doctoral Scientists and the Labour Market*. IMS Report 217. London: Institute for Manpower Studies.

Pénin, Marc. 1996. "La *Revue d'Économie Politique* ou l'essor d'une grande devancière (1887–1936)." Pp. 157–96 in *Les revues économiques en France (1751–1994)*, edited by Luc Marco. Paris: L'Harmattan.

Perez, Roland. 1998. "Les sciences de gestion à la croisée des chemins." *Économies et Sociétes* 37(8/9):583–99.

Perkin, Harold. 1989. *The Rise of Professional Society: England since 1880*. London: Routledge.

Perroux, Francois, Pierre Uri, and Jan Marczewski. 1947. *Le Revenu National*. Paris: Presses Universitaires de France.

Persky, Joseph. 2000. "The Neoclassical Advent: American Economics at the Dawn of the 20th Century." *Journal of Economic Perspectives* 14(1):95–108.

Pierson, Frank C. 1959. *The Education of American Businessmen: A Study of University-College Programs in Business Administration*. New York: McGraw-Hill.

Pierson, Paul. 1994. *Dismantling the Welfare State? Reagan, Thatcher, and the Politics of Retrenchment*. Cambridge: Cambridge University Press.

———2004. *Politics in Time: History, Institutions and Social Analysis*. Princeton, N.J.: Princeton University Press.

Pigou, Arthur Cecil. [1920] 1960. *The Economics of Welfare*. London: Macmillan.

Pirou, Gaétan. 1937. *Economie politique et facultés de droit*. Paris: Sirey.

Plowden, William. 1984. "The Higher Civil Service of Britain." Pp. 20–39 in *The Higher Civil Service in Europe and Canada: Lessons for the United States*, edited by Bruce L. R. Smith. Washington, D.C.: Brookings Institution.

Polanyi, Karl. [1944] 1957. *The Great Transformation*. Boston: Beacon Press.

Pollak, Michael. 1976. "La planification des sciences sociales." *Actes de la Recherche en Sciences Sociales* 2(2–3):105–21.

Popper, Karl. [1957] 1979. *The Poverty of Historicism*. London: Routledge and Kegan Paul.

Porter, Roger. 1983. "Economic Advice to the President: From Eisenhower to Reagan." *Political Science Quarterly* 98(3):403–26.

Porter, Theodore. 1987. "Lawless Society: Social Science and the Reinterpretation of Statistics in Germany, 1850–1880." Pp. 351–75 in *The Probabilistic Revolution*, vol.1, edited by L. Krüger, L. Daston, and M. Heidelberger. Cambridge, Mass.: MIT Press.

———. 1994. "Rigor and Practicality: Rival Ideals of Quantification in Nineteenth-Century Economics." Pp. 128–72 in *Natural Images in Economic Thought*, edited by Philip Mirowski. New York: Cambridge University Press.

———. 1995. *Trust in Numbers: The Pursuit of Objectivity in Science and Public Life*. Princeton, N.J.: Princeton University Press.

Portes, Richard. 2001. "Think Net: The CEPR Model of a Research Network." http://www.cepr.org/AboutCEPR/CEPR/CEPR_think.pdf (accessed September 11, 2007).

Posner, Richard A. 1987. "The Law and Economics Movement." *American Economic Review* 77(2):1–13.

Pouch, Thierry. 2001. *Les économistes français et le marxisme: Apogée et déclin d'un discourse critique 1950–2000*. Rennes: Presses Universitaires de Rennes.

Prasad, Monica. 2006. *The Politics of Free Markets: The Rise of Neoliberal Economic Policies in Britain, France, Germany, and the United States*. Chicago: University of Chicago Press.

Premfors, Rune. 1980. *The Politics of Higher Education in Comparative Perspective: France, Sweden, the United Kingdom*. Stockholm: Gotab.

Propper, Carol, and Partha Dasgupta. 2000. "The State of British Academic Economics." *Economic Journal* 110(464):291–92.

Prost, Antoine. 1968. *Histoire de l'enseignement en France 1800–1967*. Paris: Armand Colin.

Putnam, Robert. 1994. *Making Democracy Work: Civic Traditions in Modern Italy*. Princeton, N.J.: Princeton University Press.

Quemin, Alain. 1997. *Les commissaires-priseurs: La mutation d'une profession*. Paris: Anthropos-Economica.

Ragin, Charles. 1987. *The Comparative Method*. Berkeley: University of California Press.

Reay, Michael. 2004. *Economic Experts and Economic Knowledge*. Ph.D. diss., University of Chicago.

Reder, Melvin. 1982. "Chicago Economics: Permanence and Change." *Journal of Economic Literature* 20:1–38.

Redman, Deborah A. 1989. *Economic Methodology: A Bibliography with References to Works in the Philosophy of Science, 1860–1988*. New York: Greenwood Press.

———. 1991. *Economics and the Philosophy of Science*. New York: Oxford University Press.

Reuben, Julie A. 1996. *The Making of the Modern University*. Chicago: University of Chicago Press.

Rhoads, Steven E. 1985. *The Economist's View of the World: Governments, Markets, and Public Policy*. Cambridge: Cambridge University Press.

Ricci, David M. 1993. *The Transformation of American Politics: The New Washington and the Rise of Think Tanks*. New Haven, Conn.: Yale University Press.

Richards, Joan. 1991. "Rigor and Clarity: Foundations of Mathematics in France and England, 1800–1840." *Science in Context* 4(2):297–319.

Richardson, Theresa, and Donald Fisher, eds. 1999. *The Development of the Social Sciences in the United States and Canada: The Role of Philanthropy*. Stamford, Conn.: Ablex.

Ricketts, Martin, and Edward Shoesmith. 1990. *British Economic Opinion: A Survey of a Thousand Economists*. London: Institute of Economic Affairs.

Riecken, Henry W. 1983. "The National Science Foundation and the Social Sciences." *SSRC Items* 37(2/3):39–42.

Ringer, Fritz. 1979. *Education and Society in Modern Europe*. Bloomington: Indiana University Press.

———. 1992. *Fields of Knowledge: French Academic Culture in Comparative Perspective*. Cambridge: Cambridge University Press.

Ritschel, Daniel. 1997. *The Politics of Planning. The Debate on Economic Planning in Britain in the 1930s*. Oxford: Oxford University Press.

Robbins, Lionel. 1938. "Interpersonal Comparisons of Utility: A Comment." *Economic Journal* 48(192):635–41.

———. 1955. "The Teaching of Economics in Schools and Universities." *Economic Journal* 65(260):579–93.

———. 1984. *An Essay on the Nature and Significance of Economic Science*. New York: New York University Press.

Roberts, Richard. 1995. "A Special Place in Contemporary Economic Literature: The Rise and Fall of the British Bank Reviews, 1914–1993." *Financial History Review* 2(1):41–60.

Robinson, E.A.G. 1978. "The London and Cambridge Economic Service." *Kraus Bibliographical Bulletin* 26:218–21.

———. 1990. "Fifty-five Years on the *Royal Economic Society* Council." Pp. 161–92 in *A Century of Economics: 100 Years of the Royal Economic Society and the Economic Journal*, edited by John D. Hey and Donald Winch. Oxford: Basil Blackwell.

Robinson, Joan. 1933. *The Economics of Imperfect Competition*. London: Macmillan.

———. 1962. *Economic Philosophy*. Chicago: Aldine.

Robinson, Marshall. 1983. "The Role of the Private Foundations." *SSRC Items* 37(2/3):35–39.

Rodgers, Daniel. 1998. *Atlantic Crossings: Social Politics in a Progressive Age*. Cambridge, Mass.: Harvard University Press.

Rohrlich, Paul Egon. 1987. "Economic Culture and Foreign Policy: The Cognitive Analysis of Economic Policy Making." *International Organization* 41(1):61–92.

Rosanvallon, Pierre. 1989a. "The Development of Keynesianism in France." Pp. 171–93 in *The Political Power of Economic Ideas: Keynesianism across Nations*, edited by Peter A. Hall. Cambridge, Mass.: Harvard University Press.

———. 1989b. *Le libéralisme économique: Histoire de l'idée de marché*. Paris: Seuil.

———. 1990. *L'État en France de 1789 à nos jours*. Paris: Seuil.

Rose, Nikolas, and Peter Miller. 1992. "Political Power beyond the State: Problematics of Government." *British Journal of Sociology* 43(2):173–205.

Rose, Richard. 1984. "The Political Status of Higher Civil Servants in Britain." Pp. 136–73 in *Bureaucrats and Policy-Making: A Comparative Overview*, edited by Ezra N. Suleiman. New York: Holmes and Meier.

Ross, Dorothy. 1979. *The Origins of American Social Science: Ideas in Context*. Cambridge: Cambridge University Press.

Rothblatt, Sheldon. 1983. "The Diversification of Higher Education in England." Pp. 131–48 in *The Transformation of Higher Learning, 1860–1930: Expansion, Diversification, Social Opening, and Professionalization in England, Germany, Russia, and the United States*, edited by Konrad H. Jarausch. Chicago: University of Chicago Press.

———. 1990. "Research and British Universities." Pp. 69–76 in *The Academic Research Enterprise within the Industrialized Nations: Comparative Perspectives*. Report of a symposium by the Government-University-Industry Research Roundtable. Washington, D.C.: National Academy Press.

Rothblatt, Sheldon. 1997. *The Modern University and Its Discontents: The Fate of Newman's Legacies in Britain and America*. Cambridge: Cambridge University Press.

Rothschild, Emma. 1992. "Adam Smith and Conservative Economics." *Economic History Review* 45:247–68.

Roy, William G. 1997. *Socializing Capital: The Rise of the Large Industrial Corporation in America*. Princeton, N.J.: Princeton University Press.

Royal Economic Society. 1994. *Directory of Members*. London: Royal Economic Society.

Rudwick, Martin J. S. 1988. *The Great Devonian Controversy: The Shaping of Scientific Knowledge among Gentlemanly Specialists*. Chicago: University of Chicago Press.

Rueff, Jacques. 1947. *L'ordre social*. Paris: Librairie de Medicis.

Rueschemeyer, Dietrich. 1973. *Lawyers and Their Society: A Comparative Study of the Legal Profession in Germany and the United States*. Cambridge, Mass.: Harvard University Press.

———. 1986. "Comparing Legal Professions Cross-Nationally: From a Professions-Centered to a State-Centered Approach." *American Bar Foundation Research Journal* 3:415–46.

Rueschemeyer, Dietrich, and Van Rossem. 1996. "The Verein Für Sozialpolitik and the Fabian Society: A Study in the Sociology of Policy-Relevant Knowledge." Pp. 117–61 in *States, Social Knowledge, and the Origins of Modern Social Policies*, edited by Dietrich Rueschemeyer and Theda Skocpol. Princeton, N.J.: Princeton University Press.

Rueschemeyer, Dietrich, and Theda Skocpol, eds. 1996. *States, Social Knowledge, and the Origins of Modern Social Policies*. Princeton, N.J.: Princeton University Press.

Rutherford, Malcolm. 2000. "Institutionalism between the Wars." *Journal of Economic Issues* 34:291–303.

———. 2005. "Who's Afraid of Arthur Burns? The NBER and the Foundations." *Journal of the History of Economic Thought* 27:109–39.

———. 2007. "American Institutionalism and Its British Connections." *European Journal of the History of Economic Thought* 14(2):291–323.

———. 2008. "Chicago Economics and Institutionalism." In *The Elgar Companion to Chicago Economics*, edited by Ross Emmett. Aldershot, U.K.: Edward Elgar.

Salais, Robert, and Michael Storper. 1997. *Worlds of Production: The Action Frameworks of the Economy*. Cambridge, Mass.: Harvard University Press.

Samuelson, Paul A. 1947. *Foundations of Economic Analysis*. Cambridge, Mass.: Harvard University Press.

———. 1948. *Economics*. New York: McGraw-Hill.

———. 1955. *Economics*. 3rd ed. New York: McGraw-Hill.

———. 1962. "Economists and the History of Ideas." *American Economic Review* 52(1):1–18.

———. 1987. "Paradise Lost and Found: The Harvard ABC Barometers." *Journal of Portfolio Management* 4(Spring):4–9.

———. 1997. "Credo of a Lucky Textbook Author." *Journal of Economic Perspectives*. 11(2):153–60.

Sanderson, Michael. 1972. *The Universities and British Industry, 1870–1914*. London: Routledge and Kegan Paul.

Sarfatti-Larson, Magali. 1977. *The Rise of Professionalism*. Berkeley: University of California Press.

Sargent, J. R. 1963. "Are American Economists Better?" *Oxford Economic Papers* 15(1):1–7.

Sass, Steven A. 1982. *The Pragmatic Imagination: A History of the Wharton School, 1881–1981*. Philadelphia: University of Pennsylvania Press.

———. 1993. "Uneasy Relationship: The Business Community and Academic Economists at the University of Pennsylvania." In *Economics and Higher Learning in the Nineteenth Century: Breaking the Academic Mold*, edited by William J. Barber. New York: Transaction.

Saunders, Charles B. 1966. *The Brookings Institution: A Fifty-Year History.* Washington, D.C.: Brookings Institution.

Sauvy, Alfred. 1954. *La prévision économique.* Paris: Presses Universitaires de France.

———. 1984. *Histoire économique de la France entre les deux guerres.* 2 vols. Paris: Économica.

Schabas, Margaret. 1990. *A World Ruled by Numbers: William Stanley Jevons and the Rise of Mathematical Economics.* Princeton, N.J.: Princeton University Press.

———. 1991. "Mathematics and Economics in Victorian England." Pp. 67–83 in *The Estate of Social Knowledge,* edited by JoAnne Brown and David van Keuren. Baltimore: Johns Hopkins University Press.

Schmidt, Christian. 1999. "Economics in France: A manifold system." Pp. 125–42 in *The Development of Economics in Europe since 1945,* edited by A. W. Bob Coats. London: Routledge.

Schmidt, Vivien. 1996. *From State to Market? The Transformation of French Business and Government.* Cambridge: Cambridge University Press.

Schneiberg, Mark. 2005. "Varieties in Capitalism, Varieties of Association: Collaborative Learning in American Industry, 1900 to 1925." *Politics and Society* 1:46–87.

Schofer, Evan. 1999. "The Expansion of the Social Authority and Institutional Structure of Science in the World System, 1700–1990." PhD diss., Stanford University.

Schofer, Evan, and Marion Fourcade-Gourinchas. 2001. "The Structural Contexts of Civic Engagement: National Polities and Individual Association Membership." *American Sociological Review* 66(6):806–28.

Schultz, Henry. 1928. "Rational Economics." *American Economic Review* 18(4):643–48.

Schultze, Charles. 1977. *The Public Use of Private Interest.* Washington, D.C.: Brookings Institution.

———. 1982. "The Role and Responsibilities of the Economist in Government." *American Economic Review* 72(2):62–66.

———. 1984. "Industrial Policy: A Dissent." *Australian Bulletin of Labor* 10(3):134–143.

———. 1996. "The CEA: An Inside Voice for Mainstream Economics." *Journal of Economic Perspectives* 10(3):23–39.

Schumpeter, Joseph. [1954] 1994. *History of Economic Analysis.* Oxford: Oxford University Press.

Schweber, Libby. 1996. "Progressive Reformers, Unemployment, and the Transformation of Social Inquiry in Britain and the United States, 1880s–1920s." Pp. 163–200 in *States, Social Knowledge, and the Origins of Modern Social Policies,* edited by Dietrich Rueschemeyer and Theda Skocpol. Princeton, N.J.: Princeton University Press.

———. 2006. *Disciplining Statistics: Demography and Vital Statistics in France and England, 1830–1885.* Durham, N.C.: Duke University Press.

Seabrooke, Leonard. 2006. *The Social Sources of Financial Power: Domestic Legitimacy and International Financial Orders.* Ithaca, N.Y.: Cornell University Press.

Seligman, Erwin R. A. 1925. "Economics in the United States: A Historical Sketch." Pp. 122–60 in *Essays in Economics*. New York: Macmillan.

Sen, Amartya. 1983. *On Ethics and Economics*. Oxford: Blackwell.

———. 1992. *Inequality Reexamined*. Oxford: Oxford University Press.

Sen, Amartya, and Bernard Williams. 1982. *Utilitarianism and Beyond*. Cambridge: Cambridge University Press.

Sénat. 2001. Rapport d'information numéro 150. Fait au nom de la délégation du Sénat pour la planification sur les actes du collo "L'information économique en France est-elle satisfaisante?"

Sewell, William H., Jr. 1992. "A Theory of Structure: Duality, Agency, and Transformation." *American Journal of Sociology* 98(1):1–29.

———. 1999. "The Concept(s) of Culture." Pp. 35–61 in *Beyond the Cultural Turn: New Directions in the Study of Society and Culture*, edited by Victoria Bonnell and Lynn Hunt. Berkeley: University of California Press.

———. 2005. "The Political Unconscious of Social and Cultural History; or, Confessions of a Former Quantitative Historian." Pp. 173–206 in *The Politics of Methods in the Human Sciences*, edited by George Steinmetz. Durham, N.C.: Duke University Press.

Shackle, G.L.S. 1967. *The Years of High Theory: Invention and Tradition in Economic Thought, 1926–1959*. Cambridge: Cambridge University Press.

Shapin, Steven. 1995. "Here and Everywhere: Sociology of Scientific Knowledge." *Annual Review of Sociology* 21:289–322.

Shapin, Steven, and Simon Schaffer. 1985. *Leviathan and the Air Pump: Hobbes, Boyle and the Experimental Life*. Princeton, N.J.: Princeton University Press.

Shils, Edward. 1979. "The Order of Learning in the United States from 1865 to 1920: The Ascendancy of the Universities." Pp. 19–50 in *The Organization of Knowledge in Modern America 1860-1920*, edited by Alexandra Oleson and John Voss. Baltimore: Johns Hopkins University Press.

Shonfield, Andrew. 1965. *Modern Capitalism: The Changing Balance between Public and Private Power*. London: Oxford University Press.

Silberman, Bernard S. 1993. *Cages of Reason: The Rise of the Rational State in France, Japan, the United States and Great Britain*. Chicago: University of Chicago Press.

Silk, Leonard, E. 1960. *The Education of Businessmen*. Supplementary Paper 11. New York: Committee for Economic Development.

———. 1964. "Efficiency in the Teaching of Economics: The Product: The Problem of Communication." *American Economic Review* 54(3):595–609.

Silva, Edward T., and Sheila Slaughter. 1984. *Serving Power: The Making of the Academic Social Science Expert*. Westport, Conn.: Greenwood Press.

Simiand, François. 1912. *La méthode positive en science économique*. Paris: Alcan.

Sims, Christopher A. 1980. "Macroeconomics and Reality." *Econometrica* 48(1):1–48.

Skidelsky, Robert J. A. 1983. *John Maynard Keynes: A Biography*. Vol. 1, *Hopes Betrayed, 1883–1920*. London: Macmillan.

———. 1994. *John Maynard Keynes: A Biography*. Vol. 2, *The Economist as Saviour, 1920–1937*. London: Macmillan.

———. 1995. "The Role of Ethics in Keynes' Economics." Pp. 88–100 in *Market Capitalism and Moral Values*, edited by Samuel Brittan. London: Edward Elgar.

———. 2001. *John Maynard Keynes: A Biography*. Vol. 3, *Fighting for Britain, 1937–1946*. London: Macmillan.

Skocpol, Theda, ed. 1984. "Introduction." Pp. 1–21 in *Vision and Method in Historical Sociology*. Cambridge: Cambridge University Press.

———. 1985. "Bringing the State Back In: Strategies of Analysis in Current Research." Pp. 3–43 in *Bringing the State Back In*, edited by Peter Evans, Dietrich Rueschemeyer, and Theda Skocpol. Cambridge: Cambridge University Press.

———. 1987. "Governmental Structures, Social Science, and the Development of Economic and Social Policies." Pp. 40–50 in *Social Science Research and Government: Comparative Essays on Britain and the United States*, edited by Martin Bulmer. Cambridge: Cambridge University Press.

Skocpol, Theda, and Kenneth Finegold. 1982. "State Capacity and Economic Intervention in the Early New Deal." *Political Science Quarterly* 97:255–278.

Skocpol, Theda, and Dietrich Rueschemeyer. 1996. "Introduction." Pp. 3–13 in *States, Social Knowledge, and the Origins of Modern Social Policies*, edited by Dietrich Rueschemeyer and Theda Skocpol. Princeton, N.J.: Princeton University Press.

Skocpol, Theda, and Margaret Somers. 1980. "The Uses of Comparative History in Macrosocial Inquiry." *Comparative Studies in Society and History* 22(2):174–97.

Skowronek, Stephen. 1982. *Building a New American State: The Expansion of National Administrative Capacities, 1877–1920*. Cambridge: Cambridge University Press.

———. 1993. *The Politics Presidents Make: Leadership from John Adams to George Bush*. Cambridge, Mass.: Harvard University Press.

Smelser, Neil, and Richard Swedberg. 1994. *The Handbook of Economic Sociology*. Princeton, N.J.: Princeton University Press.

Smith, Bruce L. R. 1966. *The Rand Corporation: Case Study of a Nonprofit Advisory Corporation*. Cambridge, Mass.: Harvard University Press.

Smith, Cyril, and Otto N. Larsen. 1989. "The Criterion of 'Relevance' in the Support of Research in the Social Sciences, 1965–1985." *Minerva* 27(4):461–82.

Smith, James Allen. 1991. *The Idea Brokers: Think Tanks and the Rise of the New Policy Elite*. New York: Free Press.

Smith, Mark C. 1994. *Social Science in the Crucible: The American Debate over Objectivity and Purpose, 1918–1941*. Durham, N.C.: Duke University Press.

Snowdon, Brian and Howard Vane. 1999. *Conversations with Leading Economists: Interpreting Modern Macroeconomics*. Cheltenham, U.K.: Edward Elgar.

Soares, Joseph. 1999. *The Decline of Privilege: The Modernization of Oxford University*. Stanford, Calif.: Stanford University Press.

Social Science Research Council. 1981. *Macroeconomic Research in the United Kingdom*. London: SSRC.

Social Science Research Council, Committee on the Mathematical Training of Social Scientists. 1955. "Recommended Policies for the Mathematical Training of Social Scientists." *Items* 9(2).

Society of Business Economists. 2005. *Economists Salary Survey*. http://www.sbe.co.uk/survey/salary_survey_2005.pdf (accessed September 11, 2007).

Soffer, Reba. 1970. "The Revolution in English Social Thought, 1880–1914." *American Historical Review* 75(5):1938–64.

———. 1978. *Ethics and Society in England: The Revolution in the Social Sciences, 1870–1914*. Berkeley: University of California Press.

Solberg, Winton U., and Robert W. Tomlinson. 1997. "Academic McCarthyism and Keynesian Economics: The Bowen Controversy at the University of Illinois." *History of Political Economy* 29(1):55–81.

Solow, Robert M. 1998. "How Did Economics Get That Way and What Way Did It Get?" Pp. 57–76 in *American Academic Culture in Transformation: Fifty Years, Four Disciplines*, edited by Thomas Bender and Carl E. Schorske. Princeton, N.J.: Princeton University Press.

Solow, Robert. 2002. "Interview with Robert Solow." *The Region*. September. http:minneapolisfed.org/pubs/region/02–09/solow.cfm, (accessed December 10, 2003.)

Somers, Margaret. 2001. "Romancing the Market, Reviling the State: Historicizing Liberalism, Privatization, and the Competing Claims to Civil Society." Pp. 23–48 in *Citizenship, Markets and the State*, edited by Colin Crouch, Klaus Eder, and Damian Tambini. Oxford: Oxford University Press.

Spellman, William E., and D. Bruce Gabriel. 1978. "Graduate Students in Economics, 1940–74." *American Economic Review* 68(1):182–87.

Spengler, Joseph J. 1976. "Economics: Its Direct and Indirect Impact in America, 1776–1976." Pp. 40–76 in *Social Science in America: The First Two Hundred Years*, edited by Charles M. Bonjean, Louis Schneider, and Robert L. Lineberry. Austin: University of Texas Press.

Spenlehauer, Vincent. 2004. Pour une Déconstruction des légendes sur les rapports État/sciences sociales." Pp. 119–44 in *Les sciences sociales à L'épreuve de L'Action: Le Savant, Le Politique, et L'Europe*, edited by Bénédicte Zimmermann. Paris: Editions de la Maison des Sciences de L'Homme.

Spillman, Lynette. 2004. "Causal Reasoning, Historical Logic, and Sociological Explanation." Pp. 216–34 in *Self, Social Structure, and Beliefs: Explorations in the Sociological Thought of Neil J. Smelser*, edited by Jeff Alexander, Gary Marx, and Christine Williams. Berkeley: University of California Press.

Sraffa, Piero. 1960. *Production of Commodities by Means of Commodities: Prelude to a Critique of Economic Theory*. Cambridge: Cambridge University Press.

Starr, Paul. 1982. *The Social Transformation of American Medicine*. New York: Basic Books.

———. 1993. "Social Categories and Claims in the Liberal State." *Social Research* 59(2):263–95.

Steensland, Brian. 2007. *The Failed Welfare Revolution: America's Struggle over Guaranteed Income Policy*. Princeton, N.J.: Princeton University Press.

Stein, Herbert. 1986. "The Washington Economics Industry." *American Economic Review* 72(2):1–66.

———. 1994. *Presidential Economics: The Making of Economic Policy from Roosevelt to Clinton*. Washington, D.C.: American Enterprise Institute.

———. 1996. *The Fiscal Revolution in America: Policy in Pursuit of Reality*. 2nd ed. Washington, D.C.: American Enterprise Institute.

Steiner, Philippe. 2000. "La *Revue Économique*, 1950–1980 : La Marche vers l'orthodoxie académique?" *Revue Économique* 51(5):1009–58.

———. 2005. "Pourquoi la sociologie économique est-elle si développée en France?" *L'Année Sociologique* 55(2):391–415.

Steinmetz, George. 2005a. "Positivism and Its Others in the Social Sciences." Pp. 1–57 in *The Politics of Methods in the Human Sciences*, edited by George Steinmetz. Durham, N.C.: Duke University Press.

———. 2005b. "Sociology: Scientific Authority and the Transition to Post-Fordism: The Plausibility of Positivism in U.S. Sociology since 1945." Pp. 274–323 in *The Politics of Methods in the Human Sciences*, edited by George Steinmetz. Durham, N.C.: Duke University Press.

Steinmo, Sven. 1989. "Political Institutions and Tax Policy in the United States, Sweden, and Britain." *World Politics* 41(4):500–535.

Steinmo, Sven, Kathleen Thelen, and Frank Longstreth, eds. 1992. *Structuring Politics: Historical Institutionalism in Comparative Analysis*. Cambridge: Cambridge University Press.

Stevens, Anne. 1980. "The Higher Civil Service and Economic Policy-Making." Pp. 79–100 in *French Politics and Public Policy*, edited by Philip G. Cerny and Martin A. Schain. New York: St. Martin's Press.

Stigler, George J. 1965. "Statistical Studies in the History of Economic Thought." Pp. 31–50 in *Essays in the History of Economics*. Chicago: University of Chicago Press.

———. 1982. "The Economists and the Problem of Monopoly." *American Economic Review* 72(2):1–11.

Stryker, Robin. 1989. "Limits on Technocratization of the Law: The Elimination of the National Labor Relations Board's Division of Economic Research." *American Sociological Review* 54(3):341–58.

———. 1990. "Science, Class and the Welfare State: A Class-Centered Functional Account." *American Journal of Sociology* 96(3):684–726.

Sturges, Paul, and Claire Sturges. 1990. *Who's Who in British Economics? A Dictionary of Economists in Higher Education, Business and Government*. Aldershot, U.K.: Edward Elgar.

Sugiyama, Chuhei, and Hiroshi Mizuta. 1988. *Enlightenment and Beyond: Political Economy Comes to Japan*. Tokyo: Tokyo University Press.

Suleiman, Ezra N. 1978. *Elites in French Society: The Politics of Survival*. Princeton, N.J.: Princeton University Press.

———. 1980. *Politics, Power and Bureaucracy in France: The Administrative Elite*. Princeton, N.J.: Princeton University Press.

———. 1987. *Private Power and Centralization in France: The Notaires and the State*. Princeton, N.J.: Princeton University Press.

Summers, Lawrence. 1986. "Does the Stock Market Rationally Reflect Fundamental Values?" *Journal of Finance* 41:591–601.

Sunstein, Cass. 2002. *The Cost-Benefit State: The Future of Regulatory Protection*. Chicago: American Bar Foundation.

Swedberg, Richard. 1990. *Economics and Sociology: Redefining their Boundaries*. Princeton, N.J.: Princeton University Press.

Sweezy, Alan. 1972. "The Keynesian Revolution and Its Pioneers: The Keynesians and Government Policy, 1933–1939." *American Economic Review* 62(1/2):116–24.

Swidler, Ann. 2001. "What Anchors Cultural Practices." Pp. 74–92 in *The Practice Turn in Contemporary Theory*, edited by Theodore Schatzki. New York: Routledge.

Swidler, Ann, and Jorge Arditi. 1994. "The New Sociology of Knowledge." *Annual Review of Sociology* 20:305–40.

Szreter, S.R.S. 1993. "The Official Representation of Social Classes in Britain, the United States, and France: The Professional Model and 'Les Cadres.'" *Comparative Studies in Society and History* 35(2):285–317.

Targetti, Ferdinando. 1992. *Nicholas Kaldor: The Economics and Politics of Capitalism as a Dynamic System*. Oxford: Oxford University Press.

Tavlas, George. 1998. "Was the Monetarist Tradition Invented?" *Journal of Economic Perspectives* 12(4):211–22.

Terray, Aude. 2002. *Des Francs-tireurs aux experts: L'organisation de la prévision économique au ministère des Finances 1948–1968*. Comité pour l'Histoire économique et financière de la France. Paris: Ministère de l'Économie, des Finances et de l'Industrie.

Theakston, Kevin. 1996. *The Civil Service since 1945*. Oxford: Blackwell.

Thelen, Kathleen. 2004. *How Institutions Evolve: The Political Economy of Skills in Germany, Britain, the United States and Japan*. Cambridge: Cambridge University Press.

Thirlwall, Anthony P. 1987. *Nicholas Kaldor*. Brighton, U.K.: Wheatsheaf Books.

Thomas, Rosamund M. 1978. *The British Philosophy of Administration: A Comparison of British and American Ideas, 1900–1939*. London: Longman.

Thompson, James D. 1967. *Organizations in Action: Social Science Bases of Administrative Theory*. New York: McGraw-Hill.

Thompson, Noel. 2006. *Political Economy and the Labour Party*. New York: Routledge.

Tilly, Charles. 1984. *Big Structures, Large Processes, Huge Comparisons*. New York: Russell Sage.

Tintner, Gerhard. 1954. "The Teaching of Econometrics." *Econometrica* 22(1):77–100.

Tobin, James. 1966. *The Intellectual Revolution in U.S. Policy-Making*. Second Noel Buxton Lecture of the University of Essex, January 18. London: Longmans and Green.

———. 1976. "Hansen and Public Policy." *Quarterly Journal of Economics* 90(1):32–37.

Tobin, James, and Murray Weidenbaum. 1988. *Two Revolutions in Economic Policy: The First Economic Reports of President Kennedy and President Reagan.* Cambridge, Mass.: MIT Press.

Tocqueville, Alexis de. [1835–40] 2000. *Democracy in America.* Chicago: University of Chicago Press.

———. [1856] 1998. *The Old Regime and the Revolution.* Chicago: University of Chicago Press.

Tomlinson, Jim. 2005. "Managing the Economy, Managing the People: Britain c. 1931–1970." *Economic History Review* 58(3):555–85.

Tournès, Ludovic. 2006. "L'Institut scientifique de recherches économiques et sociales et les débuts de l'expertise économique en France." *Genèses* 65:49–70.

Trentmann, Frank. 1998. "Political Culture and Political Economy: Interest, Ideology and Free Trade." *Review of International Political Economy* 5(2):217–51.

Tribe, Keith. 1992. "The *Economic Journal* and British Economics, 1891–1940." *History of the Human Sciences* 5(4):33–58.

———. 1997. *Economic Careers: Economists and Economics in Britain 1930–1970.* New York: Routledge.

———. 2003. "The Faculty of Commerce and Manchester Economics, 1903–1944." *Manchester School* 71(6):680–710.

———. 2007 [1995]. *Strategies of Economic Order. German Economic Discourse 1750–1950.* Cambridge: Cambridge University Press.

———. Forthcoming. "Liberalism and Neoliberalism: Britain 1930–1980." In *The Making of the Neoliberal Thought Collective,* edited by Philip Mirowksi and Dieter Plehwe.

Tribe, Keith, and Alon Kadish. 1993. *The Market for Political Economy: The Advent of Economics in British University Culture, 1850–1905.* New York: Routledge.

Trow, Martin. 1993. "Comparative Perspectives on British and American Higher Education." Pp. 280–99 in *The European and American University since 1800,* edited by Sheldon Rothblatt and Björn Wittrock. Cambridge: Cambridge University Press.

Tugwell, Rexford G. 1957. *The Democratic Roosevelt.* Garden City, N.Y.: Doubleday.

Turner, Marjorie. 1989. *Joan Robinson and the Americans.* Armonk, N.Y.: M. E. Sharpe.

UNESCO. 1953. *L'enseignement des sciences sociales en France.* Paris: UNESCO.

Valdes, Juan Gabriel. 1995. *Pinochet's Economists: The Chicago School of Economics in Chile.* Cambridge: Cambridge University Press.

Van Horn, Robert, and Philip Mirowski. 2005. "The Road to a World Made Safe for Corporations: The Rise of the Chicago School." Mimeo, University of Notre Dame.

Veysey, Laurence. 1965. *Emergence of the American University.* Chicago: University of Chicago Press.

Vidal, Jean-François. 2001. "Birth and Growth of the Regulation School in the French Intellectual Context (1970–1986)." Pp. 13–48 in *Institutional Economics in France and Germany: German Ordoliberalism versus the French*

Regulation School, edited by Agnès Labrousse and Jean-Daniel Weisz. Berlin: Springer.

Vinokur, Annie. 1986. "Political Economy between Faith and Works: Saint-Simonism and the Case of Michel Chevalier." *Economies et Sociétés* 20(10):173–202.

Vogel, David. 1983. "The Power of Business in America: A Re-appraisal." *British Journal of Political Science* 13(1):19–43.

———. 1989. *Fluctuating Fortunes: The Political Power of Business in America.* New York: Basic Books.

———. 1996a. "Government-Industry Relations in the United States: An Overview." Pp. 113–37 in *Kindred Strangers: The Uneasy Relationship between Business and Politics in America.* Princeton, N.J.: Princeton University Press. Originally published in Stephen Wills and Maurice Wright, eds., *Comparative Government-Industry Relations.* Oxford: Clarendon Press, 1997.

———. 1996b. "The Power of Business in America: A Reappraisal." Pp. 268–97 in *Kindred Strangers: The Uneasy Relationship between Business and Politics in America.* Princeton, N.J.: Princeton University Press. Originally published in *British Journal of Political Science* (January 1983).

Voss, Kim. 1994. *The Making of American Exceptionalism: The Knights of Labor and Class Formation in the Nineteenth Century.* Ithaca, N.Y.: Cornell University Press.

Wagner, Peter. 1989. "Social Science and the State in Continental Western Europe: The Political Structuration of Disciplinary Discourse." *International Social Science Journal* 122:510–28.

Wagner, Peter, Carol Weiss, Björn Wittrock, and Hellmut Wollmann, eds. 1991. *Social Sciences and Modern States: National Experiences and Theoretical Crossroads.* Cambridge: Cambridge University Press.

Wagner, Peter, Björn Wittrock, and Richard Whitley, eds. 1991. *Discourses on Society: The Shaping of the Social Sciences Disciplines.* Sociology of the Sciences, no. 15. Dordrecht: Kluwer Academic Publishers.

Walras, Léon. 1965. "Notice autobiographique." Pp. 1–15 in *Correspondence of Léon Walras and Related Papers*, vol. 1, edited by William Jaffé. Amsterdam: North-Holland.

Warsh, David. 2006. *Knowledge and the Wealth of Nations: A Story of Economic Discovery.* New York: Norton.

Washington, Scott. 2003. "Principles of Racial Taxonomy." Paper presented at the Graduate Student Retreat of the Society for Comparative Research, Princeton, New Jersey, May.

Waterfield, Sir Percival. 1958. "Civil Service Recruitment." *Public Administration* 36(1):3–8.

Weiller, Jean, and Bruno Carrier. 1994. *L'économie non-conformiste en France au XXème siècle.* Paris: Presses Universitaires de France.

Weintraub, E. Roy. 2002. *How Economics Became a Mathematical Science.* Durham, NC: Duke University Press.

Weir, Margaret. 1998. "The Federal Government and Unemployment: The Frustration of Policy Innovation from the New Deal to the Great Society." Pp. 149–98 in *The Politics of Social Policy in the United States*, edited by

Margaret Weir, Ann S. Orloff, and Theda Skocpol. Princeton, N.J.: Princeton University Press.

———. 1989. "Ideas and Politics: The Acceptance of Keynesianism in Britain and the United States." Pp. 53–86 in *The Political Power of Economic Ideas: Keynesianism across Nations,* edited by Peter A. Hall. Cambridge, Mass.: Harvard University Press.

Weir, Margaret, and Theda Skocpol. 1985. "State Structures and the Possibilities for Keynesian Responses to the Great Depression in Sweden, Britain, and the United States." Pp. 107–63 in *Bringing the State Back In,* edited by Peter Evans, Dietrich Rueschemeyer, and Theda Skocpol. Cambridge: Cambridge University Press.

Weiss, Carol H., ed. 1992. *Organizations for Policy Advice: Helping Government Think.* Newbury Park, Calif.: Sage.

Weisz, George. 1983. *The Emergence of Modern Universities in France, 1863–1914.* Princeton, N.J.: Princeton University Press.

Whatmore, Richard. 1998. "'Everybody's Business': Jean-Baptiste Say's 'General Fact' Conception of Political Economy." *History of Political Economy* 30(3):451–68.

White, Leonard D. 1937. "New Opportunities for Economists and Statisticians in Federal Employment." *American Economic Review* 27(1, suppl.):210–15.

White, R. A., C. D. Billings, and R. D. Brown. 1981. "Assessing the Role of Business Schools in the Market for New Economics Ph.D.s." *Journal of Economic Education* 12:34–43.

Whitley, Richard. 1984. *The Intellectual and Social Organization of the Sciences.* Oxford: Clarendon Press.

———. 1987a. "The Rise of Modern Finance Theory: Its Characteristics as a Scientific Field and Connections to the Changing Structure of Capital Markets." *Research in the History of Economic Thought and Methodology* 4:147–78.

———. 1987b. "The Structure and Context of Economics as a Scientific Field." *Research in the History of Economic Thought and Methodology* 4:179–203.

Whitley, Richard, Alan Thomas, and Jane Marceau. 1981. "Management Education and the British Business Schools." Pp. 30–58 in *Masters of Business? Business Schools and Business Graduates in Britain and France.* London: Tavistock.

Wickham-Jones, Mark. 1992. "Monetarism and Its Critics: The University Economists' Protest of 1981." *Political Quarterly* 63(April/June):1213–22.

Wilensky, Harold. 2005. "Can Social Science Shape the Public Agenda?" *Contexts* 4(2):41–47.

Wilkinson, John. 1997. "A New Paradigm for Economic Analysis?" *Economy and Society* 26:305–39.

Williams, Raymond. 1983. *Keywords: A Vocabulary of Culture and Society.* 2nd ed. London: Oxford University Press.

Williamson, John. 1990. *Latin American Adjustment: How Much Has Happened?* Washington D.C.: Institute for International Economics.

Wilson, Graham K. 1990. *Business and Politics: A Comparative Introduction.* Chatham, N.J.: Chatham House.

Wilson, Thomas. 1984. "Otto Eckstein: Applied Economist Par Excellence." *Review of Economics and Statistics* 66(4):531–36.

Winch, Donald. 1990. "Economic Knowledge and Government in Britain: Some Historical and Comparative Reflections." Pp. 40–72 in *The State and Economic Knowledge: American and British Essays*, edited by Mary O. Furner and Barry Supple. Cambridge: Cambridge University Press.

Witte, Edwin E. 1957. "Economics and Public Policy." *American Economic Review* 47(1):1–21.

Wittrock, Björn. 1985. "Dinosaurs or Dolphins? Rise and Resurgence of the Research-Oriented University." Pp. 13–34 in *The University Research System: The Public Policies of the Home of Scientists*, edited by Björn Wittrock and Aant Elzinga. Stockholm: Almqvist and Wiksell.

———. 1989. "Social Science and State Development: Transformations of the Discourse of Modernity." *International Social Science Journal* 122:497–507.

Wittrock, Björn, and Peter Wagner. 1996. "Social Science and the Building of the Western Welfare State: Toward a Comparison of Statist and Non-statist Societies." Pp. 90–113 in *States, Social Knowledge, and the Origins of Modern Social Policies*, edited by Dietrich Rueschemeyer and Theda Skocpol. Princeton, N.J.: Princeton University Press.

Wolin, Sheldon. 2004. *Politics and Vision: Continuity and Innovation in Western Political Thought*. Princeton, N.J.: Princeton University Press.

Wood, Geoffrey. 2006. "364 Economists on Economic Policy." *Econ Journal Watch* 3(1):137–47.

Wood, Stewart. 2000. "Why 'Indicative Planning' Failed: British Industry and the Formation of the National Economic Development Council (1960–64)." *Twentieth Century British History* 11(4):431–59.

Wuthnow, Robert. 1987. *Meaning and Moral Order: Explorations in Cultural Analysis*. Berkeley: University of California Press.

Yonay, Yuval P. 1994. "When Black Boxes Crash: Competing Ideas of What Science Is in Economics, 1924–39." *Social Studies of Science* 24(1):39–80.

———. 1998. *The Struggle over the Soul of Economics: Institutionalist and Neoclassical Economists in America between the Wars*. Princeton, N.J.: Princeton University Press.

Yonay, Yuval, and Daniel Breslau. 2006. "Marketing Models: The Culture of Mathematical Economics." *Sociological Forum* 21(3):345–86.

Young, Warren, and Frederic Lee. 1993. *Oxford Economics and Oxford Economists*. London: Macmillan.

Yvert, Benoît, ed. *Dictionnaire des ministres, 1789–1989*. Paris: Perrin.

Zelizer, Julian. 2000. "The Forgotten Legacy of the New Deal: Fiscal Conservatism and the Roosevelt Administration, 1933–38." *Presidential Studies Quarterly* 30(2):331–59.

Zhao, Wei. 2004. "Institutions and Reputation Building in the Wine Market and Academia." Ph.D. diss., Duke University.

Zylberberg, André. 1990. *L'économie mathématique en France: 1870–1914*. Paris: Economica.

Zysman, John. 1977. *Political Strategies for Industrial Order: State, Market, and Industry in France*. Berkeley: University of California Press.

———. 1983. *Governments, Markets and Growth: Financial Systems and the Politics of Industrial Change*. Oxford: Martin Robertson.

Index